BTEC Level 3

edexcel

advancing learning, changing lives

INFORMATION TECHNOLOGY | LEVEL 3

Book 1 BTEC National

Karen Anderson | Alan Jarvis | Allen Kaye
Jenny Lawson | Richard McGill | Jenny Phillips | Andrew Smith

A PEARSON COMPANY

Published by Pearson Education Limited, a company incorporated in England and Wales, having its registered office at Edinburgh Gate, Harlow, Essex, CM20 2JE. Registered company number: 872828

www.pearsonschoolsandfecolleges.co.uk

Edexcel is a registered trademark of Edexcel Limited

Text © Pearson Education Limited 2010

First published 2010

13
10 9 8 7 6 5 4

British Library Cataloguing in Publication Data
A catalogue record for this book is available from the British Library.

ISBN 978 1 846909 28 3

Edited by Carol Usher and Melanie Birdsall
Designed by Wooden Ark
Typeset by Tek-Art
Original illustrations © Pearson Education Limited 2010
Cover design by Visual Philosophy, created by eMC Design
Picture research by Pearson Education Limited
Cover photo © Shutterstock/Yuri Arcurs
Back cover photos © Top Left Shutterstock/Dmitriy Shironosov; Top Right Shutterstock/Monkey Business; Pearson Education Ltd/Clark Wiseman, Studio 8 Images
Printed in Malaysia (CTP-VP)

Websites and Hotlinks
There are links to relevant websites in this book. In order to ensure that the links are up to date, that the links work, and that the sites are not inadvertently linked to sites that could be considered offensive, we have made the links available on the Pearson website at www.pearsonschoolsandfecolleges.co.uk/hotlinks. When you access the site, search for either the express code is 9283, the title BTEC Level 3 National Information Technology Student Book or ISBN 978 1 846909 28 3.

Disclaimer
This material has been published on behalf of Edexcel and offers high-quality support for the delivery of Edexcel qualifications.

This does not mean that the material is essential to achieve any Edexcel qualification, nor does it mean that it is the only suitable material available to support any Edexcel qualification. Edexcel material will not be used verbatim in setting any Edexcel examination or assessment. Any resource lists produced by Edexcel shall include this and other appropriate resources.

Copies of official specifications for all Edexcel qualifications may be found on the Edexcel website: www.edexcel.com

Contents

The following optional units are available on the Pearson Education website at www.pearsonschoolsandfecolleges.co.uk/btecnationalit using the password BTEC_Nat_IT_Web.

Also available

There are many different optional units in your BTEC Level 3 National Information Technology qualification, which you may use to form specialist pathways or to build a broader programme of learning. This student book covers all the mandatory units for the Edexcel BTEC Level 3 National Extended Diploma in Information Technology across the four pathways, but if you want a greater choice of optional units including an optional specialist unit you may be interested in Student Book 2.

Written in the same accessible style with the same useful features to support you through your learning and assessment, *BTEC Level 3 National Information Technology Student Book 2* (ISBN: 9781846909290) covers the following units:

Unit	Credit value	Unit name
17	10	Project planning with IT
18	10	Database design
20	10	Client side customisation of web pages
22	10	Developing computer games
23	10	Human computer interaction
28	10	Website production
29	10	Installing and upgrading software
30	10	Digital graphics
31	10	Computer animation
42	10	Spreadsheet modelling

Available direct from www.pearsonfe.co.uk/BTEC2010 and can be ordered from all good bookshops.

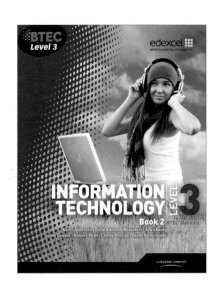

Credits

The authors and publishers would like to thank the following individuals and organisations for permission to reproduce photographs:

Shutterstock/Dmitriy Shironosov p**1**; Pearson Education Ltd/Clare Wiseman, Studio 8 p**3, 371**; Getty Images/PhotoDisk p**4, 6**; Pearson Education Ltd/Devon Olugbenga Shaw p**10**; Pearson Education Ltd/Gareth Boden p**11, 343**; Pearson Education Ltd/Rob Judges p**12, 15, 112, 128**; Shutterstock/bikeriderlondon p**16**; Shutterstock/Margot Petrowsk p**17**; Pearson Education Ltd/ Lord & Leverett p**18, 37**; Topfoto/HIP/Keystone Archives p**26(l)**; Alamy Images/Colin Young-Wolff p.**26(r)**; Shutterstock/Adriano Castelli p**33**; Shutterstock/AG Photographer p**39**; Shutterstock/ Kharidehal Abhirama Ashwin p**41, 299**; Shutterstock/Norman Chan p**51(b)**; Shutterstock/Pelham James Mitchinson p**51(t)**; iStockPhoto/Vikram Raghuvanshi p**71**; Alamy Images/CoverSpot Photography p**73**; Pearson Education Ltd/Jules Selmes p**75**; Getty Images/Stone p**76**; Shutterstock/ March Cattle p**79**; Getty Images/UpperCut Images p**95**; Shutterstock/WH Chow p**97**; Shutterstock/ ansar80 p**99**; akg-images p**100**; Topfoto p**101**; Rex Features/Jonathan Hordle p**102**; Masterfile/Guy Grenier p**103**; Shutterstock/Ragma images p**106**; Pearson Education Ltd/David Sanderson p**115**; Shutterstock/Vasily Smirnov p**122**; Shutterstock/Hakimoto Photography p**131**; Shutterstock/Supri Saharjoto p**133**; Pearson Education Ltd/Mind Studio p**135, 159, 189**; Corbis/Paul Hudson/fstop p**140**; Shutterstock/Mihai Simonia p**145**; Shutterstock/Kaspri p**151**; Shutterstock/Andres Danti p**161**; Pearson Education Ltd/Sophie Bluy p**163**; Shutterstock/Franckreporter p**191**; Shutterstock/Elena Elisseeva p**193**; Shutterstock/EDHAR p**204(t), 399**; Alamy Images/John Joannides p**204(b)**; Alamy Images/Ian Miles Flashpoint Images p**205**; Shutterstock/Brian A Jackson p**223**; Shutterstock/auremar p**225**; Shutterstock/apdesign p**227**; Shutterstock/Alvin Ganesh p**229**; Shutterstock/Alexander Kalina p**234, 245**; Alamy Images/Alex Segre p**235, 321**; Photos.com p**238**; Shutterstock/Arvind Balraman p**239**; iStockphoto/pagedesign p**252**; Photolibrary/Hemant Mehta p**255**; Shutterstock/ Valentyn Volkov p**256**; Alamy Images/Alistair Lamins p**261(t)**; Rex Features/Invista Kent Media p**261(m)**; Rex Features/Mark St George p**261(b)**; Shutterstock/diligent p**263**; Shutterstock/EML p**265**; Shutterstock/Juriah Mosin p**272**; Shutterstock/undergroundarts.co.uk p**276**; Alamy Images/ RayArt Graphics p**301**; Shutterstock/Suzanne Tucker p**303**; Shutterstock/Sergei Devyatkin p**311**; Shutterstock/macka p**312(l)**; Shutterstock/mashe p**312(r)**; Press Association Photos/Steven Day/AP p**341**; Alamy Images/1Apix p**345**; Image Source Ltd p**347, 367**; Getty Images/Riser p**356**; Corbis/ Michael Prince p**359**; Shutterstock/Monkey Business Images p**365**; Shutterstock/Home-Lab p**369**.

The authors and publishers would like to thank the following individuals and organisations for permission to reproduce photographs in the web units which can be found on the Pearson Education website at www.pearsonschoolsandfecolleges.co.uk/btecnationalit:

Unit 12 Getty Images/PhotoDisk p**1**; Getty Images/Stockbyte p**3**; Pearson Education Ltd/ Rob Judges p**10**; Pearson Education Ltd/Jules Selmes p**31**; **Unit 13** Shutterstock/Yurchyks p**1**; Getty Images/Stockbyte p**3**; Getty Images/Stockbyte p**3**; Pearson Education Ltd/Gareth Boden p**10(l,tr,br), 13**; iStockphoto/James McQuillian p**21**; Shutterstock/ostill p**33**.

The authors and publishers would like to thank the following individuals and organisations for permission to reproduce material:

p. 79 Case Study about the IATA is used by kind permission of the IATA.

pp. 110, 288 Screenshots from Skype images © are used by kind permission of Skype Limited.

p. 148 "Major Causes of Network Slowdowns" data taken from: http://articles.techrepublic.com. com/5100-10878_11-6157505.html. Used by kind permission of TechRepublic. © TechRepublic.

About your BTEC Level 3 National Information Technology

Choosing to study for a BTEC Level 3 National Information Technology qualification is a great decision to make for lots of reasons. This qualification is a further step towards a career in the IT industry. The IT industry is an exciting and constantly changing one with a wide range of opportunities – from working in computer games development to working with robotic systems or supporting scientists in combating global warming. The opportunities are endless.

Your BTEC Level 3 National in Information Technology is a **vocational** or **work-related** qualification. This doesn't mean that it will give you all the skills you need to do a job, but it does mean that you'll have the opportunity to gain specific knowledge, understanding and skills that are relevant to your future career.

What will you be doing?

The qualification is structured into **mandatory units** (ones that you must do) and your choice of **optional units**. This book contains mandatory 12 units (with a further 2 mandatory units on the Pearson Education Website – www.pearsonschoolandfecolleges.co.uk/btecnationalit). If you want a greater choice of optional units including an optional specialist unit you may be interested in *BTEC Level 3 National Information Technology Student Book 2* (ISBN: 9781846909290). How many units you do and which ones you cover depend on the type of qualification you are working towards.

- BTEC Level 3 National Certificate in Information Technology: two mandatory units plus optional units to provide a total of 30 credits (no more than 10 credits can come from optional specialist or vendor units)
- BTEC Level 3 National Subsidiary Diploma in Information Technology: two mandatory units optional units to provide a total of 60 credits (no more than 20 credits can come from optional specialist or vendor units)
- BTEC Level 3 National Diploma in Information Technology: three mandatory units plus optional units to provide a total of 120 credits (no more than 30 credits can come from optional specialist units and no more than 40 credits can come from optional vendor units)
- BTEC Level 3 National Diploma in Information Technology (Business – **B**): four mandatory units plus optional units to provide a total of 120 credits (no more than 30 credits can come from optional specialist units and no more than 40 credits can come from optional vendor units)
- BTEC Level 3 National Diploma in Information Technology (Networking and System Support – **NSS**): seven mandatory units plus optional units to provide a total of 120 credits (no more than 30 credits can come from optional specialist units and no more than 40 credits can come from optional vendor units)
- BTEC Level 3 National Diploma in Information Technology (Software Development – **SD**): four mandatory units plus optional units to provide a total of 120 credits (no more than 30 credits can come from optional specialist units and no more than 40 credits can come from optional vendor units)
- BTEC Level 3 National Extended Diploma in Information Technology: three mandatory units plus optional units to provide a total of 180 credits (no more than 40 credits can come from optional specialist units and no more than 60 credits can come from optional vendor units)
- BTEC Level 3 National Extended Diploma in Information Technology (Business – **B**): six mandatory units plus optional units to provide a total of 180 credits (no more than 40 credits can come from optional specialist units and no more than 60 credits can come from optional vendor units)
- BTEC Level 3 National Extended Diploma in Information Technology (Networking and System Support – **NSS**): eight mandatory units plus optional units to provide a total of 180 credits (no more than 40 credits can come from optional specialist units and no more than 60 credits can come from optional vendor units)
- BTEC Level 3 National Extended Diploma in Information Technology (Software Development – **SD**): six mandatory units plus optional units to provide a total of 180 credits (no more than 40 credits can come from optional specialist units and no more than 60 credits can come from optional vendor units)

The table below shows how the units covered by the books in this series cover the different types of BTEC qualifications. Green units are covered in Student Book 1, while those in yellow are covered in Student Book 2.

Unit number	Credit value	Unit name	Cert	Sub Dip	Dip	Dip (B)	Dip (NSS)	Dip (SD)	Ext Dip	Ext Dip (B)	Ext Dip (NSS)	Ext Dip (SD)
1	10	Communication and employability skills for IT	M	M	M	M	M	M	M	M	M	M
2	10	Computer systems	M	M	M	M	M	M	M	M	M	M
3	10	Information systems	O	O	M	M	M	M	M	M	M	M
4	10	Impact of the use of IT on business systems	O	O	O	M	O	O	O	M	O	O
5	10	Managing networks	O	O	O	O	M	O	O	O	M	O
6	10	Software design and development	O	O	O	O	O	M	O	O	O	M
7	10	Organisational systems security	O	O	O	O	O	O	O	M	O	O
8	10	e-Commerce	O	O	O	O	O	O	O	M	O	O
9	10	Computer networks	O	O	O	O	M	O	O	O	M	O
10	10	Communication technologies	O	O	O	O	M	O	O	O	M	O
11	10	Systems analysis and design	O	O	O	O	O	O	O	O	O	M
12	10	IT technical support	O	O	O	O	M	O	O	O	M	O
13	10	IT systems troubleshooting and repair	O	O	O	O	O	O	O	O	M	O
14	10	Event driven programming	O	O	O	O	O	O	O	O	O	M
17	10	Project planning with IT	O	O	O	O	O	O	O	O	O	O
18	10	Database design	O	O	O	O	O	O	O	O	O	O
20	10	Client side customisation of web pages	O	O	O	O	O	O	O	O	O	O
22	10	Developing computer games	O	O	O	O	O	O	O	O	O	O
23	10	Human computer interaction	O	O	O	O	O	O	O	O	O	O
28	10	Website production	O	O	O	O	O	O	O	O	O	O
29	10	Installing and upgrading software	O	O	O	O	O	O	O	O	O	O
30	10	Digital graphics	O	O	O	O	O	O	O	O	O	O
31	10	Computer animation	O	O	O	O	O	O	O	O	O	O
42	10	Spreadsheet modelling	OS	OS	OS	OS	OS	OS	OS	OS	OS	OS

M = Mandatory   O = Optional   OS = Optional Specialist

How to use this book

This book is designed to help you through your BTEC Level 3 National Information Technology course. It contains many features that will help you develop and apply your skills and knowledge in work-related situations and assist you in getting the most from your course.

Introduction

These introductions give you a snapshot of what to expect from each unit – and what you should be aiming for by the time you finish it!

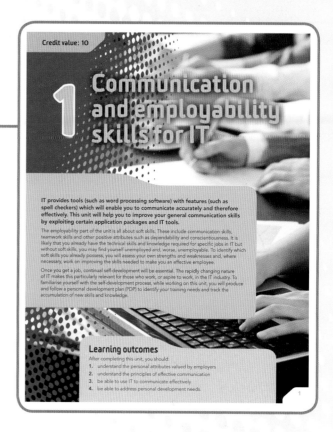

Assessment and grading criteria

This table explains what you must do to achieve each of the assessment criteria for each of the mandatory and optional units. For each assessment criterion, shown by the grade buttons **P**, **M**, **D**, etc. there is an assessment activity.

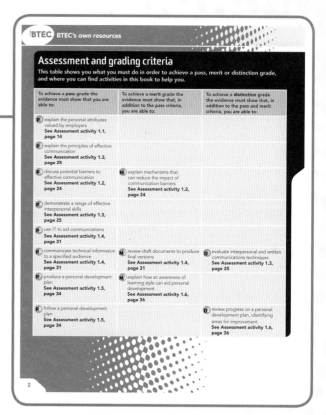

Assessment

Your tutor will set **assignments** throughout your course for you to complete. These may take a variety of forms. The important thing is that you evidence your skills and knowledge to date.

Stuck for ideas? Daunted by your first assignment? These learners have all been through it before…

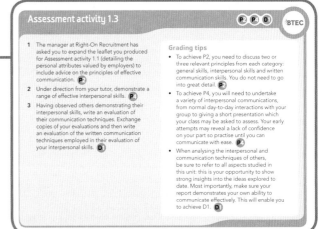

How you will be assessed

This unit will be assessed by a number of internal assignments that will be designed and marked by the staff at your centre. It may be subject to sampling by your centre's Lead Internal Verifier or an Edexcel Standards Verifier as part of Edexcel's ongoing quality assurance procedures. The assignments will be designed to allow you to show your understanding of the unit outcomes. These relate to what you should be able to do after completing this unit.

Your tutor will tell you precisely what form your assessments will take, but you could be asked to produce:
- an information booklet
- observation of your communication skills by your tutor
- detailed witness statements and written explanations of your effective use of IT.

Sam Indura, BTEC National IT learner

Where I live, we rely on seasonal trade. At Easter and during the summer months, the town is full of tourists and there are plenty of jobs. Everyone has not one, but two or three part-time jobs: serving in restaurants and shops, or working in one of the hotels or around the marina. Come the winter, though, it's dead here and money is short.

I want a career where I can be in work all year round. This unit helped me to look at myself more critically and to identify my strengths and weaknesses. I now have the confidence to promote myself and I'm working on my weaknesses.

I have always been good with computers so the IT side of communication is easy for me. I used to struggle to express myself effectively in meetings but I am now better at noticing how others 'talk' through their body language, as well as listening to what they actually say. I am also more conscious of the messages I give out simply by making certain hand gestures or standing in a particular way.

Writing up the personal development plan seemed boring at first – a real waste of time. Then, when I looked back over it and saw the progress I'd made, I realised how useful it was to keep records. I now set myself personal goals and expect to achieve them.

Over to you

- What areas of this unit might you find challenging?
- Which section of the unit are you most looking forward to?
- How can you prepare for the unit assessments?

Activities

There are different types of activities for you to do:
Assessment activities are suggestions for tasks that you might do as part of your assignment and will help you develop your knowledge, skills and understanding. **Grading tips** clearly explain what you need to do in order to achieve a pass, merit or distinction grade. There are also suggestions for activities that will give you a broader grasp of the sector, stretch your understanding and deepen your skills.

There are also suggestions for **activities** that will give you a broader grasp of the world of IT, stretch your understanding and develop your skills.

Assessment activity 1.3

1. The manager at Right-On Recruitment has asked you to expand the leaflet you produced for Assessment activity 1.1 (detailing the personal attributes valued by employers) to include advice on the principles of effective communication. **P2**
2. Under direction from your tutor, demonstrate a range of effective interpersonal skills. **P4**
3. Having observed others demonstrating their interpersonal skills, write an evaluation of their communication techniques. Exchange copies of your evaluations and then write an evaluation of the written communication techniques employed in their evaluation of your interpersonal skills. **D1**

Grading tips

- To achieve P2, you need to discuss two or three relevant principles from each category: general skills, interpersonal skills and written communication skills. You do not need to go into great detail. **P2**
- To achieve P4, you will need to undertake a variety of interpersonal communications, from normal day-to-day interactions with your group to giving a short presentation which your class may be asked to assess. Your early attempts may reveal a lack of confidence on your part so practise until you can communicate with ease. **P4**
- When analysing the interpersonal and communication techniques of others, be sure to refer to all aspects studied in this unit: this is your opportunity to show strong insights into the ideas explored to date. Most importantly, make sure your report demonstrates your own ability to communicate effectively. This will enable you to achieve D1. **D1**

How to… activities

These activities run through the steps involved in software and hardware processes, as well that you will need to carry out successfully to complete the assessment activities in this book and in your career in IT.

How to… Defragment a disk

- Select Start/All Programs/Accessories/System Tools/Disk Defragmenter. Alternatively, access this utility through the Control Panel, within the Computer Management folder (see Figure 2.20).
- Click on the Analyze button. The utility will then estimate the disk usage after defragmentation and make a recommendation either to defragment your disk, or not to, at this time.
- If you are recommended to defragment your disk, click on the Defragment button. Defragmentation will take several minutes, so you are advised to leave the PC and spend the time doing something useful!

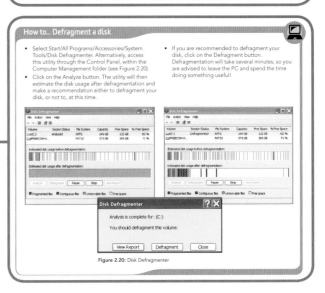

Figure 2.20: Disk Defragmenter

Personal, learning and thinking skills

Throughout your BTEC Level 3 National Information Technology course there are lots of opportunities to develop your personal, learning and thinking skills. These will help you work in a team, manage yourself effectively and develop your all-important interpersonal skills. Look out for these as you progress.

PLTS

As you work with other members of your class to demonstrate your interpersonal skills and assess the communication techniques of others, you will develop your skills as a **team worker** and an **effective participator**.

Functional skills

It's important that you have good English, Mathematics and ICT skills – you never know when you'll need them, and employers will be looking for evidence that you've got these skills too.

Functional skills

Demonstrating a range of effective interpersonal skills such as making contributions to discussions and making presentations in a range of contexts will evidence your Functional **English** skills in Speaking and Listening.

Key terms

Technical words and phrases are easy to spot. The terms and definitions are also in the glossary at the back of the book.

Key term

Independence – someone who has independence is able to act without depending on others, e.g. for financial support, approval or assistance in completing a task.

WorkSpace

Case studies provide snapshots of real workplace issues, and show how the skills and knowledge you develop during your course can help you in your career.

WorkSpace **Helen Whittaker**
Accounts Executive

Helen is an Accounts Executive working for Slick, a marketing company based in South Devon. Slick runs marketing campaigns for local businesses, creating press releases and placing adverts in local and national newspapers. Helen spends her days in meetings with clients and talking to representatives from the press. These meetings are organised by Helen's PA, who chooses a convenient time and location for each appointment.

Helen travels a lot, visiting clients and may be out of the office for days at a time. She uses her Blackberry to keep in touch with colleagues. Whenever Helen has access to a computer, for example via her laptop in a hotel room, or at an Internet cafe, she synchronises the diary on her Blackberry with that held electronically at the office.

When she is in the office, Helen looks at her emails only every two hours, so that she has blocks of uninterrupted time during which she can concentrate. She also has a 'closed door' policy which means colleagues are not able to interrupt her when she needs to be at her most creative.

Think about it!

1 How do you create the best working space for yourself?
2 How might you streamline the way in which you handle incoming emails and correspondence?
3 How do you deal with appointments?
4 How do you cope with deadlines?

Just checking

When you see this sort of activity, take stock! These quick activities and questions are there to check your knowledge. You can use them to see how much progress you've made and to identify any areas where you need to refresh your knowledge.

Edexcel's assignment tips

At the end of each unit, you'll find hints and tips to help you get the best mark you can, such as the best websites to go to, checklists to help you remember processes and useful reminders to avoid common mistakes. You might want to read this information before starting your assignment…

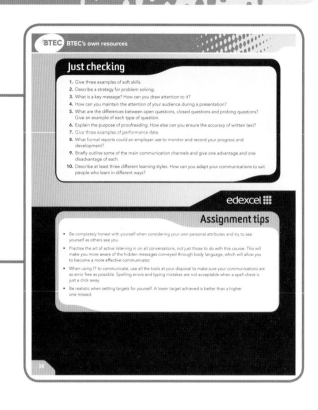

Don't miss out on these resources to help you!

Have you read your **BTEC Level 3 National Study Skills Guide**? It's full of advice on study skills, putting your assignments together and making the most of being a BTEC Information Technology learner.

work Ask your tutor about extra materials to help you through your course. The Teaching Resource Pack which accompanies this book contains interesting videos, activities, presentations and information about the world of IT.

Your book is just part of the exciting resources from Edexcel to help you succeed in your BTEC course. Visit www.edexcel.com/BTEC or www.pearsonfe.co.uk/BTEC 2010 for more details.

1 Communication and employability skills for IT

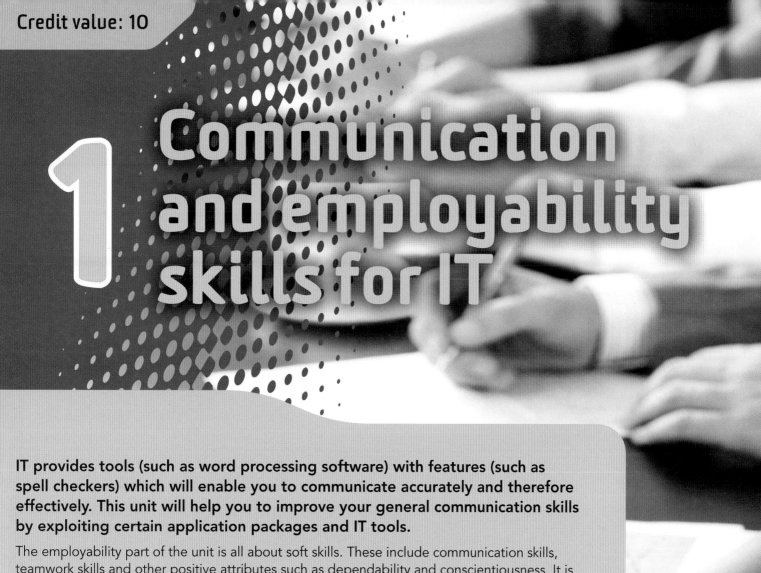

IT provides tools (such as word processing software) with features (such as spell checkers) which will enable you to communicate accurately and therefore effectively. This unit will help you to improve your general communication skills by exploiting certain application packages and IT tools.

The employability part of the unit is all about soft skills. These include communication skills, teamwork skills and other positive attributes such as dependability and conscientiousness. It is likely that you already have the technical skills and knowledge required for specific jobs in IT but without soft skills, you may find yourself unemployed and, worse, unemployable. To identify which soft skills you already possess, you will assess your own strengths and weaknesses and, where necessary, work on improving the skills needed to make you an effective employee.

Once you get a job, continual self-development will be essential. The rapidly changing nature of IT makes this particularly relevant for those who work, or aspire to work, in the IT industry. To familiarise yourself with the self-development process, while working on this unit, you will produce and follow a personal development plan (PDP) to identify your training needs and track the accumulation of new skills and knowledge.

Learning outcomes

After completing this unit, you should:

1. understand the personal attributes valued by employers
2. understand the principles of effective communication
3. be able to use IT to communicate effectively
4. be able to address personal development needs.

Assessment and grading criteria

This table shows you what you must do in order to achieve a pass, merit or distinction grade, and where you can find activities in this book to help you.

To achieve a **pass** grade the evidence must show that you are able to:	To achieve a **merit** grade the evidence must show that, in addition to the pass criteria, you are able to:	To achieve a **distinction** grade the evidence must show that, in addition to the pass and merit criteria, you are able to:
P1 explain the personal attributes valued by employers **See Assessment activity 1.1, page 14**		
P2 explain the principles of effective communication **See Assessment activity 1.3, page 25**		
P3 discuss potential barriers to effective communication **See Assessment activity 1.2, page 24**	**M1** explain mechanisms that can reduce the impact of communication barriers **See Assessment activity 1.2, page 24**	
P4 demonstrate a range of effective interpersonal skills **See Assessment activity 1.3, page 25**		
P5 use IT to aid communications **See Assessment activity 1.4, page 31**		
P6 communicate technical information to a specified audience **See Assessment activity 1.4, page 31**	**M2** review draft documents to produce final versions **See Assessment activity 1.4, page 31**	**D1** evaluate interpersonal and written communications techniques **See Assessment activity 1.3, page 25**
P7 produce a personal development plan **See Assessment activity 1.5, page 34**	**M3** explain how an awareness of learning style can aid personal development **See Assessment activity 1.6, page 36**	
P8 follow a personal development plan **See Assessment activity 1.5, page 34**		**D2** review progress on a personal development plan, identifying areas for improvement **See Assessment activity 1.6, page 36**

How you will be assessed

This unit will be assessed by a number of internal assignments that will be designed and marked by the staff at your centre. It may be subject to sampling by your centre's Lead Internal Verifier or an Edexcel Standards Verifier as part of Edexcel's ongoing quality assurance procedures. The assignments will be designed to allow you to show your understanding of the unit outcomes. These relate to what you should be able to do after completing this unit.

Your tutor will tell you precisely what form your assessments will take, but you could be asked to produce:

- an information booklet
- observation of your communication skills by your tutor
- detailed witness statements and written explanations of your effective use of IT.

Sam Indura, BTEC National IT learner

Where I live, we rely on seasonal trade. At Easter and during the summer months, the town is full of tourists and there are plenty of jobs. Everyone has not one, but two or three part-time jobs: serving in restaurants and shops, or working in one of the hotels or around the marina. Come the winter, though, it's dead here and money is short.

I want a career where I can be in work all year round. This unit helped me to look at myself more critically and to identify my strengths and weaknesses. I now have the confidence to promote myself and I'm working on my weaknesses.

I have always been good with computers so the IT side of communication is easy for me. I used to struggle to express myself effectively in meetings but I am now better at noticing how others 'talk' through their body language, as well as listening to what they actually say. I am also more conscious of the messages I give out simply by making certain hand gestures or standing in a particular way.

Writing up the personal development plan seemed boring at first – a real waste of time. Then, when I looked back over it and saw the progress I'd made, I realised how useful it was to keep records. I now set myself personal goals and expect to achieve them.

Over to you

- **What areas of this unit might you find challenging?**
- **Which section of the unit are you most looking forward to?**
- **How can you prepare for the unit assessments?**

3

1. Understand the personal attributes valued by employers

The perfect employee

Imagine you are keen on working for a particular organisation in a particular role.

- Why should the employer give the job to you?
- What are your USPs (unique selling points)?
- What makes you more suited to fill this post than any other applicant?
- What do you have to offer that the employer might value?
- What kinds of things are employers looking for in an employee?

Compare notes with others in your group. Try to identify some attributes that all employers want in an applicant.

Some attributes are specific to a given job but many apply to all jobs. Some attributes relate to you as a person, while others relate to the type of organisation that you hope to join.

The following section will consider each type of attribute in turn.

1.1 Specific attributes

Specific attributes – as opposed to general attributes (which we will look at on page 5) – fall into two broad groups: the job-related attributes necessary to carry out the job and the knowledge of the good working procedures which your employer will expect you to follow.

Job-related attributes

For some jobs, technical knowledge and skills might be necessary.

- A sales representative needs to be able to drive and to have a clean driving licence. The employer may provide a company car, but some jobs require you to have your own means of transport.
- It is courteous for airline employees to respond to passengers in the same language that the passengers have used. Therefore, some airlines demand language skills of their cabin crew.

- An IT technician who fixes hardware faults must be able to use hand tools such as screwdrivers, but will also need to be skilled in using electronic testing equipment such as a multimeter.

An employer may need you to be able to drive and to have a clean driver's licence.

You might demonstrate your technical skills by taking and passing academic or vocational qualifications, or you might have a certificate to prove that you have a special skill, e.g. you can cook or swim.

If a particular technical skill is essential to an advertised job, it should be made clear to all prospective employees. This will deter candidates without the requisite skills and prevent employers from having to waste time interviewing applicants who are not qualified for the post.

Activity: Technical skills

1 Working in groups of three or four, search the local and national papers for examples of job adverts that specify the technical skills needed for particular IT vacancies. List the attributes that employers seem to be seeking in a prospective employee.

2 Make a list of the technical skills that you have. Compare your list with others in your group and add to your own list any skills that you had forgotten. Within your group, compile a comprehensive list of technical skills that one or more of you have. For each skill, grade yourself according to your own level of competence.

Good working procedures

Working procedures can be called 'good' when they take into account health and safety and security issues.

- If you are unwell, you should stay off work until you recover. Staggering in with 'flu or a virus and giving it to everyone else in the office is counterproductive.

- The Health and Safety at Work Act (1974) requires all employees to 'take reasonable care of themselves and others who could be affected by what they do'. This Act also states that if you are an employee who has 'been injured at work, seen a dangerous occurrence, or your doctor has certified that you have a work-related reportable disease, you must inform your employer'.

- Information that you find out while doing your job is confidential. This might include personal details of customers or industry-sensitive material about the design of a product. You are expected to respect the confidentiality and security of this material.

Work attitudes

Employees work in return for a wage. However, each employee's attitude to work is important and, from the employer's point of view, a good **work ethic** is required.

1.2 General attributes

Regardless of the job and its particular requirements, there are some skills – called **soft skills** – that everyone is expected to have, to some extent. These skills make you better able to carry out the tasks for any job.

This section will look in particular at planning and organisational skills, time management, team working, verbal and written communication skills, numeracy skills and other skills such as creativity. The more competent you are in these areas, the more attractive you will appear to a prospective employer.

Planning skills

Planning involves thinking ahead to decide what you need to do to achieve a **goal** within a given timescale. You might not need to write a plan, but thinking about what you need to do and what could go wrong will help to ensure a measure of success in whatever you set out to do.

The process of planning – establishing goals, deciding on **strategy**, setting **objectives** and then matching your performance against your objectives – is a way of measuring your success. If you fail in some respect, this can help you to plan more effectively in the future.

Key terms

Work ethic – a set of values which expects the employee to arrive on time, to work diligently throughout the working day, to show initiative and to be able to work within a team.

Soft skills – skills that influence how people interact with each other, e.g. analytical thinking, creativity, diplomacy, effective communication, flexibility, leadership, listening skills, problem solving, team building and a readiness for change.

Goal – the end result towards which your effort will be directed; provides general purpose and direction.

Strategy – a systematic plan of action.

Objectives – these are similar to goals. However, goals are broad and general, whereas objectives are narrower and more precise. Goals are intangible (such as, 'improve your general fitness'), but objectives are tangible (for instance, 'practise until you can do twenty press-ups in one go').

How to... Plan

1 First, establish your goal. This should reflect your present situation (its shortfalls) and your future needs. Once you have decided on a goal that can be effectively pursued, you may wish to write this down. Some organisations frame their goals in a mission statement.

2 Next, decide on your strategy. Consider what might happen if you follow a particular course of action, and remember to take into account the people involved and any constraints such as timescale and resources.

3 Your strategy will guide you as you work towards your goals. This will lead you to a list of objectives.

Planning may involve just you. For example, you might write yourself a 'to do' list and check your progress against this on a regular basis.

- You could review your progress every Monday morning and write a fresh 'to do' list, showing all the tasks you need to complete by the end of the working day on Friday. As the week progresses, you could tick off the things that you have done and think about the remaining tasks on the list.

- You might find it more helpful to rewrite the 'to do' list every day; some tasks may have become irrelevant, while others may have become more urgent. However, your day should be spent doing tasks, rather than thinking about what to do, so the administration of your 'to do' list must not become a major task in itself!

It might prove impossible to complete all the tasks on your 'to do' list by your Friday deadline. **Prioritising** will mean that you complete the most important tasks first and should help you to make more realistic plans in future. Do not try to fit too much into your day or promise to complete work, that will prove impossible, given your available time and resources.

Microsoft® Outlook®'s Tasks feature can help you to maintain your list and prioritise your work (see Figure 1.1). Outlook® Tasks also offers a reminder feature so regular tasks automatically reappear on the list.

Planning can involve a team of people, with each member of the team agreeing to complete their own tasks within a given time frame so that the entire team achieves its objectives. The organisational skills involved in managing a team are more complex and require more sophisticated tools (see page 11).

Organisational skills

A system, or routine, can help you to complete everyday tasks efficiently. For example, if you organise your workspace so that the things you need most (pens or pencils, your calculator, a stapler, a dictionary) are within arm's reach, and keep everything tidily in its place, you will not waste time hunting for things. You may need books or folders on a shelf nearby and files arranged alphabetically in a hanging drawer. On your desk, next to the telephone, you might keep your **address book** and a **diary**.

You might find it useful to write a 'to do' list each day.

Key terms

Prioritising – identifying which tasks are most important and putting these at the top of your 'to do' list.

Address book – a book with sections for each letter of the alphabet in which addresses and other contact details are recorded under the name (usually the surname) of each person you might need to contact.

Diary – a book in which space is set out (months, weeks, days, hours, time slots) to record events (past or future). Also called an appointment diary, this provides a written record of how you have spent your time and what will be on your agenda in the future.

Set the reminder to pop up on a regular basis.

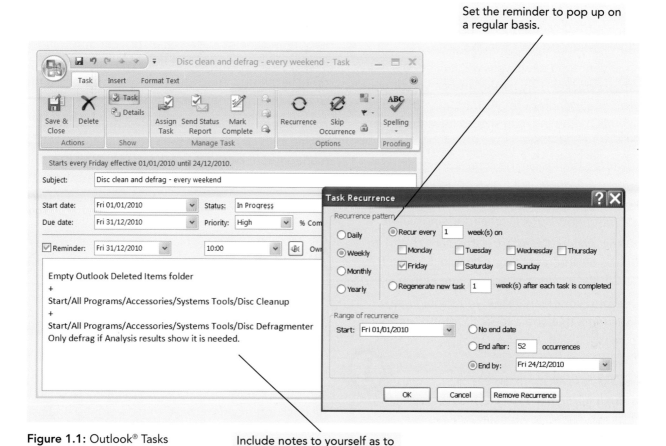

Figure 1.1: Outlook® Tasks

Include notes to yourself as to what needs to be done.

Organisational skills can be learned. First, focus on one aspect of your life that you want to organise (your workspace, your books, your CDs, your wardrobe, a social event). Then consider the purpose of organising and set yourself a **target**.

- A receptionist might write, 'I need to organise my workspace so that when someone asks me a question I can easily and quickly locate the information I need to answer. This will make me a more reliable source of information.'

- A librarian might write, 'I need to organise my books so that I can find a particular book quickly. This will be appreciated by those who visit my library.'

- An events organiser might write, 'I need to co-ordinate everyone involved in this event and ensure that everything goes according to plan.'

Once you have set your target, ask yourself what options you have. In your own workspace, you could arrange your books by type, putting fiction on one shelf and technical manuals on another shelf. By segregating the books, you can reduce the number of books you need to search through to find the one you want.

Key terms

Target – an objective or goal; something to aim for.

In-tray – a physical tray for paperwork, or an electronic Inbox such as that provided by email software like Outlook.

Time management

To make the best use of your time, you need to manage it effectively. To do this, you must:

- take control of your time – using a diary

- protect your time – space handling interruptions

- toughen up on together-time – making meetings work

- eliminate paper shuffling – getting on top of your **in-tray**.

People who offer a service (for example, a chiropodist or a piano teacher) rely on a diary to keep track of which clients they are expecting and to identify gaps where new appointments can be made. Such people need to blank out days when they are not available for work and be very careful not to double-book anyone.

If a client rings to change an appointment, this also has to be recorded carefully, rubbing out the original booking and writing in the new one.

To manage your time effectively, you will need a diary too – either a pocket diary, or the one on your iPhone® (if you own one) or computer. As long as you refer to your diary each morning, you should never forget an appointment or arrive late.

- Handwritten diaries can be small enough to carry with you everywhere (such as a pocket diary) or large enough to remain where they belong (such as an appointments book in a hairdressing salon).

- Electronic online diaries are particularly useful in a working environment. For example, Microsoft® Outlook® has a calendar feature (see Figure 1.2).

Whatever form your diary takes, you should use it to record events that you expect to attend, people you plan to meet and things you have to do. Looking at your diary will tell you what will be happening the next day, week or year and will allow you to keep track of the time you have left to do other things. An overfull diary will warn you not to take on anything extra.

Handling interruptions efficiently – from emails, phone calls or people – is an important aspect of time management because these interruptions can disrupt your work (see Table 1.1: Handling interruptions).

Did you know?

Studies have shown that on-screen interruptions announcing a new email can seriously disrupt a person's workflow.

Did you know?

Most diaries run from 1 January to 31 December, the calendar year. Academic diaries run from July one year to December the following year.

If you let yourself be distracted, you might not complete the list of tasks you'd planned to do in a day. All fresh interruptions have to be weighed against your current list of objectives. Are they more important than what you'd already set out to do?

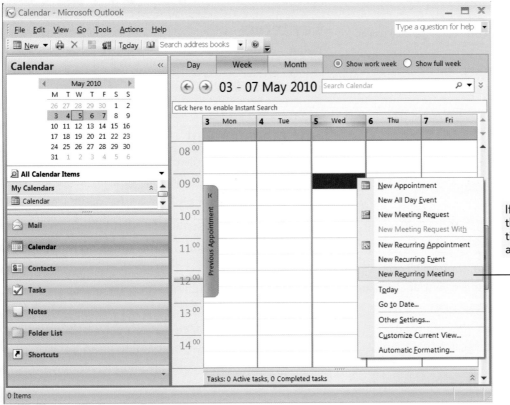

If an appointment is recurring, the calendar can set aside time for subsequent meetings automatically.

Figure 1.2: Outlook® calendar

Table 1.1: Handling interruptions

Interruption	The problem	The solution	Notes
Email	It takes time to read and respond to each email, but it also takes time to recover the momentum that was in effect before the interruption. Batching emails means there might be a longer delay in responding to any one email.	Batch the interruptions. Instead of having an announcement arrive on-screen as soon as a new email arrives, check your inbox at regular intervals, e.g. once an hour. Clear all important emails and then resume other work; resist checking your inbox again for at least another hour. Apply a priority system. Deal with the most important emails first.	Since the emails have to be processed at some point and other work needs to be completed too, the best strategy is to batch the interruptions. The time spent responding to emails is not reduced, but the quality of time spent on other tasks is improved. Leave everything else until you have completed the day's tasks.
Telephone	You have a number of telephone calls to make.	Work through them in one sitting.	List the calls you need to make, ensuring you have all the details to hand (who you are going to call, their telephone number, any paperwork that you want to discuss with them, your diary etc.).
Voicemail	While you are on the phone or away from the office, incoming callers may leave messages on your voicemail.	When you return to the office or finish making outgoing calls, check your voicemail. Prioritise your responses. Which messages need actioning now/today? Could you send an email response instead?	Telephone conversations take up more time than sending an email. Your timing may inconvenience the other person – they may already be on the phone or in a meeting – and you might end up having a voicemail conversation. An email provides a written record of your conversation.
People	If people constantly interrupt you, it can be impossible to complete a single task efficiently.	Arrive at the office an hour before anyone else and stay late? No. If you have your own office, close the door. If you have an assistant, tell them to field all interruptions, leaving you in peace for a specified period.	If you arrive early and leave late on a daily basis, there is not enough time for rest and relaxation – an essential part of anyone's day. It is important to handle interruptions in a way that does not offend anyone and yet allows you to complete your work during normal office hours. A closed door may be enough to deter casual interruptions. Some organisations encourage employees to work from home occasionally; this cuts out commuting time and helps to ensure quality working time.

Why are numeracy skills so important in a business context?

Creativity

Creativity is needed in all lines of work, not just those involving an 'artistic' output. Employees who can dream up ideas and think laterally and 'outside the box' can make major contributions to the success of an organisation. Some companies have a suggestions box – if you make a suggestion that helps to improve productivity, reduce waste or make the customers happier, you will be rewarded.

Creativity involves original thought and, for this, your mind needs space to let these ideas flow. Artists – writers, painters, musicians – have rituals to prepare themselves for creative activity. Often, they can choose when and where they work, e.g. going to a desert island or locking themselves away in a studio. Some writers work best early in the morning but spend time sharpening pencils before they write the first word of the day. Some fuel their creativity with fine wine or have loud music playing in the background. Each has his/her own way of working.

The creative process requires discipline and practice. In a team working environment, creativity has to be channelled despite background noise such as

machinery or conversation. To allow ideas to come through, you might need to create your own space within this busy environment.

1.3 Attitudes

Some skills can be learned, such as the technical skills and soft skills mentioned already. Other soft skills – such as determination, **independence**, integrity, tolerance, dependability, problem solving, leadership, confidence and self-motivation – are part and parcel of a person's temperament.

Key term

Independence – someone who has independence is able to act without depending on others, e.g. for financial support, approval or assistance in completing a task.

As each day passes, your attitudes may change.

- You may come into contact with people from different backgrounds and, by interaction with them, learn more about the motivations of others. This may give you a greater tolerance, but it may harden your existing attitudes too.

- You may find yourself giving way to peer pressure. Within any group, norms are established regarding acceptable ways of behaviour. What people wear and how they speak to each other can be influenced by peer pressure.

- You may see things differently as you grow older. It is difficult to think in the same way as a 60-year-old when you are only 30 and, to a teenager, people over 30 may seem ancient and old-fashioned in their thinking. It is only as the years pass that people change their attitudes to certain situations, simply because they are older – and maybe wiser.

The attitudes an employer expects depend very much on the job specification and conditions of working. They also depend on the people already employed – a new employee needs to fit in.

Determination

Personal attitudes are difficult to learn. Instead, if you consider yourself to be lacking in some respect, you can try hard to overcome your natural inclinations. For many attitudes, there is a spectrum ranging from 'very much so' to 'hardly at all' that might describe you.

Determination is one such attitude. How determined are you?

- Are you so relaxed that you are happy to go along with whatever anyone else suggests?
- Or are you so determined that you cannot see anyone else's point of view and simply railroad through objections?

Neither extreme is healthy! However, employers might prefer to have someone who is keen to see a job through, with the determination to overcome difficulties on the way.

Independence

An employer might advertise for 'someone who can think for themselves'. They will be looking for someone who is not totally dependent on being told what to do next and someone who can show some initiative. However, they will not want a new employee to act without checking first or consulting others as to what is normally done. Instead, common sense and a degree of flexibility should prevail.

Integrity

Integrity is essential for most jobs, for example honesty is important when handling money. However, in some jobs, you might be more successful if you can blur the truth, put a spin on things and say what people want to hear rather than telling the complete truth. In a management role, for example, a mix of kindness and sensitivity is needed when telling employees unpalatable news, such as details of the impending closure of a workplace.

Tolerance

Tolerance might be considered essential in all walks of life. To accept that each person has his or her own way of doing things, and that some are more (or less) successful than others in meeting targets, shows a level of tolerance that might be summed up as 'live and let live'. This is especially important in team working situations.

However, in positions of authority, you cannot always be tolerant and you might be expected to show no tolerance at all in certain circumstances. For example, someone who behaves in a way that might present a hazard to others must be stopped from doing so, or someone who fails to meet a deadline may be jeopardising the jobs of fellow workers.

Dependability

Reliability is a measure of how dependable you are. Most employers would prefer a worker who is reliable, who always turns up for work on time, does what is expected without complaint.

Problem solving

In any situation, some people will see only the problems they face and will be weighed down by them. Others may be quick, perhaps too quick, to see a solution. They may not appreciate the full extent of the problem.

Having an open mind and an optimistic attitude can be helpful when problem solving. If you assume that something is impossible, nine times out of ten you will prove yourself right. Similarly, if you take the attitude that nothing is impossible and are keen to look for a solution that works, you are likely to find one.

How to... Solve problems

1. Identify the problem. Write down the current situation and what is wrong. Note also what is good about the current situation – your solution must try to preserve the best aspects of the situation.

2. Identify what you are trying to achieve with the solution. This may be a long-term goal and you may need to set some intermediary targets.

3. Think of all the things you could do and what their effects might be. Will they help or hinder progress?

4. Consider known methods of solving this problem that you have seen work before. If these seem to be suitable, you might adopt them, but first set aside time to consider alternative solutions.

5. Having established your options, measure each in terms of some cost. This could be time, effort, inconvenience to others, etc.

6. Review your options again, taking into account the pros and cons of each.

7. Make a decision and carry it through as planned.

8. Review the results of your decision and note any situation that surprised you or any unexpected positive or negative outcome. Keep this review for future reference.

Leadership

Everyone is a potential leader and opportunities for leadership occur daily. However, many people lack confidence or leadership experience – they doubt that they can lead and so they do not even try. Learning how to lead includes learning how to follow, so recognising the roles and responsibilities of leaders and followers is a must for those who work within a team.

To lead well, you need to be aware of your own strengths and weaknesses. Before others will respect you as their leader, you must respect yourself. You must understand people, so that you can identify what motivates them, what rewards and values matter to them and how, as a team leader, you can inspire them with your vision of what the team can achieve.

Confidence

If you lack confidence, your approach to problem solving may be too cautious – you may not have the courage to try the best strategy. Confidence in your ability to meet the challenges you face can help you to achieve your goals. Other people's confidence in your abilities can also make a difference to how your ideas are accepted.

However, over confidence, or arrogance, may mean that you do not think things through carefully enough while planning your strategy. You may miss a vital clue or skim over an important aspect, resulting in problems at some point.

So, confidence is important, but it must be based on genuine skill levels.

Self-motivation

Some people are described as self-starters – they do not need anyone else to motivate them to do something as they have their own internal drive.

People who are not self-motivated either do very little or use up their team mates' precious energy to keep them going. Such people are not welcome in a team.

Assessment activity 1.1 P1

1 You are on work experience with the Right-On Recruitment agency and the manager that you have been job shadowing asks you to create a first draft of a leaflet to explain the personal attributes valued by employers. **P1**

Grading tip

To achieve P1, you do not need to describe the attribute – just name it and explain why it is valued. Make sure you include a range of attributes including at least one of each of the following: specific attributes, general attributes and attitudes. **P1**

PLTS

As you research the different personal attributes required by different employers, you will develop your skills as an **independent enquirer**.

Functional skills

Using a range of effective interpersonal skills, such as making contributions to discussions and making presentations in a range of contexts, will demonstrate your Functional **English** skills in Speaking and Listening.

2. Understand the principles of effective communication

2.1 Principles

The principles of effective communication depend on the type of communication that you are using. There are some that apply in general, some that relate only to interpersonal communication and others that apply specifically to written communications.

- General communication skills apply regardless of the form of communication.
- Interpersonal communication skills come into play when you are talking to someone face to face or when your message is being communicated so that the audience can see and/or hear you (even if you cannot see or hear them).
- Written communication skills apply only when you commit a communication to paper (for example, in a letter, email or press release), to a slide in a presentation or to a web page (for example, in a blog).

The following sections will look at general communication skills, interpersonal skills and how best to communicate in writing.

2.2 General communication skills

For communication to take place, there must be an audience for your message to be communicated to. Who that audience is will determine the type of language you use, the way you put your words together and how you deliver your message.

Cultural differences

Any cultural differences between you and your audience, or within your audience, will need to be addressed. Some words or signs that are acceptable in one language or culture may be misunderstood or considered offensive in another, so you might choose to use different words or gestures from the ones you would usually use.

Adapting to suit an audience

The age and composition of your audience can impact on the way you communicate with them.

Why must you be sensitive to cultural differences or age differences in your audience?

- You might raise your voice (or use a microphone to be heard) or vary your tone of voice – to modulate it – to maintain the interest of your audience.
- You might be selective in your choice of terminology, to make sure that everyone in your audience understands your message.
- You might present your message in a particular format (for example, using rhyme or music) or deliver it electronically.

Accuracy

Having adapted the content and style of your communication to meet the expectations or needs of your audience, you should next focus on the message that you are trying to convey. To win the hearts and minds of an audience, you may be tempted to stretch the truth or to make emotive statements to whip up feelings for or against some political or social issue. For some audiences, these tactics may work. However, it is usually best to stick to the truth and to include only **facts** in your message. Otherwise, you risk being shown to be a liar. If this happens, you will lose credibility and no one will listen to you – no matter how conscientious you claim to be.

When aiming to provide accurate information, you must differentiate between facts and **opinions**. Day-to-day decision making is often based on opinions, so you must make sure that you are fully informed before making any decision – especially one that may affect other people as well as yourself.

Key terms

Facts – these can be proved: they are either true or false. Data can be collected and hypotheses tested.

Opinions – these are more complex: they vary from one person to the next and can change within the same person from one day to the next. Opinions can be strong or weak and may be influenced by knowledge – or the lack of it – of relevant facts.

Engaging the audience

To maintain the interest levels of your audience, whether they are reading a report you've written or listening to a presentation, you need to apply various techniques.

Imagine listening to a speaker whose voice never varied in tone – it would soon put you to sleep! When delivering your message, written or oral, make sure that you vary your tone.

In an oral presentation, you can create interest by pausing from time to time – long enough to let the audience take in what you have said, but not so long that they think you have forgotten what you were going to say next. You can create a similar effect in written communications if you:

- vary the sentence length, using longer sentences to carry a train of thought and short punchy sentences to make a point
- use headings or bullet lists to section off or break up the message into manageable chunks.

In a face-to-face situation, you might use multimedia to hold the interest of the audience and keep their eyes from wandering to their surroundings. For example, you could show presentation slides, play music or hold up an object to illustrate a point. You could also say that there will be an opportunity to ask questions at the end

of your talk as this may encourage your audience to pay attention, thinking about what they might like to ask.

In written communications, diagrams and pictures can be used to good effect and in a presentation, animations can be used to enliven a slide show. However, you need to apply caution, since too much activity can detract from your message. Similarly, staying completely still while delivering your message may unsettle an audience, but continually pacing up and down can also be distracting. A balance is needed.

Question and answer sessions

Question and answer (Q&A) sessions can be particularly useful for clarifying points that you might have skimmed over in your presentation. You can't be sure how much your audience has understood until you hear their questions. Apart from satisfying their curiosity, you can use this feedback to improve your presentation for the next time around.

A question and answer session can also give the impression that the audience can throw any question to the speaker and that the speaker will answer it. This is not always the case.

- In broadcast Q&A sessions, the questioners often have to submit their questions beforehand so these can be vetted and the speaker may be told of the questions that will be asked so that they have time to prepare an answer.
- In face-to-face Q&A sessions, this level of control cannot be managed. However, the speaker may resort to saying what he/she wants to say – toeing the party line, so to speak – rather than actually answering the question.

Be prepared to answer questions after a presentation.

2.3 Interpersonal skills

For communication to happen, two or more people must be involved. One person expresses a message through words (spoken or written), signs, signals, facial and bodily expressions or even silence. The other person uses his/her senses (mostly sight and hearing) to gather aspects of the message.

It is important to consider how you might communicate your message to an audience and what possible barriers to communication there might be.

Methods

Verbal exchanges work for most people, but those who cannot speak may sign a message, while someone who is deaf might rely on lip reading. The recognised signing system also acts as an aid for communication with the deaf.

Techniques and cues

To express emotion in verbal communications, some change of tone is needed.

- A raised voice can indicate anger or impatience.
- A lowered voice can show fear or insecurity.

In face-to-face discussions, the tone of voice may be accompanied by some body language.

- A fist being thumped on the table conveys more force than hands that are held together as if in prayer or hanging meekly at the speaker's side.
- Folded arms across the chest may show indifference or obstinacy.

Someone who is unsighted, or at the end of a telephone line, doesn't have the extra dimension that body language offers during face-to-face communication. This person can still hear pauses though and will identify any emotion conveyed through intonation.

Positive language

The word 'Yes' is a positive response to a question. Your facial expressions – such as a smile – can also convey a positive reaction. Nodding your head, or leaning towards the speaker, conveys your agreement or willingness to listen to what is being said.

Negative language

Cutting in while another person is speaking, depending on how you do it, can convey enthusiasm

Why is negative body language a barrier to communication.

or may be seen as antagonistic. Finishing other people's sentences can be irritating and may indicate insensitivity on your part.

If you decide not to react at all and remain impassive, this also communicates a clear negative message to the speaker – you are bored and have no intention of listening.

Body language that indicates a negative attitude can act as a barrier to communication. For example, you are unlikely to persuade someone to open up and communicate with you frankly if you use closed body language and an aggressive stance.

Active engagement

Communication doesn't just happen when you are speaking – you can also communicate in several ways while the other person speaks. By paying attention and reacting to what the other person is saying, for example, with a nod or a frown, you are communicating that you hear what is being said and that you are taking note.

Once the other person has finished speaking, they may signal that you are expected to respond. They might end with a question (such as, 'Don't you agree?') or they might use body language to indicate that it is your turn to contribute to the conversation, by turning their body or inclining their head towards you. You can confirm your understanding of what has just been said by **summarising** it, before going on to make your own comments. You might also **paraphrase** what has been agreed between you.

Forgetting to turn your mobile phone off during a meeting is rude, and may be very distracting.

Key terms

Summarise – to sum up the most important points of a communication.

Paraphrase – to say again but using different words.

Open question – a question that could be answered in a variety of unanticipated ways.

Closed question – a question that expects a limited range of answers such as Yes/No.

Barriers to communication

To communicate effectively, you need to prevent, or reduce, the effect of communication barriers as much as possible. For example, for an audience to hear you, your voice should be clear and loud enough, without any distortion or interference. Therefore, it is important not to position the mouthpiece of a telephone under your chin and, in direct communication, you should face your audience.

- **Background** noise should not be underestimated. Even a slight continuous noise, such as the humming of an air conditioning unit or the ticking of a clock, can distract an audience.

- **Distractions** such as someone walking into a meeting late or leaving unexpectedly, the arrival of the tea trolley or a mobile phone beeping can interrupt the flow of thought of an audience and, momentarily, they could stop listening to you. As soon as that happens, communication will falter and you, as the speaker, might feel the need to repeat part of the message.

- **Lack of concentration** from your audience will also hinder communication. It is important to maintain concentration levels despite any distractions. The length of a conversation or communication is important – the recipient can only take in so much information at a time and anything beyond that is counterproductive. For example, a short verbal rebuke might prove useful, but the recipient is likely to lose concentration if this turns into a lecture on behaviour.

This also holds true for written communications. If you can convey your message on one page of A4, then do so. The recipient of a two-page letter will have lower concentration levels when they turn the page.

Types of question

Communication is not just two people speaking in turn. There needs to be a link between the people and questions can help to create such a link.

- An **open question** is an invitation to the other person to pick up the conversation and take control. For example, if you ask 'How are you today?' there are a multitude of possible responses. The conventional response is 'I'm fine, thanks. How are you?' whether or not this is true. During a debate on an issue, a constructive open question might be 'What do you think about this?' This invites the other person to express their views.

- **Closed questions** are expressed in such a way that the options for a reply are limited, perhaps only to 'yes' or 'no'. 'Would you like a cup of tea?' is a closed question. The question can be made less specific: 'Would you like something to drink?', but this may still result in a yes/no answer. To find out exactly what is required, you would need a follow-up question: 'What would you like to drink?'

Either form of question is acceptable during most conversations. With open questions, you may not find out what you want to know. In this case, you will need to follow up with additional questions – called

probing questions – to extract the information you want. In personal conversations, such questions might be considered unacceptable because they delve too deeply into a person's private space. In some circumstances, it may be effective to repeat questions, but this may be considered aggressive or impolite.

> ## Key term
> **Probing question** – a question that seeks out further information and narrows the responses down to the required answer.

Even closed questions can be threatening if used during an argument. 'You agree with me, don't you?' expects a yes or no answer and forces the other person to declare his or her position. A cautious response that shows diplomacy might be 'yes and no', followed up with some explanation about the points of agreement or disagreement.

Speed of response

Questions can be answered in a number of ways:

- quickly and maybe with passion
- slowly after what looks like consideration of all the issues
- something in between or not at all.

Answering a question with a question is a delaying tactic that is often used in discussions. Repeating the question back to the questioner is another delaying tactic that sometimes works.

2.4 Communicate in writing

Written communication is fundamentally different from other forms of communication. It requires special skills in the construction of the message – not least, the ability to handwrite or type. It also requires a good knowledge of the vocabulary and grammar of a language (such as English) so that the written word conveys the intended message to the audience. You cannot use visual cues such as body language, or oral cues such as tone of voice.

Writing something can seem very easy, but effective written communication is another matter. You need to understand how you can best communicate in writing and what constraints might be imposed by your working conditions. We will identify how you might use the tools at your disposal to communicate a message to your audience, minimising the risk of misunderstandings.

Guidelines

As an employee, you will be expected to follow organisational guidelines and procedures.

- You will be allocated space in which to work, and you will be given notice of the times you should attend the office and/or be available for others to contact you. You will be supplied with the communications equipment you will need in your day-to-day work, such as a computer, a telephone and stationery, and you may be given access to other essential materials such as a shared fax facility.
- There may be guidelines restricting the ways computer equipment is to be used. For example, there could be rules relating to the use of emails and faxes and the type of information that can be sent by email or fax (for reasons of confidentiality).
- There could be templates that you are required to use for your written communications, with style sheets that determine the look of any document. For example, in emails you might be required to use a standard footer with the company name and your job title or there could be a standard disclaimer.

Organisational guidelines are created to ensure a consistent and secure style of communication from those within the organisation to those outside the organisation. As a representative of the organisation you will be bound by these guidelines.

Smileys or emoticons

Smileys – also called emoticons (see Figure 1.3) – can be used to express a frame of mind. These are used in text messaging and on Internet forums and social networks like Facebook® and MSN. They are not suitable for serious communications and would be frowned upon in the workplace.

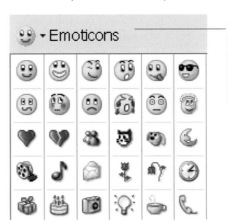

A range of emoticons is available with most forms of 'chat' or private messaging system.

Figure 1.3: Examples of emoticons taken from MSN

Key messages

Whatever form a written communication takes – report, letter, fax or email – there will be a key message to be conveyed. Within a letter, this may be flagged by the inclusion of a heading, immediately after the salutation (see Figure 1.4); electronic faxes and emails use a subject line to convey the key message (see Figure 1.5).

The heading is centred and appears just after the salutation.

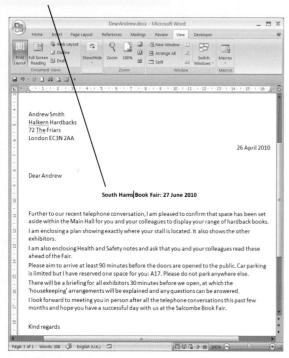

Figure 1.4: Key facts in a letter heading

Grammar and spelling

The body of a report, letter, fax or email will add substance to the key message.

• It may provide an explanation or apology.

• It may contain further information, such as directions or an itinerary, or it may request action.

Whatever the content of the communication, it is important that it is written using the correct grammar and spelling. Mistakes convey an unprofessional image to the reader and they can also create confusion if the mistakes result in the message being difficult to understand.

Word processing software offers grammar/spell checker options. Use them, but with caution (see page 30).

Structure

If the message runs to more than a line or two, make sure you structure it in a way that aids the reader's understanding.

• A logical framework with material presented in a sensible order – using headings and perhaps bullet lists – should help the reader to take in the information without a struggle and without having to read the material more than once. You might decide to number your points or present some material in bold so that it stands out.

• An illogical framework will mean that the reader has to work harder to interpret your meaning and this could result in misunderstandings.

You may be presented with templates for letters and emails, with standard wording that you are expected to adapt for specific communications with suppliers,

The Subject column indicates what the email is about.

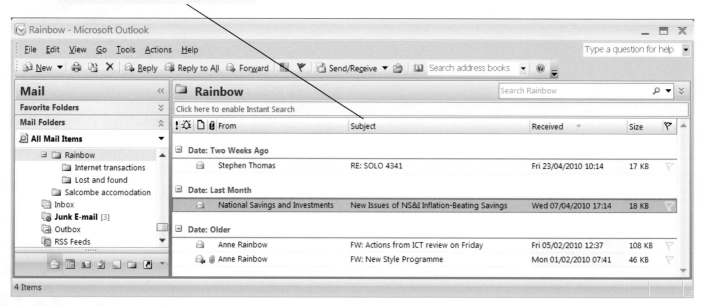

Figure 1.5: Key facts in the subject line of an email

customers and colleagues. If not, it is a good idea to reuse and adapt communications that you have used previously to convey a similar message.

Identifying relevance

When reading your report, letter or email, the recipient will try to identify relevant information within it. In a structured message, this task is made easier. However, if you have hidden relevant information within a mass of other details, the reader may miss important facts.

Underlining or emboldening important relevant information – such as the date of a meeting – is one way of ensuring that such facts are not missed. However, pruning the message so that it contains only relevant information is even more helpful to the reader.

There may be a standard way of signing off a letter that includes your official title and full contact details, for example telephone number, email address and/ or postal address. If not, adopt your own standard way which makes it clear that the communication is from you, (see Figure 1.6).

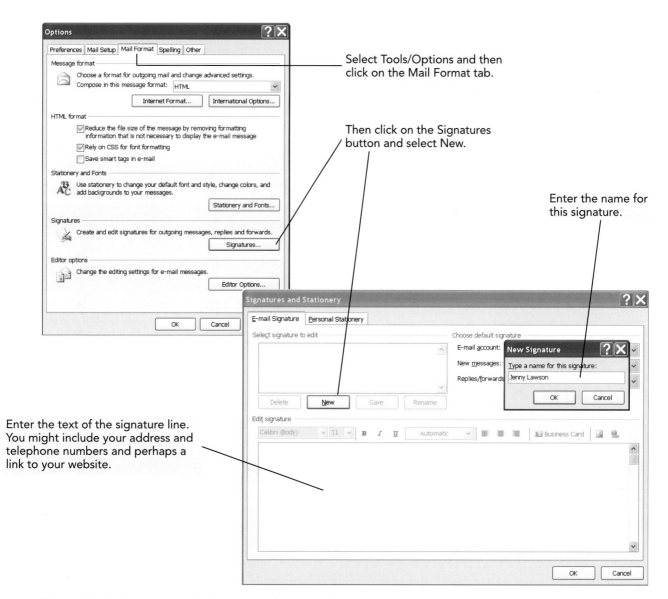

Select Tools/Options and then click on the Mail Format tab.

Then click on the Signatures button and select New.

Enter the name for this signature.

Enter the text of the signature line. You might include your address and telephone numbers and perhaps a link to your website.

Figure 1.6: Setting up a standard signature for an email

Proofreading

Before you send a written communication such as a report, text message, email or letter, it is essential to review and check your work for accuracy.

When you first create a written communication, the document is called a draft. Each time you redraft your document, you should **proofread** the text to check that you have not introduced errors. This is in addition to the use of tools such as a spell checker (see page 30).

Key term

Proofread – a process of checking, looking for errors within a written piece of text.

Finding errors in your own work is tricky – your eye reads what your brain thinks you planned to write and compensates for it. Even when there are spelling errors, your brain can make sense of the text.

There are various techniques you can try to improve your proofreading ability.

- Arrange with someone else that you will proofread their work and they will proofread yours. Some people are better at spotting errors anyway and each pair of fresh eyes is a bonus. Your reading of their work will improve your ability to spot mistakes.
- Allow time to pass before you proofread, so that you have distanced yourself from what you have written. Look at it with fresh eyes yourself.
- Read your piece more slowly than you normally would, out loud and focusing on one word at a time.
- Read the piece back, line by line.

Capitalisation

Capital letters are used at the start of a sentence (like the C in this sentence) or for proper nouns such as James and Portugal. They are also used for abbreviations, for example UK and USA and for acronyms such as WYSIWYG (what you see is what you get).

In written communications, especially text messages or emails, capitalisation of entire words or phrases is taken to mean shouting and is therefore to be avoided (unless you intend to shout).

Alternative viewpoints

Some documents can be used to present alternative viewpoints (for example, a report or a letter), and the structure of such documents must make it clear where each viewpoint starts and ends. The structure may include an introduction to explain the purpose of the document and a summary of the main points covered.

For example, a report may consider the effects of two different courses of action – a table may prove useful in presenting the pros and cons of each situation and graphs may help to show alternative results.

Note taking

You will not be alone in generating written communications in your workplace.

- Colleagues will be sending you documents, which you might need to edit before they are circulated. Alternatively, you could receive a document before a meeting which you need to review so that you are fully informed and ready to discuss the content at the meeting.
- You may receive documents from external sources, which you will need to review. For example, a supplier might present a quotation or you might commission some research to help you make a decision regarding new equipment or a course of action.

When reviewing a communication, you may find it helpful to take notes. This is especially useful when the communication is long and contains a lot of information. Note taking may involve:

- handwriting key points on a new sheet of paper
- annotating a hard copy of the document: writing in the margin, underlining key phrases or using a highlighter pen for important facts, dates or times
- using reviewing tools to annotate the electronic document with your comments (see Figure 1.7).

Electronic annotation is the most useful method. It allows you to email the document back to the originator, and, if you want to suggest changes to a Word® document, you can use Track Changes. When you email the document back to its originator, he or she can accept or reject your suggestions (see Figure 1.8) and the document can be revised in accordance with your combined wishes. Progress is made.

Highlight the text you want to comment on and click on the New Comment icon.

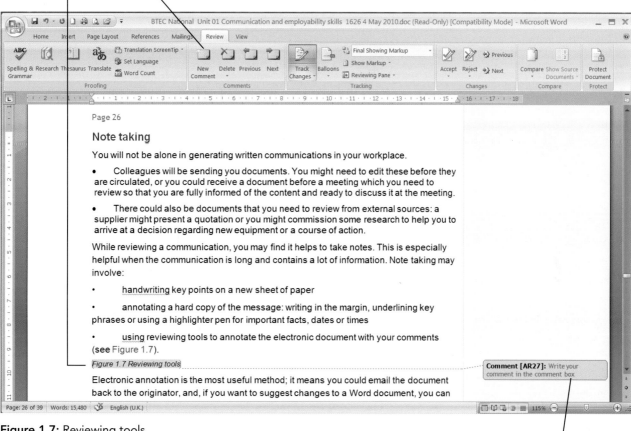

Figure 1.7: Reviewing tools

A numbered comment box will appear. Click within the comment box and write your comment there.

On the Review tab, toggle the Track Changes button on and off. When it is on, every change you make to the text is shown.

A vertical line in the left margin indicates new text has been inserted.

The way Track Changes has been set up for this document, any deleted text is shown as strike-through.

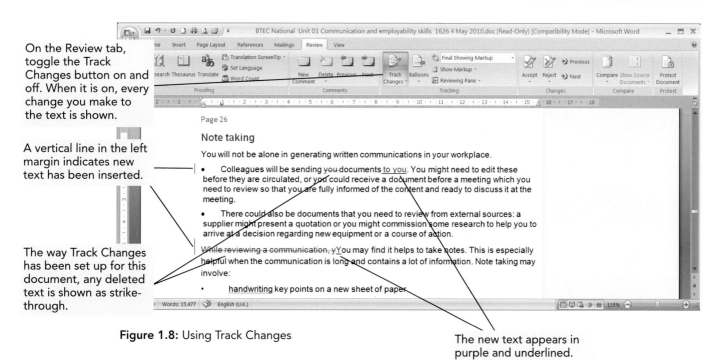

Figure 1.8: Using Track Changes

The new text appears in purple and underlined.

Assessment activity 1.2

1 You will take part in a group discussion, under direction from your tutor. During the discussion, the potential barriers to effective communication are to be discussed and demonstrated. **P3**

2 You will observe a group discussion and then write a brief report explaining mechanisms that can reduce the impact of communication barriers. **M1**

Grading tips

- To achieve P3, you must describe at least one barrier from each of: general communication skills (e.g. a diverse audience); interpersonal skills (e.g. background noise); written communications (e.g. using an inappropriate structure). **P3**

- You will have witnessed at least one barrier from each of general communication skills, interpersonal skills and written communications. To achieve M1, you should explain – not just describe – the mechanisms which may be used to reduce the impact of these barriers and why you think each may work. **M1**

PLTS

As you take part in a group discussion, you will develop your skills as a **team worker** and an **effective participator**. In your explanation of the ways in which barriers to communication can be overcome, you will demonstrate your skills as a **creative thinker**.

Functional skills

Using a range of effective interpersonal skills, such as making contributions to discussions and making presentations in a range of contexts, will demonstrate your Functional **English** skills in Speaking and Listening.

Assessment activity 1.3  BTEC

1 The manager at Right-On Recruitment has asked you to expand the leaflet you produced for Assessment activity 1.1 (detailing the personal attributes valued by employers) to include advice on the principles of effective communication. **P2**

2 Under direction from your tutor, demonstrate a range of effective interpersonal skills. **P4**

3 Having observed others demonstrating their interpersonal skills, write an evaluation of their communication techniques. Exchange copies of your evaluations and then write an evaluation of the written communication techniques employed in their evaluation of your interpersonal skills. **D1**

Grading tips

- To achieve P2, you need to discuss two or three relevant principles from each category: general skills, interpersonal skills and written communication skills. You do not need to go into great detail. **P2**

- To achieve P4, you will need to undertake a variety of interpersonal communications, from normal day-to-day interactions with your group to giving a short presentation which your class may be asked to assess. Your early attempts may reveal a lack of confidence on your part so practise until you can communicate with ease. **P4**

- When analysing the interpersonal and communication techniques of others, be sure to refer to all aspects studied in this unit: this is your opportunity to show strong insights into the ideas explored to date. Most importantly, make sure your report demonstrates your own ability to communicate effectively. This will enable you to achieve D1. **D1**

PLTS

As you work with other members of your class to demonstrate your interpersonal skills and assess the communication techniques of others, you will develop your skills as a **team worker** and an **effective participator**.

Functional skills

Using a range of effective interpersonal skills, such as making contributions to discussions and making presentations in a range of contexts, will demonstrate your Functional **English** skills in Speaking and Listening.

3. Be able to use IT to communicate effectively

Activity: In the good old days

Politicians used to canvass for support by standing on a soapbox in the town square and declaring their manifestos.

Later, prospective MPs used cars with loudspeakers on the roof to tour their constituency, urging their supporters to come out and vote.

In 2008, US President-Elect Barack Obama used email to reach voters during his campaign for office and in 2010 UK politicians followed suit.

- Look back over the past 100 years and identify changes in communication methods – radio, television, mobile technology and the Internet – and consider how these developments have impacted on politics.

- In what way can the social networks of today, such as Facebook® and Twitter, be deployed to create momentum in an election?

How have developments in communication affected political campaign methods?

3.1 Communication channels

A number of communication channels are available, each suited to a particular type of message, as shown below.

Table 1.3: Communication channels

Communication channel	Description/Examples	Benefits	Disadvantages
Word-processed documents	Presented on paper and/ or on screen Can include text, tables and still images Reports, business letters, newspapers and magazines	Hard copy is portable: you don't need to have access to a computer Hard copy can form a permanent record (e.g. for minutes of a meeting that need to be authorised as true) With on-screen documents, you can use the search option to locate particular information within the document	For a hard copy, the document has to be printed, which uses costly resources (e.g. paper and ink) You need a computer to view the document on-screen Some people find it more difficult to navigate through an electronic document – they cannot memorise where something was on a page
Presentations	A slide show Can be viewed with or without a presenter being there	Usually a short and snappy way of conveying key points, especially when used to illustrate a verbal presentation	Requires presentation hardware: a computer screen, whiteboard and/or projector

cont.

Table 1.3: Communication channels *cont.*

Communication channel	Description/Examples	Benefits	Disadvantages
Email	Electronic message Can include attachments such as a Word® document	Can be sent to more than one recipient at the same time Speedier than 'snail mail' (the traditional postal service)	Sender and recipient both need to subscribe to an email service Need access to the Internet while sending/receiving emails
Web pages	Can include audio and moving images Written in HTML code and/or scripting language such as Java™	Available online to all Internet users Interactivity may be provided, giving the visitor to the site a more rewarding experience while accessing the information Updating a website can be achieved very quickly, compared to the time it might take to republish a book (for example)	Requires skill in creating the elements of the web page and knitting them together to build a coherent, user-friendly website A computer with Internet access is needed to upload updated web pages
Blogs	An online journal, displaying frequent and chronological comments and thoughts for all to see	Offers the same benefits as a web page and provides insight into one person's view of life Individuals can access a worldwide readership without going through the medium of a publisher or the complexities of setting up a website	Same disadvantages as web pages, except that software is available to help the blogger
Vlogs	A medium for distributing video content Usually accompanied by text, image and metadata to provide a context or overview for the video	Offers the same benefits as a web page Allows individuals with little web development experience to air their views on the Internet	Same disadvantages as web pages
Podcasts	A method of publishing files (especially large audio files) to the Internet	Subscribers receive new files automatically Allows subscribers to decide what they hear and/or watch and when	Internet access is necessary for downloading files Users need to subscribe to a feed
Video conferencing	A way for many people, located in different places, to communicate 'face to face' without actually leaving their desks	Saves travelling time Costs of setting up and maintaining video conferencing are more than recouped by savings in travel and subsistence costs of delegates	Technical expertise is required to set up the audio and video links

Key terms

Blog – stands for weblog.

Vlog – a blog which uses video as its primary presentation format.

Podcast – a media file distributed over the Internet for playback on portable media players and personal computers. The term originates from Apple®'s iPod® and the word broadcasting.

3.2 Software

Let's now review four types of standard software that you'll use to communicate your message: word-processing software, presentation packages, email software and specialist software for the visually impaired.

Word-processing software

With word-processing software, you can enter, edit, format, save and print out text-based documents.

- Text can be entered via the keyboard and you can also adapt materials from secondary sources – you could copy and paste text from another document or from a web page or you could scan in text and convert it into a Word® document.

- Editing involves inserting, amending or deleting text to reword the document. It is achieved by inserting new text (keying it in or pasting it into place from elsewhere), amending the text (typing over it while using Overtype mode or pasting over existing material) or deleting text.

- Text can be formatted on one of two levels: **character formatting** or **paragraph formatting**.

- Because you can save your work, you can begin a letter or report one day and then work on it again at some later date. You can retrieve the finished document at an even later date and use it to create another document. For example, an annual report has the same basic structure each year – it is just the details that change. Having set up a report in the required style, the following year's report should take less time to produce.

- A word-processed document can be printed. You can preview the document before you print it, so you can proofread what you have written on-screen without wasting paper. You can also fine tune the settings for margins and horizontal/vertical spacing to create the best visual effect on the page.

Key terms

Character formatting – affects only those characters selected and can be used to highlight individual words. For example, to make important material stand out, you could change the font colour or present the material in italic, bold or underlined.

Paragraph formatting – affects the entire paragraph and is used to control the spacing of lines within, before and after the paragraph. It sets the basic look of the text (font style and size) and may be incorporated into a style sheet or template.

Presentation packages

A presentation package facilitates the construction of a sequence of slides, in the order you want to display them, with notes. Templates for a range of slide layouts let you incorporate bullet lists, tables and images. You can also incorporate other media (sound and video) or animations (see Figure 1.9).

The presentation package then offers various ways of running the presentation:

On the Animations tab, click on Custom Animation.

Select the text you want to animate and then choose what effects you want for it.

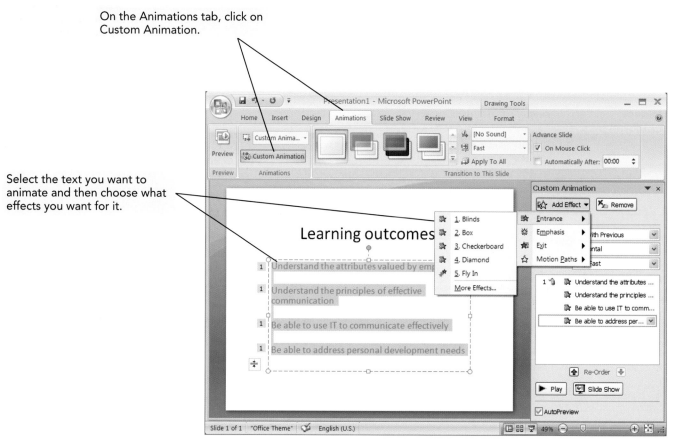

Figure 1.9: Options for animation

- on a whiteboard, with you controlling the transition from one slide to the next while you talk
- running continuously at a pace to suit most viewers, so that you do not need to be present
- with interactivity, allowing the viewer to decide when to view the next slide.

Email software

Email software is provided by Internet Service Providers (ISPs) who offer email as part of the Internet connection deal. You can also install an email client on your computer, such as Microsoft® Outlook®, which – while you are online – downloads incoming emails into your Inbox and uploads outgoing emails from your Outbox.

Whichever version of software you use, there are functions for composing a new email, replying to an incoming email and forwarding an incoming email. Having set up an email, you can attach documents to it and send it to more than one person (see Figure 1.10).

You can set up an address book to hold the email addresses of people you want to send emails to. You can set this up using data which arrives with the email (the email includes the address of the person who sent it). You can also set up distribution lists which allow you to send emails to a particular group of people.

Specialist software

Specialist software is available, for example for the visually impaired. You might think that the visually impaired cannot see a computer, a presentation

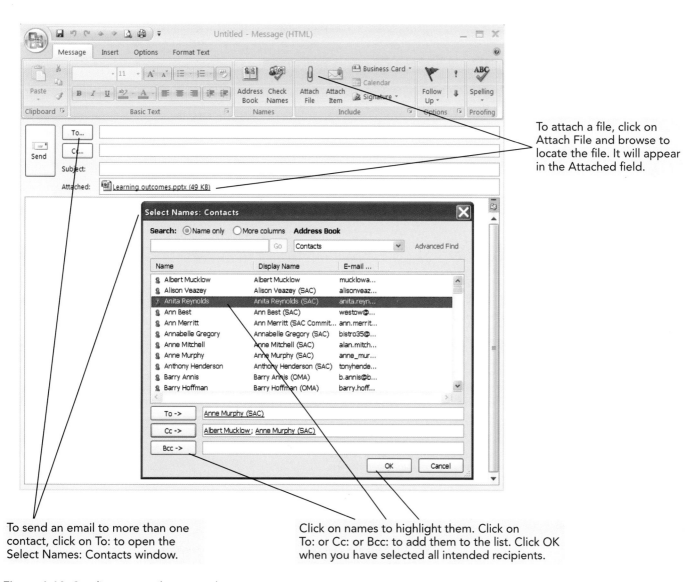

To attach a file, click on Attach File and browse to locate the file. It will appear in the Attached field.

To send an email to more than one contact, click on To: to open the Select Names: Contacts window.

Click on names to highlight them. Click on To: or Cc: or Bcc: to add them to the list. Click OK when you have selected all intended recipients.

Figure 1.10: Sending an email to more than one person

screen or a hard copy of a document. However, visual impairment covers a whole spectrum of sight problems.

- Some individuals are only slightly affected, while others are totally blind and cannot distinguish light from dark.
- Some people lose their sight through trauma, as a result of war or through disease. Most people are affected by deteriorating vision with advancing age.

Whether visual impairment comes about quickly or over time, IT can offer solutions to those who need help.

- Text readers, for example, can be used to convert material that has arrived in text form (by email or as an attached document) into an aural output which can be heard.
- Hardware has also been developed to help. A Braille printer has an embosser that punches dots on to paper rather than printing characters in ink. Braille printers connect to the computer in the same way as text printers, using a serial or parallel port. You can also buy Braille translation software that translates printed text into Braille.

3.3 Review documents

Having written the first draft of a document, the review stage begins.

One of the challenges in written communication is to use a varied and rich vocabulary. You need to be understood by your audience – no jargon! – and yet you need to choose the best possible words to convey your message. To provide a variety of vocabulary you might use a **thesaurus** (see Figure 1.11).

To make sure that you spell words correctly, you might use a **spell checker** (see Figure 1.12) which will flag a mistake like 'hwere' instead of 'where'. However, it is important to note that a spell checker will accept 'were' instead of 'where' because both words appear in the dictionary.

Key terms

Thesaurus – similar to a dictionary but, instead of giving meanings, it lists words with the same meaning.

Spell checker – compares your words with those listed in a dictionary, to ensure that they are spelled correctly.

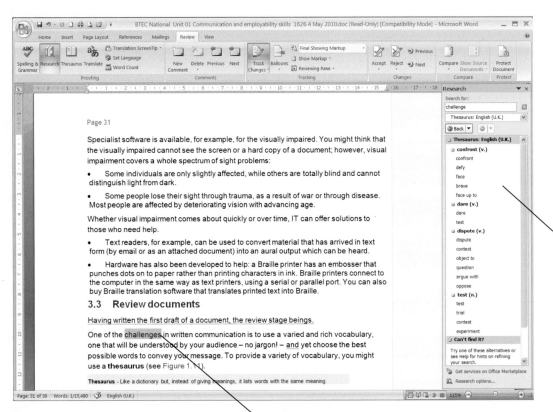

Figure 1.11: An electronic thesaurus

Highlight the word you want to replace, right click and select Synonyms/Thesaurus [or press the Thesaurus button, or key Shift/F7].

Because 'challenges' is plural, you are offered 'challenge' and, if you click on that, then the panel offers alternative words, dividing them into verbs and nouns.

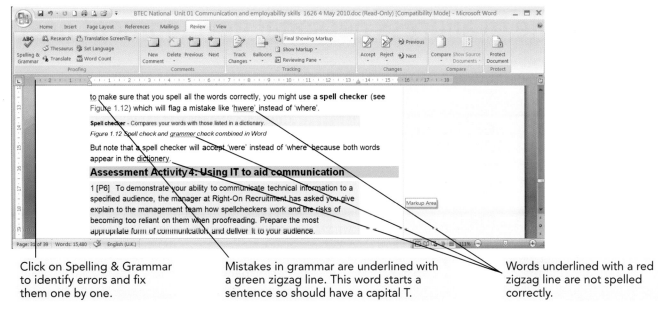

Click on Spelling & Grammar to identify errors and fix them one by one.

Mistakes in grammar are underlined with a green zigzag line. This word starts a sentence so should have a capital T.

Words underlined with a red zigzag line are not spelled correctly.

Figure 1.12: Spell check and grammar check combined in Microsoft® Word®.

Assessment activity 1.4   P5 P6 M2   BTEC

1 To demonstrate your ability to communicate technical information to a specified audience, the manager at Right-On Recruitment has asked you to explain to the management team how spell checkers work and outline the risks of becoming too reliant on them when proofreading. Prepare the most appropriate form of communication and deliver it to your audience. **P6**

2 Demonstrate your technical skills by using IT as an aid to the communication for Question 1 or for some other communication. **P5**

3 Your manager at Right-On Recruitment has asked you to review the draft leaflet created for Assessment activity 1.1 to produce a final version for distribution to fellow students. **M2**

Grading tips

- The technical information you provide for P6 does not have to be IT-related, so you could communicate on a topic relevant to another course you are studying, or on some aspect of your life outside school. Choose the form and style of communication carefully to ensure it is appropriate, considering the subject material and your audience. **P6**

- To achieve P5, you should use at least two proofing tools (such as spell check and thesaurus), plus one other tool that your software offers. **P5**

- When reviewing the document, you do not need to use the standard proofreading marks, but you must annotate your early draft(s) to show what changes were to be made. Evidence for M2 could come from the review of another document altogether, either one of your own creations or someone else's work. **M2**

PLTS

As you review your own and others' draft documents in order to identify improvements, you will develop your skills as an **effective participator**.

Functional skills

Communicating technical information to a specified audience will demonstrate your Functional **English** skills as you present information in ways that are fit for purpose and audience.

Using IT to aid communication will demonstrate your Functional **ICT** skills in that you select and use IT to communicate and exchange information safely, responsibly and effectively.

4. Be able to address personal development needs

When you're in full-time employment – when your boss is deciding who to promote and how much of a rise you deserve – you will most likely be put through an appraisal system that identifies your plus and minus points, and monitors and reviews your progress formally on a regular basis.

Now, though, you have an opportunity to find out how your personal learning style might have helped or hindered you in the past and to address your personal development needs – without risking a salary freeze!

Personal development means building on your strengths and managing your weaknesses.

- What are your strengths?
- What are your weaknesses?

4.1 Identification of need

Development needs are, by their very nature, personal. They apply to a single individual and each individual may have completely different development needs from his/her colleague.

To discover your personal development needs the first step is self-assessment.

This section also considers assessment by others, such as a formal report from a line manager, customer feedback and other performance data that an employer may choose to collect.

Formal reports

Formal reports provide your employer with an opportunity to record your progress within the organisation.

- **Appraisal meeting notes:** a properly conducted appraisal, and the notes recorded from this, can help people to progress in their job and make improvements in their work, adding to increased self-esteem and job satisfaction. The appraisal report could list any decisions that are made to train you or to redirect your energies through promotion, demotion or sideways moves. If your behaviour, or performance, is less than satisfactory, this may also be recorded, together with targets that you are expected to achieve and that, by negotiation, you agree to meet. If you then fail to meet agreed targets, you may be dismissed.

- **Customer feedback:** some organisations encourage customers to provide feedback about employees. Guests of a hotel chain, for example, may be invited to complete a questionnaire about the levels of service experienced during their stay. This can reflect well or badly on specific groups of employees, such as the reception staff, the housekeeping team or the bar/restaurant staff.

- **Performance data:** some organisations collect data to record the performance of individual employees. A supermarket, for example, can record how quickly a checkout worker scans products, how many customers are served during one shift and what turnover is taken during that shift. Each of these measures, taken in isolation, may not seem very fair. One customer might buy a lot of low-priced items, all of which are bulky, resulting in a slower scanning process. Another customer might find that an egg has broken and the completion of the transaction will be delayed while a fresh box is fetched. As with any statistical analysis, the sample group must be large enough to represent the entire population if the data is to prove useful. Over a long enough period of time, one checkout operator can be compared against another.

Self-assessment

Self-assessment is an essential part of personal development planning.

During this course, you will have had opportunities to consider your own strengths and weaknesses, your best and worst traits, and those of others in your group. There should also have been opportunities for others to express their opinion of you and for you to assess others and tell them what you think of them.

What others see in you tends to be what you choose to reveal about yourself. You have the option to hide certain traits and to promote the ones that you want others to recognise in you. The same goes for other people. So, in assessing someone else, you should be aware that you are only seeing what that person chooses to reveal. They may have hidden qualities that are revealed at certain times – perhaps in times of stress or when that person has the confidence to be more honest with you.

For personal development planning to be successful, you must be honest with yourself. If you cannot see your own faults, you cannot overcome them. Enlisting the help of others might help you to see yourself differently and more objectively.

4.2 Records

This section reviews two types of records: personal development plans (PDPs) and appraisal records.

Target setting

While completing this unit, you should have produced and followed a PDP. The process of thinking about your future and your plans (and setting short-term, medium-term and long-term goals) should have given you an insight into how useful PDPs can be. It is essential to think about what to do and to plan how you will achieve your goals. It is also important to record these goals and any objectives that you establish and to note the progress that you make. This will enable you to monitor your progress and set more realistic targets in future.

Appraisal records

For an employer, appraisal records are important as a way of recording what you and your manager plan for the coming year. They are useful for recording work and training goals and for identifying areas for improvement. See also the section on Formal reports on page 32.

4.3 Addressing needs

There are a range of options open to an individual to address needs that have been identified during an assessment process.

Job shadowing

Job shadowing is particularly useful for work experience, when you are trying to decide what career path to follow. It involves accompanying someone throughout their working day and observing what they are doing at all times. This provides useful insights into the stresses and strains of the job and how the person doing it copes with their workload and any interruptions.

If there is time, the person who is being shadowed can give a running commentary on what is happening. Sometimes, though, this is not practical, especially if other people, such as a customer or supplier during some delicate negotiation, could overhear what is being said. If this is the case, a debriefing session can be used afterwards to explain what was going on.

Team meetings

Some learning comes from talking with colleagues and watching them at work. This can happen during team meetings or while attending events outside the organisation such as conferences.

Most industries hold annual events. What can you learn by meeting with people working in the same trade or profession?

Attending events

Most industries hold annual events in which people in the same trade or profession gather at some central venue. These events provide an important opportunity to catch up on the latest developments, to share expertise and to find out what competitors are doing.

Training

If your job requires knowledge and skills that you don't yet have, you may be asked to attend a formal course. This course may be delivered within your organisation – internal training – or you may be sent off-site for external training.

The training may lead to qualifications for which you have to pass an examination. Examinations, such as those taken by bankers and those in insurance, are set to establish a standard of knowledge and performance expected of those within the industry. Within the IT industry, Microsoft® offers a number of certifications that can confirm your understanding of one or more of their products. Holding such a certificate can prove your level of expertise.

Assessment activity 1.5 BTEC

1 Having completed an analysis of your strengths and weaknesses, produce a personal development plan. **P7**

2 Follow your personal development plan and keep a record of what you do, when you do it and the levels of success or failure experienced. **P8**

Grading tips

- To achieve P7, you must be completely honest in your analysis of your strengths and weaknesses. Only then can you produce a plan that suits you. Include realistic timescales within your plan so that you can expect to be successful in whatever it is you are planning. **P7**

- To achieve P8, make a note of your progress on a regular basis. Writing everything up at the end of the course would be a terrible chore and your experiences would no longer be fresh in your mind. Instead, try to write something each day, as you would a blog, and make a note each time you experience something new. This will allow you to produce a lively and honest record. **P8**

PLTS

As you evaluate your own strengths and weaknesses and produce a personal development plan, you will develop your skills as a **self-manager**.

Functional skills

Producing your own personal development plan will demonstrate your Functional **English** Writing skills.

4.4 Learning styles

Learning styles vary from one person to the next and no two people learn in the same way. However, studies of groups of individuals and learning styles have resulted in terms being coined to describe different types of learners, such as: active/reflective, sensory/intuitive, visual/verbal, sequential/global.

- **Active learners** enjoy working in groups and like to try various solutions to problems in order to find out what works. They prefer to handle objects and to do physical experiments. **Reflective learners** prefer to figure out a problem on their own. They think things through, evaluate the various options and learn by analysis.
- **Sensory learners** look for facts first and prefer concrete, practical and procedural information. **Intuitive learners** look for meaning and prefer conceptual, innovative and theoretical information.
- **Visual learners** understand drawings (for example a spider diagram) that represent information. **Verbal learners** like to hear or read information and understand best explanations that use words.
- **Sequential learners** need information presented in a linear and orderly manner. They piece together the details to understand the bigger picture. **Global learners** see the bigger picture first and then fill in the details systematically. This is called a holistic approach to learning.

A number of models have been developed to describe how people study, how they perceive information, how they process information and how they organise and present what they have learned.

The perception stage relies on:

- sight (visual cues)
- hearing (auditory cues)
- other sensations, including touch, temperature and movement (kinaesthetic cues).

Each of these three types of cue (visual, auditory and kinaesthetic) appeals to some people, but not to others, so the way in which information is presented can affect how people perceive it.

- An auditory learner is most comfortable absorbing information that they have heard or discussed.
- A kinaesthetic learner prefers to learn through practical classes and hands-on activities, rather than by reading books and listening to lectures.

Most people can learn using a mixture of visual, auditory and kinaesthetic cues.

Having acquired information, how you process it mentally (by thinking about it and memorising it) can also vary. When grasping facts, you might prefer to deal with concrete, practical examples or you might be happier with abstract concepts and generalisations.

In ordering information, some people prefer to receive facts in a logical, sequential way so that they can build up a picture one step at a time. Others prefer an overview straightaway, so they can grasp the big picture first and then focus on the details. Some people engage with the information they have gathered by active experimentation, while others prefer to let things sink in through reflective observation.

In organising what you know, you may adopt a holistic overview or engage in detailed and logical analysis. When presenting information to share with others, you might tend to give verbal explanations, while someone else might use images.

Identification of preferred style

A number of quiz-type analyses have been devised to help people to identify their preferred learning style. Your answers to a number of seemingly simple questions build a profile of you and you can then be given feedback as to what learning styles suit you best.

Knowing your own preferred learning style

Tutors are trained to recognise learning styles and should present information to their classes in a variety of ways so that all learners benefit, regardless of their preferred learning style. However, if you find it difficult to grasp a subject, or find a lesson boring, you might need to adapt your way of listening or note taking so as to make the best of the lesson. For example, if your tutor presents you with a handout that you find hard to understand, try transferring the facts into a tabular format or a spider diagram, or present the data in some other way that makes it clearer to you.

The onus is on you to make the most of whatever your tutor presents, but giving feedback to the tutor may help them too. Ask questions if anything is not clear. Offer the tutor your version of the data – they may suggest giving a copy of what you have produced to other learners. Similarly, you might learn from how others take notes or represent the information they get from the tutor.

Understanding others' preferred learning style

Because each individual has his or her own preferred learning style, the way in which a team of people learns can be quite complex. Presented with a brief, such as an A4 sheet of written instructions, some of the team will very quickly grasp the facts of the problem to be solved. Others will need it explained differently, perhaps by using a diagram or talking it through.

So long as each person understands what is expected before work commences, the team should prove effective. However, any communications between team members need to take into account variations in preferred learning style, otherwise misunderstandings can occur which may hinder progress.

Assessment activity 1.6   BTEC

1   Explain how an awareness of learning style can aid personal development. **M3**

2   Review your progress on your personal development plan, identifying areas for improvement. **D2**

Grading tips

- To achieve M3, answer the question: 'If you know your preferred learning style, how can this help you to make your learning more effective?' You may offer a personal perspective or a more general perspective. **M3**

- Identify one particular weakness and focus on improving your technique in that area to provide evidence for D2. Choose a weakness you genuinely want to overcome and set yourself realistic targets. Your review can then close with a note of your success. **D2**

PLTS

This Assessment activity will allow you to develop your skills as a **reflective learner**, as you evaluate your experiences (showing an awareness of learning style) and review your progress, highlighting areas for improvement.

Functional skills

Using a range of effective interpersonal skills, such as making contributions to discussions and making presentations in a range of contexts, will demonstrate your Functional **English** skills in Speaking and Listening.

Helen Whittaker

Accounts Executive

Helen is an Accounts Executive working for Slick, a marketing company based in South Devon. Slick runs marketing campaigns for local businesses, creating press releases and placing adverts in local and national newspapers. Helen spends her days in meetings with clients and talking to representatives from the press. These meetings are organised by Helen's PA, who chooses a convenient time and location for each appointment.

Helen travels a lot, visiting clients and may be out of the office for days at a time. She uses her Blackberry to keep in touch with colleagues. Whenever Helen has access to a computer, for example via her laptop in a hotel room, or at an Internet cafe, she synchronises the diary on her Blackberry with that held electronically at the office.

When she is in the office, Helen looks at her emails only every two hours, so that she has blocks of uninterrupted time during which she can concentrate. She also has a 'closed door' policy which means colleagues are not able to interrupt her when she needs to be at her most creative.

Think about it!

1 How do you create the best working space for yourself?
2 How might you streamline the way in which you handle incoming emails and correspondence?
3 How do you deal with appointments?
4 How do you cope with deadlines?

Just checking

1. Give three examples of soft skills.
2. Describe a strategy for problem solving.
3. What is a key message? How can you draw attention to it?
4. How can you maintain the attention of your audience during a presentation?
5. What are the differences between open questions, closed questions and probing questions? Give an example of each type of question.
6. Explain the purpose of proofreading. How else can you ensure the accuracy of written text?
7. Give three examples of performance data.
8. What formal reports could an employer use to monitor and record your progress and development?
9. Briefly outline some of the main communication channels and give one advantage and one disadvantage of each.
10. Describe at least three different learning styles. How can you adapt your communications to suit people who learn in different ways?

edexcel ⠿

Assignment tips

- Be completely honest with yourself when considering your own personal attributes and try to see yourself as others see you.

- Practise the art of active listening in on all conversations, not just those to do with this course. This will make you more aware of the hidden messages conveyed through body language, which will allow you to become a more effective communicator.

- When using IT to communicate, use all the tools at your disposal to make sure your communications are as error free as possible. Spelling errors and typing mistakes are not acceptable when a spell check is just a click away.

- Be realistic when setting targets for yourself. A lower target achieved is better than a higher one missed.

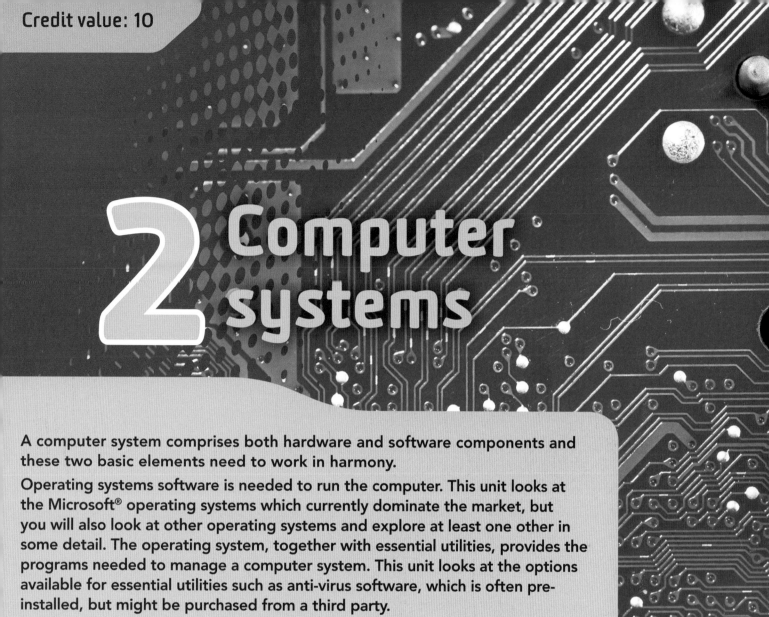

2 Computer systems

A computer system comprises both hardware and software components and these two basic elements need to work in harmony.

Operating systems software is needed to run the computer. This unit looks at the Microsoft® operating systems which currently dominate the market, but you will also look at other operating systems and explore at least one other in some detail. The operating system, together with essential utilities, provides the programs needed to manage a computer system. This unit looks at the options available for essential utilities such as anti-virus software, which is often pre-installed, but might be purchased from a third party.

Manufacturers of hardware offer a wide range of models, each with its own specification. This unit reviews the many hardware components of a computer system and how they interact.

Deciding which particular model is appropriate for a given situation depends on a variety of factors. You will explore these factors so that you can make informed choices when selecting the components for a system.

Technicians also need the skills required to set up and carry out routine maintenance of computer systems. Although this unit does not cover fault finding and repair (covered in Units 12 and 13), it includes the basic maintenance skills that would normally be expected of most IT professionals.

Learning outcomes

After completing this unit you should:

1. understand the components of computer systems
2. be able to recommend computer systems for a business purpose
3. be able to set up and maintain computer systems.

Assessment and grading criteria

This table shows you what you must do in order to achieve a pass, merit or distinction grade, and where you can find activities in this book to help you.

To achieve a **pass** grade the evidence must show that you are able to:	To achieve a **merit** grade the evidence must show that, in addition to the pass criteria, you are able to:	To achieve a **distinction** grade the evidence must show that, in addition to the pass and merit criteria, you are able to:
P1 explain the function of computer hardware components **See Assessment activity 2.1, page 55**		
P2 explain the purpose of operating systems **See Assessment activity 2.1, page 55**	**M1** compare the features and functions of different operating systems **See Assessment activity 2.1, page 55**	
P3 explain the purpose of different software utilities **See Assessment activity 2.1, page 55**		**D1** explain how software utilities can improve the performance of computer systems **See Assessment activity 2.1, page 55**
P4 recommend a computer system for a given business purpose **See Assessment activity 2.2, page 57**	**M2** justify choice of computer system to meet a given business purpose **See Assessment activity 2.2, page 57**	
P5 set up a standalone computer system, installing hardware and software components **See Assessment activity 2.3, page 70**		
P6 configure a computer system to meet user needs **See Assessment activity 2.3, page 70**		
P7 test a configured computer system for functionality **See Assessment activity 2.3, page 70**	**M3** evaluate the performance of a computer system **See Assessment activity 2.3, page 70**	**D2** explain and justify improvements that could be made to a computer system **See Assessment activity 2.3, page 70**
P8 undertake routine maintenance tasks on a standalone computer system **See Assessment activity 2.3, page 70**		

How you will be assessed

This unit will be assessed by a number of internal assignments that will be designed and marked by the staff at your centre. It may be subject to sampling by your centre's Lead Internal Verifier or an Edexcel Standards Verifier as part of Edexcel's ongoing quality assurance procedures. The assignments will be designed to allow you to show your understanding of the unit outcomes. These relate to what you should be able to do after completing this unit.

Your tutor will tell you precisely what form your assessments will take, but you could be asked to produce:

- diagrams, notes and comparative tables
- a presentation with supporting notes
- witness statements and observation records of your skills in installing components
- screen shots and test records.

Priya Patel, BTEC National IT learner

I've always enjoyed working on computers at school and at home, but whenever we bought a new computer, my elder brother or my Dad would decide what we needed. I was never consulted and I didn't have the confidence to voice an opinion about what we might buy next.

Completing this unit has given me time and the motivation to find out much more about all the component parts of a computer system. I now understand all the technical jargon and can recommend systems to suit different business purposes.

I had also not really had much to do with the maintenance of computers that I used. Now though, I appreciate what needs to be done and when, so that my hardware lasts for longer and my system works more efficiently.

Over to you

- **Do you already know how to set up – and maintain – a computer?**
- **How familiar are you with the technical details associated with hardware and software?**
- **Do you understand all the computer jargon?**
- **How confident would you be if asked by a friend to recommend what computer they should buy?**

1. Understand the components of computer systems

The perfect computer

Just imagine you've won the lottery or the premium bonds! If money was no object, what computer would you buy?

- What make and model of computer would you choose?
- What mix of hardware would you order?
- What operating system would you prefer to use?
- What software would you want to install?

Of course, everything depends on your planned use of the computer system, so think about that too.

Compare notes with others in your group. Did you all agree on the same configuration? If not, why not?

1.1 Internal system unit components

This section will look at what's inside the box and what options you might have when purchasing a new computer system.

Processors

The processor is a chip housed on the motherboard and is the 'heart' of a computer system – it controls everything. It contains the circuitry which processes the instructions in the computer programs by interpreting them into actual movements of bits of data within the computer memory.

The control circuitry pulls data in via the various ports, directs it along data buses, stores it within the memory, performs calculations on it and sends the results of processing to a visual display unit (VDU) screen, to a printer or to a secondary storage device for more processing at a later date.

Computer manufacturers constantly seek to improve the processor by increasing its capabilities (that is the types of instructions that it can process) and its speed.

With each new development of the processor chip, the voltage that the processor requires has also been reduced. This makes the processor more reliable because it does not get so hot. The memory capacity has also increased, as has the size of the cache (see page 49).

Did you know?

The speed of a processor is measured in GHz – the higher the number, the faster the processor works.

Figure 2.1: Processor configuration

Motherboard

The motherboard is the most important component within a PC system. It is a **PCB** (printed circuit board) that houses many of the essential parts of the PC and all connections between the PC and any peripherals go through it.

BIOS

The **BIOS** is a collection of software utilities that forms part of the operating system. It is usually on a **ROM** chip that comes with the computer, called the ROM BIOS.

Being on ROM, the BIOS is not affected by power failure and makes it possible for the computer to boot itself. So, what does the BIOS do?

- The BIOS boots up the PC, that is it starts up the PC every time it is turned on.

- The BIOS checks the actual hardware configuration against the configuration data. It ensures the integrity of the computer system and can therefore prove to be the most important diagnostic tool available to you.

- The BIOS handles the input and output of the computer, allowing the operating system to use particular features of hardware within the configuration.

Case study: Anne's laptop (1)

The hardware of a computer system – the main components and the **peripherals** – can be found either within the processor box or attached to the computer by some cabling.

There are also peripherals which do not need cabling and which rely on wireless or infrared to transmit data between processor and peripheral and vice versa. For each type of peripheral, there is a **port** on the processor to which it is connected, either through a cable or via a wireless link.

Anne has a laptop and this is linked via **USB** cabling to a mouse, a printer, a hard drive and a webcam.

According to the system information on Anne's laptop, she has a Dell™ Precision M6300 with Intel® Core™ 2 Duo CPU T7770 processor running at 2.40 **GHz** with 3.50 GB of **RAM** (see Figure 2.1 on page 42).

1 Find out what processor is at the heart of your computer. What is its speed? List its other characteristics.

2 Research the Internet to find out more of the history of the chip. What are the most popular chips today? What are their basic characteristics? Present your findings as a table showing the development of the chip from early Pentium® days to the present.

Key terms

PCB – stands for printed circuit board.

BIOS – stands for basic input/output system.

ROM – stands for read only memory.

Peripheral – any device, such as a printer, attached to a computer to expand its functionality.

Port – provides the link between peripheral and the CPU (central processing unit).

USB (universal serial bus) – a higher-speed serial connection standard that supports low-speed devices (e.g. mice, keyboards, scanners) and higher-speed devices (e.g. digital cameras).

GHz (gigahertz) – hertz are named after Heinrich Rudolf Hertz (1857–1894), a German physicist who studied electromagnetic radiation. Hertz are a measurement of frequency in cycles per second – 1 hertz is one cycle per second.

Giga – one billion. When measuring computer data, giga means 2^{30} (= 1073,741,824), which is the power of 2 closest to one billion.

RAM – stands for random access memory.

When the computer is turned on, its memory is empty, apart from one set of hardwired instructions that are located at an address called the jump address. These important few instructions, when executed, will load the BIOS into memory. So, the computer 'jumps' to the jump address, starts executing instructions and this results in the BIOS being loaded.

The loading of the BIOS is part of the booting up process during which the configuration of the computer is checked (during the **POST** process) and the operating system loaded, so that everything is ready for the user to start work.

Activity: Motherboards

1 Find out what type of motherboard you have installed on your computer. Locate the BIOS ROM chip on a motherboard. What make of BIOS ROM is it?

2 Identify the main components on a motherboard. Draw a diagram to show the position of the processor chip, the BIOS chip, the battery, the power supply connector, the memory slots, the expansion slots, the ports and other important components. Look at how components are slotted into place.

3 Turn on your computer and watch the POST process. Note what happens if one part of your system is not working or has been disconnected (such as a LAN cable).

Power supply

Within a PC, the **PSU** is a black or silver coloured box, with a fan inside it and cables coming from it.

Did you know?

So that PCs may be used worldwide, there may be a 110/220V selector switch on the PSU.

The main job of the PSU is to supply power to the various components of the PC. There are two types of power: internal and external.

- The external power via the socket provides **AC** of 110–220V.
- The internal power needed by the various components within the PC is either 5V or 12V of **DC**.

Key terms

POST – stands for power-on self test. It is a hardware diagnostic routine that is run during the start-up boot sequence and checks configuration settings of the computer.

PSU – stands for power supply unit.

AC – stands for alternating current. It is a type of electricity. The direction of the current alternates (very quickly), providing an efficient way of supplying power over long distances.

DC – stands for direct current. A different type of electricity, where the power runs from negative charge to positive charge, always in the same direction. This works for battery-powered devices where the power has only a short distance to travel.

Since PC components work on DC and the power from the wall socket supplies AC, the PSU has to convert AC to DC. So, the PSU converts the incoming supply of power to one that is needed – the right type and at the required voltage.

Activity: PSU

1 Locate the PSU within your desktop computer's processor box. Note the leads that run from the PSU to other devices. Draw a diagram to illustrate the connections.

2 Find out what voltages different peripherals (such as a monitor, printer and mouse) require. How are these devices powered?

3 Check the type and power of the battery that is located on the motherboard. What is this battery used to power?

4 Find out how a laptop is powered when there is no connection to the mains supply.

Fan and heat sink or cooling

The airflow and cooling system may seem a minor design point but, like a car engine, if the chips within the PC become overheated, they may fail. Some components, such as 3D video cards, generate a lot of heat and these can affect other chips close to them. So, the placement of essential chips (like the CPU!) has to be carefully decided, all within a limited amount of space on the motherboard.

Early PCs, cooled by airflow within the case created by a fan in the PSU, relied on cool air being sucked into the case by the fan. For later models of PC, a **heat sink** or **processor cooling fan** (or both) were attached to the CPU. To make the system even more efficient, the PSU fan was reversed so that it acted as an extractor, pulling hot air out of the PC case.

Modern chips, such as the Pentium® processor, present special problems – they become much hotter than previous designs of chip and so need a careful heat dissipation system. Otherwise, they can overheat and fail.

Activity: Cooling

1   Locate the processor on a motherboard. What cooling device is used?

2   Research the Internet for data on heat sinks. What materials might these be made from?

3   Research the Internet to find out what happens (and at what temperature) if the fan stops working on a PC, or the heat sink is removed or not connected properly to the processor chip.

Hard drive configuration and controllers

The hard drive for a computer, together with a drive for CDs and DVDs, are usually located within the processor box. However, an external hard drive can provide additional secondary storage and may also be used as a backup device.

Hard drives, wherever they are located, are **IDE** devices, controlled by an IDE controller.

Key terms

Heat sink – a device attached to the processor chip that has lots of fins so that its surface area is maximised and the heat transfer from the chip is maximised. It draws heat from the processor and therefore keeps its temperature down.

Processor cooling fan – a tiny fan attached to the processor chip or heat sink to prevent it from overheating.

IDE – stands for integrated drive electronics. It refers to a standard electronic interface between a computer motherboard's data paths (or buses) and the computer's disk storage devices, based on the IBM PC ISA (industry standard architecture) 16-bit bus standard.

SATA – stands for serial advanced technology attachment. This is a computer bus interface for connecting host bus adapters to mass storage devices such as hard disk drives and optical drives.

Did you know?

An enhanced version of IDE called EIDE (enhanced IDE) was superseded by **SATA** which is now used in most new computers.

There are two types of IDE controller – primary and secondary. The hard drive is normally attached to the primary IDE controller (the IDE1 connector). A CD drive (or DVD drive or another hard drive) can then be attached to the secondary channel (the IDE2 connector) on the motherboard.

Each IDE ribbon, attached to either one of these controllers, can support two drives. To know which data relates to which drive, each drive is identified as either the master drive or the slave drive.

- **Master drive:** handles all the traffic on the IDE cable. Its controller retains its own data and passes on data to the slave drive.

- **Slave drive:** sees only the data that is passed to it by the master drive. (NB There does not have to be a slave drive if there is only one drive attached to the cable.)

Case study: Anne's laptop (2)

Anne's laptop has a three-port SATA storage controller (see Figure 2.2). The Device Manager also reveals Anne's laptop is configured for an HP® Officejet 6100 series printer, a Logitech® Quickcam™ Express #5 and a Smartcard Reader.

1 Check the ports available on your computer. List them and the devices that can be attached to them.

2 Research the Internet for information on SATA controllers.

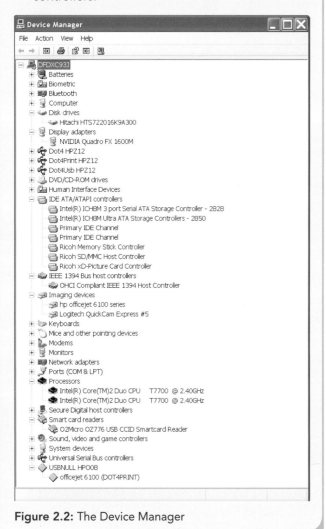

Figure 2.2: The Device Manager

Activity: Hard drives

1 Locate the hard drive within your PC. Check which IDE channel is being used for it. Check the master/slave settings.

2 Identify any other backing storage devices attached to your computer. Which are internal? Which are external? How are they connected to the processor?

Not all peripherals need a cable to link them to the port – some use wireless or infrared technology. However, a variety of ports are available so that a range of peripherals, each with differing needs, may be attached to the processor (see Figure 2.3).

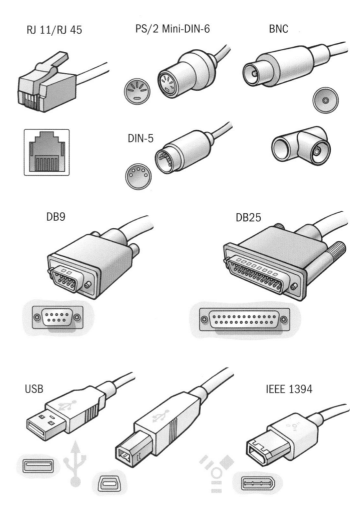

Figure 2.3: Ports and connectors

For example, if cabling is used, the transfer of data to and from the peripheral will be one of two types:

- **serial transmission** – 1 bit at a time and the cable is usually circular in cross-section

- **parallel transmission** – 1 byte (8 bits) at a time. This cabling looks like a ribbon, the wires being laid side by side.

The simplest devices such as mouse and keyboard only need serial connection. Others, such as printers, benefit from the two-way communication of parallel connections. However, nowadays, you're more likely to see a printer connected via a fast serial port using a USB connector, this being a faster option than the old ribbon connection.

The serial and parallel ports on the PC are very different, as are the connectors that fit into them (see Figure 2.4).

- The **serial port** conforms to the **RS-232c** standard. It requires a 25-pin male port, but PCs only use 9 of these pins so it can be, and often is, replaced by a 9-pin male port.

- The **parallel port** on the PC, for example for a printer, offers a female 25-pin DB (databus) connector. A male 25-pin DB connector on one end of the printer ribbon cable will clip or screw into place. At the other end of the cable, at the printer end, is the 36-pin Centronics connector.

USB was designed to make the installation of slow peripherals, such as the mouse, joystick, keyboard and scanners – and other devices, such as printers, digital cameras and digital telephones – as easy as possible. Nowadays, the USB host controller is included in the chipset and this recognises when you plug a device into a USB port and allows **hot swapping** of devices.

There may be as many as four or more USB ports supported by a motherboard (see Figure 2.5).

Key terms

RS-232c – stands for Reference Standard 232 revision c.

Hot swapping – connecting (or disconnecting) a peripheral while the PC is turned on.

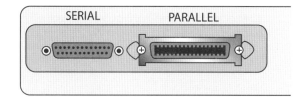

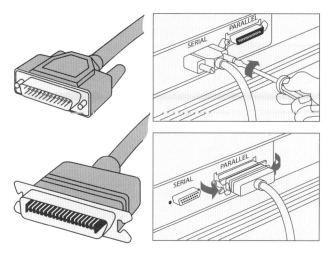

Figure 2.4: Serial and parallel connectors

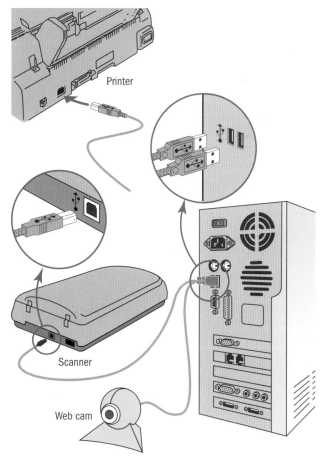

Figure 2.5: USB port and connector

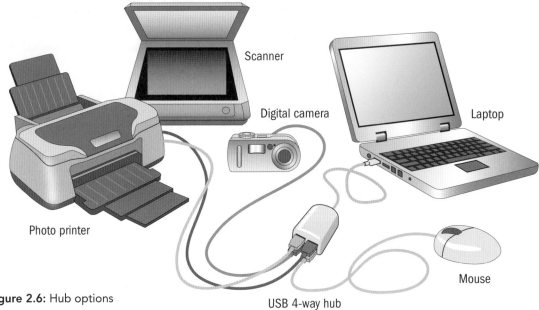

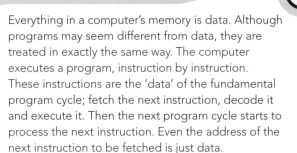

Figure 2.6: Hub options

It is also possible to link the devices in a 'daisy chain' so that the PC may have many more devices attached – each device provides the USB port to the next device in the chain. Another option is to have a USB hub, into which devices can be plugged (see Figure 2.6).

For a wireless mouse, a connector (called a notebook receiver) may be attached to a USB port – the mouse is then battery-operated.

Generally, transmission via a serial port is a slow, inexpensive method of data transfer. USB is faster than standard serial and an optical serial connection may transfer at an even faster rate, faster than a parallel connection. So, parallel transmission is usually, but not always, faster than serial transmission.

Activity: Peripherals

1 Research the Internet to find out when the mouse was first introduced. Prepare a presentation to show the development of technologies for pointing devices from then until the present day.

2 Which peripheral is the most recent invention? Obtain details of its functionality and cost.

Internal memory

Internal memory is used for two main purposes – to store programs that are being run and to store the data that the program works on.

Did you know?

Everything in a computer's memory is data. Although programs may seem different from data, they are treated in exactly the same way. The computer executes a program, instruction by instruction. These instructions are the 'data' of the fundamental program cycle; fetch the next instruction, decode it and execute it. Then the next program cycle starts to process the next instruction. Even the address of the next instruction to be fetched is just data.

There are two main types of memory within the PC – RAM (random access memory), which is volatile, and ROM (read only memory), which is non-volatile. Volatile memory loses its data when the power is turned off. So, for example, when your computer crashes and you have to turn it off and restart it, whatever changes you made to a document since it was last saved (either by you or using an Autosave function) are lost. Like other memory, both RAM and ROM are measured in bytes or, more likely, GB (gigabytes).

Did you know?

Programs that are written and stored in RAM are called software – the instructions can be overwritten. To preserve data and/or program instructions for use later, these have to be stored either on ROM (see page 49) or to a secondary storage device such as a hard disk (see page 51).

RAM memory chips provide a form of memory that offers the same **access time** for allocations within it (hence the term 'random access'). The time it takes to fetch a program instruction affects the speed at which an application can run. For optimum performance, the 'page' of code that is being executed is brought from the backing storage location (for example on the hard disk) into RAM. When these instructions have been executed, the next page is swapped into position. Having a greater amount of RAM results in there being space for more instructions that can be held close to the processor at any one time and this reduces the amount of time spent swapping pages into and out of RAM.

A 'crash' can result when the processor spends its time swapping pages rather than executing the instructions – this can happen if you try to run too many applications at the same time, each of them needing its own page space in RAM.

> **Did you know?** ⓘ
>
> The RO in ROM stands for 'read only' but, depending on the type of ROM, you may or may not be able to write to it.

ROM is non-volatile memory. It does not lose its data when the power supply is off, so it can be used to store data and/or instructions (called **firmware**) that are needed when you next turn on, for example for the BIOS chip.

There is one other type of memory which is a fast memory that is used as a data buffer between the CPU and RAM and is called the **cache memory**.

- Internal cache is located inside the CPU chip – also called primary cache or on-die cache.
- External cache is also on the motherboard but not within the CPU chip – also called secondary cache.

Cache memory can also be categorised according to its closeness (proximity) to the CPU.

- Level 1 (L1) cache is closest to the CPU and, like internal cache, is housed within the CPU chip.
- Level 2 (L2) cache is not so close – it may also be on the CPU chip (just behind the L1 cache) or it may be external cache.

Why is cache memory needed? Central to the operation of a PC is the communication between the CPU and RAM. These two components (like many others in a computer) work at differing speeds.

- The CPU works in megahertz (millionths of seconds).
- The RAM works in nanoseconds (billionths of seconds).

Even though the RAM is so much quicker, it takes time to find the data that is needed and bring it via the data bus to the CPU for processing. To aid the process, the CPU interacts with the RAM by having a series of **wait states** – it actually pauses for a while to allow the data that it wants to be transferred from RAM into the registers within the CPU. Data may be coming from far away, for example from a hard disk, and so it has to be transferred from the disk to RAM and then from RAM to the CPU. So, extra wait states may be necessary.

Even when the data is within RAM, there is a delay in transferring data within the PC called **latency**. Wherever the data is, the CPU has to wait – and an idle CPU is not acceptable!

Key terms

Access time – the length of time that RAM takes to write data (or to read it) once the request has been received from the processor. This is measured in nanoseconds (ns) – the fewer ns, the faster the RAM.

Firmware – the name given to the instructions encoded onto ROM chips. Unlike software, once written it cannot be changed.

Cache memory – a fast memory that is used as a data buffer between the CPU and RAM.

Wait state – a time of inactivity for the CPU to allow other devices to catch up with it.

Latency – a time delay that could be better used, for example for processing.

The cache memory is there to solve this problem. It acts as a buffer, and holds data that the CPU will need, for example things that are used a lot. Like a printer buffer, the cache memory makes up for the mismatch between the speeds of the CPU and RAM.

Caching involves some guesswork by the system which has to decide what the CPU will need next.

This guesswork uses the principle of **locality of reference** and a good guess results in a more effective use of CPU time.

- A good guess for the disk cache is that it will be whatever comes next on the disk.
- For the internal cache, a good guess would be whatever lies in the next section of RAM.

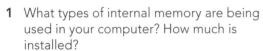

Activity: Internal memory – cache memory

1 What types of internal memory are being used in your computer? How much is installed?

2 Research the Internet to find out how much cache memory is used in a number of PCs with different specifications.

Specialised cards

Expansion slots allow the life of a computer to be extended, since new technology can be added as it becomes available. They allow you to add specialised cards to your PC, for example for a **modem**, a sound card and/or an **NIC**.

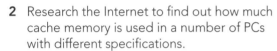

Activity: Specialised cards

1 Locate the expansion slots within your PC and list the expansion cards already in the slots.

2 Repeat this activity on other PCs, noting differences between the form factors (shape and size) of the motherboards and the cards that are present in the slots.

3 For one video card, visit the manufacturer's website and find out as much as you can about the card. Compare notes with others in your group.

4 Research the Internet to find out about video adapter card standards: MDA, CGA, EGA, VGA and AVGA. Discover what resolution they support and how many colours they can display.

Key terms

Locality of reference – guesswork principle used by the caching system. There are three types of locality: temporal, spatial and sequential. Temporal locality assumes that if a resource (for example a program instruction or a data item) is referenced now, then it will be referenced again soon. Spatial locality recognises that most program instructions are found in routines and that these routines are usually close together and also that the data fields are close together. It assumes that the likelihood of referencing a resource is higher if a resource near it has been referenced. Sequential locality assumes that memory will be accessed sequentially.

Modem (modulator/**dem**odulator) – is a device that encodes digital information signals into analog carrier signals and vice versa and transmits information over a phone line.

NIC – stands for network interface card.

Input/Output devices (I/O devices) – input devices allow a computer user to enter information on to a computer. Output devices enable information to leave a system in many forms, e.g. audio, visual, printed documents etc. Computer input or output devices are known as peripherals.

1.2 Peripherals

Peripherals fall into two groups.

- **Input devices** such as a keyboard, camera or scanner provide a way for the user to put data into the processor and to give commands (for example a pointing device, like a mouse, to click on the application you want to open or to select an option from a menu).

- **Output devices** such as a monitor, printer or plotter present the results of any processing to the user.

Did you know?

Storage devices – also known as the backing store are both input and output devices but are not peripherals. They provide a place, other than the RAM or ROM memory within the PC, to store data. They also provide portability, allowing data (and software) to be transferred from one PC to another, for example on a CD-ROM.

According to their type (serial or parallel), input and output devices need to be connected to the processor using appropriate cabling (e.g. coaxial, optical, twisted pair) to an appropriate port or configured as wireless devices.

1.3 Backing storage

Primary storage, located within the computer, is relatively small and the majority of it is lost when the computer is switched off.

- To create a more permanent store for data (including software), a **secondary storage** device or backing store is needed, such as a hard drive.
- To create a portable store for data, offline storage devices are needed: CD-ROMs, DVDs, memory sticks, etc. These are sometimes referred to as **tertiary storage**.

There is a variety of types of backing store now available to the PC user such as magnetic discs and optical discs, the newer **pen drives** and **flash memory cards**.

What type of memory card readers are on the market today?

Did you know?

Flash memory cards evolved from EPROM (erasable programmable read only memory) and the process called flashing, which involves overwriting what was once considered to be a write-once medium.

To access the data on a flash memory card, a card reader is plugged into the USB port and the card is slotted into the reader. Because there are lots of different shapes and sizes of flash memory card and each one needs a reader with the right shape slot before the data can be transferred, there is also a range of readers available. There are also some readers available which accept more than one size of card – these have several slots. Laptops invariably have a memory slot and this will take a Type II memory card.

Portable and fixed drives

In the design of early computers, the drives (that is the readers) were located within the casing. Hard disks were fixed within the casing but other media formats (such as magnetic tape and floppy disks) provided portable ways of storing data. More recently, external hard drives have been developed and this has brought with it the option to move a hard drive (and the hard disk within it) from one computer to another. Similarly, pen drives and card readers, both of which plug into the USB port, provide a portable solution to data storage. With the increased capacity and compact format of these devices, it is now possible to enjoy portability for large amounts of data.

Key terms

Primary storage – the memory of the computer.

Secondary storage – a backing store that remains with the computer and provides a greater capacity than the processor can offer.

Tertiary storage – a store that is destined for transfer to another computer or archiving and needs to be on a portable medium.

Pen drives – small devices that can be used to transfer files between USB-compatible systems and provide a high-capacity alternative to CD-ROMs. They are plugged directly into the USB port and need no batteries for power.

Flash memory cards – a portable medium for data. Commonly used in digital cameras, they can hold your photos until you upload them to your computer or output them to a photo printer.

What is the largest amount of memory you can find available on a pen drive?

Performance factors

When deciding what storage device to use, a number of factors need to be taken into account.

- How much data will the device hold? What is its maximum capacity?
- How fast can the data be stored on (written to) the device?
- How fast can the data be retrieved (read) from the device?

The performance of a system can be monitored using a **profiler**.

Activity: Portable storage devices

1 Investigate the market for pen drive products. Produce a table to show their promised performance factors and include costings. Compare your findings with others in your group.

2 Research the Internet for data on flash memory cards. Find out which reader(s) is/are compatible with the cards, and compare their performance factors, for example transmission speeds.

1.4 Operating system software

At the very heart of any computer system is the operating system software.

Operating system examples

There are several operating systems on offer:

- **DOS** was originally the name of an operating system developed by IBM for a line of business computers. The first personal computer version of DOS, called PC-DOS, but now more commonly referred to as DOS, was developed for IBM® by Bill Gates, who then set up Microsoft® Corporation. It is a non-graphical line-oriented command or menu-driven operating system, with a relatively simple interface which lacks the 'friendly' user interface of the **WIMP** environment.
- **LINUX** is a Unix-type operating system originally created by Linus Torvalds with the assistance of developers around the world. The source code for Linux is freely available to anyone with Internet access.

Key terms

Profiler – a performance analysis tool that measures the behaviour of a program while it is running.

DOS – stands for disk operating system.

WIMP – stands for windows, icons, mouse, pointer. It is used to describe a GUI system. The windows are used to show running programs, the icons to start programs, the mouse to control the system and the pointer is an arrow on screen to show the position of the mouse.

- **Windows®** is a WIMP environment system developed by Microsoft® Corporation and sold under licence. It is used on IBM®-compatible PCs. The first Windows operating system was simply an application – a user interface – that ran on top of the MS-DOS operating system.
- **MAC OS** is a parallel system of software developed by Apple® for those users who choose not to follow the IBM-PC hardware route.

Command line and GUI operating systems

Prior to the introduction of the WIMP environment, early computers relied on command line interpreters. The operating system responded to individual commands keyed in by the user. When it had finished doing whatever was asked of it, the user was presented with the command line prompt (usually including a > symbol) and the computer then waited for the next instruction. The user needed to have a high level of knowledge, particularly in how to give the commands in the DOS language.

When Windows®-based operating systems were introduced, instead of entering a command, the user now indicated their selection or decision by clicking on an option in a menu, pressing a button or completing boxes on a form. The interface became far more user-friendly and it opened up the use of computers to people who had not learned how to program a computer.

Operating system functions and services

The operating system includes a number of accessory programs which offer machine and peripheral management, security and file management. To access these functions and services, you might – on a Windows® computer – press Start/All Programs/Accessories/Systems Tools and then you might run Disk Cleanup or Disk Defragmenter, both of which provide ways of tidying up your disk space (see page 54).

Device drivers

For each peripheral device, a device driver is needed to interface between the processor and the peripheral. The driver acts as a decoder, so the data is interpreted correctly. Installing device drivers is necessary when new hardware is installed (see page 58).

Features

In choosing which operating system to use, you must take into consideration what features are on offer and which ones are most important for you.

- Does the operating system let you customise what you see on the screen and how you interact with the computer?
- Does it provide support for connectivity of portable media?
- What provisions are there to ensure tight security of the computer system?
- What guarantees do you have of stability and reliability?
- How easy is it to manage the computer system?
- What utilities are included?
- How much does it cost?
- What after-sales support is on offer for the user?

1.5 Software utilities

Software utilities offer security in the form of virus protection and firewalls, McAfee®'s Total Protection Service and ZoneAlarm® Antivirus.

To visit the McAfee® and ZoneAlarm® websites, go to Hotlinks.

Virus protection

PCs can be attacked by **viruses**, **worms** and **trojans** arriving with emails or during access to the Internet.

Anti-virus software checks for intruders. It attempts to trace viruses by spotting the **virus signature**. Meanwhile, virus writers adopt cloaking techniques such as **polymorphing**.

Almost as soon as virus writers invent new viruses, so do anti-virus software vendors produce updated versions of their software.

The anti-virus software vendors maintain a database of information about viruses, their profiles and signatures. Users who subscribe to an online anti-virus protection service may have this database downloaded to their PC automatically each time an update is released. Other users may receive an email telling them that an update is available.

Having the most up-to-date virus information file, scanning regularly and avoiding opening emails that may contain viruses is the best advice. The main defence against viruses is to subscribe to a reliable software vendor's virus protection service. If the software detects a virus, a pop-up screen may offer options to quarantine the file (that is move it so it can do no harm), to repair the file (that is delete the virus but retain the file) or to delete the file.

Anti-virus software vendors may offer to create a rescue disk – a bootable disk that also contains anti-virus software. If a virus-infected system won't boot, a rescue disk may solve the problem. Write-protecting the disk may prevent it from becoming infected with a virus.

Key terms

Virus – (so-called because it spreads by replicating itself) a program that is designed to erase data and corrupt files.

Worm – a type of virus that can forward emails (and the worm) to all your contacts using data from your address book.

Trojan – a malicious program that pretends to be a benign application, but purposely does something the user does not expect. Trojans are technically not viruses since they do not replicate, but can be just as destructive. If left in a computer system, provides 'back door' access to the hard drive and data.

Virus signature – a sequence of characters which the anti-virus software gleans by analysing the virus code.

Polymorphing – a virus that is designed to change its appearance, size and signature each time it infects another PC (just as cells in a diseased human mutate), thus making it harder for anti-virus software to recognise it.

Firewalls

Firewalls build a protective barrier around computers that are connected to a network, so that only authorised programs can access data on a particular workstation.

The user can control exactly which software is allowed to pass data in and out of the system. For example, automatic updates might be allowed for some installed software.

For more on firewalls, see *Unit 5: Managing networks*, page 155.

Cleanup tools

Over a period of time, a PC becomes cluttered with data that you do not need.

- **Removal of cookies:** Each time you visit a new website and register so that you can receive newsletter updates or make a purchase, a cookie is most likely left on your PC so that the site can recognise you the next time you visit. These cookies are useful as they save you entering your details again. However, you may have cookies for websites that you never intend to visit again, so you might decide you would prefer to remove them (all) from your system.

- **Internet history:** Each time you request a page on the Internet, a copy of that page is retained in the Temporary Internet Files folder. This is useful because when you use the Back and Forward buttons, the web page does not need to be downloaded afresh. However, the space taken up by these pages can accumulate.

- **Defragmentation:** Each time you save a file, the space on your hard disk begins to fill. When files are deleted, some space becomes available, which appears as 'gaps' on the map of the disk. There may come a time when a file you want to save will not fit into an available gap. The system copes with this by fragmenting the file and storing the fragments wherever it can. Unfortunately, additional space is

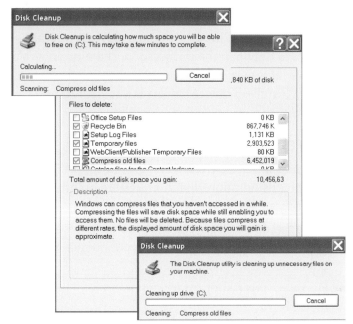

Figure 2.7: Disk Cleanup

taken up noting the whereabouts of the fragments. Before long, the organisation of files on the disk is a mess!

Cleanup tools can be used to solve the clutter problem. Disk Cleanup scans a drive and presents a list of files you might like to delete (see Figure 2.7), while Disk Defragmenter rearranges files so that the gaps are used up systematically, leaving available space in contiguous (that is connecting) strings.

Drive formatting

For storage media to be recognised by your computer so that it can be used to store data files, it has to be initialised or 'formatted'.

There are two stages.

- **Physical (low-level) formatting** tests the surface, scanning for imperfections and setting aside those sectors that cannot be used.

- **Logical (high-level) formatting** prepares the disk by setting up a file system which then defines how files and folders will be stored and accessed.

The high-level formatting process writes material to allow the operating system to interact with the disk – the **boot sector**, the **root directory table** and the **FAT** table.

Key terms

Boot sector – set aside to hold data about how data is organised on the disk, such as the number of sectors, the number of sectors per track, the number of bytes per sector, the number of FATs, the size of the root directory and the program needed to load the operating system. This last item is the program that searches and loads files needed to boot the disk – if these files are missing, the disk is unbootable.

Root directory table – has an entry for each file on the disk, the name of the file and the file extension, the file attribute, the date and time that the file was created or last updated, the position where the start of this file is to be found on the disk (cluster number) and the length of the file.

FAT – stands for file allocation table.

Did you know?

Since the clusters are too short to store whole files of data, a file will be stored in a number of clusters and these need not be consecutive on the disk. The file is then called fragmented. Keeping track of the many fragments of a file falls to the FAT. It records which clusters are used for which files. Defragmentation (see page 54) is a process which tidies up the disk, reusing the disk space more efficiently after some files have been deleted.

A disk utility program can be used to format or reformat a disk and this will create a seemingly blank, empty disk for storing your files, apparently destroying everything that was previously on that disk. However, the old data is still on the disk. The files don't show on the directory because they are no longer included in the directory structure.

Activity: Software utilities

1 Identify two different providers of anti-virus software. Do they also provide firewall protection?

2 For one provider of firewall protection, find out what is available for the user. Make notes.

3 Use the Disk Cleanup tool to rid your PC of unwanted files.

4 Find out how to format disks on your PC. Make notes.

Did you know?

If you format a disk or just delete files from a disk, you – or someone else – could gain access to the data using a utility such as Norton™ Disk Doctor.

Assessment activity 2.1

1 For your computer system, or one identified by your tutor, list the hardware components and, using one or more diagrams and/or photographs with supporting notes, explain the function of each component. **P1**

2 Jamil is about to buy a new computer system, but isn't sure what make to choose – Microsoft® Windows® or an Apple® Macintosh®.

(a) Explain the purpose of operating systems. **P2**

(b) Compare the features and functions of different operating systems. **M1**

3 Jamil is also unclear about software utilities.

(a) Using a tabular format or otherwise, explain the purpose of different software utilities. **P3**

(b) Explain how software utilities can improve the performance of computer systems. **D1**

Grading tips

- You might produce a web page with hot spots over different components explaining what the components are. Make sure you identify the communication between components. **P1**

- Include an outline of the basic functions of operating systems explaining how they are used to facilitate users. **P2**

- You will need to refer to at least two different operating systems. **M1**

- Include at least one example of each of these types of utility: security, cleanup tools and drive formatting. **P3**

- When you consider the benefits of computer performance created by using software utilities, give reasons for possible improvements from using a specific utility. **D1**

PLTS

Specifying suitable components to meet user requirements demonstrates that you are a **reflective learner** because you can plan solutions to complex tasks by analysing the necessary stages involved.

Functional skills

Explaining and justifying choices to a business demonstrates your Functional **English** skills as you can combine and present information which is fit for purpose.

2. Be able to recommend computer systems for a business purpose

Activity: The best buy

Refer back to the 'perfect computer' you planned to buy, had you been lucky enough to win the lottery or the premium bonds (see page 42).

- What were your priorities in deciding on the make and model of computer? List the factors of importance to you.

- What helped you to decide which software to include in your specification? Identify the factors that persuaded you one way or another.

- How much did you take into account your own competence on a computer or your own special needs?

Compare notes with others in your group. Are your priorities the same? If not, why not?

2.1 Considerations for selection

When deciding which make and model of computer to purchase and the configuration to construct (how much memory, which peripherals and so on), you should consider a number of factors. The final decision might have to be a compromise – perhaps because you have to keep within a budget – and the priority you give to each factor will, of course, depend on the relative importance of each one.

Cost

Cost is usually a deciding factor in any purchase, not just computers. You should aim to buy the best specification within your budget. Computers are constantly being developed (faster memories, larger capacity, new and exciting peripherals), so to buy something that ignores the latest technologies will mean that your system is out of date as soon as you have bought it.

Savings can be made by buying from a company that offers lower prices, but these have to be judged against intangible considerations, such as whether the kit is going to prove reliable and whether there will be any backup support after you have completed the sale.

User requirements

The primary consideration is fitness for purpose. The computer system must meet the needs of the user. Ascertaining the needs of the user is essential before any decisions are made as to what to recommend.

- **Operating software:** Some users have a preference for a particular operating system (such as Microsoft® Windows®) and may not wish to change to an unfamiliar one (such as an Apple® Macintosh®) and vice versa. There are options though within these vendors' ranges, for example Microsoft® Windows Vista® versus Windows XP®, and a user may prefer one to another for ease of use or familiarity reasons. The availability of a preferred operating system may limit the range of models available.

- **Application software:** Application software will need to be installed so that the user can perform the tasks that he or she wants to do on the computer, for example writing letters or reports using word-processing, doing design work using painting and drawing packages, processing financial data using spreadsheets or maintaining records using a database. Most application software will run on both Windows® and Apple® Macintosh® machines so this should not be a limiting factor.

- **Network sharing:** The system configuration might need to include necessary hardware and software to connect to a network such as the Internet.

- **Need for maintenance:** Hardware vendors may offer a maintenance agreement and software vendors may also offer online support for the user.

Did you know?

Often a computer vendor 'bundles' application software with the hardware, trying to make the complete system attractive to a wider market of potential purchasers. These packaged systems may be targeted towards business users, while others might be described as home entertainment systems. Within the bundle, there will be essential software, but also possibly some software for which the user has no need.

- **Outputs required:** The user may require specialist output such as the highest-quality graphics or sound systems.

- **Integration with other systems:** The necessary hardware and software might need to be integrated with other existing or planned systems, for example a home entertainment system.

- **Processing power:** It is essential to include enough processing power to create a usable, fast-moving system. A slow processor may result in a system that does not meet the user's requirements at all.

- **Storage capacity:** It is also essential to ensure sufficient RAM to run the largest of programs and to store data (maybe videos or images).

- **Accessibility for disabled users:** Some users have special needs. Visually impaired people may need to rely on their sense of hearing and the computer system will need to be set up to produce voice output as appropriate. Users with some physical disability may need special peripherals to replace the conventional mouse and/or keyboard.

- **IT competence of the intended user:** Novice users can be catered for by choosing a user-friendly operating system and installing bundled software which will offer a consistent user interface. Once the user has learned how to use one application the other applications will become easier to learn too. For expert users, any system will suffice, but more sophisticated applications might be needed, such as web design applications.

- **Training requirements:** Regardless of the competence of a user, training will help the user to make the best use of the hardware and software. Some vendors provide on-screen help screens, others offer training videos and sometimes these are free or perhaps free for a limited period.

Assessment activity 2.2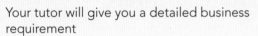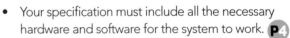

Your tutor will give you a detailed business requirement

1 Recommend a computer system that meets the needs of this particular business. You may present your recommendation as a written report or as a presentation. **P4**

2 Justify your choice of computer system to meet the given business purpose. **M2**

Grading tips

- Your specification must include all the necessary hardware and software for the system to work. **P4**

- Suggest at least one alternative set up and discuss why the alternative(s) could also be appropriate. Explain your reasoning (for example cost) clearly, making reference to the user need, and justifying any optional extras that you have recommended. **M2**

PLTS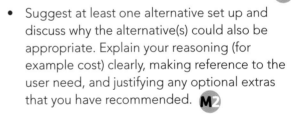

When you are identifying questions to answer and problems to resolve (for example when specifying suitable components to meet user requirements), or when you are planning and carrying out research, appreciating the consequences of decisions (for example when selecting suitable components to meet user requirements) you are demonstrating your skills as an **independent enquirer**.

Functional skills

Specifying suitable components to meet user requirements demonstrates your Functional **ICT** skills as it shows that you can plan solutions to complex tasks by analysing the necessary stages.

3. Be able to set up and maintain computer systems

Activity: Safety first

Do you know how to wire a plug? There are three coloured wires to be connected:

- the green and yellow Earth
- the blue Neutral
- the brown Live.

To help you remember the positioning of these wires:

- BL = Bottom Left = Blue
- BR = Bottom Right = Brown.

The third wire then goes at the top. But what would happen if you wired it incorrectly? Luckily, new plugs come with a handy diagram showing what goes where (see Figure 2.8).

Similarly, when connecting and setting up a computer system, it is a good idea to read all the available manuals for each component.

- What risks are there in connecting and setting up a computer system?
- How can you protect yourself from harm?
- What advice can you give others to ensure their safety?

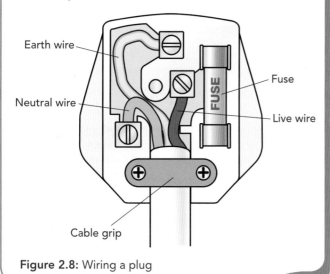

Figure 2.8: Wiring a plug

3.1 Connect and set up

In the process of connecting and setting up a computer system, you will be handling many separate items of equipment, such as a monitor, a printer, a modem/router, a keyboard, a mouse, speakers, a microphone, perhaps some RAM and a hard drive.

For each item, you need to identify how it is to be connected to the processor and what cabling may be needed.

Activity: A computer set-up

Your tutor will tell you which computer set-up to study.

1. Draw a sketch showing all the components and the connections between them.
2. On your diagram, label each component (such as monitor, printer, modem/router, keyboard, mouse, speakers and microphone).
3. Label each connection between components and describe the types of connectors (for example USB, serial, parallel).
4. Swap diagrams and computers with one of your group. Compare notes and check that you both agree with how you have described each computer set-up.

3.2 Install hardware

Nowadays, the installation of new peripherals is relatively straightforward. The vendors supply all the items that you need – the device, any connectors, a CD with the set-up software and any drivers that you might need. They normally also provide step-by-step instructions that you should follow carefully.

The usual method is to install relevant software first and then to attach the hardware, which will then be recognised. However, modern operating systems are sophisticated enough to spot when you have attached a new device.

Before you are ready to install new hardware, you need to have installed internal components and to have an operating system installed (see page 60). However, having installed the device, you may need to do some customisation to make it suit the user.

- For a printer, you might want to make it the default printer (see Figure 2.9).
- For a mouse, you might want to set the speed of response or perhaps make it usable for a left-handed operator.

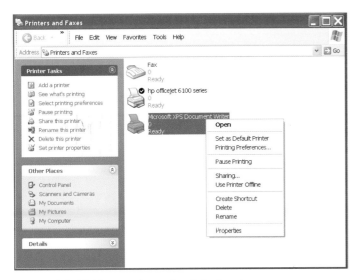

Figure 2.9: Making a printer the default printer

The Control Panel includes an option to Add Hardware (see Figure 2.10). This software will then guide you through the process of configuration.

The installation of internal components, such as a graphics card, sound card or CD/DVD drive, requires a little more expertise than is needed to install a peripheral. You also need to take more care, as

accessing the inside of a processor box carries a risk, both to you and to the computer.

Some devices, such as the hard drive, have to be connected to the motherboard and PSU using cabling – this makes installation similar to an external peripheral, the only difference being that they are housed within the box. Other devices, such as the cards available for graphics and networking, have to be fitted into the appropriate slot.

How to... Add/Remove a video card

1   Check that you know which slot you are going to use and that you have the correct board for your PC.

2   Be careful to handle the card by its non-connecting edges. Otherwise, you may leave traces of grease and/or dirt from your fingers.

3   Gently place the video card into the slot and press it into place.

4   To remove a card, release the locking mechanism and then slide the card gently out of its slot.

Figure 2.10: The Add Hardware Wizard

3.3 Install software

Once all the necessary hardware is in place and suitably connected, it is time for the software to be installed.

- **Operating system software:** Most computers come with operating system software such as Windows® already installed. However, if you don't buy in this way, you will have to install it yourself.

- **Application software:** Once the operating system is in place, you can install the application software such as Microsoft® Office®.

- **Security software:** Then you should consider security software such as virus checkers and firewalls – certainly before connecting to the Internet.

- **Device drivers** (see page 53) will be needed for peripherals such as printers.

- **Directory/folder structures:** Although you can manage for a while without doing so, it's wise to create appropriate directory/folder structures so that finding files at a later date is made easier.

3.4 Configure

Having installed software, the next stage is to configure the system to suit the user.

- **BIOS configuration:** You have the option to determine the BIOS configuration and might set a BIOS password or edit the power management options. To access the BIOS configuration, when you first turn your computer on, notice the message in the top right-hand corner which tells you which function keys can be used to interrupt the boot process and give you access to the BIOS configuration.

- **Anti-virus software:** Editing anti-virus configurations is necessary to determine the frequency and timing of virus scans. Some operating systems include free anti-virus software or you may have installed your own third-party software. Either way, you need to decide what scans you require (Figure 2.11).

- **Desktop:** Editing the desktop – for example changing the icon size, the font size, the text colour, the background, icon choice – personalises the desktop for the user. These are controlled through the Control Panel/Task Bar and Start Menu (see Figure 2.12).

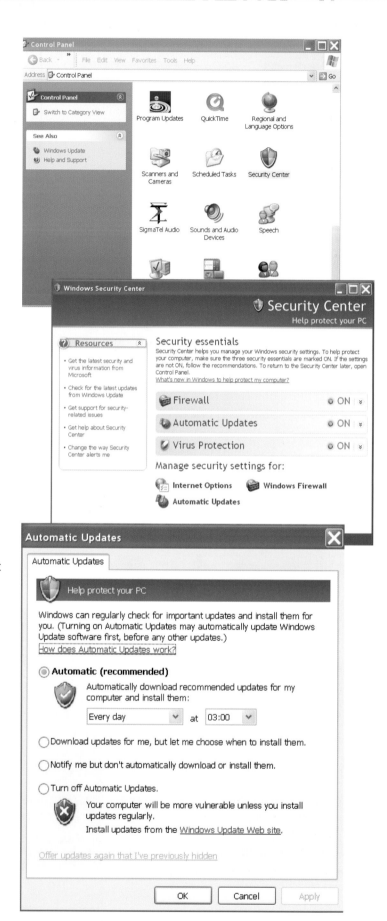

Figure 2.11: Editing anti-virus configurations

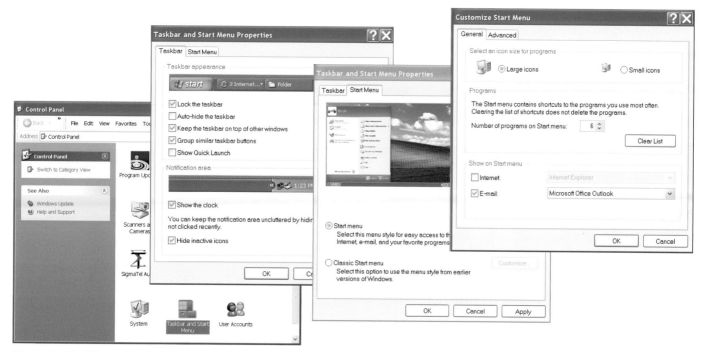

Figure 2.12: Editing the desktop

Case study: Anne's laptop (3)

When Anne turns her computer on, if she presses F2 as soon as the start-up screen appears, this takes her into the BIOS set-up sequence of screens, and she has the option to change the BIOS password and edit the power management options.

1. Watch the process of a computer starting up and note which function keys can be used to enter the BIOS set-up routines.

2. Restart the computer and press the necessary function key to interrupt the boot process.

3. Note what settings you might change.

4. Repeat this process on a different make or model of computer and compare the options made available to you.

- **Start-up:** Creating start-up options can save time. By identifying which applications are to be opened every time the computer is switched on or restarted, the user is saved the task of opening every application individually. The Startup Folder is accessed through the Start Panel (see Figure 2.13). Moving shortcuts to this folder will result in those applications being opened on start-up. If you change your mind, deleting the shortcut will

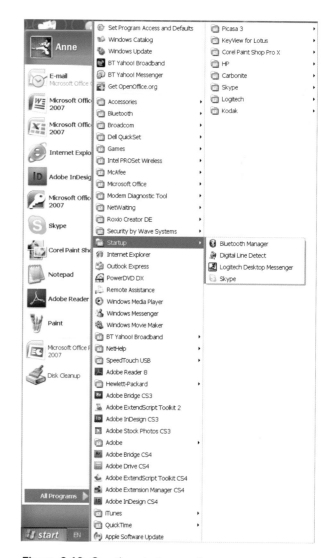

Figure 2.13: Creating start-up options

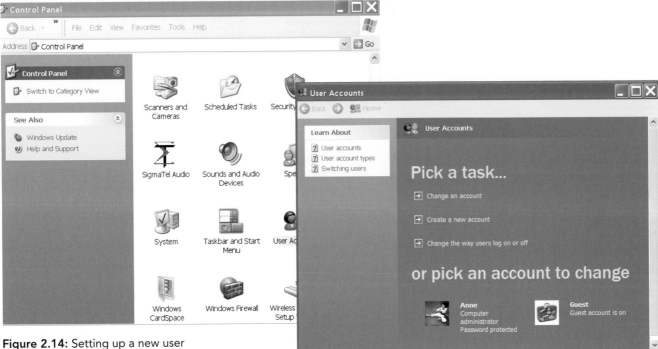

Figure 2.14: Setting up a new user

remove the application from the start-up sequence. It does not remove the application from your computer – to do this you'd have to use Add/Remove Programs.

- **File sharing/permissions:** Setting file sharing/permissions is essential if you plan to have more than one user on the same computer and you want to prevent one user from looking at another user's files. First you will need to set up each user; see Control Panel/User Accounts (see Figure 2.14). Then each user will have their own workspace and can access files in the shared workspace. To make a folder available for sharing, drag it to the shared workspace (Figure 2.15).

- **Application toolbars:** A final touch in the configure process is to create and reconfigure application toolbars so that the user is presented with the most commonly used icons, rather than the set of menus determined by the software vendor. This is done within the application software (see Figure 2.16).

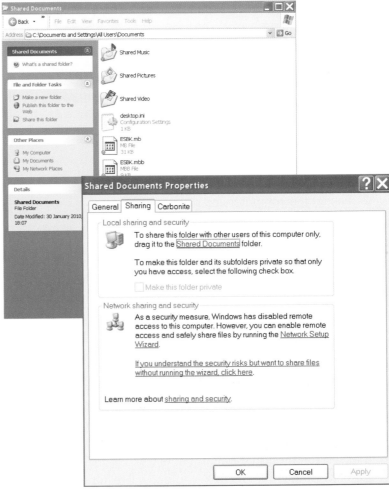

Figure 2.15: Sharing folders

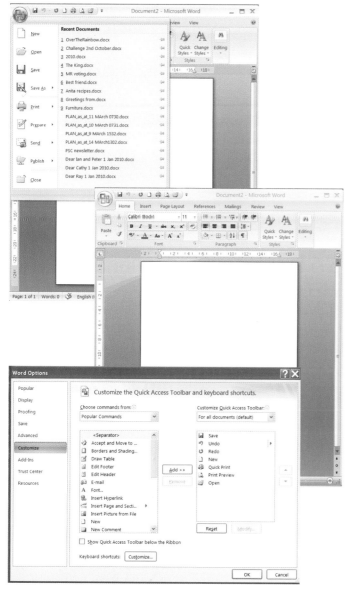

Figure 2.16: Configuring toolbars

3.5 Testing

Once the hardware and software have been installed and any customisation done, you must check that the system works.

- Do the software applications open and work as intended?
- Are the default folder settings correct?
- Do the desktop shortcuts go to the right place?
- Are the correct device drivers installed?
- Are the correct default paper sizes set for printing?
- Do the menu options work as intended?
- Is the correct date and time set? If not, fix it as shown in Figure 2.17.

Activity: Investigating a computer set-up

Your tutor will tell you which computer set-up to study.

1. Find out what anti-virus software is installed and the current settings for frequency of virus scans.

2. Note the current desktop settings – the icon size, font size, colour and background – or take screen grabs to illustrate them. Identify what settings you might change.

3. Find out what software automatically opens on start up.

4. Check what users are permitted to use the computer and what files might be available for shared use.

5. Note the current application toolbars or take screen grabs to illustrate them. Identify what you might want to change.

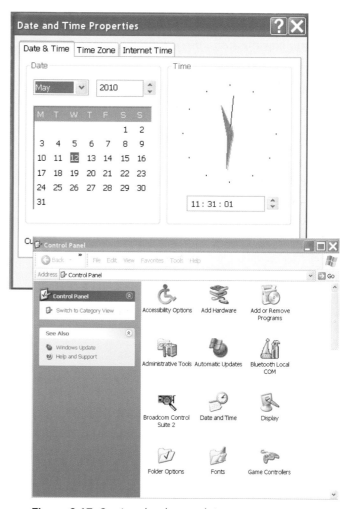

Figure 2.17: Setting the date and time

Activity: Installing hardware

Your tutor will tell you which new item of hardware to install.

1 Read the documentation that is supplied by the manufacturer. Check that you have everything you need – the installation CD, any cabling, any media. Ask your tutor any questions you need answered before starting the installation.

2 Following the instructions supplied with the hardware and, using either the Add Hardware option on the Control Panel, or relying on your operating system to recognise the new hardware, install the new item.

3 Restart your computer and check that it works with the new item of hardware.

4 Configure the new item of hardware in some way, changing an option or setting a default.

Activity: Installing software

Your tutor will tell you which new item of software to install.

1 Read the documentation that is supplied by the vendor. Check that you have everything you need – the software CD or the location on the Internet for the download. Ask your tutor any questions you need answered before starting the installation.

2 Follow the instructions supplied, entering reference numbers where requested to do so.

3 Restart your computer and check that it works with the new item of software.

4 Configure the new software in some way, changing an option or setting a default.

Activity: Testing an installation

Your tutor will tell you which installation – hardware and or software – to test.

1 For each item of hardware or software indicated, list the checks that you intend to do, to make sure it works as you might expect.

2 Work systematically through your list, checking the functionality and noting any problems that you encounter.

3 Report back to your tutor, in writing or verbally, on what you have discovered during the checking process.

4 According to instructions from your tutor, fix any faults or shortcomings that you have discovered.

3.6 Routine maintenance

Maintenance is an essential part of running a computer system. Its aim is to prevent problems arising and to save time when diagnosing and fixing faults. It can also extend the life of your PC.

Just how regularly the maintenance tasks are performed depends on the task – maintenance could be daily, weekly, monthly or annually, or whenever necessary, as suggested in Table 2.1. If the air in which the PC operates is dusty or smoky, even more frequent cleaning will be necessary.

Table 2.1: Preventive maintenance schedule

Frequency	Maintenance task
Daily	Virus scan of memory and your hard disk
	Take backup of changed data files
Weekly	Clean mouse (ball and rollers) and check for wear
	Clean keyboard, checking for stuck keys
	Clean monitor screen
	Clean printer
	Delete temporary files (Disk Cleanup)
	Defragment hard disk and recover lost clusters
Monthly	Clean outside of case
	Take complete backup of data files
Annually	Check motherboard: reseat chips if necessary
	Clean adapter card contacts with contact cleaner and reseat
As required	Record and backup CMOS set-up configuration
	Keep written record of hardware and software configuration

For some routine maintenance tasks, the computer can remain powered up (for example cleaning the mouse) or must be powered up (for example to do a virus check). For others, it is necessary to power down, i.e. switch off the computer (for example when cleaning the monitor). As soon as you have completed the maintenance task, make sure that the PC still works!

Some hardware can – and needs to be – cleaned (casings, mouse rollers, etc.), but some hardware is sealed so your maintenance is restricted to 'cleaning' using software (for example deleting temporary files off the hard disk).

It is possible to use software to remind you when to carry out essential maintenance tasks. Software such as Microsoft® Outlook® offers a feature where you can set up a task and reminders at times to suit you (see Figure 1.1, Unit 1, page 7). If you prefer, you can schedule the task to happen automatically (see Figure 2.18).

This is especially advisable for essential tasks such as making backups. However, the backup software will usually allow the details of the task (what has to be backed up) to be set once, rather than every time you decide to do a backup. For example, using Carbonite™ online backup, you can update your backup automatically or set it to backup at a regular time every day. To visit the Carbonite™ website go to Hotlinks.

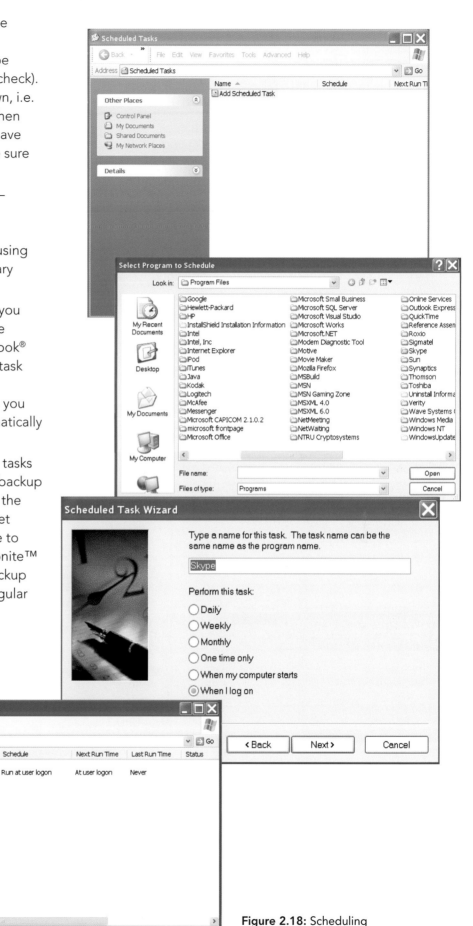

Figure 2.18: Scheduling

Organisation and naming of files

Maintaining the hardware and software so that you have a fully functioning computer system is essential, but your file management is also important, otherwise you might not be able to find your documents.

Microsoft® offers some standard folders to encourage users to be systematic when saving files. For example, the My Pictures folder is for your images and photos. Within the My Pictures folder, you would be advised to set up additional folders, perhaps according to the subject of the photos or the date on which they were taken (Figure 2.19). Otherwise, you will soon find you cannot track down a particular shot without trawling through every photo you have ever taken.

You could put all your documents in the My Documents folder. If you save more than 40 files in any one place, there will be too many to view in one dialog box, so to select a file you will have to scroll up and down to find it. For this reason, it makes more sense to create folders within the My Documents

folder. No two users will have the same arrangement, but you should use logic when organising your folder structure – a logic that makes sense to you.

Many people use their computers partly for work and partly for pleasure. If a computer is used for work purposes, a sensible way of organising files could be to have one folder per client. If there are many clients, it might help to group the clients in some way and to create folders within folders. In this way, a hierarchy of folders can be built up and you can browse through the hierarchy to locate the client and then the particular file that you want to work on.

Backup procedures

Having worked on documents and filed them in appropriate folders, if disaster were to hit your system – a power surge which blows components, a house fire or a flood – how would you pick up from where you left off? You should have a system of backing up important documents and data, so that you can recover from such a disaster.

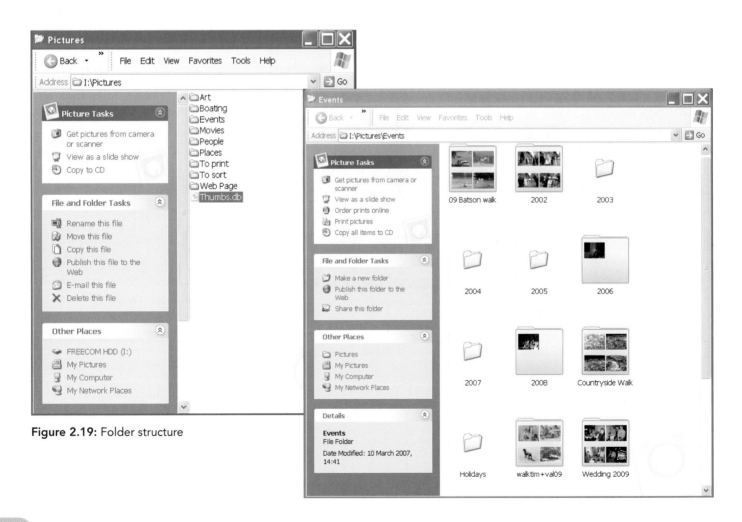

Figure 2.19: Folder structure

Some operating systems incorporate a backup utility, while others are available from third party suppliers.

The scheduling of backups needs to match the relative importance of the data being backed up. If something rarely changes, it only needs to be backed up infrequently, but if something changes by the minute, it probably needs backing up daily or even more frequently.

Backups are considered in other units: see *Unit 5: Managing networks*, pages 149–150.

Backup media

Backups could be saved to your own hard disk but, if anything happened to the disk, all files might be lost including the backups. So, it makes sense to back up onto an alternative device such as another hard disk, or to an online service such as Carbonite.

Automatic scheduling and deletion of unwanted data

There is a limit to how much you can store on one computer. You could resort to storing data on external drives, but you should ask yourself questions such as: 'Do I really need an electronic copy of a letter I wrote to a client eight years ago?'

Did you know?

Emptying the Recycle Bin is one of the things offered in a Disk Cleanup (see page 54).

Until the Recycle Bin is emptied, you have the option to retrieve the file, so you can change your mind!

When files are first deleted, they go to the Recycle Bin – they are not actually deleted from your computer. It is only when the Recycle Bin is emptied that the space they take up is freed for other files.

Archiving

Archiving is the process of setting to one side, usually in a **compressed** form, files that have not been accessed for some time. Old data could be archived for a period, just in case it is needed at a later date but, eventually, some files should be deleted.

Key term

Compression – involves reducing the size of the file by coding it more efficiently into fewer bits of data.

Activity: File management

1 Review the structure of folders on your computer. Does it make sense to you? Is it easy for you to find documents?

2 Review the ages of files stored on your computer. Should you delete some files to free up space?

Defragmentation

Some maintenance, such as disk cleaning and defragmentation, ought to be done by the user, rather than relying on technical support.

Defragmentation is best carried out after a disk cleanup, so that all the unneeded files have been deleted before the tidying up process is done.

Deleting temporary files

Temporary files are created each time you visit a web page (see Internet history on page 54) and each time you open a document or spreadsheet. When you save the document or spreadsheet successfully under the same name or another name, the temporary file is deleted automatically. However, if your computer crashes any open files may be retained as temporary files. During the Disk Clean up process, you will be offered the option to delete temporary files (Figure 2.7 on page 54) and this is an essential part of a maintenance programme.

How to... Defragment a disk

- Select Start/All Programs/Accessories/System Tools/Disk Defragmenter. Alternatively, access this utility through the Control Panel, within the Computer Management folder (see Figure 2.20).
- Click on the Analyze button. The utility will then estimate the disk usage after defragmentation and make a recommendation either to defragment your disk, or not to, at this time.

- If you are recommended to defragment your disk, click on the Defragment button. Defragmentation will take several minutes, so you are advised to leave the PC and spend the time doing something useful!

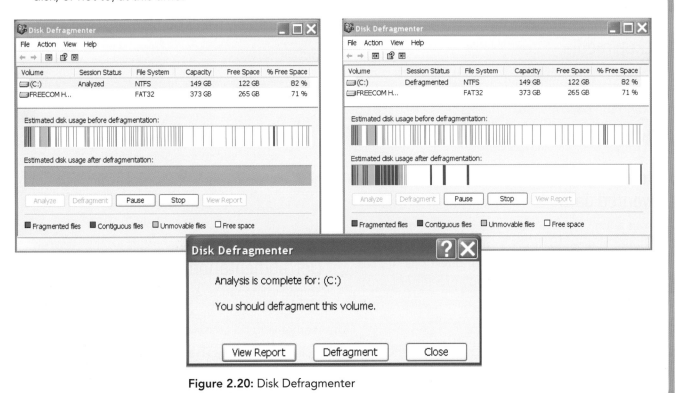

Figure 2.20: Disk Defragmenter

Cleaning hardware

Like any machine, a PC needs some attention on a regular basis, if only to keep the keyboard, mouse, display screen equipment (DSE) and ventilation grills clean. Computers attract a lot of dust. If dust settles on the outside, it soon forms a grimy layer of dirt which is unsightly. If it settles on the inside, it can block airways, preventing the cooling mechanism from working properly. Overheated components may then fail.

When choosing cleaning equipment, you should be wary of potential health risks to you in using these products, as well as selecting the right type of product for the task in hand. For example, many of the chemical solvents are poisonous and may need special handling.

With any chemical product that you buy, you should be given a material safety data sheet (MSDS) – or something similar, for example as part of the label. This lists important advice to help you to handle and use the product correctly and safely. It lists its toxicity, any health effects, first aid measures (for example if you were to ingest some accidentally), how to store the product, how to dispose of it and what to do if the chemical is spilt. Information about the hazards of chemical cleaners is also available on the Internet.

The cheapest liquid cleaning compound is water. Used carefully, it can be used to clean cases, but you must be sure not to wet the electronic parts of the PC.

Water can be mixed with a general purpose cleaner and this may be necessary if the casing has not been cleaned for some time and dirt has built up.

The most expensive option, but the safest for your PC, is isopropyl alcohol. This chemical can be used to clean the PC case, the keyboard case and keys and any other similar casing on your PC. It removes dirt and then evaporates so the equipment does not become wet. It can harm you, though, so be sure to read the instructions carefully – and follow them!

A variety of cleaning equipment is needed.

- **Soft lint-free cloth:** This can be used for cleaning glass and plastic surfaces of components.

- **Paper towels:** These may also be useful, especially to mop up any spillages.

- **Cotton buds or swabs:** These might be useful, for example for cleaning the contact points inside a mouse, but take care they do not leave deposits.

- **Non-static brush or probe:** This, and/or a small flat-bladed screwdriver, can be used to dislodge stubborn bits of dirt, for example on the mouse rollers.

- **Compressed air:** This comes in an aerosol can and may be used to clean fans, grills or keyboards. To direct the air more precisely, use the long thin plastic tube, taking care to blow the air in a direction that will take the dust away from the PC.

- **Non-static vacuum cleaners:** Vacuuming the inside of a PC can remove a lot of the dust that collects. Some small cleaners include brush heads ideal for the purpose. However, it is important to use non-static vacuum cleaners.

Activity: Hardware maintenance – cleaning

1 Research the Internet to discover what dangers are involved in using isopropyl alcohol.

2 You will give a PC a spring clean and you are to time how long it takes.

   (a) Examine the PC to see what you think needs cleaning. Make a list of the tasks you intend to do and assemble the cleaning materials that you plan to use. Obtain approval from your tutor before starting.

   (b) Clean each component separately and then check that the PC still works before moving on to clean the next component.

   (c) Tick each item on your task list, noting how long it took to do.

   (d) Draw up a maintenance list for future cleaning of this PC. Estimate how much time per week will be needed.

Replacing consumables

Consumables are resources that are used up in a process, such as printer paper, ink or toner cartridges. These consumables need replacing – without a supply the computer system cannot output data via the printer.

Replacing damaged components

Wear and tear and accidental damage – a cup of coffee spilt on a keyboard for example – may result in your having to replace a damaged component. The circumstances of the damage ought to be recorded and the lesson learned.

Activity: Software maintenance

1 Establish a routine of software maintenance for your own PC. Utilise software such as Outlook® to set up reminders for yourself.

2 Set up a scheduled task for some aspect of your software maintenance, for example a daily backup.

3 For one item of software, check the Internet for the availability of an upgrade. How much will it cost? And what will the download involve you doing?

4 Check whether a hard disk requires defragmentation and, if it does, choose the option to complete the defragmentation. Take screenshots of the disk usage before and after defragmentation to show the effect.

5 Research the Internet for compression software. Identify one such utility and experiment with compressing files. Which files are reduced in size the most?

Assessment activity 2.3

P5 P6 P7 M3 D2 P8 BTEC

1 Your tutor will instruct you to set up a standalone computer system, installing at least one hardware component and at least one software component. **P5**

2 Your tutor will instruct you to configure in some way a computer system to meet user needs. **P6**

3 Test a configured computer system for functionality, taking screen shots as appropriate. **P7**

4 Evaluate the performance of a computer system. **M3**

5 Explain and justify improvements that could be made to a computer system. **D2**

6 Undertake routine maintenance tasks on a standalone computer system. **P8**

Grading tips

- Make sure that you observe all necessary safety measures. **P5**

- Try to complete the task without undue prompting from your tutor. Prepare by practising beforehand: setting left/right hand buttons on a mouse, setting power saving options, changing the screen resolution, changing the desktop theme, changing the default language setting and changing default folder locations. **P6**

- You should prepare a test plan and present it together with your test results. Include an explanation of any test failures, with reasons. **P7**

- When carrying out tests, make sure you evaluate the configuration of the system against the user's requirements. **M3**

- Offer suggestions on how the system could be improved, considering costs involved and the potential benefits to be gained. **D2**

- Take screenshots as evidence of the routine maintenance tasks that you have completed to include with the witness statement. Evidence can also be given in the form of photographs or videos. **P8**

PLTS

When you organise your time and resources, prioritising actions when setting up, testing and maintaining the system, you are demonstrating your skills as a **self-manager**.

When you support conclusions, using reasoned arguments and evidence (for example when justifying a choice of computer system), you are demonstrating your skills as an **independent enquirer**.

Functional skills

When you are connecting hardware safely to a computer system, testing for functionality, configuring software for a given user requirement and maintaining the system, it demonstrates your Functional **ICT** skills by showing that you can select, interact with and use IT systems safely and securely for a complex task in non-routine and unfamiliar contexts.

Khalid@Whizzworld

Information desk

Khalid works on the information desk at WhizzWorld and his job is to help customers who have already bought a computer system and are having problems with it.

Sometimes someone comes to the information desk because they are thinking about buying a computer and need guidance as to which one to purchase.

It can be bewildering for the prospective customer. WhizzWorld stock all the well-known makes of computer such as Microsoft® and Apple® Macintosh® and a full range of peripherals such as screens and printers. There is also a wide range of software available and Khalid is expected to know which software products are compatible with which hardware ranges.

The latest products are always exciting to try out and Khalid often attends courses so he knows all there is to know about the WhizzWorld's range of computerware.

Think about it!

1 List five factors you might take into account when recommending a computer system to a particular user.

2 Why might a user insist on a particular brand of operating system?

3 Why is it essential to aim for the maximum processing power and storage capacity that can be afforded?

4 What is a bundle of software? What are the advantages and disadvantages of purchasing a bundle?

5 What is the advantage of choosing a software vendor which offers online training as part of purchase price?

Just checking

1. Explain these terms: peripheral, port, BIOS, PCB and PSU.
2. What purpose is served by the POST?
3. Explain the purpose of an expansion slot and give three examples of cards found in one.
4. Explain how viruses, trojans and worms can infect a PC and how this can be avoided.
5. List five tasks that might be included in a maintenance schedule.
6. What is the purpose of the defragmentation utility?
7. Under what circumstances should you use water while cleaning your computer?
8. What functions does the PSU serve?
9. What is an RJ-11 connector used for?
10. Explain these terms: processor speed, clock rate and access time.

edexcel

Assignment tips

- Pool information with others in your group. You can learn from them as much as they can learn from you.
- The Internet will provide you with all the additional information you might need. Just use Google® or some other search engine and key in a term, for example 'SATA'. Be careful, though, to check the validity of a website.
- When watching a presentation given by your tutor, or one of your classmates, be aware of how they present the information on the slides, how they talk along with the slides (referring to notes as necessary) and how they hold your attention throughout the talk. Learn from what works well and, when you are required to make a presentation, avoid making the mistakes that you notice in others.

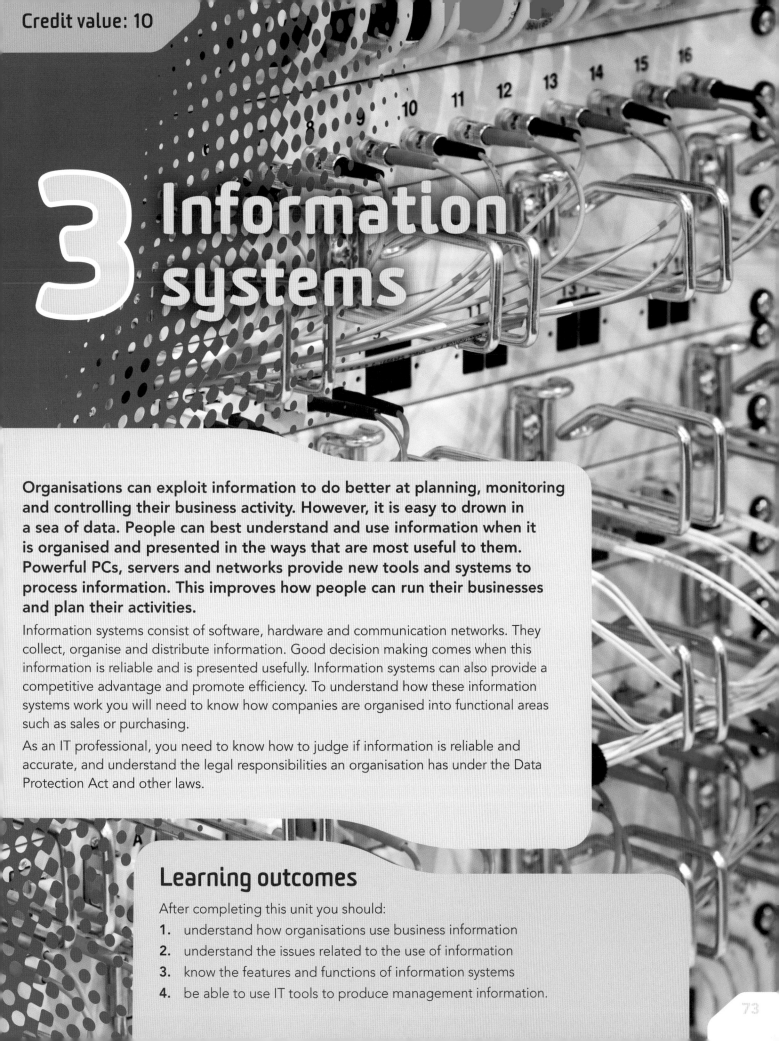

3 Information systems

Organisations can exploit information to do better at planning, monitoring and controlling their business activity. However, it is easy to drown in a sea of data. People can best understand and use information when it is organised and presented in the ways that are most useful to them. Powerful PCs, servers and networks provide new tools and systems to process information. This improves how people can run their businesses and plan their activities.

Information systems consist of software, hardware and communication networks. They collect, organise and distribute information. Good decision making comes when this information is reliable and is presented usefully. Information systems can also provide a competitive advantage and promote efficiency. To understand how these information systems work you will need to know how companies are organised into functional areas such as sales or purchasing.

As an IT professional, you need to know how to judge if information is reliable and accurate, and understand the legal responsibilities an organisation has under the Data Protection Act and other laws.

Learning outcomes

After completing this unit you should:
1. understand how organisations use business information
2. understand the issues related to the use of information
3. know the features and functions of information systems
4. be able to use IT tools to produce management information.

Assessment and grading criteria

This table shows you what you must do in order to achieve a pass, merit or distinction grade, and where you can find activities in this book to help you.

To achieve a **pass** grade the evidence must show that you are able to:	To achieve a **merit** grade the evidence must show that, in addition to the pass criteria, you are able to:	To achieve a **distinction** grade the evidence must show that, in addition to the pass and merit criteria, you are able to:
P1 explain how organisations use information **See Assessment activity 3.1, page 83**	**M1** illustrate the information flow between different functional areas **See Assessment activity 3.1, page 83**	**D1** explain how an organisation could improve the quality of its business information **See Assessment activity 3.1, page 83**
P2 discuss the characteristics of good information **See Assessment activity 3.1, page 83**		
P3 explain the issues related to the use of information **See Assessment activity 3.2, page 87**	**M2** assess how issues related to the use of information affect an organisation **See Assessment activity 3.2, page 87**	
P4 describe the features and functions of information systems **See Assessment activity 3.1, page 83**		
P5 identify the information systems used in a specified organisation **See Assessment activity 3.1, page 83**		
P6 select information to support a business decision-making process **See Assessment activity 3.3, page 94**		**D2** justify the information selected to support a business decision-making process **See Assessment activity 3.3, page 94**
P7 use IT tools to produce management information **See Assessment activity 3.3, page 94**	**M3** generate valid, accurate and useful information **See Assessment activity 3.3, page 94**	

How you will be assessed

This unit will be assessed by a number of internal assignments that will be designed and marked by the staff at your centre. It may be subject to sampling by your centre's Lead Internal Verifier or an Edexcel Standards Verifier as part of Edexcel's ongoing quality assurance procedures. The assignments will be designed to allow you to show your understanding of the unit outcomes. These relate to what you should be able to do after completing this unit.

Your tutor will tell you precisely what form your assessments will take, but you could be asked to produce:

- presentations
- case studies
- practical tasks
- written assignments.

Jade Williams, BTEC National IT learner

This unit gives you a good insight into how IT works with a business. For example, when most of us go into a shop we just buy something and think nothing of it. This unit makes you think about the effect your buying has. It goes through the systems that are used.

The first assignment showed me the difference between information and data, which I just thought were two different words. I found the assessment easy, but the higher grades were harder, especially the distinctions, as they needed a lot more depth and understanding

I found that in my part-time job at Sainsbury's it has made a difference to my understanding. I use a scanner to check stock levels on the shelves and I didn't used to think about it. Now, I know why I scan the gaps and what low product quantities do to the systems, tracking the storeroom and re-ordering stock.

This unit shows you how to process data and make it presentable to others so it can be read easily. You also learn how to break down an organisation into smaller sections and see what information goes where by using data flow diagrams. This can improve how businesses are run and how they plan their activities.

Information systems consist of software, hardware and communication networks. They collect, organise and distribute information. They can also increase profits and promote efficiency. Right now, this hasn't made any difference to me outside of work, but I know it will help in job interviews as it will be a lot easier to talk about how company IT systems work.

At the start of the course, I thought it didn't have much practical work in it so would be boring, but now I understand why the theory is important.

Over to you

- **What part does the scanner take in Sainsbury's information systems?**
- **Find examples of information that is clearly presented and information that is poorly presented.**
- **What information do you think might be communicated between sites by information systems?**

1. Understand how organisations use business information

Ethical information

Companies hold a lot of information for different purposes, which can be accessed by members of staff as part of their job, but which might also be useful information that could be used in other ways.

What do you think are the rights and wrongs of these situations?

- A bank employee finds out how much money is in the bank account of someone owing money to their partner's business, claiming to be broke.

- An employee finds out that their company has received a lot of complaints regarding pollution of a local river and sends this information to the local newspaper.

- An employee has a friend who is tendering for work from their employer and tells the friend how much has been quoted in the other tenders that have been received for this work.

Are there any situations where you think whistle blowing on an organisation is the right thing to do?

1.1 Types of information

Two main types of data are considered here: **qualitative** and **quantitative**.

Key terms

Qualitative – personal and subjective.

Quantitative – factual, often number-based, obtained through well-defined processes.

Case study: Fast food customer satisfaction survey

Diana works for a company that runs customer satisfaction surveys for a fast food chain. She visits their stores and carries out surveys with customers. She records their responses, which are used by the store and company management to make improvements.

Here are some of the questions that Diana asks customers. For each question, decide whether the information obtained will be qualitative or quantitative. The first two have been done for you to get you started. Add some more questions of your own and do the same for these questions.

1 How long did you wait to place your order? (quantitative)
2 Was your server friendly? (qualitative)
3 Was your server well groomed?
4 How long did you wait for your order to be delivered?

5 How clean was the store?
6 Was your server wearing a name badge?
7 How tasty was your food?

Primary data

Primary data is data that you collect yourself. You may do this by direct observation, surveys, interviews or logs. You should be able to rely on primary data because you know where it came from. You also know what you have done to the data to process it.

Secondary data

Secondary data is data that you collect from external sources such as:

- the Internet
- television
- written articles in journals, magazines and newspapers
- stories told to you verbally.

You should rely less on secondary data because you cannot be certain how accurate it is. It may also include bias because of a point its author is trying to make.

Primary data is often expensive and difficult to get hold of. However, you can trust it. Secondary data is usually cheaper and easier to collect, but you may not be certain of its accuracy or scope.

1.2 Purposes of information

Organisations use business information in many ways to help them become more effective. Four of the most important ways are operational support, analysis, decision making and gaining advantage. This section explains each of these terms and gives examples of how a business might use them.

Operational support

When monitoring and controlling its activities a business can make immediate use of the information from its operational support system to make its minute-by-minute or hour-by-hour decisions. For a restaurant, for example, some of their products are freshly prepared, while others are cooked in batches or need time to defrost. If customer orders are recorded on an **EPOS** system, then an operational support system can alert the restaurant management as to when they need to cook or defrost more bulk products.

Key term

EPOS – stands for electronic point of sale. It is an automated till system used in many shops and restaurants.

Analysis

Analysis is where the business regularly does the same or similar processing of its data. This is typically to identify patterns or trends and to monitor the business. A business might produce a weekly sales and costs report. This would show a trend of whether profits are increasing or decreasing and whether increased sales drive up costs.

For example, a restaurant chain might use analysis to compare the performance of similar restaurants, to compare one restaurant against the regional or national average or to identify the impact of a promotion on sales and costs. Analysis may also be used to identify patterns, such as the increase in sales at Christmas or Easter.

Analysis can be a powerful tool to predict sales and demand in the future, which in turn helps the organisation to know how much stock to buy in, what staffing is required and what advertising needs there are.

Decision making

Information systems can support decision making when a problem or issue arises and management needs to take action to resolve it. This is typically done on an ad hoc basis as problems arise. Management can take these decisions at various levels – operational, tactical or strategic.

For example, the management of the restaurant chain might want to reduce costs. They might decide to do this by a reduction in the hours that some of their restaurants are open. They could decide when to close the restaurants by looking at information on sales and costs by hour of the day, by day of the week and by branch. They could open later, or close earlier, if sales less direct costs were low. This could be operational (for one branch), tactical (for a group of branches) or strategic (for a region or nationally).

Gaining advantage

This is the opposite to resolving a problem, in that it is about taking advantage of external or internal events. It is done on an ad hoc basis as and when opportunities arise. It is also used to identify patterns or trends, this time with the aim of making decisions to benefit from these events.

For example, how should the restaurant respond when the local football team gains promotion to the premier league? Should management employ more staff or open longer on match days? Should they advertise more at the club ground? Or should they do special promotions?

Another example is if a competing chain goes out of business. What actions should the restaurants near to their former competitor take? What might be the effect of taking these actions?

1.3 Sources of information

Internal information

Within a business, each department produces information which is of value to other departments.

Often, putting this information together right across the business gives valuable insights to the senior management of the company. Table 3.1 gives some examples of the information that different departments in an organisation might produce.

External information

There is also a lot of information available externally to organisations that can help them in their decision making. Table 3.2 gives some examples.

Table 3.1 Internal information

Organisational department	Type of information produced
Administration	In some organisations, some, or all, of the data production tasks mentioned below are done and/or stored by a central administration department
Finance	Information about revenues or income, costs or expenditure, assets or capital items, liabilities or known future costs and investments
Manufacturing	Information about what resources are used and the timescales in which input products are turned into output products
Marketing	Information on the organisation's customers, either individually or grouped by category of customer; may also be responsible for the definition and description of the products and how these are grouped as brands
Personnel/HR	Information about the people that the organisation employs, such as their contact details, jobs, grades and skills
Purchasing	Information based on purchase orders about who supplies which products to the organisation, how often and for what price

Table 3.2 External information

Source of external information	Type of information available
Commercially provided databases	Many information businesses take publicly available data, add in their knowledge of an industry and process that information to provide information. A simple example is in newspaper publishing. Most newspapers make their current content available free on the Internet. They can profit from the archives by adding powerful search functions and then charging to search for groups of historic stories
Government	Many governments, both central and local, require organisations to provide them with a great deal of data. Once the government has processed and summarised this data, the information can often be reused. However, as it is produced primarily for government purposes, this is not always timely or detailed enough for other uses
Research	Many consultants with a deep knowledge of a particular industry know exactly where to look and who to contact to find needed information. Organisations can use this external research to find advice or information to improve their decisions
Trade groupings	Almost all trades have formed groupings of businesses in that trade to influence others for the benefit of their trade

Case study: Trade groupings

A good example of a trade grouping is IATA (International Air Transport Association), which is the trade grouping for the airline industry. Its aims are summarised as follows.

- IATA simplifies travel processes for passengers.
- IATA allows airlines to operate safely, securely, efficiently and economically.
- IATA serves as an intermediary between airlines and passenger agents.
- A large network of suppliers gathered by IATA provides solid expertise to airlines in a variety of industry solutions.
- IATA informs governments about the complexities of the aviation industry to ensure better long-term decisions.

1 What information might IATA supply to its member airlines?

2 What information might IATA supply to passengers?

3 What information might IATA supply to governments?

Activity: Organisations and information

1 Consider several organisations of your choice. These could be, for example your local council, a college, a shop, or a restaurant.

2 What types of information is each organisation likely to need?

3 Where could each organisation get the necessary information from?

4 In each organisation, which departments are involved in collecting and processing the different types of information?

5 What are the similarities and differences in information needs between the organisations you have selected?

Reliability of data sources

There are many sources of data, both good and bad, so it is important to understand how reliable your data sources are. Obviously, data from a reliable source can be trusted and so important decisions can be based upon it.

Usually, the most reliable data is that which you or your organisation has created. But often the need is for external data that can be used to help plan operations or assist in other decision making.

The old adage 'you get what you pay for' can apply here, with free data being particularly suspect, although the government does publish a lot of trustworthy data.

There are many commercial databases that an organisation may choose to purchase from their providers, especially if the data has direct relevance, such as detailed information about potential clients in a geographical area.

Reliability is often related to quantity, so a large, targeted dataset from a trustworthy source can be valuable to an organisation.

1.4 Good information

Information is of the most use if it has the following characteristics.

- **Valid:** It should be unbiased, representative and verifiable.
- **Reliable:** How well does it fit in with other facts you already know? How well do you trust this source of data?
- **Timely:** Information should be available when it is needed for decision making and not some time afterwards.
- **Fit for purpose:** Was this information provided for the purpose for which it is now being used?

For example, a monthly budget prepared six months before the start of the year may not be of much use in forecasting the remaining spend for the last two months of the year.

- **Accessible:** You must be able to do calculations with the data. For example, a printed report may be valuable, but if it contains a lot of data you would not want to have to key it all in again in order to perform calculations.

- **Cost-effective:** The cost of capturing and producing the data should be very much less than the value of the decisions made on that data. It is said that the cost to business of government laws to capture data is often greater than the benefit gained from these laws.

- **Sufficiently accurate:** Information needs to be accurate enough, but not necessarily completely exact. If you are calculating whether you can afford to buy a car, you will need to know how much capital you have available and how much you can spend per month. You will also need to know the expected monthly total running costs and the cost of the car. However, these costs do not need to be exact as there will be some flexibility, for example you could reduce your monthly mileage to reduce your monthly costs or buy a cheaper car to reduce the monthly loan repayment cost.

- **Relevance:** There is no point in capturing information if it is not relevant to the decisions you want to make from it.

- **Having the right level of detail:** You need to capture enough detail for the purpose that is required, but no more. If you manage your household accounts, it is unlikely that you will record every postage stamp purchased or every item in your shopping basket. You are more likely to record just the totals.

- **From a source in which the user has confidence:** You need to know how believable it is. For a news item, you are more likely to accept a story reported in several national newspapers rather than one on an individual's web page.

- **Understandable by the user:** It must be at the user's level. For example, share-buying advice in a weekend newspaper for the general public might have one paragraph for each share. At the other extreme, financial analysts advising pension funds with billions of pounds of assets would give much more detailed recommendations.

Two competing retail chains developed sales information systems to help their management have the right stock in their stores at the right prices.

- One system captured detailed data from the till systems of every store every night. It provided detailed sales figures for local and regional management by 07:00 the following morning. This gave them an excellent way to manage sales, though it was not completely accurate as it didn't account for returns or exchanges.

- The second system tracked all goods from ordering from a supplier through to customer delivery and possible return. Its main purpose was to provide the company's monthly financial accounts. This was, however, less successful as a sales information system than the first system, as it was several days, and often weeks, before sales information was available in a suitable form for management to take sales decisions.

1 List the advantages to the retail chain of the first system.
2 List the advantages to the retail chain of the second system.
3 List the types of retail store that would prefer the first system and those that would prefer the second system.

1.5 Business functional areas

As well as being sources of information, parts of a business want to gain a good understanding of how they perform. They want to use this information to help them to perform better. This section gives examples of the sorts of things they might do. It builds on the information you saw in Table 3.1 (page 78).

Sales

The sales department is interested in what products they have sold, to whom and for how much. Sales analyses are of great use to the sales department. These could include data on sales organised by:

- product and product group
- store, location or outlet and various groupings by geography, store size and organisation hierarchy
- salesperson, for bonus purposes
- customer and customer type.

Each of these might be organised by time of day or day of week, or as a comparison against the previous week, month or year.

Purchasing

The purchasing department is interested mainly in how their suppliers perform. They would analyse them by price, by lead-time, by fewest problems and by product availability. The best supplier would have one of the cheapest prices, deliver quickly and reliably, not give problems with product quality or paperwork and always have the products needed available.

Manufacturing

The manufacturing department wants to show how efficient the business is. This means that they analyse how well they use their staff and machinery, how well they produce the most successful products, how they minimise wastage and how well they can react to changing demands.

Marketing

The marketing team is interested in analysing the customers and competitors. Like sales, they are interested in sales by customer and customer type. They may well have segmented the customers into types such as 'wealthy pensioners' and 'trendy teenagers'. They may also have segmented their addresses into groups such as 'rural farming' and 'affluent suburbs'.

They are interested in which products sell best to which customer type, for advertising and promotional purposes. They will also do external competitor analyses. These may focus on what competitors are doing to attract the most profitable customers.

Finance

The information from the finance department is often split. Financial accounting is concerned with what money the organisation has, that is its income and expenditure. Management accounting is concerned with *how* the money is spent. For example, the management accounts of a college would say how much money each subject department has spent.

Personnel

The human resources, or personnel department, analyses information about the people that the organisation employs. They will monitor staff turnover, average staff wages, average days off sick and hours worked in order to comply with labour laws and staff agreements.

Administration

If there is a central administration department, they may prepare reports that apply to the whole organisation. They may also prepare and use some of the departmental reports.

1.6 Information flows

Information flow is the movement of information relevant to the business, from where it is produced to where it can be actioned. For any organisation, speedy, efficient information flow is very important to its success.

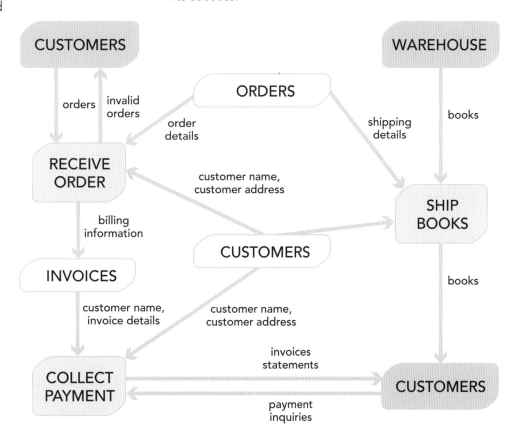

Figure 3.1: Data flows in a book ordering system

Internal information flows

Within most organisations, there are three types of information flow.

- **Downwards:** Senior management informs the rest of the organisation about decisions taken and the direction of the company.
- **Upwards:** The staff of the organisation report to management on their progress and on any successes and problems that management need to address.
- **Across:** Information is passed between different parts of the organisation so that they can work together to achieve their common goals.

For example, an IT department has information flows to and from the parts of the organisation for which it develops or maintains systems. It maintains a help desk to record and resolve day-to-day problems with systems used by other departments. The management of the IT department holds a weekly meeting with departments that use IT services in order to report on progress and identify trends.

Information flows to external bodies

Information also flows out of an organisation. Almost all organisations will provide information to their customers. This may be targeted to individual customers (such as a bank statement or utility bill), to a group of customers (such as a council's report on its performance) or to all customers (such as a public company's annual report). In the past, this information would always have been delivered in printed form, but is now increasingly likely to be delivered via the Internet.

Information also flows to suppliers and many organisations are also legally required to send large amounts of information to government bodies.

Information flow diagrams

An information flow diagram shows the steps involved in data flow – it includes where data is originally produced, where it is turned into information and where decisions are made on that data.

Figure 3.2 shows the steps involved in an information system from the past reporting on aircraft movements.

1. Take-offs and landings are observed.
2. Reports are manually entered.
3. Information derived is vague and non-specific.

Figure 3.3 shows the steps involved in an information system today, turning aircraft movement data into aircraft punctuality information.

1. Aircraft movement (data).
2. Time and other movement details entered into a local computer.
3. External body records aircraft movement data. Movement data validated, processed into information, sorted and stored centrally.
4. Screens and reports produced analysing movements in many ways.
5. Analysts take action on information.

Figure 3.2: Information flow – aircraft punctuality management long ago

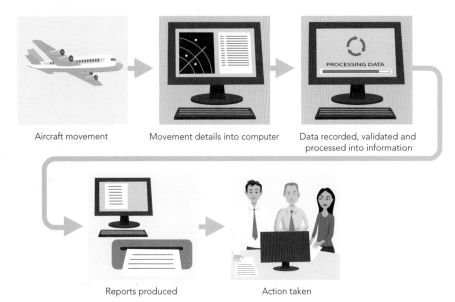

Aircraft movement   Movement details into computer   Data recorded, validated and processed into information

Reports produced   Action taken

Figure 3.3: Information flow diagram – aircraft punctuality management today

Assessment activity 3.1

P1 P2 P4 P5 M1 D1   **BTEC**

You are working in the publicity department office of a large bank as a junior publicity and media officer. After a recent financial rescue from the government, the bank is starting a publicity campaign to explain to the public the good work it does.

You have been allocated some tasks to help prepare for a set of roadshow materials that are to be set up in shopping malls throughout the country.

1 Prepare a poster entitled 'Good information' to explain how the best information should be valid, reliable, timely, fit for purpose, accessible, cost-effective, accurate, relevant, have the right level of detail, be from a reliable source and understandable by the user. **P2**

2 Prepare a brochure entitled 'How to improve the quality of business information' targeted at small businesses, explaining how to make the best of their information.

The brochure should include your task 1 poster as an image, with sections to cover these areas, explaining how an appreciation of each of the aspects of information can improve its quality:

- Types of information
- Purposes of information
- Sources of information. **D1**

3 Prepare a poster entitled 'Using information' to show how data is transformed into information by organisations. The poster needs to identify some ways that organisations use their information. **P1**

4 Prepare a slide show presentation entitled 'Information systems' which can run as a continuous loop on roadshow computers. The presentation needs to have four sections:

- Features and functions of information systems, including what data is, who uses information systems, as well as the hardware, software and telecommunications used by these systems. Include slides about input, storage, processing, output, control/feedback loops, closed and open systems **P4**

- Types of information systems – for a named organisation, including the management information systems and other information systems, such as marketing, financial and human resources the organisation actually operates **P5**

- Business functional areas – including sales, purchasing, manufacturing, marketing, finance, personnel and administration **M1**

- Information flows – using suitable diagrams to show both internal information flows and information flows to external bodies. **M1**

Grading tips

- The poster needs to explain how organisations use information. **P1**

- This poster could give a realistic example for each of the attributes of good information shown on it. **P2**

- Structure your presentation into sections for both the features and functions of information systems with follow-on slides to give more detail. **P4**

- Make sure you name the organisation using the information systems in these slides. **P5**

- You need to identify some different functional areas and how information flows between them. **M1**

- You will need to provide appropriate examples to support your explanation of types, purposes and sources of information. **D1**

PLTS

You will show yourself to be an **effective participator** when you present a persuasive case for action suggesting additions and improvements to the management of information.

Functional skills

You will practise your Functional **ICT** skills by finding and selecting information Functional skills when you use appropriate search techniques to locate and select relevant information.

2. Understand the issues related to the use of information

2.1 Legal issues

There are many laws that affect the use of information. Three of these are the:

- Data Protection Act (1998)
- Freedom of Information Act (2000)
- Computer Misuse Act (1990).

Data Protection Act (1998)

The Data Protection Act (1998) provides a framework to ensure that personal information is handled properly. It also gives individuals the right to know what information is held about them.

The Act works in two ways. Anyone who processes personal information must register with the DPA registrar and comply with eight principles. These make sure that personal information is:

- fairly and lawfully processed
- processed for limited purposes
- adequate, relevant and not excessive
- accurate and up to date
- not kept for longer than is necessary
- processed in line with your rights
- secure
- not transferred to other countries without adequate protection.

The Act also provides individuals with important rights. These include the right to find out what personal information is held on computer and most paper records.

Freedom of Information Act (2000)

The Freedom of Information Act (2000) deals with access to official information. It gives individuals or organisations the right to ask for information from any public authority, including central and local government, the police, the NHS and colleges and schools. They then have 20 days to provide the information requested. They may refuse if the information is exempt from the Act. Examples of exemption are if releasing the information could prejudice national security or damage commercial interests.

Computer Misuse Act (1990)

The Computer Misuse Act (1990) details three offences:

- unauthorised access to any computer program or data – the most common form of this is using someone else's user ID and password
- unauthorised access with intent to commit a serious crime
- unauthorised modification of computer contents. This means impairing the operation of a computer, a program or the reliability of data. It also includes preventing access to any program or data. Examples of this are the introduction of a virus, modifying or destroying another user's files or changing financial or administrative data.

Some minor changes to tighten up this Act were introduced as a small part of the Police and Justice Act (2006). This made unauthorised acts with intent to impair the operation of a computer illegal.

2.2 Ethical issues

Codes of practice

Many organisations will have a code of practice to make it clear what uses can be made of their computing facilities. The main uses will be to support the purpose of the organisation, but a code of practice will often define the extent to which private use of the computer system is permitted. Examples of items included in a code of practice are as follows.

- **Use of email:** Threatening or harassing emails are usually banned, as well as spamming or producing large numbers of unsolicited emails. Limited use of email for private purposes is often allowed.
- **Use of the Internet:** Inappropriate classes of websites, such as pornography or gambling, are usually banned, either by the code of practice or by filtering software. Limited Internet use for personal purposes is often allowed, as this can be difficult to distinguish from professional research. Where an organisation has its own web server, there are often strict rules as to what can be posted to it. There may be exceptions for clearly identified personal pages.

- **Whistle blowing:** Codes of practice will often protect computer users who draw management's attention to other users' misuse of the system. The codes will certainly protect IT administrators who run the servers and will often be the first to detect misuse.

Activity: Codes of practice

1 Find examples of computer codes of practice, either from your college or by carrying out Internet research.
2 Produce a code of practice for a top secret military or government establishment.
3 Produce a code of practice for a small web design or computer consultancy company.
4 List the areas in which these codes are similar. List the areas in which they differ significantly. Explain the reasons for the areas where they differ.

Organisational policies

An organisation's policies may have a significant effect on how it treats information. An organisation with a strong hierarchy that operates on a need-to-know basis is likely to impose policies restricting access to information. For example, it may keep its databases, files and email servers in a secure central data centre. IT security and data centre staff may put in place tight controls on who can access or update this data.

A decentralised organisation with decentralised computing is also likely to have restricted access to information, but this time for geographical reasons. There may be few security restrictions on access to files, databases or email on each site. However, there may be limited or no direct connectivity between sites. This could prevent staff at one location accessing information held at another location, even though the company would be happy for them to do so.

Information ownership

The department that produced the data should own every field of data in every record. They should have the responsibility for making sure that it is entered into the computer system in a timely way, that it is correct and that it is consistent.

Information ownership is much more complex. Many data owners may have supplied the original data that has been processed to produce this information. The often arbitrary way of allocating ownership is that the department responsible for defining or running the program that produces the information owns it. Except for internal IT information such as computer network performance, it is not a good idea to make the IT department responsible for information ownership. They are its guardians rather than its owners.

2.3 Operational issues

Security of information

System users expect the IT department to keep its information secure. This means that it is safe from unauthorised or unexpected access, alteration or destruction. It is management's responsibility to specify who can look at and update information. In small organisations with a simple structure, management may decide that anyone in the organisation can look at any information or that people on an authorised list may update information.

Many organisations have much more complex rules. Management may require a log of who has made updates or accessed information. It is usually the responsibility of the IT department to advise on security and to implement the chosen rules.

For more on Security, see *Unit 5: Managing networks*, page 146.

Backups

It is good practice to make frequent **backups** of information in case of physical or processing problems. This may be a full backup of all information or a partial backup of just the information that has changed since the last full backup. The IT department should occasionally practise a recovery or restore from the full backup of all the information. They should then apply any partial backup to make sure it works.

Key term

Backup – a copy of the data that is kept in case anything should happen to the original. The term 'back up' is also used as a verb.

Health and safety

Although information systems are relatively low risk, there are a few health and safety issues that must be addressed. There are regulations that apply to screens and monitors, their positioning and usage. Keyboards, mice, chairs and tables must be appropriately positioned. Computer users are entitled to eye tests. They should have breaks away from the computer. All existing office and other workplace environment laws apply to using information systems.

Organisational policies

Many organisations have policies for the use of information systems that their staff should follow. These may range from keeping information confidential within the company to the procedures to follow for correcting any information that appears to be wrong.

Business continuance plan

IT is at the heart of how many organisations operate and should therefore be an important part of any business continuance plan (BCP) to plan how operations can continue if any major part of an IT system should fail.

The IT department should have things set up so that if there is a major failure, they will be able to continue to provide a service, even though a more limited one. A good example is to provide a dual network, attaching alternate terminals to each network. Then, if there is a complete failure of one network, half the terminals will continue to work.

The organisation needs to make decisions regarding their BCP. For example, a retailer may decide to have more tills, or point of sale terminals, than strictly necessary in order to allow for failure. They may also decide to have two servers in the back office driving the tills, rather than one, in case of server failure. However, do not expect the BCP to cover every eventuality.

Costs

Whether an organisation is a business with a focus on costs, a government organisation whose aim is to deliver the best possible service within a fixed budget, or a not-for-profit charity, it is important to manage the costs of an IT system. The total benefits of an IT system should greatly exceed the total costs. There are two important areas you should consider when costing an IT project.

- **Additional resources required:** The introduction of a new system often entails the one-off costs of new equipment purchase and installation, and user testing and training. In the IT department there are often more resources needed and so there will be ongoing costs to run a new system.

- **Cost of development:** This is usually a large part of the budget for a new computer system. There will also be ongoing costs once the system is running for minor changes to keep the system in line with the organisation's needs.

Impact of increasing sophistication of systems

Early information systems often just automated existing manual processes. This meant that little user training was needed and the software was relatively simple. Today's computing power means that systems are now becoming increasingly sophisticated. They need the following.

- **More trained personnel:** Users often need training in how to use the equipment, the basic computing features, the processes brought in with a new computer system and the transactions, queries and reports that form the new system.

Case study: Business continuance plan

A business has its offices in an area that is liable to flooding. It therefore decides to install the servers for its information systems on the fourth floor of the building, in case the ground floor or basement ever floods. One day, the staff arrive to find water cascading through all the floors of the building due to a leak. The building is closed for several weeks while the leak is fixed and the building dries out and is cleaned. The BCP planners had not known there was

a large air-conditioning water reservoir on the roof of the building and this had burst.

1 What actions might be in the BCP for that building and system?
2 What could have been done to prevent this incident?
3 Once the leak had happened, how could its effects have been minimised?

- **More complex software:** Modern development software hides a lot of complexity from the application builder. This means they can focus on the business problems that the new system will solve and create overall better and more complex systems. However, when there are problems, it may need both a development software expert and a business software expert to work together to fix them.

Activity: Customer information and constraints

Focus on an organisation that uses customer information. This could be one of the organisations you studied for the activity on page 79, or another organisation. You should consider legal, ethical, operational and other constraints.

1 What constraints affect the way the organisation uses customer information?

2 How does the organisation deal with these constraints?

Assessment activity 3.2

 BTEC

You are working in the publicity department office of a large bank as a junior publicity and media officer. After a recent financial rescue from the government, the bank started a publicity campaign to explain to the public the good work it does.

You were set some tasks preparing for a roadshow that was set up in shopping malls throughout the country. Visitor feedback from the show has identified a need for some extra material to be added to the bank's website.

This extra material is to show how the bank is aware of, and deals with, issues around the collection and processing of information.

1 You are to produce some pages that could be used on the bank website to explain:

- legal issues **P3**
- ethical issues **P3**
- operational issues. **M2**

2 The legal issues web page needs to summarise these relevant data protection legislations:

- Data Protection Act (1998)

- Freedom of Information Act (2000)
- Computer Misuse Act (1990). **P3**

3 The ethical issues web page needs to summarise the bank's codes of practice regarding staff use of email, Internet and whistle blowing. **P3**

4 The operational issues web page needs to explain how the bank keeps information secure. This should include backups, organisational policies, the bank's continuance plans and the impact of increasing sophistication of systems on large organisations such as banks. **M2**

Grading tips

- Include brief summaries of how legislation affects the use of information. **P3**

- Include what an organisation must do to respond to any issues related to the use of information. **M2**

PLTS

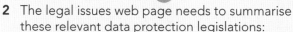

You will show yourself to be an **independent enquirer** when you identify questions to answer and problems to resolve when explaining how organisations manipulate and use information.

You can also show yourself to be an **independent enquirer** when you plan and carry out research, appreciating the consequences of decisions when investigating the use of information by organisations.

Functional skills

You will practise the **ICT** finding and selecting information Functional skill when you select information from a variety of sources to meet requirements of a complex task by selecting information to support a business decision-making process.

3. Know the features and functions of information systems

3.1 Features of information systems

An information system has five parts: data, people, hardware, software and telecommunications.

Data

The data input to the system must be as accurate as it can be, subject to its cost and timescales for capture. It should then be stored in the most logical way. This often differs from how the data is input. The data then needs to be summarised to create information in a way that best meets the needs of the system's users – this may not necessarily be the most logical way or the easiest or cheapest for the IT team.

People

People are involved both in capturing the data and in exploiting the information. It is important to motivate those who capture the data by highlighting the value that the exploited data brings to the organisation.

Hardware

In a small organisation, the **MIS** may run on just the sales or finance director's PC. In larger businesses, it usually runs on a server, either shared or dedicated, with Internet or intranet access for those who need it. It is unusual to require specialised hardware.

> **Key term**
>
> **MIS** – stands for management information system.

Software

The simplest MIS can be built using standard software. However, most MIS use specialised software, which has the most common features of an MIS already built in. The developer configures this by describing the database and its structure, where the data comes from, how to summarise the data and what standard queries will be required. The cost of this software varies widely. The cheapest offers limited functions for one PC.

The most expensive is highly functional, providing high performance and many features for hundreds or thousands of users and vast amounts of data.

Telecommunications

An MIS may be delivered across the Internet, though this sometimes brings difficult security questions. Many MIS are delivered across an intranet within a company's firewall for protection from competitors and others seeking this valuable management information. Occasionally, a dedicated telecommunications network is used to provide the utmost security.

3.2 Functions of information systems

An information system has four functions: input, storage, processing, output. There is often also a control or feedback loop so that system output can affect future input, as shown in Figure 3.4.

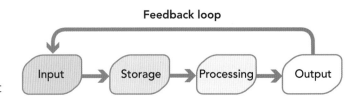

Figure 3.4: Information systems functions

Input

Input to an information system has two parts:

- There is the detailed data which is stored and processed and forms the basis for the output from the system.
- Then the user must also tell the system what sort of analyses they want from the system. Sometimes this is hidden from the user and the IT department sets this up in advance of users using the system.

Storage

The data should be stored at the most detailed level possible. The IT department may also choose to store various summaries of data for ease of use and consistency. The IT department should take regular backups of the data. Some of these should be kept in a different location in case of disaster.

Processing

Processing is what turns data into information. At its simplest, it may just be adding up all of the individual items sold by a supermarket and producing totals by store, by product, by time of day or by any other classification. At its most complex a computer program, or the user, will perform complex calculations, make assumptions about missing data and select criteria to include or exclude. For example, a complex mathematical model might be used as part of a stock control system – as well as looking at sales, this might consider lead times, the cost of being out of stock, the effect of the weather and expected future demands.

Output

Output can be in two formats: graphical and textual. **Graphical output** is often the best for seeing the big picture, understanding trends and presenting the information to management. **Textual output** is best where it is important to analyse the detail and to know exact values. A common way of using both formats is to use graphical output to identify areas of interest, then to use graphical again to focus in on the details and to switch to textual output to see the lowest level of detail.

Key terms

Graphical output – information that is presented as charts, diagrams, graphs or pictures.

Textual output – information that is presented as characters, numbers or text.

Closed system – an information system where the outputs are fixed.

Open system – information system where the user has a wide choice in how to present the output.

Output is best presented in the form that each user wants. For example, for supermarket sales a product manager mainly wants to see sales by product or product group. The store managers are mainly interested in what is happening in their own store. A regional manager wants to see what is happening across all stores in their region. The default output for each of these users should be the one that they are interested in.

Control and feedback loops

A control or feedback loop is what happens in the organisation as a result of the output from an information system. It should have some effect, direct or not, on future inputs to the information system.

An automated example is a data feed of actual sales data to a computerised stock control system. This could note which products have increasing sales and reorder these products from suppliers in order to reduce the likelihood of being out of stock. A similar example is management looking at the sales reports to see which products are selling well and which are not. To maximise profit, they might choose to increase the price of the products that are selling well and reduce the price or offer a promotion on those that are not selling well.

Closed and open systems

In a **closed system**, the user may have some choice about what to report on, but they are limited to predefined output formats. These are often easy to use. They mainly use graphical formats and are often aimed at management.

In an **open system**, there is often great flexibility on what to report on and the format in which the information is output. This powerfulness may mean that significant training is needed before the systems can be effectively used. Open systems are aimed more at analysts. They typically use both graphical and textual formats.

3.3 Transformation of data into information

You will have already heard the terms 'data' and 'information' and may have thought them different words for the same thing, as they have similar meanings. There is, however, a big difference between them as information is obtained from data.

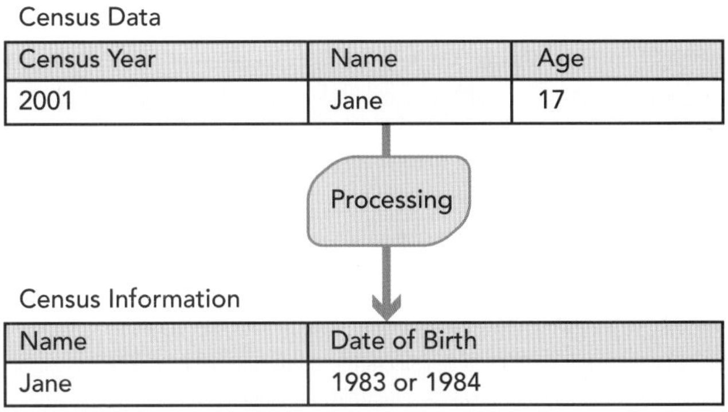

Census Data

Census Year	Name	Age
2001	Jane	17

Processing

Census Information

Name	Date of Birth
Jane	1983 or 1984

Figure 3.5: Diagram showing data in and data out

An example of data could be a massive list of items sold by a supermarket during five years. Information obtained from this raw data might be which items have changed sales patterns over this period.

When data into transformed into information, there are usually these stages.

- **Collection:** Data is taken from where it is generated or available and is checked or validated to make sure that it is as accurate, consistent and complete as it needs to be.
- **Storage:** The data is kept for the longer term. It is often on disk, either on a personal computer or on a server. It may be on a magnetic card, a flash drive, a CD-ROM, a DVD, magnetic tape or other electronic device. Prior to the widespread use of computers, paper was the most common form of data storage and paper is still in use for small manual systems.
- **Processing and manipulation:** At this stage the input data is turned into information ready for output. At its simplest, this may just involve producing totals or averages. At its most complex, more than 90 per cent of the complexity of a system may be in this stage.
- **Retrieval:** The required information from the processing and manipulation stage, with support from the input, is brought back into the computer from storage.
- **Presentation:** The information is output or presented in the way that the user wants to see it. It can have graphics or text or both. It will most likely be presented on a screen or monitor and sent to a printer or to another output device.

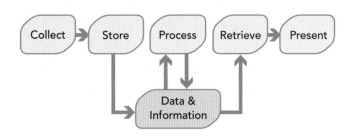

Figure 3.6: Turning data into information

3.4 Types of information system

Almost all departments of an organisation can make effective use of an information system. Here are some of the more common examples where many businesses have benefited.

Marketing systems

Many of the first examples of information systems were in marketing and sales.

- **Sales performance:** If a business could identify where and why its sales were increasing, then it could apply those conditions elsewhere with the same effect. For example, a retail chain might run an advertising campaign or a reduced price offer in one shop or a small number of shops. An information system could identify how successful this was. A chain of shops or hotels could have a programme of refurbishing their properties. An information system could show how successful this programme was in increasing business.
- **Competitors:** Typical competitive activities include selling competing products, opening competing stores and reducing prices. As competitors introduce these changes, an information system can show what effect these changes have. A business can also make similar changes specifically to compete and the system could identify the effect of these changes.

Financial systems

Once a business has an information system to help manage income or revenue, the next area to address is often expenditure or costs.

- **Financial costs:** Spreadsheets can be used to help manage regular costs. However, information systems will more easily find trends and unusual patterns. Typical questions they could answer are: Do costs regularly surge or drop at the start or end of the year? Which over-spends are gradual? Which are caused by one large unexpected or excessive item?
- **Investment returns:** A bank or investment company wants to understand its portfolio of investments. Some investments are high risk, but potentially high return. Some are low risk, but with low return. Some offer no return at all, but increase the capital value of the investment. An information system will help identify the investments that fall into each category.

Human resources systems

Human resources (HR) departments often produce a lot of analyses and so may have an information system to help them.

- **Staffing:** One of the goals of an organisation may be to have the right number of people doing the right work with the right skills. An information system can identify staff and skill shortages and excesses. It can also identify staff turnover, age, gender and experience profiles.

- **Professional development:** This is an extension from staffing – it covers the organisation's needs, staff training, and skills and experience for professional development. Analysis of this can identify suitable candidates for jobs and potential training opportunities for staff.

3.5 Management information systems (MIS)

Features

A management information system (MIS) is a decision support system in which the form of input query and response is predetermined. It is often summarised from an information system. It is used where management wants to ask the same question frequently, though perhaps about different subjects. Here are two typical questions:

- List the top ten stores for sales this month, by product type, together with last month's data and the percentage change. (This would help management review its flagship stores.)

- For a particular store, list this month's average sales by day of week and by product type. (This would help store management plan the staff needed at different times. It could also help them understand their sales – for example, it might show that groceries sell best on Fridays, wines, beers and spirits on Saturdays and home improvement items on Sundays.)

Benefits

A benefit of an MIS is that it is easy to use by senior management, as much of the complexity is hidden from them. The answers are often provided as both tables and graphics and for import into a spreadsheet for flexibility. An MIS also typically provides answers very quickly.

Effectiveness criteria

For an MIS to be effective it must meet these criteria.

- **Accuracy:** It must be as accurate as any other source of this information.

- **Sustainability:** The information must be reliably available, week by week and month by month.

- **Consistent timelines:** Where information is displayed by time period, then these times must be consistent. For example, for a store that is open 24 hours a day, it needs to be decided when the day's sales start (for example at midnight or at 04:00 when the till system is backed up and reset). For a UK-based international operation, is the time based on UK local time or is it based on the local time in each country?

- **Confidence:** The users must have confidence in the MIS for it to be used. This means that any faults found with the data, processes or computer system must be quickly put right. The users need to be informed of the upgrade and reassured that it has improved the quality of the system.

Case study: Where in the world are we?

An international organisation reduced its sales management overheads by merging its African sales division into the UK division. The IT department had to change their MIS to attribute all African sales to the UK. The operations department then decided that part of their New York operation should be allocated to the European division. This was more complex as all New York sales and some operations remained with the New York division.

Geographic changes often happen with information systems. One of the best ways to cope with this is to have supporting data that relates divisions with their names and what forms them. It is then easier to add or take away the parts that change and to rename the divisions.

1 What are the advantages of summarising data, for example by division, before making it available to the users?

2 What are the advantages of every query going to the detailed data to produce the information?

3 What could the IT department do to reduce the effect of such changes?

4. Be able to use IT tools to produce management information

IT tools offer organisations powerful assistance in understanding the marketplace and how well the organisation is performing.

4.1 Tools

Databases

At the heart of every information system is a database. One of the first tasks in developing an information system is to design the data model. A data model (see Figure 3.7a)) describes every piece of information stored in the system, what it means and how it relates to the rest of the data. It is a business document and could apply just as well to a manual system based on paper stores.

A database (see Figure 3.7b)) is where all the data described by the data model is actually stored, usually on disk. It has indexes to speed access to frequently-used data and pointers from one piece of data to another.

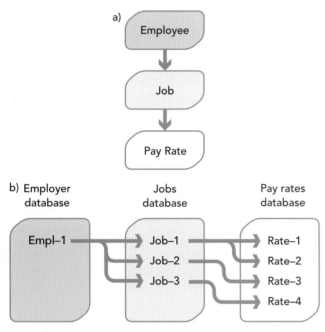

Figure 3.7: a) Data model; b) Database showing linked tables or files

Artificial intelligence and expert systems

Artificial intelligence (AI) and expert systems have rules, which may be changed, to model business actions taken by an expert. A good example of this is an airline fare management system. The business objective is to sell all the seats on a flight for the most money. High demand increases the price of a ticket or fare, while low demand reduces it. This expert system increases the fare each time a ticket is sold. If no seats are sold, it reduces the price as the date of the flight approaches. Rules will say how quickly the price changes and if there is a maximum or minimum fare for the flight.

Again select an organisation that you know.

1 Describe the features and key elements of a management information system (MIS).

2 Show how and where it supports the functional areas of your chosen organisation.

3 For your chosen organisation compare, with examples, how useful different tools might be for processing information to support effective business decision making.

4 Evaluate a range of these tools noted in question 3 with respect to their support in decision making.

5 Explain the purpose and operation of data mining and predictive modelling.

Predictive modelling

Predictive modelling is an expectation of many information systems as it gives the organisation help in understanding what the future may hold. The information system uses old historical data to create a model, allowing the organisation to see what is likely to happen in the future. Within predictive modelling there may be parameters that can be adjusted to allow for different situations, such as worse than expected sales, the effects of taking on extra staff, etc.

Internet

Most systems today provide Internet access to them. Some may be for general public or subscriber use. Many are restricted to members of the organisation and will be protected, often by a user ID and password. Providing access from the Internet reduces many of the network issues that an organisation may face. Internet access can also reduce development time, as part of the system can be built using one of the many easy-to-use Internet development tools.

Data mining systems

An example of another tool is a data mining system. When directed by an expert user, this finds patterns in sets of data. Sometimes these patterns are known, but it is of greatest value when they are not. Sometimes they are used to identify groups of customers.

For example, a supermarket may know its total sales and total customers per day. However, this simple statistic hides the fact that a large number of its customers come in to buy just a newspaper and maybe a few low-value items. This means that the average sale per customer will be much less than the value of a weekly shopping trolley.

Activity: Tools

By searching the Internet, or using information provided by your tutor, research information system tools that are available.
1   List the type of tools that you find.
2   What does each tool do? Give an example of where it might be used.

4.2 Gather information

An information system without information is not very useful, so data has to be identified and gathered. The first part of this process is to define what is actually required.

Define the requirement

It is important to define the requirement, so you know exactly what information is needed. Often this starts with the outputs required from the system. Without the requirements, there might not be enough data gathered to make the system work, or there might be too much detail in the information produced, adding to the cost and processing with no useful benefit.

Establish sources of information

When the requirements are known, you need to establish the sources of information, which is where the data is to be found.

The sources need to meet the requirements, with enough detail and accuracy as well as meeting any other constraints such as cost or timeliness.

Define other factors to be considered

Other factors or constraints such as cost, access to the data and personnel need to be considered, understood and defined.

Timeliness is often important as information has to be available when it's needed. Late information can be totally useless, especially if decisions need to be made on it.

Select information

It may be necessary to select information used in the system from a wider collection of data, for example if the information is sourced from questionnaires there might be some sheets which have been badly completed and are obviously unreliable, so should be excluded from the data used.

4.3 Analyse information

When analysing information you need to look for validity, accuracy, currency and relevance to ensure the information is reliable and useful.

Validity

Valid information is useful for your purposes because it meets the requirements.

Accuracy

Accuracy is always useful and is helpful towards producing reliable outputs from the information system. Accuracy can be lost when data is transferred from paper to a computer system by mis-typing or from scanning errors using **OCR** or **OMR** technologies.

Key terms

OCR – stands for optical character recognition. When a document is scanned into a computer system the software translates the scan into a document with editable text.

OMR – stands for optical mark recognition. When multiple-choice sheets are scanned into a computer system the software translates the respondents' marks into a spreadsheet or database.

Currency

Currency is how up-to-date or current the information is. Obviously out-of-date information is not nearly as useful as current data.

Relevance

Information needs to be relevant. If an organisation produces a range of cakes then information on last year's car sales by another organisation is not relevant or useful.

Identify alternatives

There might be alternative sources of information you can identify that would be useful to the organisation, saving some, or all, of the cost of gathering information and processing.

4.4 Management information

Management information systems produce information which is usually available both on-screen and in the form of written reports.

Reports

Information is often printed as a report. There are many types of report, according to the varied needs of different types of organisations.

The sales report is regular and holds very important information for every organisation that sells products or services. This information is the starting point for many important decisions such as how much stock is needed, what staffing is required and much, much more.

A college may use a report with enrolment statistics for basic planning, such as how rooms and teaching staff will be allocated during the academic year.

A new business could benefit from a marketing analysis report to help understand the marketplace and how to position the business. This can be useful for decisions such as whether to set up as a brick (with premises) or click (using the internet to sell) business, or a mixture of these approaches.

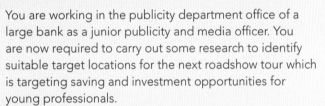

Assessment activity 3.3

You are working in the publicity department office of a large bank as a junior publicity and media officer. You are now required to carry out some research to identify suitable target locations for the next roadshow tour which is targeting saving and investment opportunities for young professionals.

These locations should be in areas where there are likely to be substantial numbers of young people in professional employment. This research will produce some reports identifying likely locations for the roadshow to set up.

Identify a dataset to process into information for your reports. The data you will need for these tasks can be found using the nomisweb data (go to Hotlinks and click on this unit) or you may use any other appropriate sources. Download your data into a spreadsheet or database.

1 Produce some notes on where the dataset was found and why it was selected. **P6**

2 Use a spreadsheet or database for processing the data you find into useful management information identifying some suitable locations where the roadshow is likely to find young professional workers. **P7**

3 You have been asked to produce a front sheet to your reports explaining how the information you generate is valid, accurate and useful. This will ideally be a single page, two pages maximum, so management reading the reports can understand the validity of your findings. **M3**

4 Produce a substantial email to your team leader justifying the information you selected to support these business decision-making processes. **D2**

Grading tips

- Be careful to select information that is substantial enough for your reports. **P6**
- The IT tools to produce management information could be a spreadsheet, database or other MIS tool. **P7**
- The reports you generate must be valid, accurate and useful. **M3**
- To justify the information you selected, you could explain what information you rejected with reasons. **D2**

PLTS

You will show yourself to be an **independent enquirer** by analysing and evaluating information, judging its relevance and value when using IT tools to produce management information.

Functional skills

Your **ICT** skills are demonstrated by developing and refining information using appropriate software to meet requirements of a complex task using IT tools to produce valid, accurate and useful information.

Shahanara Begum

Systems Analyst

Hi, my name is Shahanara. I'm a systems analyst in the regional office of a large insurance company. We have a team of four systems analysts here. Our main role is to help design new IT solutions to improve business efficiency and productivity.

We work closely with the user departments, examining the existing business models and flows of data, discussing our findings and designing appropriate improved IT solutions. We then produce an outline design and costing for a new IT system, defining the operations the system will perform and how data will be viewed by the user. Once it is approved, we work closely with the programming team to implement the solution. I spend a lot of time in meetings, liaising with users and department managers.

Our existing systems work well, but we still need to keep analysing them, identifying options for potential solutions and assessing them for both technical and business suitability. The outcome of analysis is to create solutions to quite complex problems, with proposals for modified or replacement systems, feasibility reports and ensuring that budgets are adhered to and deadlines met.

I am also involved in writing user manuals and providing training to users of our new systems.

It is good to have a role in the organisation that actually makes a difference. I help to give managers better understanding to aid their decisions and to make our users more productive.

Think about it!

1 Why do you think Shahanara needs to be in lots of meetings?

2 In what ways do you think an information system might be improved?

3 Why do you think a systems analyst is expected to write user manuals?

Just checking

1. What are examples of primary and secondary data?
2. What are the three offences of the Computer Misuse Act (1990)?
3. What might appear in a code of practice for Internet usage?
4. What health and safety issues might apply to an information system?
5. What are the typical benefits of an MIS?
6. What is predictive modelling?
7. What are the possible disadvantages of using secondary data?
8. What is the difference between data and information?
9. How might a marketing department use an information system?
10. How might a finance department use an information system?

edexcel

Assignment tips

- You must explain how information is used by organisations.
- You can discuss the characteristics of good information by giving some examples of why data is important and how information can meet these needs.
- Explain both the legal and ethical issues related to the use of information.
- You must describe both the features and functions of information systems.
- There must be a named organisation for this evidence.
- You need to select information that you can use to produce useful reports.
- You need to actually use IT tools such as a spreadsheet or database to produce useful management information.
- You could use a data flow diagram to illustrate information flows between different functional areas.
- Assess both what an organisation should do and what an organisation must do regarding issues related to the use of information.
- You need to generate valid, accurate and useful information from your spreadsheet or database.
- You might find it useful to have some solid examples of how an organisation could improve the quality of its business information.
- The information you select must be justified, perhaps by explaining why you chose it and why you rejected other information.

Credit value: 10

4

Impact of the use of IT on business systems

Keeping up to date with this ever-changing world has a huge impact on businesses and their managers and employees.

In this unit you will identify organisational challenges, such as the re-engineering of systems, the need for constant upskilling of the workforce and dealing with redundant skills and employees. You will explore the benefits of IT developments, such as reduced business start-up costs, increased opportunities for global companies using e-commerce and access to greater outsourcing and geosourcing.

While working through this unit, you will learn to recognise which IT developments have an impact on organisations in both positive and negative ways. You will report on why and how organisations adapt their activities in response to these developments.

You will learn about the potential risks to business systems through the use of IT and examples of how organisations can manage that risk. Finally, you will be given opportunities to consider how organisational business systems may be improved by the introduction of new technologies and propose an improvement to a business system through the use of IT.

Learning outcomes

After completing this unit you should:

1. understand the effect of developments in information technology on organisations
2. understand how organisations respond to information technology developments
3. be able to propose improvements to business systems using IT.

Assessment and grading criteria

This table shows you what you must do in order to achieve a pass, merit or distinction grade, and where you can find activities in this book to help you.

To achieve a **pass** grade the evidence must show that you are able to:	To achieve a **merit** grade the evidence must show that, in addition to the pass criteria, you are able to:	To achieve a **distinction** grade the evidence must show that, in addition to the pass and merit criteria, you are able to:
P1 explain the reasons for upgrading IT systems in an organisation **See Assessment activity 4.1, page 119**	**M1** examine why an organisation needs to keep pace with IT developments **See Assessment activity 4.1, page 119**	
P2 explain the impact of IT developments on an organisation **See Assessment activity 4.1, page 119**		**D1** evaluate the impact of IT developments on an organisation **See Assessment activity 4.1, page 119**
P3 explain how organisations respond to information technology developments **See Assessment activity 4.2, page 127**		
P4 explain how an organisation can manage risk when using IT technology **See Assessment activity 4.2, page 127**		
P5 describe recent IT developments **See Assessment activity 4.1, page 119**	**M2** suggest how recent developments may improve a business system **See Assessment activity 4.1, page 119**	
P6 produce a proposal for an IT-enabled improvement to a business system **See Assessment activity 4.3, page 130**	**M3** demonstrate originality in proposing an IT-enabled improvement **See Assessment activity 4.3, page 130**	**D2** fully justify proposals for an IT-enabled improvement **See Assessment activity 4.3, page 130**

How you will be assessed

This unit will be assessed by a number of internal assignments that will be designed and marked by the staff at your centre. It may be subject to sampling by your centre's Lead Internal Verifier or an Edexcel Standards Verifier as part of Edexcel's ongoing quality assurance procedures. The assignments will be designed to allow you to show your understanding of the unit outcomes. These relate to what you should be able to do after completing this unit.

Your tutor will tell you precisely what form your assessments will take, but you could be asked to produce:

- presentation
- business proposal in a report
- case study (comparing advantages with disadvantages)
- podcast
- short film.

Romana Waheed, BTEC National IT learner

As a 17-year-old girl brought up in the Middle East I am enjoying learning about the developments that industry has encountered through technology. This unit has helped me realise that no matter where I might work around the world, or in what type of industry, I will be able to use my skills. I particularly enjoyed the Case study (page 107) which really motivated me to investigate different types of organisations that use assistive technology to help anyone with a disability. This means that anyone can develop the skills they need to get a job related to their interests.

By working through this unit it got me thinking about the exciting ways that industry has changed over the years. I'm also more considerate about people's feelings where they may feel threatened about being left behind and how industry has to adapt to support its workforce. I was really excited to learn how I could get a merit by being creative and then push myself to get a distinction by thinking more critically and being analytical. I can now use those skills in the other areas of my work and do the very best I can to help me get a place at university.

Over to you

- **Do you, or someone you know, use specialist electronic equipment to do something you wouldn't normally be able to do? How would you do the same task without technology?**
- **Talk to someone who studied at least 20 years ago about their experiences and the tools they used. What was different then?**
- **What aspirations do you have after completing this course?**

1. Understand the effect of developments in information technology on organisations

Start up

How techno-savvy are you?

Make a list of all the technology you can use.

- Don't forget to include practical devices at home, not just items you use for fun.
- Think about the technology you rely upon in your social life.
- What item of technology has helped you the most with your homework?

Before you can measure the impact IT developments have on organisations, you need to identify what developments have taken place – for example, increases in power, performance, capacity of systems and physical size of equipment.

Did you know?

There is more computing power in a mobile phone of today than there was in the entire Apollo moon landing mission in 1969.

One area that has benefited greatly from developments in IT is the world of medicine. The identification of illness and injury using equipment such as **MRI** and laser eye surgery and keyhole surgery are widely used. Equipment such as pacemakers, and procedures for kidney dialysis or cataract eye surgery, are also made more effective by the use of IT. Airports are now using iris recognition immigration system (IRIS) as a more secure and fraud-resistant way of checking a person's identity, while the range of assistive technology for those with disabilities is wide and ever developing.

Key term

MRI – stands for magnetic resonance imaging, which enables investigations without surgery by generating images of living tissues inside the human body.

Try to imagine what it would have been like when mainframe computers used to fill a whole room.

1.1 Hardware

This subsection explores the developments in hardware and computer systems that have evolved because of companies such as Dell™, Microsoft® and Google®.

How have the developments in hardware and systems helped the IT industry since the 1980s?

Activity: Our technologial world

1 Use the list you were asked to make at the beginning of this chapter of the range of technology you currently own or use.
2 Identify all the devices that you didn't own or use a year ago. Do the same for every device up to five years ago.
3 Identify the computing power in each of the items you have listed, for example memory, features or speed).
4 Select two items from your list and search for the nearest comparison available five years ago. Make notes on the differences to each item, such as its features, capacity, memory, speed, size and weight.
5 Identify which items (or features of your items) on your list were not available five years ago.
6 Compare the results with your peers.

Key terms

GPS – stands for global positioning system.
PSU – stands for power supply unit.

Since the founding of Dell™ in 1984 the organisation has grown to be the world's largest computer firm, selling hardware and computer systems by mail order. Systems have evolved and are still developing rapidly, while the costs for these systems appear to tumble. The availability of cheaper computers, offering more for the price, has extended access to IT to a wider range of consumers. Keeping up to date with this ever-changing world has a huge impact on businesses and their managers and employees.

The development of Internet search engines, as a free tool to find resources using key words, has extended the popularity of computers so they are now a must-have commodity worldwide. Google® is a particularly popular search engine and has become a hugely profitable organisation. More recent arrivals include Bing™ and Zhift.

Other recent developments in hardware and systems have led to greater flexibility (for example the ability to use a mobile phone for access to the Internet, emails, radio frequencies and **GPS**) and compatibility with storage devices such as USB drives. There are still gaps in the compatibility of hardware. For example, some storage devices, such as memory cards in cameras, might only be compatible with a computer, or television, of the same make.

Many organisations now rely on technology in the everyday running of their business, to the extent that when the system crashes, operations come to a standstill. Regular updates to computer systems are carried out in an attempt to maintain and increase efficiency, reliability and productivity.

Traditional skills are often replaced with automated systems which are quicker and able to produce a standardised product, for example knitwear, embroidery, fashion goods, pottery, artwork and ready meals.

Increasing power and capacity

Due to the increasing power in computers, the speed at which information is processed is faster, so computers can perform more tasks in the same amount of time.

The power supply to the computer (via the **PSU**), is fed to the motherboard and to the peripherals, etc. (See *Unit 2: Computer Systems*, page 44, for details of how the PSU controls the voltage supplied to an individual component.) In terms of capacity, Moore's Law illustrates a long-term trend of increased capacity by dramatic rates. Moore's Law was a result of a speech given in the mid-1960s by Gordon Moore, inventor of Intel, in which he made links between the capability processing speed and memory capacity. He predicted the trend for an increase in transistor counts, which has enabled planning in research and development of computing hardware.

Table 4.1: Technological developments in relation to specification and cost

Product/model	Year introduced	Approx cost	Power*	Performance** (main memory)
Commodore™ 64	1982	£350	1 MHz	64K RAM
BBC B Micro	Early 1980s	£500	2 MHz	32K RAM
Amstrad PCW	1984	£125	4 MHz	64K RAM
Amiga 1000	1985	£900	7.14 MHz	256K RAM
Dell™ PC	2006	£529	Up to 3 GHz	Up to 4GB (up to 1000GB internal storage)
HP Pavilion	2010	£379	3.2 GHz	320GB

* speed of processor ** memory of RAM plus operating system capability

How has power and capacity of computers changed since the 1980s?

While power and capacity has increased, the cost has fallen. By mass production and sophistication in the manufacturing process the cost of the manufacture has reduced considerably.

Activity: The quarter of a century change

Table 4.1 compares a few of the early home computers with a typical computer available in 2010. Look at how far computers have advanced over the years. For example, the Commodore™ 64 with its 64K memory caused quite a sensation back in the early 1980s when home computers started to appear, whereas today computers with 250GB storage are readily available. Notice, not only the differences in cost, but also in storage methods.

1 Replicate Table 4.1 as a spreadsheet and include additional columns:

   a Removable storage device (for example tape streamers, CDs, USB drives, memory cards, DVDs, Blu-Ray discs)

   b Storage capacity.

2 Share your findings and sources with others in your group.

3 Discuss why some storage devices would be more appropriate for personal use and which would be more suitable for business use and why.

Computer platforms

With the ever-growing range of software applications, computer **platforms** are also increasing in capacity and sophistication.

The platform could be the processor running the operating system (such as Windows Vista®) or it could be a UNIX® computer running on an Ethernet network.

Case study: Super-fast broadband

BT are in the process of updating their telecommunication systems to cope with the ever-increasing demand for broadband and speed. Fiber optic cable installations are being launched in stages around the country. To check out their latest news go to Hotlinks and click on this unit. The government has set a target for all households to have super-fast broadband by 2020. You can read ISP Review's article on Hotlinks.

1   How will businesses benefit from this development?

2   How will faster broadband impact on efficiency in the workplace?

3   What disruptions are possible while these developments are taking place?

Key terms

Platform – the foundation around which a system is developed.

Architecture – the internal structure of a computer, including hardware, firmware, assembler, kernel and operating system, plus applications.

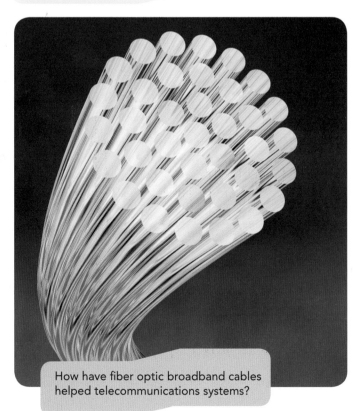

How have fiber optic broadband cables helped telecommunications systems?

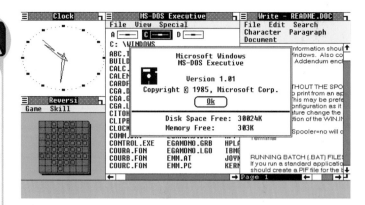

Figure 4.1: Windows version 1.0

The introduction of the Apple® Macintosh® in 1984 with its graphical user interface and Microsoft® Windows® version 1.0 (see Figure 4.1) in November 1985 revolutionised computer use and set the course for the way computers are used today. Nowadays, almost all software is Windows®-based, with Windows® and its associated software dominating the market.

Typical platforms include the computer's **architecture**, operating system and programming languages. Computer platforms have evolved due to the need to support applications.

Developments in computer operating systems and collaboration between rival manufacturers have led to software in different versions to run on your chosen platform, for example Microsoft® Office® for Mac®.

Choice is a good thing. People should be able to choose the systems, software and hardware to suit themselves and their organisations. However, with so much available it is difficult to select the most suitable. As individuals we tend to be driven by what we perceive to be trendy. New products play on desire to be up to date and huge amounts of revenue are generated by this desire. Software and hardware manufacturers are constantly striving to introduce new features to the marketplace. Reasons include demands by users for improvements to current models and versions, keeping up with competitors, the introduction of gimmicks and progress arising from research. Some systems and software do not interact with any other systems than their own, so when organisations need to upgrade their software or system it may be necessary to keep to their current supplier to keep costs down. Many will choose familiarity as a reason to remain with their current manufacturer or supplier.

Activity: Architecture

What operating system do you use? Do you know the programming language used? Discuss and compare with another learner. You may find that the college or learning environment uses a different system from one you might use at home or possibly at work. Why is that? Which do you prefer and why?

Communication technologies

Nowadays, people want and expect to be able to communicate at any time and in any place. A variety of platforms make this possible, including **PDAs**, **Blackberries**, **CCTV** and **smart chips** in credit card formats. These devices are accessible across networks by wireless or wired methods.

The latest developments provide collaboration between devices such as PDAs, Blackberries and mobile phones with cameras, access to the Internet and other multimedia, for example virtual games such as tennis, golf and other activities. Robotics, **haptic** and multi-sensory technology are no longer alien terms and exciting developments are being made through further research.

Did you know?

Microsoft® bought a version of DOS from which it developed its programming languages and own operating system.

Advancements in devices include networks for backing up data over Ethernet cables and remotely via **Bluetooth**, email and **EDI**.

Key terms

PDA – stands for personal digital assistant. PDAs are hand-held computers.

Blackberry™ – the trade name for a mobile phone which combines a keyboard and a large screen and is used liked a PDA.

CCTV – stands for closed circuit television.

Smart chip – is an integrated circuit card which can store data, identification, process applications and even monetary values.

Haptic technology – touch screen technology which is extremely common in everyday technology in the home and business and can even carried around in your pocket.

Bluetooth – a wireless device enabling connection and an exchange of information.

EDI – stands for electronic data interchange.

Activity: Developments to operating systems

1 Carry out research, using the Internet and other sources, to identify developments to operating systems (for example, there have been over 27 versions of Windows® since its initiation).

2 Put your findings into a spreadsheet (example shown in Table 4.2). As well as Microsoft® systems, also include operating systems from other developers.

3 Share your findings with others in your group.

4 Now look specifically at Microsoft Office® 2003 and compare it with Microsoft Office® 2007. Make a list of differences.

5 Discuss with another learner.
 • What do you consider has improved? How?
 • Which version do you prefer?
 • Why would you upgrade your system?
 • Could you upgrade just by purchasing Office® 2007? What is the cost?
 • Do your opinions differ? If so, how?

Table 4.2: Developments to operating systems

OPERATING SYSTEMS				
Date first available	Producer	Name and version	Screenshot	Source of information

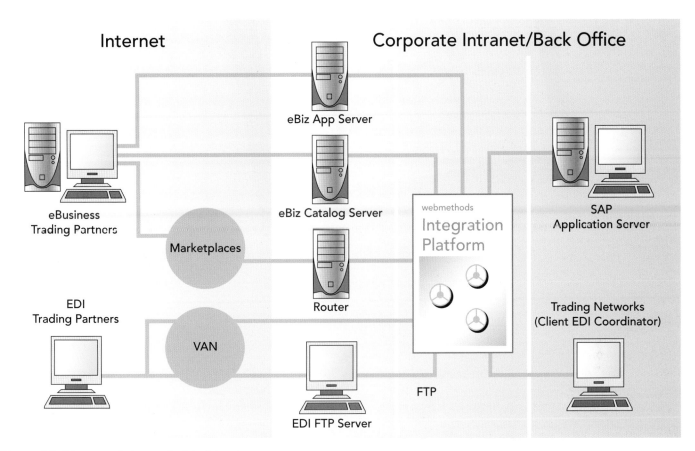

Figure 4.2: Diagram of electronic data interchange

Bluetooth enables communication between devices such as computers and mobile phones. Data is also transferable between organisations by EDI which uses standard data formats to communicate between businesses, for example to exchange orders and invoices electronically in a standard format – swiftly, accurately and without using paper. Communication across our planet is readily available via satellite navigation systems. Satellite navigation (GPS – see page 101) has rapidly become a more widely available and affordable commodity and is now in common usage by people in their cars.

1.2 Software

As systems become more powerful, a wider range of application software can be supported. In addition, many companies use bespoke or specialist software to support their businesses.

Specialist databases and MIS (management information systems) are used to log sales and purchases, monitor stock levels and manage production. Customer relationship management (CRM) systems are used by many organisations to develop confidence in customers when multiple personnel carry out the same tasks in large organisations.

Computer aided design (**CAD**) is a drawing application and an example of sophisticated software. It enables architects, car designers and kitchen designers to produce technical drawings using a computer. These 2D drawings can be manipulated and viewed as if in 3D using digital prototyping.

Key term

CAD – stands for computer aided design.

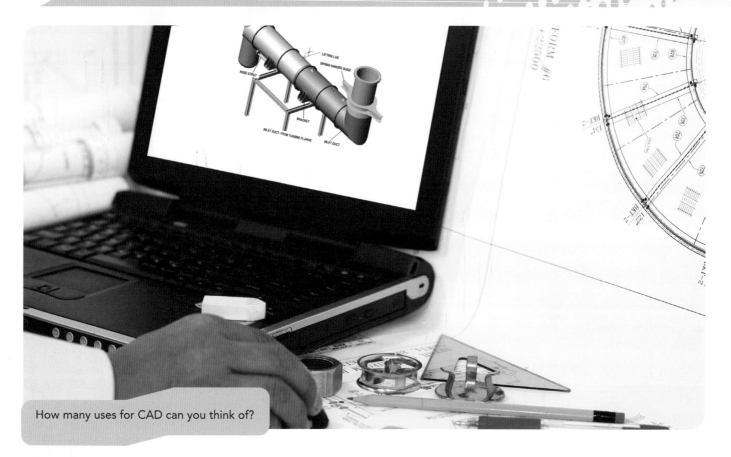

How many uses for CAD can you think of?

Integration of application software

Software is becoming increasingly sophisticated. For example, software is now available that allows users to include video clips and background music in presentations, download and mix music or create their own DVDs. Producing podcasts and designing web pages have become much simpler processes and free software such as Picasa™ from Google® and Microsoft® Photo Story® can be downloaded to turn digital photographs into electronic photo albums with soundtracks, titles and captions.

Some software integrates with other software, for example some bespoke databases integrate with Microsoft® Excel® in order to migrate data out of the database into a spreadsheet, perhaps to analyse data further or to produce a graph. A common method for doing this is by using a **CSV** format.

As specialist software is developed, it is easy to assume that skilled professionals are a dying breed, as the software can now do their work for them. However, it is still important to have the background knowledge to use software correctly. For example, a draughts-person still needs to know how to produce a detailed drawing, even though the software now does most of the work. Similarly, an accountant needs to understand how double-entry bookkeeping works in order to get the most out of a computerised accounts package such as Sage or Pegasus. In fact, a different set of skills is needed to keep up to date with technology.

Key term

CSV – stands for comma separated value. It presents data in comma delimited text file format.

Activity: Just how many applications?

1 Make a list of the software applications on your computer system, some of which you might have never used.

2 Identify who makes each application and what it does. Note the version number of each application. Why do you think some computers have different versions from others?

3 List what can be done to update a version. What is the cost? Would you need to upgrade your computer's memory capacity to upgrade?

4 Compare your list with others from your group.

Case study: Assistive technology

Assistive technology has produced an extraordinary array of devices and the ingenuity of some products is startling, reported *Computer Weekly* in early 2008. (Go to Hotlinks to see the article). For example, with the aid of a small pipe that operates a two-state switch, a person with little or no ability to move can do everything an able-bodied person can do with a computer, simply by sipping and puffing on the mouthpiece.

Some developments are at the cutting edge of technology. For example, gaze-tracking technology uses a camera to track the movement of a user's pupils to detect where they are looking. By doing

this it allows them to control a pointer, select options and operate an on-screen keyboard. Take a look at a *New Scientist*'s report on this technology by going to Hotlinks and clicking on this unit.

1 Who do you know who would benefit from assistive technology?

2 How would gaze-tracking technology support people with disabilities in carrying out everyday tasks?

3 What other types of assistive technology can you find? Share your findings with another learner.

An important question is whether we are becoming too IT dependent. For example, a comparison between the mental arithmetic abilities of people under 20 and people over 40 might have quite different results, showing that young people are no longer learning these skills.

Specialist support software

Organisations can select from a range of specialised support software, for example to enable remote access, call logging or to identify network traffic. Some specialist support software enables organisations to identify the reasons for increases or decreases in product sales and this information helps them to find out ways to improve performance. Another example is software that supports people with disabilities or learning difficulties.

Other specialist support software includes management information systems (Figure 4.3) for collating and analysing data internally and remote diagnostic software that enables manufacturers of large plant (construction machinery) to monitor the performance of their machinery and swiftly diagnose a problem and provide a solution.

Car manufacturers such as Mercedes include an automated service recall in their cars – the software

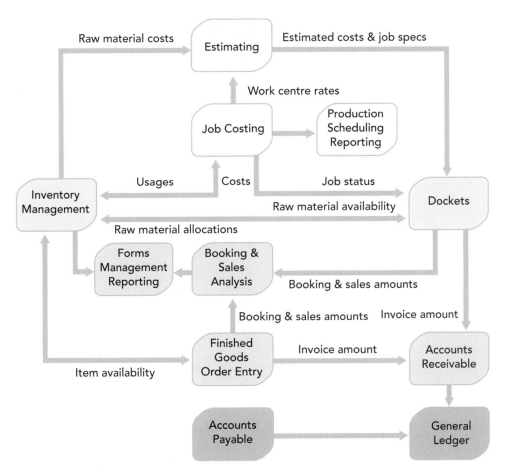

Figure 4.3: Management information system

calculates when a service is due, based on the way the car is driven. The display in the car shows the driver how many miles are left before the next service and a warning when a service is almost due.

Unfortunately, not all specialist software has proved to be effective. Examples include the databases developed for the National Health Service (NHS), the Child Support Agency (CSA), the national crime database and the air traffic control computer system.

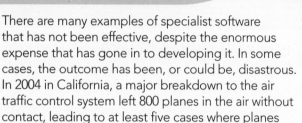

Case study: Specialised software disasters

There are many examples of specialist software that has not been effective, despite the enormous expense that has gone in to developing it. In some cases, the outcome has been, or could be, disastrous. In 2004 in California, a major breakdown to the air traffic control system left 800 planes in the air without contact, leading to at least five cases where planes came dangerously close to each other (go to Hotlinks and click on this unit to find out more).

The NHS has been criticised on several occasions after databases have failed or confidential information has been shared in error. In 2004 there was much criticism of the multi-billion pound spending to install a new computer system. Also, in early 2010, letters were sent to patients in error containing confidential information about other people. (To read about these cases go to Hotlinks.)

1 In each case, identify what went wrong and why.
   - Was it because the system was too big, staff were not trained well enough or the designers and developers did not identify accurately the needs of the organisation?
   - Maybe the system became larger than ever anticipated and the budget ran out. Perhaps the large sums of money spent gave credibility to the system and so assumptions were made that it must provide the solution.

2 What improvements would you recommend?

Also refer to the sections on specialised software in *Unit 3: Information Systems*.

Other examples of specialist software include **decision support software** and **expert systems**.

Support systems comprise processes, people and software, whereas decisions support systems (often

called business intelligence) are designed to enhance the business decision-making process with supporting analyses (reports or graphs).

E-commerce

With the rapid growth of the Internet (for public use) and intranets (for private use), many people now have easy access to a huge resource of information. Both require specialist software to operate them. Search engines are available to locate information. Of these Google® is the most popular, according to current statistics.

The use of the Internet has enabled organisations to promote their products and services easily, swiftly and relatively cheaply when compared with more traditional methods. Credit card technology has allowed online shopping to grow rapidly from year to year. Amazon®, eBay™ and online banking are just a few examples of **e-commerce**.

Key terms

Decision support software – software that is designed to help users compile useful information from raw data in order to solve problems and make decisions.

Expert systems – software that is designed to perform tasks that would usually be performed by a human expert. They provide clear answers to questions without any further analysis needed by the user.

E-commerce – trade carried out online.

Firewall – a software filter which prevents unauthorised access to the computer.

Did you know?

Tesco introduced online grocery shopping to be delivered to your door in 1996 and since then other supermarkets have followed suit.

The Internet provides consumers with flexibility such as online repeat prescriptions and electronic voting. Specialist security software (such as Norton™, McAfee®, Spyware Doctor, Net Nanny and many others) offer protection to both software and hardware. Some offer complete Internet security, while others provide a **firewall** and protection against some viruses. (For more on firewalls, see page 54.)

The section on **cyber crime** later in this unit (see pages 123–24) explores the threats to organisations as a result of the development of IT as well as the risks if organisations choose not to move with the times.

There is more discussion of this topic in *Unit 8: E-commerce*.

Did you know?

There might be an over-reliance on information posted on the Internet and, in particular, its credibility. Anyone can put any information they want on the Internet and just because it appears there doesn't make it true. The easy access to information on the Internet can result in some people believing that they are experts in a field, even though the information they have found there might be inaccurate.

Did you know?

You must never share your personal logins with anyone else, Your personal identity could be abused, your virtual property tampered with, misused or taken. Treat your password like your toothbrush – don't share it with anyone.

Activity: Today it is here, but yesterday it wasn't

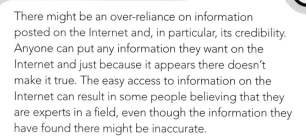

1 Ask your grandparents or anyone you know of the older generation (i.e. grandparent or great-grandparent age) what technological developments and changes they have experienced in their lifetime.

2 Make a list of all the technology they had when they were your age and the stages in their lives when new technology became available to them. Ask them what technology they use, what they don't use, and why/why not?

3 Compare the list with the list you made of the range of technology you currently own or use for the start-up activity on page 100.

4 Discuss with your peers – what changes did they identify?

1.3 Reasons for upgrading systems

This section explores why organisations need to upgrade systems.

External pressures

External environmental factors contribute to the need for change. Some of these factors are **legislative** and some are financial.

Changing regulatory and legal frameworks

Changing **regulatory** and legal frameworks impacts on organisations. The way an organisation interprets legislation, or regulatory frameworks, determines the content of internal policy. For example, laws governing illegal file sharing have led to most schools and employers banning the use of **P2P file sharing**, even if the files shared are legal or open-source.

The legislation relating to checks on people who work with children and vulnerable adults is undergoing change and relevant employers will need to ensure they keep up to date with the changes. Legislation on equality of opportunity is also undergoing change with the October 2010 consolidation of equality laws into the Single Equality Act. Another change is the October 2010 raising of the minimum wage, which in the current economic climate could have a major impact on the finances of some businesses.

Other policies will be in place for legal reasons, such as ensuring equipment is regularly tested for safety (**PAT**) or compliance with the Data Protection Act (1998).

Other examples of legislation that will have an impact on company policies include the Display Screen Regulations (1992), Computer Misuse Act (1990) and the Disability Discrimination Act (DDA, 2005), which requires organisations to supply suitable equipment for employees who have a disability, or specific need, to help them carry out their jobs, for example. a tracker ball for a user with arthritis or wrist rests to help prevent **RSI**.

Key terms

Cyber crime – a crime committed over the Internet or a virtual crime.

Legislative – refers to a legal requirement.

Regulatory – refers to a rule or policy that is not a government law, but is a requirement.

P2P file-sharing – programs that are shared between people (P2P = peer to peer) where users don't own a program or a file but pay a small subscription.

PAT – stands for portable appliance testing.

RSI – stands for repetitive strain injury. It is a condition suffered by many PC users.

A company may also have a policy to make its website accessible to people with disabilities. In the USA this is a legal requirement and in this country there are elements of the DDA which legislate for web accessibility. Tools, such as Bobby, can be used to check and improve on the accessibility of a website. (To learn more go to Hotlinks and click on this unit.)

Accessibility issues include legibility of text, the amount of white space and text alternatives for images.

Did you know?

The Royal National Institute for the Blind (RNIB) reports that the DDA makes it compulsory that all web pages are accessible to visually impaired people.

Activity: What's in a policy?

1   Name three policies that directly affect you. (These could be policies that are in force in your school or college or perhaps in a part-time job or a club or organisation to which you belong.)

2   Select one policy and write in your own words what it means. Is the policy based on any legislation?

3   Identify one other policy that is backed up by legislation and identify the legislation, for example if it is mentioned in a policy document that you have been given, you can highlight this.

4   Compare your findings with your peers.

Keeping up with competitors

There is increased potential for competition by global companies at local level using e-commerce. This has enabled organisations operating online to acquire business from more traditional traders. For example, online grocery shopping was started by Tesco, which rapidly took business from its competitors. Other supermarkets soon followed suit and if they had not done so, they would have undoubtedly lost more business.

An example of online competition being seen as a particular threat was the introduction of electronic mail (email) and its possible impact on the Royal Mail. As yet, email has not resulted in the demise of the traditional postal service.

Did you know?

Skype™ (see Figure 4.4) is an example of a service offering free or cheap worldwide telephone calls to standard landline numbers using broadband and video.

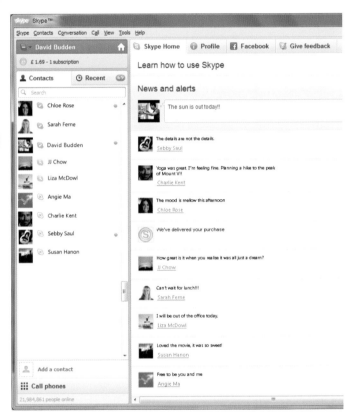

Figure 4.4: Skype™

Enhanced business opportunities

Developments in technology have led to a host of business opportunities and a range of organisations have emerged to take advantage of those opportunities. You will read examples in the subsection on security (page 117). A seemingly endless list of business opportunities have arisen through the use of the Internet. This has enabled businesses to set up without the need for large amounts of capital for premises or equipment. Many distributors of products may not even have warehouses to hold stock but act as a 'go-between' by brokering demand with supply. One such example is that of Dominic McVey who, in 1998 at the age of 13, started trading aluminium scooters over the Internet. By the age of 15 he was making huge sums of money. (Read more about him by going to Hotlinks.)

Increasing globalisation

Developments, such as increased access to the Internet, email and video conferencing mean that organisations can very easily and quickly identify other suppliers or distributors of their products located almost anywhere in the world. This is called **globalisation**. However, the same applies to rival organisations, which could result in increased competition and loss of business. So organisations need to ensure that they exploit the benefits of the technology available in the most effective way, to reduce costs and increase efficiency while not reducing quality.

Potential for outsourcing

Outsourcing means paying a third party to provide a service that would normally be performed by a member of staff employed directly by the organisation, for example an IT technician. When an organisation has to cut costs, perhaps to allocate more of its budget to increasing or updating technology, it might choose to use outsourcing and/or **geosourcing**.

Outsourcing to provide technical support for an organisation might prove to be more cost-effective than running an IT department. Buying in ongoing specialist support, rather than paying for a full-time member of staff who might require regular training to keep up to date with the changes in technology, could save the organisation money. If the organisation can find the expertise needed in a location where labour is cheaper, irrespective of distance, this is called geosourcing, for example locating call centres in India.

Improving customer service

Throughout this section the emphasis has been on reducing costs by outsourcing locally or internationally. The most important aspect of an organisation's operations is the customer. If a product can be manufactured and delivered in a shorter **lead time** without compromising its quality then the customer is likely be satisfied. If the organisation passes on any of the cost savings then the customer is more likely to return or recommend the product to others. This form of marketing is far more powerful than any other and generally free. An organisation's prime aim is to continually strive to improve customer service. Further gratification can be gained by freeing up time and resource to increase productivity, a win-win scenario.

1.4 Benefits

Organisations need to have a strategy for dealing with the challenges brought about by IT developments. They can do this by carrying out a cost–benefit analysis of the current IT system. The results of this analysis can be used to inform decisions about how to develop the system. The organisation can compare the cost of updating the system with the cost of discarding and replacing it (**re-engineering the system**).

When deciding on their strategy, the organisation needs to consider the cost, as well as the quality, speed and service of the system. Once a decision is made, the organisation should measure the impact, for example the benefits to the organisation due to an increase in productivity, resulting in increased profit and efficiency.

Productivity gains

Productivity gains can be made by using a range of automated manufacturing processes and developments in customer support (see page 113). Although the initial outlay for automating processes in industry can be extremely high, they can result in large productivity gains. Robots and machinery can be operational 24 hours a day, seven days a week.

Key terms

Globalisation – having access to products and services from a wider range of sources around the world from which to select the most desirable according to what the organisation seeks.

Outsourcing – paying a third party to provide a service that would normally be performed by a member of staff.

Geosourcing – the process of seeking expert skills at the best possible price regardless of location.

Lead time – the amount of time taken before delivering a service or product.

Re-engineer the system – a phrase that means starting again with a new system rather than attempting a quick fix.

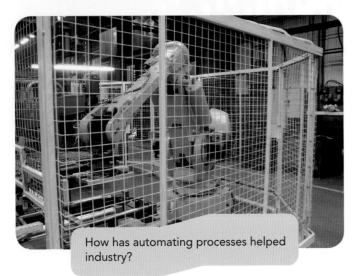

How has automating processes helped industry?

Machinery doesn't take tea breaks or lunch breaks. While it may need some time off 'sick' (for essential maintenance or repairs), it never expects to go on holiday. Productivity is usually constant and the organisation can therefore rely on the amount and quality of work the machinery will carry out.

This makes it is easier for an organisation to calculate how many products it will make, how much they will cost to make and the length of time it will take to make them. However, there will be regular maintenance costs to ensure the equipment doesn't break down and costs to keep up to date with new developments and further enhance productivity.

Cost reduction

Developments in IT are allowing reduced costs for some services and products, for example the cost of automated services is often less than the cost of staff. One example of IT being used to reduce costs is the use of video phones by news journalists to make up-to-the-minute reports. This saves the cost of a large camera crew, all the supporting staff and their travel and **subsistence** costs.

Organisations that operate mostly online also benefit from reductions in cost – they generally do not have the high overhead costs of bricks-and-mortar businesses, such as high street premises, large numbers of sales staff, well-presented stores etc.

Key term

Subsistence – living requirements, for example accommodation, food, drink.

Increased profitability

Developments in technology have led to smarter ways of working and in the manufacturing industry, for example, have enabled parts and products to be produced by machines rather than everything being made by hand. As a result, productivity is increased, consistency in quality is often higher so there is less wastage, more products can be sold and profits rise as a result. Those organisations that choose not to replace manual labour with automated technology or to invest in the technology where costs might be high, can still benefit by leasing or buying components that have been mass produced and make savings that way.

Efficiency

By introducing more automated processes and exploiting technology in business activities, organisations should become more efficient. Examples include mail order catalogues and stores that use the Internet as another means of selling their products, for example clothes, books, CDs, electrical goods, furniture and food. Consumers can make choices about where and how they make purchases.

Organisations become more efficient in servicing orders when they use EDI systems that can process orders, take payment for the product and inform the accounts system. The system identifies whether the item is in stock, reduces the current stock level by the number that is ordered and has the ability to reorder stocks automatically when levels become low.

Some organisations do not physically need to stock a product, in which case the system sends the order direct to the supplier who will dispatch the product direct.

Improved management information

As a result of the changes in IT and the development of specialised systems to manage information, organisations are able to track and analyse productivity more easily.

Did you know?

MIS can monitor the stock of components and hence maintain the flow of productivity. Sales invoices can be generated swiftly and accounts reconciled to provide an up-to-date and accurate picture of the state of the organisation. This results in smarter pricing of products and services in attempts to remain competitive.

IT systems mean that organisations are likely to have a great deal more control over the performance of their businesses. Improved MIS enable managers to monitor the efficiency and effectiveness of performance. Globalisation enables organisations to locate alternative suppliers who could provide more competitive products and therefore save them money. The use of automated manufacturing processes results in a more consistent and reliable output, contributing to organisations retaining control.

Improved customer service

Some organisations have adapted to provide enhanced customer service and support. However, some consumers are confused by the technology used and have difficulty coping with the new style of customer service. They might lack the level of skill required to access an organisation's website, for example. Where an organisation relies entirely on customers using the Internet, for example to refer to **FAQ** sites, this could be detrimental to the growth of sales for its products or services. So, it is a good idea for organisations to provide alternatives for customers who prefer to use more traditional styles of customer support, such as speaking to an adviser on the telephone.

Synergy and integration of systems

The developments that have taken place in IT, how they impact on organisations and how (and if) organisations have adapted their practices accordingly, also rely on the **synergy** and integration of systems. In this subsection we look at how an organisation can bring together these systems and developments so as to benefit the organisation.

Organisations cannot work effectively when their systems do not work in harmony with each other. One simple example: organisations replace their computers with up-to-date models that include USB drives, but no longer contain CD/DVD drives. However, if staff have files stored on CDs, these files cannot be accessed on the new system.

Key terms

FAQ – stands for frequently asked questions.

Synergy – when two or more elements (in this case computer systems) work together with positive results, the combined effect being greater than the sum of the individual effects.

Integrated system – enables access to separate network management systems by linking them together.

Activity: How do you score?

1 Ask your friends and family if they still have files stored on media they cannot access, such as floppy disks or possibly tapes.

2 Make a list of all the different types of storage media you can identify. What is stored? Is it needed or missed?

3 Find out if you can restore the data that is on the media. Share your results with your friends and family.

Effective **integrated systems** tend to be found in those organisations that opt for EDI or management information systems in order to streamline procedures. (For more on integrated systems, go to page 117.)

Did you know?

Vinyl records are also storage media.

Activity: Ahead of the times

1 How would you ensure that the desire to have the latest technology does not hinder general working practices? For example, should a business upgrade all its computers every year to the most powerful specification with the latest software? What would be the impact of this on the continuity of the business and effectiveness of its employees?

2 Compile a checklist, or flow chart, of stages to follow prior to upgrading existing systems. Discuss with another member of your class to test it out.

1.5 Impact

Developments in IT have had a major impact on the way organisations operate. Few organisations in the developed world are able to survive in a competitive market without utilising IT in some way.

New technologies are being developed all the time and organisations are often compelled to upgrade their computer systems if only to keep up with the competition.

To cope with the challenges facing organisations and to monitor the effectiveness of the IT system, an organisation should implement a **technical infrastructure**.

Key term

Technical infrastructure – the development of the management's underlying structure.

A technical infrastructure includes producing reports on the effectiveness of the system, analysing performance and making recommendations for improvements. For example, a recommendation might be to provide staff training on using software and how this should be done, whether by internal IT support staff or by external training providers. Other recommendations might be to re-engineer the system and a proposal would need to justify the reasons for this along with the costs and the benefits to the organisation as a whole.

Activity: My technical infrastructure

Put yourself in the position of an IT support technician within the organisation where you study. Your team has been asked to write a proposal that shows how the organisation should keep up to date with developments, including the cost and justification for any changes.

1   Look at the sorts of challenges that the organisation faces and technical developments they might consider. Research the Internet for details of recent developments and costs of new devices and software. Make notes.
    Tip: You could build on the costs you produced for the activity (The quarter of a century change) on page 102. Add in the cost of items such as surge protection, anti-virus software, Internet costs and setting up a new website.

2   Using clear and jargon-free language, present your findings in a short report including details (and images where appropriate) of your proposal (devices, software, costs, preferred suppliers, etc.). Identify the benefits to the organisation for change and the impact of not changing.

Cost

Organisations looking to upgrade their systems will have to consider the cost. Most organisations will have a budget and the desire to upgrade may be outweighed by the amount of money they are able to spend. Some organisations might take the view that they will make cut-backs in other areas of their organisational budget in order to upgrade their systems or invest in more technology. Managers are likely to carry out a cost–benefit analysis to justify any additional spending. As mentioned earlier, the use of technology could benefit an organisation by increasing profitability, but it might also result in redundancies. They also have to consider costs that are indirectly associated with the increase or upgrading of technology, such as upskilling staff.

Did you know?

The growth in technology often means a reduction in cost.

Impact on procedures

All organisations require sound and robust procedures in order to function efficiently. Some businesses use external companies to validate their quality procedures and systems. When ways of working change, or the tools and in this case the computer systems and associated software change, procedures need adjusting to accommodate that change. All change is challenging to manage. One factor that makes coping with change difficult is the time it takes to put new procedures or staff into place. This also has a cost implication, for example a receptionist in a doctor's surgery who has been used to keeping a paper appointments book is likely to have a fairly simple, although not foolproof, system for making changes to appointments. With the introduction of an electronic system the basic procedure will no longer be effective.

Impact on staff

The fast pace of change brought about by developments in IT requires organisations to recognise the need for upskilling and training the workforce. Specialist skills are needed to use IT, for example the company may need someone who can use Dreamweaver® to design web pages.

Fewer organisations employ secretaries today and so staff and managers are increasingly expected to be administrators in addition to their main job role, for example sales representative, marketing manager, financial director. This will mean that they will need IT skills in using administrative software, such as word processing and spreadsheets. However, the cost of managers carrying out their own administrative tasks may be greater to the organisation per hour than that of employing administrative staff.

It is highly unlikely that the workforce (staff and managers) can simply 'pick up and run' with the introduction of new systems, software and even apparently basic or simple devices. Staff might be moved into jobs they do not particularly want and they might not have the necessary skills to carry out their new jobs efficiently and effectively straight away. There may be resistance from staff. Not everyone adapts to change easily.

Why is training important to IT staff?

Activity: Training needs analysis

1 Identify a local organisation and look at their organisational structure to identify the roles and responsibilities of the staff.

2 Select three different organisational roles: one director or manager and two different administrative or support roles. Identify the skills that each of these employees needs in order to operate the technology that has changed in the last three years.

3 Produce a training plan for each of these employees. For example, an administrator who has been using Windows XP® and Office® 2003 is likely to require training on more recent operating systems and changes introduced in the latest version of Office®. There might be a training need for remote workers or sales representatives to learn how to use PDAs or how to access the organisation's network remotely. The IT technician might require training on new systems or networking.

Dealing with redundancies

Changes to the ways in which an organisation operates impact on the number of staff it requires or can afford. Organisations must deal with redundant skills and employees in order to avoid unnecessary costs. For example, if an organisation is considering moving towards a paper-less office or outsourcing some of its services, it needs to think carefully about the job role (not the person) being made redundant and whether the salary saved benefits the business sufficiently.

The organisation will have to balance different considerations in order to decide which roles to make redundant. In addition, there are the overhead costs to consider such as office space, resources and possibly company cars. The organisation might benefit financially from making a director redundant, but also risks losing expertise. The organisation also needs to consider any redundancy payment it will have to offer – the size of this will depend on the length of time the employee has been with the organisation and also the size of their current salary.

Some organisations ask for volunteers to take redundancy.

Balancing core employees with contractors and outsourced staff

When considering staff reductions, changes to job roles and outsourcing of services, a strategy is needed before making any change to the staffing structure. For example, if all the sales staff are made redundant, who will sell the company's products? Devising a suitable strategy will create a delay and therefore has a cost implication.

Consideration of the balance of core employees (those who are employed by the company as a minimum for the organisation to operate effectively) against those who are contracted or outsourced is important.

Core employees are permanently employed by the organisation and receive a regular salary. They are an ongoing cost to the organisation. Contractors (those who are outsourced) are not on the payroll and therefore are not an ongoing cost (although are likely to cost more per hour). Outsourced staff might include those on temporary contracts – these could be long-term contracts, but are not permanent. These staff will not be subject to the same terms and conditions as those on permanent contracts and are likely to be less cost-effective.

Relying on contractors, or outsourcing services, is not necessarily the most efficient way to run an organisation. Employed staff are likely to be more loyal and generally more available. Organisations might identify that a reasonable number of core employees, together with some outsourced staff, will provide an efficient and effective working model. However, changes to the way organisations are staffed might result in the staffing structure being **flattened**.

Enabling home and remote working

Another way for an organisation to cut costs is to encourage staff to work from home. Some staff

Key term

Flattened – (also called delayering) the reduction in the number of levels of staff and managers.

(such as sales representatives) benefit from working remotely instead of rushing back to the office after visiting customers to write reports, submit sales orders or attend meetings face to face. With the use of mobile technology, such as netbooks and smartbooks, laptops, 3G mobile video phones, intranet, email and video conferencing, sales and support staff can spend more time with customers and less time in the office.

Some issues might arise with staff working from home, for example how managers can monitor the productivity of people who are not in the office and the effect on the individual or the family caused by intrusion into their environment. There are also technical challenges involved in setting up all the necessary equipment at home and maintaining and servicing it.

Dealing with the impact of regular restructuring on staff

Organisations face many challenges brought about by change, such as:

- the cost of keeping up to date with developments (changes to equipment and resources)
- changes to the environment (setting, location, culture)
- and changes in human resources (number of staff and the skill levels needed).

All of these will impact on organisational structures.

Changes in staffing structures and reductions in staff impact on the cost and time taken to carry out changes. Those who are working remotely are not easily accessible to discuss and solve problems face to face. Staff who are promoted as a result of the restructuring might not be ready for a higher-level position such as a management role. They might be ill-equipped to manage staff and the employees they are responsible for might resent their promotion, becoming difficult and uncooperative.

Where new teams are formed they might be less productive than the previous teams. This is because effective teams are made up of people with a range of personality types, skills and job roles who adapt their behaviour in order to accommodate changes. Organisations need to clearly define individual roles and responsibilities in such a way that everyone understands who does what. They also need to train individuals so they can build on their existing skills and knowledge in order to take on new roles and sets of duties.

Integration of legacy systems

As technology develops along with associated software, existing systems – also known as legacy systems – may become redundant if they are not compatible with the updated versions or new technology. In these cases, organisations may choose to replace, or increase, their technology to support their business practices. It is not always the case that an organisation has no choice but to replace everything. Other factors may feature such as the cost to upgrade against the cost to replace. Replacement may be the quicker option, although not always. It is dependent upon the length of time for the new system to be implemented and fully

operational. There may be teething problems. Also, upgrading may require the current system to be out of service for a period of time. Some decide to replace for cosmetic reasons, for example large monitors and towers replaced with laptops, bringing with it the additional benefit of portability.

Security

You learned previously about how organisations are using technology to promote their products and services. With this brings a number of security concerns that organisations need to manage. For example, any organisation taking a credit card payment will need to be sure they get their money. They will want to make sure organisational information is not shared with the wrong people. Banks have been exposed to computer hackers and in China, bank hackers have been sentenced to death. Even Tim Berners-Lee (the inventor of the Internet) is listed as a hacker and it seems that as fast as security software is developed other ways

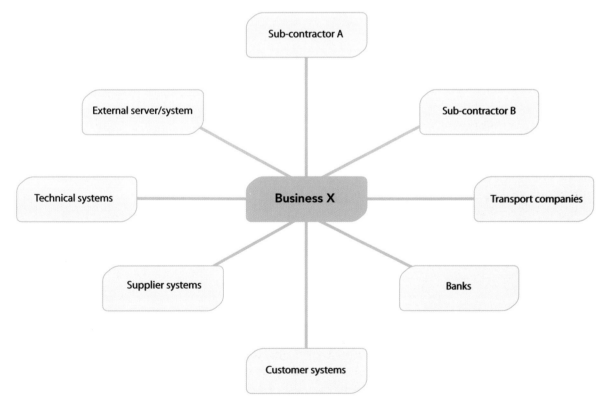

Figure 4.5: An example of an integrated system

of breaking that security are being discovered. (Read an IT Security article by visiting Hotlinks and clicking on this unit.)

You have already read about specialist security software and other means of protection available (see page 108). A fundamental process for increasing security of systems is to ensure that dedicated user IDs with passwords are provided, and that organisation policies emphasise the importance of not disclosing those details to anyone. Some say 'you should treat your password like your toothbrush'.

In terms of shared systems, the use of restricted and permitted access rights is important. For example, if everyone had access to the full use of a system, it could be argued there is little need for passwords. Restricted access rights do help secure data which might be sensitive, confidential or simply to avoid accidental damage to the data or system. Use of a hierarchical system allows different permissions to administrators of systems compared to those of data entry clerks, for example. You will have restricted access rights in your place of study or work, and a wider range of access, perhaps as administrator, of your home computer.

Legal requirements

As you have read in the subsection about changing legal and regulatory frameworks (page 109), organisations need to comply with legal requirements set by government and other bodies. Two examples of such requirements – Copyright and the Data

Protection Act – cause organisations many challenges, as they try to ensure compliance while not restricting access to what is needed by the right people.

Data protection is often used as a reason for not sharing information. In many cases this is correct, but an organisation needs to be confident that data is not used for any other purpose than the one(s) stated. So if, for example, customers' names and addresses are kept in a database, how can a company be sure the information is safe and only shared appropriately? Specialist software might be required or the use of limited access rights to individuals might be used.

There have been many examples where information has been shared, sometimes quite innocently, for example a passing comment across the office or a phone number given out in error over the phone. Many larger organisations announce they record conversations, usually to measure customer service, but this can also be used to gather information which could be used in other ways.

Rules also apply regarding where, when and how long data are stored. Different rules apply to different types of data, for example financial and personal. Organisations have benefitted from storing data technologically as it saves considerable space and is generally safer than storing mountains of paper. However, different sets of risks accompany electronic storage, such as storing next to a magnetic field and wiping off the information stored, or not having the hardware to read the data on an old medium such as a floppy disk and microfiche.

Assessment activity 4.1

You are the IT manager for a medium-sized family firm called Full of Beans, which employs 50 staff. You manage an IT administrator and two technicians. The firm makes and sells bean bags of all shapes and sizes. You have identified a problem in the organisation – the IT systems and equipment are out of date, slow and often unreliable. As a result, sales have fallen and the company is facing some potentially difficult times ahead.

The business has been slow to move with the times. The accounts clerk and other administrators are using bespoke systems that work in isolation from the sales and buying departments. The production section also has its own system, much of which is paper-based. The delays between departments in knowing what

the others are doing is also having an impact on the efficiency of the organisation.

The owner has agreed that you should identify a way to improve the current situation. It is your job to try to save the day by carrying out research in order to put a proposal for a new system to your boss.

1 As IT manager, you will describe recent IT developments. **P5** **M2**

2 Explain the reasons for upgrading systems in an organisation. **P1** **M1**

3 Explain the impact of IT developments on an organisation. **P2** **D1**

Grading tips

- To achieve a pass, you should look at recent developments within the last 2–3 years and produce a report or summary. **P5**

- Look through computer magazines, as well as websites, to find information about the latest developments. Remember to concentrate on business systems and not on gaming or social networking developments. **P5**

- To achieve a merit you should suggest how recent developments may improve a business system. This could be an extension of your report or a separate document. **M2**

- You could produce a table awarding stars or points under various categories such as cost, speed and usability. **P5**

- To help you achieve a merit, you need to examine why an organisation such as Full of Beans needs to keep pace of IT developments.

You might consider producing a case study which provides a comparison between 'this is now' and 'this is how it could be'. Make sure you highlight the benefits very clearly. You need to explain why an organisation such as Full of Beans feels that change in necessary. **P1** **M1**

- To achieve a distinction you need to evaluate the impact of IT developments on an organisation. You should evaluate the benefits of change when weighted against the risks. A good way of presenting this is to do a cost–benefit analysis. **P2** **D1**

- Make sure you keep all your records clearly labelled so you can refer back when working on the other Assignment activities in this unit. Anything that might be slightly useful is worth keeping for now.

PLTS

By independently researching developments in the IT industry you will demonstrate that you are a **self-manager**. By producing a case study comparing a company's IT systems ('this is now' to 'this is how it could be') you can demonstrate that you are a **creative thinker**.

Functional skills

When carrying out research, you are likely to use both your **English** and **IT** Functional skills as you use books and the Internet as primary sources. By using a variety of means to communicate your business case you will be demonstrating your level of **English** Functional skills. Ensure the language you use is clear, at the right level and jargon-free. Proofread and check your grammar and punctuation.

2. Understand how organisations respond to information technology developments

This section aims to help you to understand how organisations adapt their activities to respond to developments in IT.

2.1 Responses

Adapting business processes

With the expansion of technology globally, organisations are exploiting the ways in which technology can benefit their business. For example, the introduction of **loyalty cards** in the first instance by Tesco in 1995, where returning customers are rewarded with points and prizes, has also played its part in increasing sales. The loyalty cards of a supermarket chain encourage customers to patronise its stores or drive out of their way to purchase petrol from its garages. Supermarket loyalty cards have been suggested as a factor in the demise of corner shops – how can the small-time grocer or butcher compete with multinational purchasing power (reduced buying costs) or offer **payback** in return for loyalty?

Another example of payback is when you make a purchase online and the supplier follows up with a personalised email inviting you to take advantage of a percentage reduction next time you make a purchase. This promotion is exploited further by allocating a limited timescale to the offer, tempting you to buy now in order to take advantage of the offer, whether you want (or can afford) it or not.

Key terms

Loyalty card – looks like a credit card and identifies its owner and the provider of the card. It can be used to store points or discounts.

Payback – reward in some form or another for using an organisation's product or service.

Viral marketing – marketing that relies on social networks passing on product or service information from person to person.

Sales and marketing strategies for global opportunities

The ability to market an organisation's products on the Internet results in swifter and cheaper global opportunities. Sales representatives can negotiate business deals over the telephone, by email and by conference and video calls, therefore avoiding the delay and cost of lengthy travel. This results in some business deals being closed more quickly and a proportion, if not all, of the cost savings being passed on to the customer – this makes the organisation more competitive.

Another form of online marketing is **viral marketing**, which offers inducements or incentives to pass on the message about a product or service.

Some organisations have been innovative in relaunching existing products to keep up with changing times and make use of the new technology available. One successful example of this is the relaunch of Monopoly, the classic board game that has been around for decades. The new version of the game has no paper money – instead it features calculators and debit cards for buying property around London.

Charitable organisations such as the Poppy Foundation are also keeping up with technology. There is now the opportunity to download the poppy as an icon for display on a mobile phone. To find out more about this visit Hotlinks.

Activity: Does charity begin at home?

1 Identify other charitable organisations which have adapted or exploited information technology. Carry out your research and remember to identify your sources.

2 Find out when the organisations made the developments and how these developments might benefit the organisations. Share your findings with the group.

Not all viral marketing campaigns are malicious – some are quite welcome and work well because they build a sense of community among recipients, who actually want to pass on the message. Viral marketing works particularly well among groups with highly developed social networks, such as teenagers.

Activity: What value social networking?

You would be 'hard pushed' to find an organisation that doesn't have Internet access. However, how they choose to use it and who they give it to varies. For example, the organisation where you are studying will use the Internet for marketing their services and products, but will have a number of rules about what you can access. Why is that?

1   Do you belong to a social network? What proportion of your time is spent virtual networking and socialising as opposed to face-to-face interaction?

2   What protocols should you follow in order to be safe, particularly when using social network sites?

3   What are key areas of which to be aware when 'meeting new friends' on the Internet?

4   Make a list of 'keeping safe' protocols to discuss with other learners. Do you all agree? If not, why not?

Many organisations make arrangements with other organisations to promote each other's products or services on their websites. Here are two examples of when this might be helpful – both for the customer and the organisation.

- A camera supplier might sell only digital cameras and not printers. It could therefore have a link to another website that sells printers that are compatible with its cameras.

- You might buy a computer from one website and follow a link to another website where you can buy software or peripherals to go with it.

The use of pop-ups is one type of Internet advertising that is not particularly popular with consumers, as they appear without the user's permission and have to be closed. The Internet also contains some shocking advertisements that would not be acceptable to television audiences.

Spam emails, such as follow-up emails from an online purchase, are another example of online marketing. This type of marketing is often unscrupulous, with organisations imposing their advertising on consumers without their permission. Some of this marketing can have unsavoury content or relate to unsavoury products and can be very difficult to stop.

The use of specialist software (see page 107) can monitor or log sales. When an organisation monitors sales of a product, it gains a greater understanding of the impact of the product on consumers. It gains better and quicker feedback through the ordering process and therefore can adapt the product range to meet the demands of consumers. This is called **mass customisation**.

One way major organisations can find out what customers want is by tracking individual purchases through the use of loyalty cards (see page 120). Specialist software is used to identify other, similar products that the consumers might be persuaded to buy. In this way, the organisation can tailor the vouchers and offers that are sent to individual consumers, guiding and tempting them to buy more. For the consumers this can feel like Big Brother is watching them and taking note of everything that they do.

Purchasing strategies for automated ordering

As a result of developments that make it easier for organisations to talk to each other through their systems, automated ordering becomes easier and quicker. One such example is the systems that large superstores use to monitor the stock on the shelves – tracking sales and using EDI for automatic reordering before stock runs out. Calculations are carried out in an attempt to avoid stocks running out at critical times based on the likelihood of products selling at peak times. An effective system calculates the optimum level of stock in relation to storage capacity and with the least impact on **cash flow**.

These new purchasing mechanisms are also referred to as channel management, as all the different potential channels to market are managed. Organisations decide how to sell their products and services – through catalogues, over the phone, on the Internet, etc. – choosing the method that seems to be the most effective.

Key terms

Mass customisation – efficiently mass producing goods and services for customers that have individual needs

Cash flow – refers to ready funds that are available within a business for spending.

Customer support processes for online systems

Most people have experienced first hand how new technology has changed the way organisations provide customer support, for example when asking for guidance on how to use a new mobile phone or a new computer or game console. These developments have enabled access to customer support through a number of channels, such as logging a query on the organisation's website using the 'contact us' section, sending emails or simply searching for an answer on the FAQs page.

However, sometimes technological advancements have resulted in a less satisfactory level of customer service for consumers.

Technology has resulted in many organisations using automated telephone systems to deal with customer transactions and queries. It can be very frustrating to be instructed to 'press 3, press 2, then 5...', and then be told to hold for several minutes, perhaps being cut off without your query being resolved. Such systems tend to be very unpopular with customers.

Some organisations employ support staff who read from a script and are therefore not able to answer questions directly – they simply read back what is on the script. It is likely that some organisations have adopted these approaches because they are cheaper and in some cases so consumers can access support out of usual working hours.

Financial systems for secure funds transfer

With users moving money between bank accounts using online transactions (e-banking), the opportunities for hackers to steal funds has increased. (This is explored further in the section on cyber crime on page 123.) Therefore, software is required to provide security for transfer of funds. A firewall is one method of providing some security (see page 125).

The introduction of chip and pin was intended to provide a secure way of using a credit card. Inserting a personal, private pin number instead of signing for goods is an attempt to prevent signature fraud. Unfortunately, the outcome has not proved to be entirely fraud-free and some would argue that vendors simply shifted the responsibility away from themselves and on to the purchaser. If you let anyone know your pin, you are to blame, as the vendor does not have to check signatures any more.

With more attempts by fraudsters to access our online bank account details, apart from security software developments, additional protocols are available to customers in order to gain access to their bank accounts. These include a security device sent by the bank which generates a unique number to enter, in addition to security codes and passwords. Other methods include sending the bank a message via a secure system confirming the instructions with the bank. For some customers, these extensive security measures are considered too time-consuming and not worth the additional security they can provide. (For more on secure payment systems, see page 126.)

Automating manufacturing processes

There have been tremendous changes in the way we work over the last 20 years. For example, the introduction of the fax machine in the mid-1980s was a major technological advancement to communications. Before this, there had been little development impacting on administrators other than the electric typewriter.

Now there can hardly be a business in the UK that does not rely on highly sophisticated networked computers, running a range of software applications for performing a variety of tasks.

In the manufacturing industries, the introduction of robots has automated some of the tedious jobs that manual workers used to carry out. For example, the car industry uses robots to build and spray paint cars.

What effect has automating manufacturing processes had on the workers in the industry?

The Formula 1 motor sports industry uses programmable machinery to carry out dangerous and precision tasks in the manufacture of a racing car, such as cutting sheet metal, welding and other precision processes. However, these highly specialist car manufacturers (such as Ferrari, McLaren and Mercedes) combine both automated and manual processes due to the fine precision engineering used in producing these cars. Other car manufacturers such as Rolls Royce and Aston Martin also prefer to retain a large proportion of the hand-built craftsman approach.

Robots are used for highly dangerous activities such as in radioactive areas and drilling undersea for oil.

Robots are not just used for dangerous manufacturing processes. For example, sweet manufacturers use automated machinery to make their confectionery and often to pack the products.

Activity: Sweet tooth

1   Identify some confectionery organisations that use automated processes in their manufacturing. What manual processes have these replaced? One such example could be Cadbury.

2   Choose one organisation from the ones you have identified. What can you find out about the organisation's productivity rate? Has it increased since introducing automated processes? If so, why?

3   Write a short report on the benefits of using automated processes in your chosen organisation and identify any disadvantages.

No response

This subsection considers how organisations need to manage their services in response to IT developments. It considers an organisation's output in relation to meeting demand and how improvements can be made to increase effectiveness. It looks at financial viability and stability and the way in which information is communicated internally and externally.

Of course not every organisation is an 'early adopter' and they may not respond to developments in IT either in the short term or even longer term. In some ways this is a sensible strategy. It means that others test out the technology first and future developments are introduced to address problematic areas or weaknesses. This tends to be a strategy of some

major software companies. Another reason, which is confirmed repeatedly, is that when first introduced, new technology is more expensive. We have seen prices tumble consistently across technological items.

In some cases developments are imposed upon organisations, for example public sector organisations such as the NHS. Some like to continue with their tried and tested systems, even if they are not as effective. For example some, although possibly very few, organisations still use fax machines for urgent information due to the sensitivity of the content or their nervousness about sending information over the Internet using email. Not everyone uses email and some companies, including many educational establishments, block email access – although this is not considered to be a well thought-out strategy.

Technological developments also may not be deemed cost-effective, or organisations may feel that staff have insufficient skills to adapt quickly and prefer minimum disruption to the business. There is likely to be some resistance where external bodies, such as unions, perceive the introduction of a particular technology as impacting negatively on staffing numbers, resulting in possible redundancies.

2.2 Managing risk

This subsection explores the risks that accompany developments in IT and ways to manage these risks. Risks are both threats and opportunities. You will need to consider the risks involved both in implementing IT developments and in not making any changes in response to technology developments.

Cyber crime

The increase in developments in IT, and in particular the use of the Internet (e-commerce), brings with it the risk of cyber crime. There are cases of Internet fraud where consumers' credit card details are stolen, despite chip and pin which was introduced to increase the security of buying using debit and credit cards. Hackers can also 'break into' bank accounts and steal money by moving it to other bank accounts.

The dark side of e-commerce is that unlawful purchases can be made from undesirable sites and unscrupulous organisations can offer illegal wares to the general public and adult products to under-age consumers. This is a difficult area to police and it is recognised as a major issue.

There is also the risk of share prices being influenced by Internet communications. For example, there are message boards for virtual dialogues about share prices. The information about shares posted on a message board might be nothing more than rumour or gossip, but ultimately it can devalue or increase share values.

Did you know?

Cyber crime is one of the fastest growing criminal activities on the planet.

Activity: Preventative measures

1   Identify how some websites have introduced an additional security measure for purchases made by credit card. What does it claim to do and how does it work? Share and discuss your findings.

2   Identify at least five different types of equipment available which claim to help to reduce risk to injury when using technology. Discuss with your peers.

Diverting financial assets

There are several different ways in which financial assets can be diverted. Criminals are able to transfer sums of money ('megabyte money') across the Internet easily and quickly. This illegal activity is made easier due to the high volume of financial transactions made online – it can be difficult to identify and trace individual transactions on a global scale.

Sabotage of communications

Deliberate sabotage of communication systems mainly occurs through viruses, which might be sent as, for example, email attachments. Software bugs are also a threat and, although non-malicious, the attack is likely to be as of much a risk to software or a system as a virus attack. Bugs are likely to occur where software is introduced prematurely onto the market with insufficient testing. It can be very tempting for developers to launch their software onto the market too early in an attempt to gain the edge over their competitors.

To protect our technological service against virus attacks, security software should be installed on home and work computers. The computer you use at your school/college or training provider will have at least one form of preventive or blocking device (see the section on firewalls on page 125).

Wireless telecommunications are also subject to sabotage. In a recent case Nigeria considered withdrawing its new mobile network from Ghana due to sabotage. Sabotage has been blamed for disruptions to mobile telephone services in the Caribbean, while T-Mobile and AT&T were fined for unsecure voicemails (to read the related *Cellular News* articles go to Hotlinks).

Intellectual property theft

There are two main types of business: those that provide a service and those that make and/or sell products. Some organisations have exclusive rights to a design of their product which they have patented. Patented products cannot be copied by anyone else. Many creative works and products are not patented, but are protected by copyright law, for example paintings, images, literary articles such as novels and poems.

The owner of the patent or copyright to a product owns the rights to make or reproduce the product and no one else can do this without permission.

When a person or organisation copies or uses patented or copyright material without the owner's permission, this is called stealing **intellectual property**. This is a particular problem with copyright material that is made available on the Internet. Many people are tempted to copy and paste information from the Internet and pass it off as their own work – however, this is an illegal activity and is known as plagiarism.

Activity: Copycat

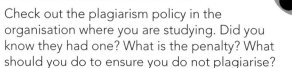

Check out the plagiarism policy in the organisation where you are studying. Did you know they had one? What is the penalty? What should you do to ensure you do not plagiarise?

Key term

Intellectual property – patented products protected by copyright. It is described as 'intellectual' because it has been thought up by someone and the idea belongs to that person.

Internet search engines can be used to help combat plagiarism, as they can search vast amounts of text to match plagiarised material very quickly.

For further information on security issues, see *Unit 5: Managing networks*, page 146.

Access control methods

Access to computers is usually secured by the need to insert a password to log in. With the use of the Internet and, in particular, the rapid increase in the use of wireless connection, there is a need to security-enable the connection to prevent unauthorised users obtaining access. This is done by selecting the security-enable option during the set-up of the connection.

It a wireless connection remains unsecured, an unauthorised user could connect not only without having to pay, but could access private information such as emails and bank account details.

One of the ways that criminals gain people's bank details is by **phishing**. This involves sending out spam emails claiming to be from the recipient's bank (see Figure 4.6). These hoax emails inform the recipients that they must immediately check their bank details due to a security error. The success of these emails relies on some receivers following a link and entering their bank details (including login and password), which then allows the criminals to access the bank account and withdraw funds. Banks now give warnings to their customers not to act on these emails and to report them to the bank.

> **Did you know?**
>
>
> Your organisation, tutor or examination board might use specialist software to check your work is not copied.

Denial of service attacks

Not only are deliberate attacks made on computer systems, but there are also non-malicious attacks such as the interruption to the operation of a network. Denial of service can happen when a site is bombarded with requests for a page and the site jams.

You will find more about denial of service attacks in *Unit 7: Organisational systems security*.

> **Activity: Keep your hands off!**
>
> 1 Identify an example where stealing of intellectual property has occurred. Explain what happens as a result of this type of theft.
>
> 2 Find out the laws that are in place to protect intellectual property.
>
> 3 Share your findings with a partner.
>
> 4 Discuss with a partner how you would feel if you read someone else's assignment and found that it contained some of your words? Why would you feel this way? What could you do about it?
>
> Hint: A good place to start is by searching for case studies on world news websites. If you have seen the TV programme 'Dragons' Den' you may have picked up some ideas there.

> **Key term**
>
> **Phishing** – when criminals send out fraudulent emails that claim to be from a legitimate company with the aim of obtaining the recipient's personal details and committing identity theft.

Preventive technologies

Preventive technologies can aid the management of risks. Preventive measures include systems that monitor compliance with data protection and firewall software that can prevent access to certain undesirable websites.

Firewalls

Firewall hardware, or software, that limits access to, and between, networks is one method to improve the level of security. Firewalls use filters to block unauthorised material and potentially dangerous attacks such as viruses from entering the system.

Dear valued customer of TrustedBank,

We have recieved notice that you have recently attempted to withdraw the following amount from your checking account while in another country: $135.25.

If this information is not correct, someone unknown may have access to your account. As a safety measure, please visit our website via the link below to verify your personal information:

http://www.trustedbank.com/general/custverifyinfo.asp

Once you have done this, our fraud department will work to resolve this discrepency. We are happy you have chosen us to do business with.

Thank you,
TrustedBank

Member FDIC © 2005 TrustedBank, Inc

Figure 4.6: Phishing for bank details

Secure payment systems

You may be familiar with some secure payment systems such as PayPal. With so many attempts to access our money it is often difficult to tell whether the websites we use are secure or not. You have been learning about phishing and the wiser we become the more clever the scams are at fooling us into believing otherwise. There are many sites aimed to help us, but how do we know that these sites are what they claim to be? The padlock on a website is meant to confirm that site is secure (see Figure 4.7) which you may have seen if you use online banking.

Figure 4.7: Padlock for secure sites

Sites, such as PayPal, also offer the VeriSign® Identity Protection Network (VIP) as an additional layer of security when logging into the site. There are many websites giving guidance and advice on security of websites, such as the Windows® site (go to Hotlinks and click on this unit).

Disaster recovery

As previously explored, a number of risks and threats to personal and business data exist. Organisations and individuals should have a plan for ensuring that information stored electronically is not only secure, but also backed up. Individuals should frequently and regularly back up data. For organisations, it is necessary to retain files such as financial accounts and to back up these files before and after each month end, as well as annually.

Individuals may have a very simple plan for restoring a file accidentally deleted. It may be an informal plan that they remember and carry out automatically.

Organisations should have a formal disaster recovery plan setting out clearly what they should do in the event of a range of disastrous scenarios. For example, an organisation would need to have plans for more complex activities such as how to restore last month's accounts if they are accidentally overwritten or become corrupt. Specialist accounting software often has a simple process for restoring accounts, but it is important that examples are considered, solutions explored and processes identified that can be clearly followed and are made readily available to those concerned.

You can learn more about disaster recovery in *Unit 7: Organisational systems security*.

Activity:
The computer says no

Check out the BBC news article entitled *Organs removed for transplant without consent*. What went wrong – was it a software disaster? How could this have been prevented?

Corporate electronic data retention is a complex area. Decisions have to be made regarding the types of documents to be saved and the information contained within them. The protocols for retention are likely to be identified within a retention policy.

Each organisation should also have a system for backing up everything on the system (including emails) and ensure that backups are not kept on the premises (in case of fire or theft). Data protection does not only apply to file servers, but also to PDAs. Remote data centres provide this type of service.

Risks can also present opportunities, particularly for companies that produce products to help manage risk or provide technical support. Risks become threats only when organisations choose not to move with the times.

Assessment activity 4.2

Your first assessment activity asked you to provide your boss at Full of Beans with information on recent IT developments, the reasons for upgrading systems in an organisation and the impact of IT developments on an organisation.

1   This time you need to explain how organisations such as Full of Beans can respond to IT developments. **P3**

2   Explain how such an organisation can manage risk when using IT. **P4**

Grading tips

- Use what you produced for the Assessment activity 4.1 as a starting point. You might decide to enhance any case studies you produced or presentations you gave and demonstrate your findings in innovative ways. For instance, you could take examples of current practice, such as the manual recording of figures, and show how technology could present and store larger amounts of data and provide results more quickly. You could provide examples of organisations without technology and those with technology – one approach might be to explore the working environment. **P3**

- When promoting ways to manage risk, you might again choose to represent scenarios. Ensure you consider all sides of the argument – the pros and cons. Use real examples to further your case. **P4**

PLTS

By evaluating the quality of the information you provided previously and adapting it accordingly, you will be demonstrating your ability as a **reflective learner**. By asking questions and gathering information to further improve what you are developing your skills as an **independent enquirer**.

Functional skills

Your second assessment activity will also require you to apply Functional Skills in **English** to meet industry standards. Components 1, 2 and 3 will be covered through your research, discussions with your colleagues and managers, then the results of your findings presented in a variety of ways. Functional Skills in **ICT** will be applied in many ways and should you choose to present figures of how data is stored and the size of data, you will have opportunities to demonstrate some aspects of Functional Skills in **Mathematics**.

3. Be able to propose improvements to business systems using IT

3.1 IT developments

Throughout this chapter, you have been learning about the recent developments in technology and the relationship between those developments and business. You have been given opportunities to carry out research, engage in activities and challenge your understanding. In this final section you will be given opportunities to consider improvement proposals using the knowledge gained throughout the chapter.

Recent developments

Business are benefitting, not only from improvements to technology, but also the choice of new applications entering the market on an almost daily basis. One such example of the range and flexibility of new applications available is in relation to mobile technology and in particular through mobile phones. Consider how businesses rely on the fact that their workforce operating away from the office, perhaps on the road or from home, are able to keep in contact with their office, staff and records.

How have off-the-shelf systems helped to support businesses?

Communicating has been made easier through a variety of media. Much of the communication relies on wireless technologies and workforce efficiency is improved as a result. For example, commuters are able to access business documents or arrange appointments while travelling by train. Planning of future journeys is made simpler by accessing websites and there are even applications to help you plan your meals and order the groceries. Operating systems have become more sophisticated, and simpler to use, with users no longer needing knowledge of computer programming just to access the software, as was the case back in the 1980s.

We have been exploring the innovative software platforms that enable businesses access to a wider variety of software, removing the restrictions of previous years. We don't know what the future holds, but we can be fairly confident that future developments will continue to be innovative.

3.2 IT improvements
Developments

One major benefit of the developments in IT is the opportunity to buy off-the-shelf systems that support many business requirements. Integrated systems, such as customer relationship and management information systems, provide access to a range of information that would be previously be stored on paper. Whether countless trees will be saved is unknown but worth considering.

Databases are simpler to use and provide filtered information in report or graphical formats, which are easier to interpret. To improve efficiency, businesses can increase their network, or incorporate a range of communication technologies for personnel on the move, around the globe. Smaller businesses, particularly a small trade such as a plumber, builder or electrician, might wish to explore having a **web presence** to promote their business more widely during tough, economic times.

Key term

Web presence – visibility through a website; promoting a product, service, company or individual(s) by featuring their 'presence' on the Internet. Another meaning can be a 'digital footprint' e.g. the number of hits to a website.

Businesses of any size will require management reports which can be more easily (and remotely) produced using technology. By logging all business transactions, generating reports is not only simple, but also provides a more efficient approach to business practice. For example, a business using an accounting package can generate standard reports such as expenditure, cash flow and income.

3.3 Business systems

Functions

Business personnel who travel to meet customers and promote their company's products and services can function more efficiently and be better informed by using Customer Relationship Management (CRM) software. Providing the data is current and accurate of course, the system is capable of providing information on recent and past customer purchases, prices paid and discounts given. The benefits of having this information at your fingertips are many but, in particular, customers who are recognised and whose history is known feel valued.

Businesses not only rely on customers, but also suppliers. Supplier relationship management (SRM) systems monitor the viability and vulnerability of suppliers. This means that suppliers who are vital to a business can be measured in terms of their reliability and cost-efficiency. A method of identifying which suppliers are less reliable or cost-effective is crucial for a business to operate effectively.

Technology developments have resulted in a series of management systems which support organisations throughout the business process. A business involved in product development might choose to use a system for project managing the product from idea to design to prototype and then right through to sales. Technology enables analysis of productivity, flags up deadlines, calculates ongoing costs against budgets and helps identify cost savings and viability of the product. Businesses can then make the decision as to whether or not the product is a viable proposition or whether it should be scrapped or refined.

Systems also exist to manage service delivery. A service delivery platform helps manage a range of technologies required to deliver a service. For example, a system such as this could identify how other technologies, for example TVs and mobile phones, can be deployed to deliver a specific service.

All business requires people to operate. People management systems are more likely to be used by larger organisations to manage their personnel records. In much smaller organisations, a basic system can be implemented using standard software.

Any business providing a product or a service needs some form of stock control system. These systems are used to monitor and control the movements of stock. For example, an Internet cafe needs to ensure that sufficient stocks of consumables are available to meet customer demand. More sophisticated systems also analyse the demand of different products to help avoid wastage and satisfy needs which could vary at different times of the day, week or season.

Finance systems vary in sophistication and as referred to earlier in this section, accountancy software such as Sage can be used for smaller businesses to manage their income, expenditure and any VAT. Some systems include the facility for managing the payment calculations of staff, although dedicated systems for **PAYE** also exist.

> ## Key term
>
> **PAYE** – stands for pay as you earn. A system that enables an employer to deduct your tax and National Insurance contributions at source. Depending on any other income, you may be required to complete a tax return to pay any additional tax which has not been collected by your employer.

Factors, such as size of the organisation, number of employees and variations in the way in which they are paid (for example salary, hourly rates, bonus or commission payments) are likely to determine the type of finance system used. Larger financial systems operate at global level for organisations such as banks, to control and regulate financial operations.

Assessment activity 4.3 · P6 M3 D2 · BTEC

Since presenting your first proposal to the owner and other members of the board at Full of Beans, you have been asked to work with the sales and marketing department to meet their IT needs.

Both the sales manager and the marketing manager are relatives of the owner and are unfamiliar with the power of IT. Marketing is still carried out by leaflet drops and adverts in the paper, while sales staff travel long distances, knocking on doors to drum up business.

You need to produce a proposal for an IT-enabled improvement to a business system. **P6 M3 D2**

One approach you might consider to accommodate the range of your audience could be to provide an interactive proposal so the managers could experience the benefit and impact of those proposals. **M3**

It might help your justification if you provided case studies or anecdotes from other sources. If you provided these in digital format and your audience could see or hear evidence from other sources, they might be more convinced. **D2**

Grading tips

- Your final proposal will be a continuation and refinement of the proposal you have been working on through this chapter. By reflecting back on your earlier work you should be able to improve on the content and the way it is presented. Check the language and terminology to ensure it is understandable and not too technical, as it needs to suit the audience. Ensure your reasoned arguments are sound. **P6**

- The proposal that you present should be fit for purpose, but may be the simplest and most obvious solution. **P6**

- The proposal should be sufficiently detailed to show how the improvement would fit in the existing system. **P6**

- To achieve a merit you need to present your proposal innovatively and creatively. It will need to be original, so don't be tempted to copy someone else's idea, although the technology you use might be the same. Consider the range of people in Full of Beans and their skills levels. **M3**

- To achieve a distinction you should include details such as cost, inputs, effects on staff and other knock-on effects as appropriate. **D2**

PLTS

When presenting and defending your conclusions you are developing your skills as an **independent enquirer**. When considering adapting presentation and language approaches to meet the challenges and influences faced by the sales and marketing teams you are demonstrating your skills as a **creative thinker.**

Functional skills

Your final assessment once again provides opportunities to apply Functional Skills in **English** and **ICT** across many of the components. In particular, when you present your proposal using creative and innovative ways, you could demonstrate a wider range of ICT skills. Should you strive to gain a distinction you will have opportunities to demonstrate your Functional **Mathematics** skills too.

Jamal Lewis
Small Business Owner

Jamal has been running a fairly successful catering business on a small scale, providing healthy, lunchtime snacks to local industry.

He gets up early every day to ensure he is first in the queue at the bakery, then travels to the greengrocers and butchers to ensure he buys what his regular customers request, although he doesn't always manage to get what they want and this results in wastage or fewer sales. Jamal then has to travel back to make the snacks, occasionally taking a diversion to buy the packaging needed to transport the snacks. Although he buys drinks from the cash and carry in bulk, he still has to make another trip at weekends to bulk-buy consumables that aren't immediately perishable.

For most of the weekends Jamal catches up on paperwork, checks stock, works out what is likely to be needed the following week and disposes of perishable goods.

Jamal feels he has worked incredibly hard and it is about time he was able to reap the rewards of building his business while ensuring it continues to develop. He has considered taking on help and perhaps advertising for more business, but doesn't know how he will manage. He is not sure which parts of the business he could hand over or what he could do to be more efficient. He is worried if he takes on help, that the cost will be too high without expanding his business and is also concerned about losing control.

Think about it!

1 What would your advice to Jamal be?

2 How could Jamal use technology to cut down his workload without costing him too much?

3 Which parts could Jamal hand over to have the greatest impact in terms of cost, efficiency and time?

4 In what ways could Jamal use technology to maintain control and monitor effectiveness yet reduce his workload, while developing his business?

5 How would you present your advice to Jamal and provide him with a plan of how to move forward without overwhelming him?

Just checking

1. What is the difference between regulatory and legislative policies?
2. Describe geosourcing and how it differs from outsourcing.
3. Give examples of how organisations can cut costs.
4. Give three examples of why staff might require upskilling.
5. What are the differences between contractors and employed staff?
6. Name at least two companies that have helped IT evolve.
7. Give three examples of specialist support software and their purpose.
8. How can organisations prevent unwanted or unauthorised access to electronic data?
9. What is the term that describes theft over the Internet?
10. Why could using Internet restrict growth of sales for a company?
11. What are the benefits and challenges that customers experience when organisations use technology to provide their customer service?
12. Where can cost savings be made because of developments in technology?
13. How do mobile technologies benefit commuters and other business activities?
14. What are the benefits in having systems such as a customer relationship management software?

edexcel :::

Assignment tips

- Do keep a portfolio of useful articles, case studies, information and notes. Start by dividing up the sections of the portfolio by topic, for example using sections or subsections from this book. File as soon as you have anything. Your portfolio does not have to comprise printed out copies – it can be in hard-copy, electronic form, or both. If storing your information electronically, use the same definitions and dividers as you do with your physical portfolio, so you can find everything more easily.

- Do use all the opportunities and information you can from other sessions or experiences. If you are in part-time work, apply what you are learning to the workplace. If you are studying Functional Skills or another unit or even qualification, relate what you are learning to and from those other units. Gather information from lots of different places and in different ways. For example, ask people in business, check with your organisation and try out your suggestions with someone whose opinion you value.

- Do not rely on others to do the work for you, nor copy others' work (whether you know the individual or not) without their permission or citing the source. Do not rely on being able to go back and trace the source of your information. Do always check the actual source – Wikipedia, for example, is a collection of information which can be derived from anywhere or anyone and is not necessarily verified as accurate. If a reference is given, trace the reference back and make sure you will be able to find it again. A web link may change and not be available next time you look.

- Several websites have been provided throughout the book. Make sure you always keep a note of the URL or book, page, author, title and year to cite in your work. In addition, there are some links to case studies you might find useful on Hotlinks: Cisco, BSI Group, European Commission – Environment, Health and Safety Executive.

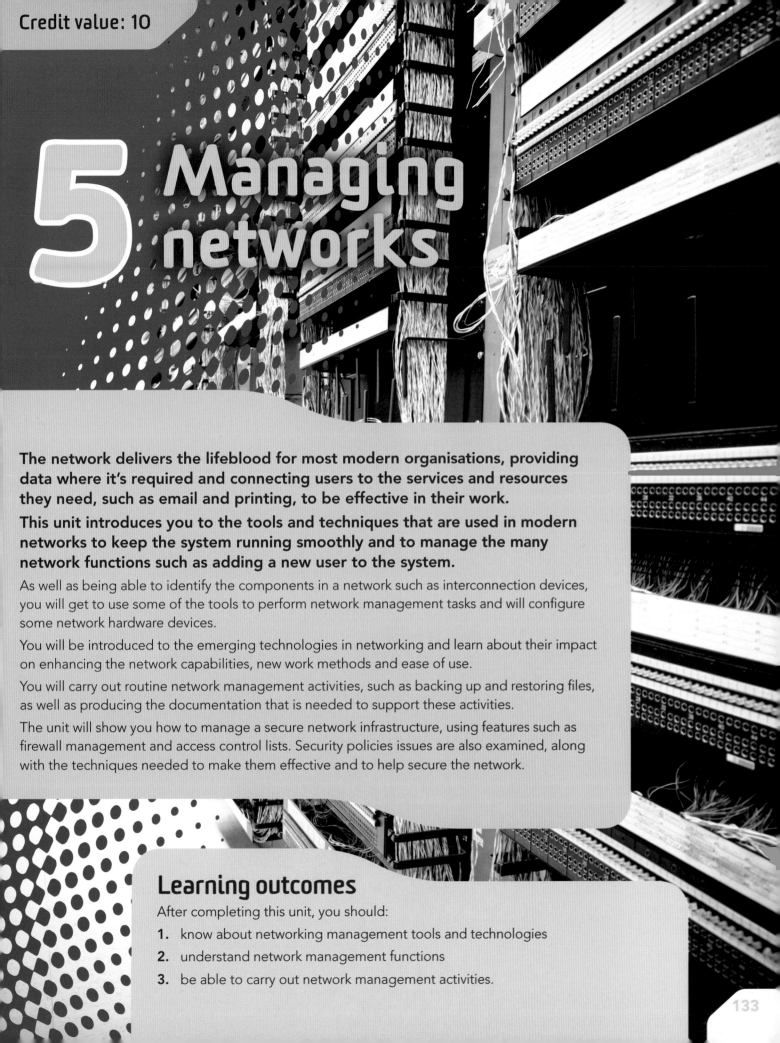

Credit value: 10

5 Managing networks

The network delivers the lifeblood for most modern organisations, providing data where it's required and connecting users to the services and resources they need, such as email and printing, to be effective in their work.

This unit introduces you to the tools and techniques that are used in modern networks to keep the system running smoothly and to manage the many network functions such as adding a new user to the system.

As well as being able to identify the components in a network such as interconnection devices, you will get to use some of the tools to perform network management tasks and will configure some network hardware devices.

You will be introduced to the emerging technologies in networking and learn about their impact on enhancing the network capabilities, new work methods and ease of use.

You will carry out routine network management activities, such as backing up and restoring files, as well as producing the documentation that is needed to support these activities.

The unit will show you how to manage a secure network infrastructure, using features such as firewall management and access control lists. Security policies issues are also examined, along with the techniques needed to make them effective and to help secure the network.

Learning outcomes

After completing this unit, you should:

1. know about networking management tools and technologies
2. understand network management functions
3. be able to carry out network management activities.

Assessment and grading criteria

This table shows you what you must do in order to achieve a pass, merit or distinction grade, and where you can find activities in this book to help you.

To achieve a **pass** grade the evidence must show that you are able to:	To achieve a **merit** grade the evidence must show that, in addition to the pass criteria, you are able to:	To achieve a **distinction** grade the evidence must show that, in addition to the pass and merit criteria, you are able to:
P1 describe network technologies **See Assessment activity 5.1, page 142**		
P2 outline the purpose of networking tools **See Assessment activity 5.3, page 158**		
P3 identify emerging network technologies **See Assessment activity 5.1, page 142**	**M1** describe the potential impact of emerging network technologies **See Assessment activity 5.1, page 142**	
P4 explain the functions of network management **See Assessment activity 5.2, page 149**	**M2** explain the goals of fault management **See Assessment activity 5.2, page 149**	**D1** justify the inclusion of routine performance management activities within a network managers role **See Assessment activity 5.2, page 149**
P5 interrogate a network to identify the network assets and their configuration **See Assessment activity 5.3, page 158**		
P6 undertake routine network management tasks **See Assessment activity 5.3, page 158**	**M3** keep accurate records of network management tasks **See Assessment activity 5.3, page 158**	**D2** design a network security policy for a small organisation **See Assessment activity 5.2, page 149**

How you will be assessed

This unit will be assessed by a number of internal assignments that will be designed and marked by the staff at your centre. It may be subject to sampling by your centre's Lead Internal Verifier or an Edexcel Standards Verifier as part of Edexcel's ongoing quality assurance procedures. The assignments will be designed to allow you to show your understanding of the unit outcomes. These relate to what you should be able to do after completing this unit.

Your tutor will tell you precisely what form your assessments will take, but you could be asked to produce:

- presentations
- case studies
- practical tasks
- written assignments.

Alex Young, BTEC National IT learner

This was an easy unit with a lot of theory and some practical lab work so we could get hands-on experience. We found out about the different types of networks and how to set them up and which situations they were best in.

We had to look at considerations when designing a network and the issues that have to be thought about during the planning. We found out about the good and bad points of different operating systems. I decided I don't like Vista®. It was good to find out about mobile networking and how laptops are used now.

We had three assignments, with the pass criteria easy, but it was a lot more difficult for distinction. It was good to use some network tools, including Wireshark, NMap and the command prompt.

I think this unit has helped me decide to look for a career in networking. I am looking forward to being able to work with a real system and to help develop it.

I have set up a client–server network at home now. It was hard to do, but brilliant experience and I'm sure it will be useful later. I believe networks are going to be a good area to work in, as more and more companies depend on them. I want to be part of that.

Over to you

- **Why do you think Alex does not like Vista®?**
- **Find the names of three network tools and briefly describe what they do.**
- **What is a client–server network system?**

1. Know about networking management tools and technologies

Emerging technologies

There are some very powerful emerging technologies for modern networks including:

- video on demand
- greater storage capacity
- mobile working with laptops
- home working.

What do think are the impacts of these technologies? What are the good and bad aspects of each of these?

IT networking professionals need to know about networking management tools and technologies, appreciate which networking operating systems are available, the role of **protocols**, the components used in a network and the impacts from emerging technologies.

1.1 Network technologies

Every network uses a network operating system and protocols to allow the computers and devices to talk to each other. The operating system connects the software to computer hardware, allows users to operate their computers and controls the network. Protocols are used when devices connect to each other, handling the connection speed, data transfers and error checking.

The layout of the network is how it is physically implemented, that is whether it is wireless or cabled. If cabled, the network will have a topology, the logical structure of the networked connections.

There will be devices in the network. These are the hardware components such as switches, which allow the components to connect together and communicate.

1.2 Networking operating systems

An operating system is present on every computer, connecting the hardware to software and the user. PCs mostly use Windows® and Apple® computers use MacOS®. A network operating system (NOS) also allows computers to connect together into a network, sharing resources such as printers and disk space, as well as running services such as emails. Examples of network operating systems include Windows® and Linux. Many business networks use Windows Server® as the main NOS. Linux is an **open source** NOS that has a strong user base, but is not used as much as Windows®.

Windows

Microsoft® Windows® is the market-leading operating system for both PCs and business networks. PCs usually have Windows® installed on them when purchased, so this is the operating system that is most familiar to users.

Key terms

Protocol – devices and computer systems use protocols to communicate together so they use the same error checking, data transfer speeds and share other standards, such as data packet structures.

Open source – when the source code of software is available to anyone using the software. Source code is the actual code written by the programmers who created the software, so open source software can be changed to exactly meet the needs of users or to fix bugs.

Business networks are usually **client–server networks** and can use versions of Windows® for both the clients and servers.

Professional versions of the PC Windows® operating system have client services built in, that need to be configured if the PC is to be used on a client–server network. Windows Server® is the version of Windows® used to control a client–server network.

Linux

Linux was designed from the beginning to be a networking operating system and can be configured as a **peer-to-peer network** or client–server. The definitive website for Linux (go to Hotlinks and click on this unit to access the website) includes free downloads of this open-source operating system, with lots of support. Although Linux is freeware, there are several suppliers who sell their own versions of it, usually bundling in their own utilities to make it easier to install and use.

1.3 Networking protocols

A protocol is a set of rules that allow devices to communicate together and exchange data. There are many protocols of interest to networking professionals, including Simple Network Management Protocol (SNMP) and Internet Control Message Protocol (ICMP).

SNMPv3

Simple Network Management Protocol version 3 (SNMPv3) is a protocol that is widely used in networks to control devices such as routers. Version 3 of this protocol provides better security than previous SNMP releases.

SNMP is the technology behind a lot of network operator consoles, showing the status of devices on-screen and allowing the operator to reconfigure devices when needed.

ICMP

The ICMP is used with **TCP/IP** networks to pass back error messages such as not finding a server. Some network utilities, such as the traceroute command, are based on ICMP.

1.4 Layout

There is a broad divide between the layout of cabled (wired) and wireless systems as there are several topologies (structures) used for cabled systems.

Key terms

Client–server networks – when the server (or servers) control the network and allow clients to log on to the network. The control the server has over the network makes this the network system of choice for most organisations.

Peer-to-peer networks – the opposite to a client–server network, with no server controlling the network. Each computer has equal rights and can share folders, printers or other resources. This is the network system of choice for most homes.

TCP/IP – stands for transport control protocol/Internet protocol. It is the very widely used protocol for the Internet, intranets and networks, allowing websites and web surfers to connect and share data.

FDDI – stands for fiber distributed data interface, a standard using optical fiber to connect the network together.

Topologies

The topology is the shape or structure of a cabled network. The current topology standards are:

- **star:** used in many small networks with a single switch
- **tree:** used by many larger organisations to join their stars together
- **ring:** used with **FDDI** for fast fiber optic networks
- **mesh:** used by BT for their telephone network.

(See Figure 5.1.)

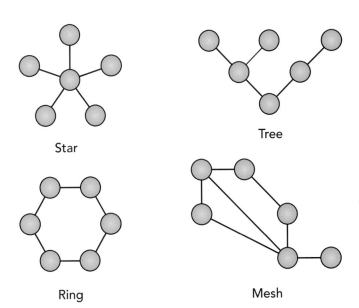

Figure 5.1: Network topologies

Key terms

Switch – a switch is a box with a number of RJ45 network ports (sockets) used to connect networked devices together. RJ45 is the usual connection plug on network cabling.

WiFi – a common method for wireless networking used by laptops, printers and many computers, based upon the IEEE 802.11 standards provided by the WiFi Alliance, initially advertised in 2003 as 'The standard for wireless fidelity'.

WLAN – wireless LAN (local area network) usually following WiFi standards.

WiMAX – stands for worldwide interoperability for microwave access

MAN – a metropolitan area network (MAN) is a network connecting LANs in an area that might be as small as a campus or as large as a city. A MAN could use wireless, or leased circuits, to allow the system to communicate.

Intranet – like the Internet, but running on an organisation's network rather that the worldwide web. Many organisations use their intranet to help communications with staff with news, support forms, holiday request forms and many other useful resources.

Star

Each computer in the network uses the same **switch** to connect to the other computers and devices such as printers.

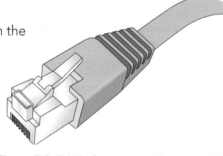

Figure 5.2: RJ45 plugs on an Ethernet cable

Tree

This is the most common topology used by larger organisations as it joins the switches together into a large network that works well and is easy to administer.

Ring

This topology is used with FDDI for fast fiber optic networks which can stretch for miles between the networked computers and devices.

Mesh

The mesh topology is used by BT for their telephone network. A mesh has many possible routes between devices connected to it. Routers are used by computers to find the best path (route) for data

to travel between them. Mesh topologies are very resilient to damage. If, for example, road works broke a BT connection, the system would route phone calls around the fault to maintain the telephone service.

Cabling

The are many different main types of cabling for current systems with a wide range of speeds and possible distances for the cable runs (see Table 5.1).

Wireless

Wireless layouts have become popular because of their flexibility and ease of setting up as there is no need to install trunking and cable runs. The **WiFi** standard (802.11) is built into most modern laptops, making it very easy for them to connect to an office network or WiFi hot spot in a hotel, train or cafe.

Whereas WiFi is the accepted standard for **WLAN** (wireless LAN), there are also wireless technologies such as **WiMAX** available for city-wide networking (**MAN**) and providers such as Gaiacom Ltd offer nation-wide wireless networking solutions between cities.

1.5 Network devices

A network device is any item of hardware that is part of a network.

Servers

The servers control every aspect of the network. Some networks only have one server, but larger networks have several servers, each controlling an aspect of the network such as Internet access.

These types of servers are often used in business networks.

- **Application servers:** supply the software applications opened by users of the network.
- **Audio/video servers:** bring multimedia to users by streaming video to them.
- **Fax servers:** fax documents out and receive incoming faxes.
- **FTP servers:** move files securely between computer systems.
- **Groupware servers:** enable users to collaborate using the Internet or a corporate **intranet** and to work together.
- **Mail servers:** move and store emails for corporate networks.

Table 5.1: Types of cabling (Information compiled using: http://www.networkdictionary.com as a source of information)

Term	Standard	Specifications	Medium	Speed	Distance
Ethernet	10BaseT	IEEE 802.3i	CAT5 UTP	10 **Mbps**	100 m
Ethernet	10BaseFB 10BaseFL 10BaseFP	IEEE 802	3j Fiber	10 Mbps	2000 m 2000 m 500 m
Fast Ethernet	100BaseT	IEEE 802.3u	CAT5 UTP	100 Mbps	100m
Fast Ethernet	100BaseFX	IEEE 802.3u	MMF MMF SMF	100 Mbps 100 Mbps 100 Mbps	412 m HD 2 km FD 20 km FD
Gigabit Ethernet	1000BaseT	IEEE 802.3ab	CAT6 UTP	1 **Gbps**	100 m
Gigabit Ethernet	1000BaseCX	IEEE 802.3z	Shielded, balanced coax	1 Gbps	25 m
Gigabit Ethernet	1000BaseSX	IEEE 802.3z	MMF 850nm MMF 850nm	1 Gbps 1 Gbps	550 m 275 m
Gigabit Ethernet	1000BaseLX	IEEE 802.3z	SMF 1300nm MMF 1300nm MMF 1300nm	1 Gbps 1 Gbps 1 Gbps	5000 m 550 m 550 m
Gigabit Ethernet	1000BaseLH	IEEE 802.3z	SMF 1300nm MMF 1300nm	1 Gbps	10 km 550 m
10Gigabit Ethernet	10GBaseS 10GbaseL 10GbaseE (Each has R or W mode where R is for dark fiber and W is for SONET) (10GBaseX)	IEEE 802.3ae	MMF 850nm SMF 1310nm SMF 1550nm	9.95 Gbps 12.5 Gbps 10.3 Gbps	300 m 10 km 40 km
10Gigabit Ethernet	10GBaseT	IEEE 802.3an	UTP	10 Gbps	100 m
10Gigabit Ethernet	10GBaseCX4	IEEE 802.3ak	thin twin-axial cables	4 x 2.5 Gbps	25 m

Abbreviations key

HD = half duplex   FD = full duplex   SMF = single-mode fibre   MMF = multimode fibre
UTP = unshielded twisted pair   CWDM = coarse wavelength division multiplexing
CAT5 = category 5 UTP   CAT6 = category 6 UTP   Mbps = megabits per second
Gbps = gigabits per second

Key terms

Mbps – stands for megabits per second. Approximately a million bits can be transmitted through the media in one second. (Remember, elsewhere data size is measured in bytes and there are 8 bits in a byte.)

Gbps – stands for gigabits per second. Approximately a thousand million bits can be transmitted through the media in one second.

A server may be a tower, blade or rack mounted. This is a rack mounted server.

Activity:
Server vs gaming PC

Visit the Dell™ website by going to Hotlinks. Look at their server products, found on the small and medium business web pages.

Compare the specification of a tower server with a high-performance gaming PC from the Dell™ Alienware range.

1 What features does the tower server have that the gaming PC does not?

2 What features does the gaming PC have that the tower server does not?

3 Write a short piece that could be used in an advert to summarise and sell the tower server.

4 Write a short piece that could be used in an advert to summarise and sell the gaming PC.

- **Proxy servers:** filter web requests to block unwanted websites, improve performance and share connections between users and the Internet.

- **Telnet servers:** allow users to log on to a host computer and perform tasks as if they're working on the host.

- **Web servers:** provide web content to browsers visiting the site from inside or outside the network.

Server hardware may be blades, rack mounted or a tower. A tower server is similar to a desktop PC, but with some specialist features that help to make it secure and reliable.

Blade and rack are both modular systems, using an enclosure (blade) or cabinet (rack) to hold the server module(s).

Server software will be a network operating system that has been configured to deliver the role of the server type.

Workstations

There will be many workstations for the users to log into and carry out their work. A workstation is simply a computer attached to the network that is there for people to use. It needs to have a specification powerful enough to meet the needs of the user, but usually has a modest specification with good reliability and low price.

Interconnection devices

The interconnection devices are used to connect the parts of a network together.

An interconnection device may be a:

- **repeater:** to boost the signal of a cable so it can reach a farther distance

- **bridge:** to connect local area networks together, usually on the same site

- **router:** to find a route to send data between systems, usually over distance.

Network cards

Many computers in a network have a network card to connect them to the network. Other networked computers have on-board networking, where these circuits are built into the motherboard.

A wired network solution uses a network cable, usually with a RJ45 socket. A wireless network solution uses a radio-based connection, usually WiFi and so does not need cabling.

Vendor-specific hardware

Vendor-specific means that the component will only work with hardware from the same manufacturer, such as a HP® Jet-direct card which can only plug into a HP® printer to connect it to the network. Vendor-specific hardware is not very common now, as standards for hardware are quite open, with networks able to mix and match components from different manufacturers.

1.6 Networking tools

There is a wide choice of networking tools to help network operators and administrators control and solve problems with their network.

Purpose

The purpose of a networking tool can be to manage:

- **faults:** to detect where problems are and to fix them
- **performance:** to understand how well the network is working and to assist in configuring it to work even better.

Examples of networking tools

HP OpenView

HP OpenView is a collection of network management tools that are widely used in modern networks. These tools allow fast diagnosis and repair of IT problems, as well as automatic data collection and problem fixing.

CiscoWorks

CiscoWorks is a suite of network management tools that help configure, administer, monitor and troubleshoot Cisco networks. They can quickly identify and fix network problems and improve network security through integration with access control services and auditing network-level changes.

Wireshark

Wireshark is a network protocol analyser and is widely used by many industries and educational institutions. It runs on Windows®, Linux, OS X, Solaris, FreeBSD, NetBSD and many other network systems. Live data can be read from Ethernet, IEEE 802.11, PPP/HDLC, ATM, Bluetooth®, USB, token ring, frame relay, FDDI, and others (depending on your platform). Captured network data can be browsed in different ways using colours to help understanding. Output can be exported to XML, PostScript®, CSV, or plain text.

System software

Using system software such as MS Operations Manager it is possible to find **network assets** and track their performance.

1.7 Emerging technologies

As an IT professional, you need to be aware of the developments in hardware and software that affect networked systems.

Key terms

Network assets – any components (such as switches) that are used in the network.

Bandwidth – term used to define how quickly data can travel through a communication media. High bandwidth is a general term describing a fast communication, often fast enough to support video.

Server virtualisation

There has been a strong trend recently towards server virtualisation. This is where several servers run on the same computer. The great advantage of server virtualisation is a more efficient use of hardware because there is no need to buy a separate computer for each server.

Video on demand

Video on demand is when the user is able to select a video and then see it straight away. Faster computers and faster data transfer rates have made video on demand increasingly popular, with more and more systems offering this service.

Users of these services are varied – they may be logged onto a network, visiting a website, or at home using any of the video on demand products available to view on the television. There is an increasing expectation for modern systems to provide high **bandwidth** services such as this to meet user demand for near-broadcast image quality.

1.8 Impact of emerging technologies

As well as recognising modern trends and developments you need to appreciate the impact they have, not only on the network management but also on the people involved with using them and anyone else who is affected by these emerging technologies.

Enhanced capabilities

Newly emerging technologies provide enhanced capabilities to networks such as:

- faster speed due to the improvements in components providing faster data transfers and quicker devices
- greater storage capacity, with larger hard disks and more memory

- improved control, with network operators and administrators finding it much easier to see when devices are working correctly and drill down on poorly performing devices to identify problems and correct them.

New working methods

New technologies can bring new work methods. There is now a real choice for a lot of people regarding how they work. New working methods also bring change they have to embrace.

- **Mobile working:** This usually involves using a laptop and taking work to clients or other places outside the office. Many hotels and public places offer WiFi hot spots so mobile workers can connect through the Internet to their organisation's network.

- **Home working:** This method is used when there is no need for a worker to go into the office. It may involve using a specialised workstation from home that securely connects to the organisation's network and is locked down to prevent other usage. Alternatively, home workers may use their own computer to log on to their employer's system.

- **Web-centric applications:** These are Internet-based systems that allow employees to log on and work from almost anywhere. A web-centric application might allow employees to access a database system to look up client details and to update as required.

Ease of use

An expected benefit of emerging technologies is improved ease of use, with easier access to the organisation's systems from different places and more control over them.

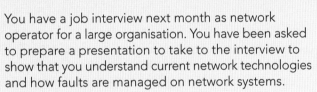

Assessment activity 5.1 P1 P3 M1 BTEC

You have a job interview next month as network operator for a large organisation. You have been asked to prepare a presentation to take to the interview to show that you understand current network technologies and how faults are managed on network systems.

1 Produce a section in your presentation covering these network technologies:
- networking operating systems
- networking protocols
- network layouts
- network devices. **P1**

2 Add some slides to your presentation identifying and describing three emerging network technologies. These might be server virtualisation, video on demand, IPv6 or any other emerging network technology you find interesting. **P3**

3 You are expected to be able to answer questions describing the potential impact of emerging network technologies. Produce some notes as a document describing these impacts. Use the following sub-headings:
- Enhanced capabilities
- New work methods
- Ease of use. **M1**

Grading tips

- Create a section for each of the network technologies, describe the technology. Then use two example products from each technology to complete your descriptions. **P1**

- For each of the emerging network technologies you identify give an example of where it could be used and the benefits the technology brings. **P3**

- You could describe the potential impact of emerging network technologies from the perspective of the people affected by them. **M1**

PLTS

You will be a **creative thinker** when you generate your ideas and explore possibilities identifying the potential impact of emerging technologies. As an **independent enquirer**, you will plan and carry out research, appreciating the consequences of your decisions when identifying the emerging technologies.

Functional skills

Selecting appropriate sources of information to match the requirements of the tasks you are set demonstrates your Functional **English** skills.

2. Understand network management functions

There are many network management functions that help administrators and operators manage and configure networks to keep them running effectively.

Configuration

Network configuration is a major aspect of setting up a network and it will be tweaked regularly to improve performance and to respond to any problems that occur.

- Network devices, such as switches and routers, need to be configured so they can work and communicate together.
- User accounts need to be configured to allow them to access the resources they need such as printers and networked folders.
- Application software needs to be configured to use the correct templates, user folders and anything else the software needs to run correctly on the network.
- The virus checking software needs to be configured on when to scan, how to deal with any viruses detected and where scanning reports are to be sent.

Fault management

The network is the vital part of IT systems for most organisations and if it fails there can be massive problems.

Fault management offers a range of techniques to keep the network up and running and to minimise the possibility of failure. If the network does fail then these techniques can help bring it back to life quickly, with minimal down time.

There are fault management systems that help network reliability by monitoring how the system is performing, triggering alarms if performance deteriorates in any of the monitored areas. If an alarm is triggered, the operator can take action before the problem becomes a serious issue and causes a network fault. For example, an alarm could be set on performance degradation for a network device such as a switch. If the alarm is triggered, the operator could run tests on the switch and reconfigure it in the evening, when the users have left work, so their work is not disrupted and the network is kept working.

Fault management needs devices to be remotely controlled, so the operator can reboot or reconfigure from a **centralised console**.

Key terms

Centralised console – used by a network operator to control the network. A few years ago, network operators would have needed to use several consoles to control separate parts of the network. In current systems these are centralised into one or two consoles.

App – shorthand term for a software application.

Account management

A network user account is used by a network to allocate rights, such as which network folders a user can access when they log on. These accounts require management tools to help the network administrator set up new users and to make any changes needed to the existing user accounts.

A large network will have a large number of user accounts, so users are grouped with other members who have similar rights. At the start of the academic year a school or college will need to set up hundreds of new users, but as all of these will be in a user group, the network management tools will make it quick, accurate and easy to set up these new user accounts.

Similarly, a change to the user group will affect all the users in that group, for example if two hundred learners need to use a new software application, then one change to their user group will enable access to the **app** for all of them.

Performance variables

To manage a network, so that it is performs well and is reliable, involves a lot of skill and experience. An understanding of the performance variables is an essential ingredient in this.

Performance variables are the figures that measure how important parts of the network are performing. Network tools will report back to the network manager about how different parts of the system are performing and will also show historical figures, so current performance can be compared with previous levels of performance. This gives the network manager useful information, especially if parts of the network show deteriorating, or improving, network performance.

Lower performance will give some cause for concern. The network manager will need to find out why. Devices may need to be reconfigured or replaced to bring the performance back to the expected levels.

Improving performance can be due to changes the networking team have made to device configurations, so the performance variables can confirm such changes worked.

Performance variables can include:

- network throughput
- user response times
- line utilisation.

Network throughput

Network throughput is a measure of how quickly data can travel through the network. A simple way to measure this might be to copy a large file from one part of the network to another and measure how long this takes. Unfortunately, such a test would give an overly optimistic speed, as in the real world network throughput is influenced by anything else that is in the cabling and what the computers in the network are being used for. So, network throughput is better measured by network testing tools such as Iperf (see Figure 5.3), Bwping and others.

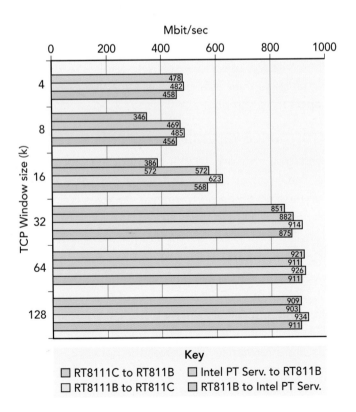

Figure 5.3: Iperf showing server speed comparisons

Key terms

GUI – a graphical user interface (GUI) is the name given to systems such as Windows® or MacOS® where the computer is controlled with a mouse.

TCP/UDP – Transmission Control Protocol/User Datagram Protocol (TCP/UDP) is used for streaming audio and video, voice over (VOIP) and videoconferencing.

Datagram – a self-contained chunk of data including the information needed for routing it from the source to destination computers.

BSD license – a software distribution license from Berkeley Software Distribution (BSD), which is an open source license. The BSD license means the software can be reused and sold without need for payment to BSD, although the software still needs to show a copyright message acknowledging the original source.

- **Iperf:** This has a **GUI** interface and is used to measure **TCP/UDP** bandwidth. It is open source software, able to be used with Linux, Unix® and Windows® systems. It can be set to different **datagram** sizes, producing results for datagram throughputs and packet loss. Iperf is a good tool for comparing the performances of wired and wireless networks.

- **Bwping:** This is a command line tool used to measure bandwidth and response times between two hosts using ICMP (see page 137) to echo request replies. It can be included, under a **BSD license**, in other products, and has been used in Mac OSX®.

Data throughputs in a network can be measured using these units:

- Kilobits per second (Kbps) or 1000 bits per second
- Megabits per second (Mbps) (1,000,000 bits)
- Gigabits per second (Gbps) (1,000,000,000 bits)
- Terabits per second (Tbps) (1,000,000,000,000 bits)
- Petabits per second (Pbps) (1,000,000,000,000,000 bits).

Sometimes the network throughput is measured using bytes instead of bits. This has an impact on capitalisations in the unit acronyms and the number 1024 is used instead of 1000 to scale the units:

- Kilo bytes per second (KBps) or 1024 bytes per second
- Mega bytes per second (MBps) or 1,048,576 bytes per second (1024 x 1024)
- Giga bytes per second (GBps) or 1,073,741,824 bytes per second

- Tera bytes per second (TBps) or 1.09951E+12 bytes per second
- Peta bytes per second (PBps) or 1.1259E+15 bytes per second.

User response times

The user response times are a measure of how quick the network is for the users, who will have an impression of how responsive, or slow, the network is in use. Using a network tool such as Nimsoft's Monitoring Solution can provide numbers to measure and monitor user response times.

The Nimsoft Monitoring Solution (NMS) enables organisations to measure the levels of performance end users actually receive from the IT infrastructure. NMS features two end-user response monitoring solutions, active monitoring and passive monitoring which can be used together, at the same time, if the best monitoring is required. Active monitoring uses software probes on remote computers to report back on their performance. Passive monitoring inspects **packets** in the network to measure the intervals between requests and their responses.

Key term

Packet – a formatted block of data sent over networks and the Internet. A packet contains the addresses of sender and destination, the data and error checking. The maximum size for an IP packet is 64KB.

Line utilisation

Line utilisation is how much data is loaded onto the network cabling and can be shown as a graph so the network manager can see any times when attempts were made to overload the cabling and also if the cabling was underused. This, in turn, gives useful information for decisions on when to upgrade cabling or consider alternative ways of structuring the network infrastructure to help it run better.

IBM® can provide the NetView Performance Monitor (NPM) network tool, which has a network performance feature producing line utilisation reports. An important aspect of configuring this tool is to set the line threshold setting, which is the maximum acceptable load value before performance begins to degrade. NPM can produce graphs to show peaks in line usage.

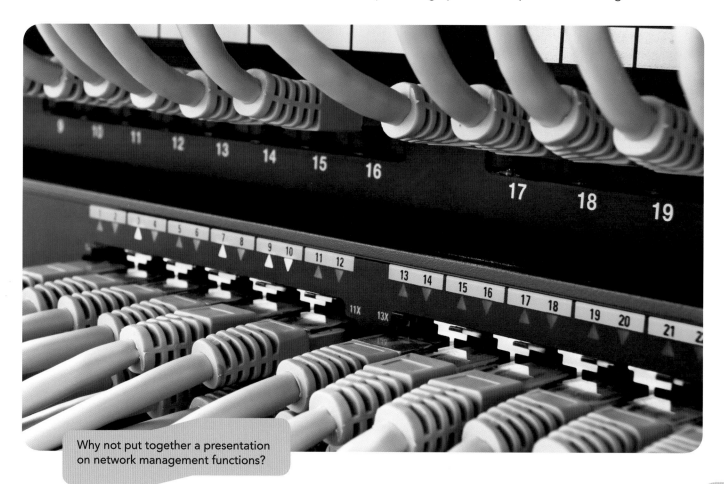

Why not put together a presentation on network management functions?

Other activities for setting up a network

The other network management activities undertaken when a network is first set up include:

- planning
- designing
- installing.

Setting up a network can be a complex project, as there are a lot of tasks to manage. Project-planning techniques can help coordinate and track these tasks.

Planning

The first stage in any IT project should be planning. When setting up a network the planning will involve understanding what is wanted from the network in order to know which components will be needed.

This planning will identify how many workstations are needed and the number of servers needed to run the proposed network. Connections between the workstations and servers will have to be chosen, wired or wireless, with the data communication standards and speeds. Planning will also identify what peripherals, such as printers, are needed, as well as any other services the network will be required to provide, such as VOIP (Voice Over Internet Protocol, allowing telephone calls using network hardware) or the Internet.

At this stage, a budget should be agreed and equipment costed.

For more on project-planning techniques, see *Student Book 2, Unit 17: Project planning with IT.*

Designing

After planning, the network needs to be designed. The design includes the layout and locations of the components. It clarifies where cables are to be run, where power points are needed, where the workstations, printers, servers and other devices are to be located. The design will also clarify the software and configurations that are needed.

Floor plans help to ensure that everything (including the users themselves) will fit into the available space. They are also a powerful and useful way to communicate to the people involved in the installation where everything will go.

Designing a network is time well spent because it will be a lot easier and faster to install the network if everyone

involved in the installation knows what they're doing and where the devices are to be set up. Decisions left until the point of installation usually waste a lot of time and money, as tasks are half completed and then need to be restarted when foreseeable problems occur.

Installing

Installation is when the network is connected, plugged in and brought to life. Many network installations have run over time and over budget because of inadequate planning, usually when simple problems, which should have been considered and solved before starting the install, are encountered.

Installation often starts with the cabling needed for the new system. Mains power sockets must be in place for equipment. **Trunking** will be needed around the rooms for network cabling if the network is cabled and sockets installed to connect workstations and servers to the cables.

Network operations

After the network has been installed it needs to be operated. Network operations include:

- security
- data logging
- checking performance and traffic.

Network operations keep the network running and respond to any problems that occur.

Security

Security is an important issue for every networked system, as threats can come from many directions and in many forms, including the Internet, staff, fires, thefts, floods and hardware failures.

Different types of threat to **network security** need different types of defence. The Internet is a powerful way to promote an organisation and to communicate with customers, but there are a lot of viruses out

Key terms

Trunking – conduit used in IT rooms to hold the cabling and RJ45 network ports. Trunking is often made from plastic and is usually attached to the walls at desk height.

Network security – protecting the network from threats to the data contained within it and threats to the software configurations that keep it running effectively.

there and a lot of **hackers** who are trying to enter the network. A firewall and virus checkers are necessary security measures against these threats.

Staff can be a danger to network security. They can corrupt data accidentally by making typing errors or deliberately if they dislike the organisation and are planning to leave. Security measures for this are to do regular backups and to configure user accounts so that users cannot see or change any data beyond the requirements of their job.

Staff can also introduce viruses to the network by opening infected emails or by visiting infected websites. To protect the network from this threat, security measures include the application of organisational policies that give staff responsibility for safe computing practices. A firewall, to prevent viruses entering the network from the Internet, and a virus checker, to detect any viruses that enter from other sources such as pen drives, should also be installed.

Fire, theft, flood and hardware failure are all risks to the hardware and data they contain. The best security measure for these risks is to back up the data regularly and to keep the backups in a secure location away from the systems. Backups kept in a shelf in the server room in a building that burns to the ground will be of little use. Some organisations keep their backups in a fire-proof safe. Other organisations keep their backups in a secure place that is off-site, in another location.

Some organisations enter into a reciprocal agreement with a partner organisation, so that if either of them has a major disaster, the partner's computer system can be used for a short while to keep operations running until a replacement system can be brought on-stream.

Did you know?

Flooding is a real risk to computer systems, even if the premises are a long way from the nearest river or coastline. This is because office buildings have water pipes that are often above the ceilings of offices. If a water pipe bursts there is a very good chance that any equipment below will get drenched.

Data logging

Data logging can be useful in identifying causes of problems in computer systems. The data logging

Key term

Hackers – people who are skilled in IT and who like to gain access to networks they have no right to. This might be to obtain confidential information about the organisation and clients or to steal money, although some simply hack for the fun of it.

software (such as the Advanced TCP/IP Data Logger from AGG Software) records all the data and interactions passing through a particular point in a system, usually part of a communication to, or from, a device such as a keyboard and display on which data is transitory. If there is a system failure, it may be possible to reconstruct the situation that caused the problem by carefully examining the data log.

Data logs are usually very temporary and get deleted if not needed, so if data is logged in a troublesome part of a computer system then most of the logs where the problem did not reappear would be deleted. However, it is useful to keep one or two data logs of parts where no problem is found to help identify what has caused a problem in another part.

Checking performance and traffic

IT professionals who manage networks need to be aware of traffic running through the system and to keep checking performance. There are many software tools available to check traffic and performance, including Microsoft®'s Network Monitor® to measure traffic with usage and Paessler's Traffic Grapher to provide current and historic bandwidth usage data for the network.

Checking performance and traffic helps network managers to:

- understand normal performance
- measure the effects of new devices installed to improve performance
- recognise when performance is reduced
- recognise when devices are giving problems
- recognise if there are regular times when performance drops, to gain an understanding of the cause and supply appropriate fixes.

Table 5.2 shows some of the major causes of network slowdowns with actions that can be taken to resolve them.

Table 5.2: Major causes of network slowdowns (Source: Tech Republic)

Cause	Effect	Solution
Bad network interface cards (NICs)	Intermittent network errors	Visually inspect the card's LED link lights
Failing switches/routers	Network slowdowns and strange occurrences, such as attempts to connect to secure (HTTPS) sites fail	Reboot the switches/routers
Daisy chaining where network expansion has been by plugging another switch into an existing switch	Slow network	Replace daisy chained switches with single switches having enough ports
NetBIOS conflicts	Shared files inaccessible, increased network congestion	Ensure older Windows® systems all receive the most recent service packs
IP conflicts	Network slowdowns or computers not able to access network	Configure IP addresses
Excessive network-based applications	Slow network	Implement hardware-based web filtering tools to prevent applications from overwhelming available network bandwidth
Spyware infestation	Security breached	Decent anti-spyware application and gateway-based protection
Virus infestation	Slow network and corrupted data	Firewalls, Windows® updates and antivirus programs are properly configured and maintained
Insufficient bandwidth	Slow network	Upgrade existing NICs, cabling and devices to 10/100/1000 Mbps equipment
DNS errors	Network failures and generally slow performance	Placing DNS servers as close to network systems as possible; also, always check to ensure systems are configured to use the proper DNS servers

Reporting

Reporting is a useful network management function to help communicate network usage and performance to the network administrators and other managers in the organisation.

These reports can be obtained from the network operating system, such as Windows Server®, or from any of the many software tools, such as the NetQoS® Performance Center, which provides reporting for application response time, traffic analysis, packet analysis and device performance.

Assessment activity 5.2

The job interview went well and you got appointed to the position of network operator with a large organisation. Your line manager has been asked to produce a report for the board of directors explaining network management to them, so you have been asked to produce the report for your manager to edit before she passes it on to the board.

1 Produce a report explaining the functions of network management. This will contain sub-headings for sections:
   - configuration
   - fault management
   - account management
   - performance variables
   - security
   - data logging
   - checking performance and traffic
   - reporting. **P4**

2 Add explanations to each section of the goals of these aspects of fault management. **M2**

3 Add to your report a justification for the inclusion of routine performance management activities within a network manager's role. **D1**

4 Add to your report your recommendations for a network security policy for a smaller organisation. This could include firewall management, access control lists, device hardening, continuous policy review, user rights and when to periodically review them. **D2**

Grading tips

- For each of the functions of network management produce up to two paragraphs of explanation. **P4**

- The goals of fault management could be explained by adding a section to each section of the report. **M2**

- For the justification of routine performance management activities you could explain what these are and then outline their benefits. **D1**

- Use the guidance for Task 3 to design your network security policy for a small organisation, including a brief explanation of the benefit of each policy. **D2**

PLTS

You need to be an **independent enquirer** to support your conclusions, using reasoned arguments and evidence justifying the routine management activities.

Functional skills

You will practise your **ICT** Functional skills by using ICT to plan solutions to complex tasks by analysing the necessary stages – when undertaking routine maintenance activities.

3. Be able to carry out network management activities

You will need to gain some hands-on experience of routine network management activities in this unit.

3.1 Regular maintenance activities

Every network has regular tasks that have to be carried out to keep it secure and running smoothly.

Backups

Every network should have a regular and reliable backup regime in place to safeguard the data held on the servers. The regularity of backing up depends upon what the network is used for and how much the data changes every day or week. Many organisations back up every day, some twice a day, while others back up every week.

These backups are often made to DAT tape cartridges or external hard disk. Optical DVD or CD disks are cheaper and can be used for backups, but they are easily damaged and not trusted by some IT professionals.

Backups can be made to a remote backup service through the Internet to another system that provides this service. Many organisations have data that is sensitive and private and so may be unwilling to trust a third party supplier to provide space for backups. Those that do, often **encrypt** the data they send for backup to help protect it.

Many network servers have **RAID** hard drive systems, which can spread data across several disk drives, effectively backing up the data as it is written to the disk. Some RAID systems allow hot-swapping of hard drives, so a faulty disk can be replaced without switching the server off and the RAID can rebuild the data that was on the replaced drive.

RAID systems still need backing up, as there are a lot of risks such as fire or theft which RAID would not be able to protect against.

Organisations should practice restoring backed up files to a computer system that is new to the data from time to time, to check that the backups are working effectively. It could be reckless folly to regularly back up data without ever checking it can be restored.

The traditional way to back up is to use a son, father, grandfather rotation on the backup tapes (see Table 5.3). In this system three tapes are used in rotation. When a new backup is made, the tape used for this becomes the son. The next time a backup is made, a fresh tape is used which now becomes the son, with the old son renamed to father. The next backup uses a fresh tape which now becomes the son, with the old son renamed to father and the old father renamed to grandfather. The next backup reuses the grandfather, over-writing the backup data there and becoming the

new son, with the old son renamed to father and the old father renamed to grandfather.

There are lots of ways that backups can be organised, often using several cycles with a daily cycle, a weekly cycle and a monthly cycle. A different set of tapes would be used for each cycle.

User accounts

There has to be a user account for every person who is able to log on to the network. Each user account has an ID (identification) which is unique to the user. The ID is associated with rights for the user to define which network services, such as printers or applications, are available to them. The account also has a password that should be changed regularly, unlike the ID which stays the same. User accounts are usually set up so that the user is forced to change their password regularly, perhaps every month.

The network administrator will not be able to see any of the user passwords, but does have the power to reset or change the password. This is useful for when a user forgets their password.

Every new user needs an account so they can log on to the network and access the network services they need for their job. Most networks use grouping for network accounts, such as sales or accounts, so creating a new account means adding the new user to the most appropriate group. This means that the new user will

Table 5.3: Son, father, grandfather rotation on backup tapes

	Tape A	Tape B	Tape C
Names of tapes after first backup of the system	Son	(still blank)	(still blank)
Names of tapes after the next system backup	Father	Son	(still blank)
Names of tapes after the next system backup	Grandfather	Father	Son
Names of tapes after the next system backup	Son (overwrites old Grandfather data)	Grandfather	Father

What do you need to think about when writing login scripts?

have similar rights on the network to others in the same group, such as accessing a shared database.

Using account groups, makes adding a new user and administering the user accounts quick and easy. A change to a user group can affect all the users, so a network administrator could add rights to a new network service, such as new intranet pages, to hundreds of users in one action.

When someone leaves the organisation their user account needs to be deleted. This is simple good housekeeping as there is no point in keeping the accounts which are no longer live or active. Old accounts also pose a security risk as they could be used by someone for negative purposes.

Login scripts

A login script is run every time you log on to a network. It does useful actions, such as detect which computer you have logged on to then connect you to the local printer. Designing and developing login scripts requires an understanding of using the **command prompt** and a scripting language for batch files such as VBscript or PHP.

Batch files have always been used with PCs. In the days of DOS they could automate DOS commands. A batch file named autoexec.bat has always been used to help set up a computer when it first boots up and is still present in modern Windows® systems. Each line in the batch file is a command or a comment.

> ### Key terms
>
> **Command prompt** – this is a window that can be opened in Windows computers, equivalent to the old DOS prompt where operating system commands can be typed into the C:\>_ prompt.
>
> **Ipconfig (IP configuration)** – a utility program included with Windows that is used from the command line to show the IP address of the computer running the utility and can show some other network information such as the domain name.

- Comments are used to self-document the batch file to explain what the section in the batch file does. Comment lines start with rem in VBscript.
- Commands may be from the scripting language or may be actual commands that could be typed into a command prompt. This works well for networks as a lot of the programs and utilities, such as **ipconfig** are command line driven.

The code uses these commands:

- **rem** to start a comment
- **ipconfig >"%userprofile%\ipconfig.txt"** to run the ipconfig program and send the output from this into a text file in the user profile named ipconfig.txt
- **echo** to show words on the screen

- **findstr "192.168.22.254" "%userprofile%\ ipconfig.txt"** to look for 192.168.22.254 in the text file named ipconfig.txt in user profile, setting errorlevel to 1 if not found
- **if not errorlevel 1 goto UK** to jump to the label UK if appropriate
- **goto next** to jump to the label next.

Note that a colon (**:**) appears at the start of every label name.

Virus scans

A network will have a multi-user version of an effective virus checker installed. Virus scans will be set up to run regularly and automatically on all the servers and workstations in the network with automatic updates of the virus signature definition files. These are needed by the virus checker software to keep up to date with all the new viruses that have been found since the last update. Every manufacturer of virus checking software runs an online updating service for their virus checkers so that anyone who uses the virus checker can bring it up to date with the best ways of dealing with every known virus. It is therefore important that the virus signature definition files are regularly updated.

The way the virus checker software responds to any virus threats found is likely to be configured differently on a network from how it is on domestic computer systems in your home. The virus checker on a network will be configured to notify the network administrator, who will be very interested in any virus that is found and will want to investigate where it came from and any other impact it has.

File cleanup

Good management of a network will include regular file cleanups, where any temporary files are deleted and user disk spaces are cleared of old, unwanted files. Temporary files can be left behind after a software installation or when a program closes unexpectedly after a crash, or if the computer is switched off at the mains instead of being closed down through the operating system.

Large numbers of temporary files can be a cause for concern as they are often there because of a problem elsewhere, so the network manager should investigate what they are and what caused them. If

they were caused by crashes, the manager is likely to take remedial action to reconfigure the system, or if they were caused by people inadvertently abusing the network, the manager can schedule some user training.

Old user files are best deleted by the user, as they know best what they no longer need. The network manager may run reports on disk usage then contact any users who are using a lot of disk space. The users can also be asked regularly to delete any old or unwanted documents.

Other maintenance activities

There is a wide variety of tools that network managers can use to manage performance or fault find, so every network should have appropriate tools for these tasks:

- managing performance
- fault finding
- finding network assets
- tracking device performance
- system testing.

3.2 Tools

Managing performance and fault finding

Tools to manage performance or fault find include HP OpenView (see page 141) and SNMP (simple network management protocol).

SNMP is a widely used standard to help identify devices in a network, how they are performing and to control them. It uses a manager/agent model consisting of an SNMP manager, an SNMP agent, a database of management information, managed SNMP devices and the network protocol. The operator uses the SNMP manager. The SNMP agent connects the SNMP manager to the physical device(s) in the network.

SNMP uses an SNMP Management Information Base (MIB) with a small set of commands to interrogate and control devices.

Finding network assets and tracking performance

System software such as MS Operations Manager® (see Figure 5.4) can find network assets and track their performance.

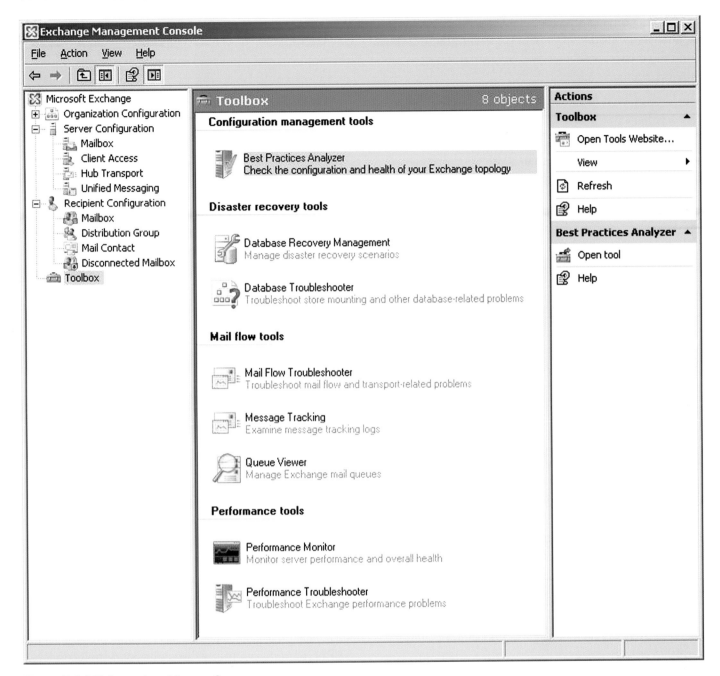

Figure 5.4: MS Operations Manager®

3.3 Documentation

Documentation should record everything important that happens to the network. This is helpful in fault finding and to recover lost or corrupted data.

The organisation should have a network documentation policy detailing what aspects of the network need documentation, especially the servers. This policy will communicate to each administrator exactly what is expected of them in their documentation.

Network documentation will have some or all of these sections:

- topology diagram
- server names, roles and IP addresses
- change log for each server
- software versions and proof of licenses
- hardware components
- active directory
- backup procedures.

The topology diagram will include each network segment, the routers connecting the various segments, and the servers, gateways and other major pieces of networking hardware.

The change logs for servers are useful because when a server fails, the failure can often be traced to a recent change.

Hardware components such as switches, routers and gateways documentation should include information such as the configurations and passwords.

Active Directory documentation should include domain names, site structure, the Active Directory hierarchy and contents of each group policy.

Work logs

Work logs are used to keep records of jobs or programs that are run on the network. They are useful as they can help to recreate data if a corruption occurs, as the log will identify which data was changed and from what source.

Resources logs

These logs record the resources used, perhaps for internal billing or charging between departments, such as paying for paper or toner used by a printer.

System testing

The system testing should check and record performance levels. As well tracking current performance, records provide valuable information for comparison purposes if there are problems in the future.

3.4 Configuration options

Configuration is when options are set for the software to work in a particular way such as the default locations of document files for separate users.

Configuring user accounts

The user accounts control how people can log on to the network, as well as what they can see or change on the network and the resources that are available to them. The network administrator chooses which server hosts the user accounts and configures these settings to enable the network rights the user needs for their job.

Drive mappings

There will be several drive mappings on your network. This is where folders on a server are given names which make them look like hard drives to the user. Mapping drives simplifies them and makes them easy to use. The actual name for a folder available to users on a network could be long and difficult to remember, whereas if the folder is mapped to a drive, it will simply be to drive S: or similar.

Most networks map to drive letters that are easy to remember with letters such as H: for the home drive or S: for a drive shared between users.

Virus scanning options

Virus scanning software options need to be set to respond to any viruses found by automatically dealing with the threat (deleting or **quarantining** the virus or infected file) and notifying the network management. The network manager needs to be alerted to any problems found by the virus checker, so that the causes can be investigated and action taken to prevent it happening again.

3.5 Security features

Security is important to every network. The network must be kept running and the data on it protected from unauthorised access, corruption or loss.

Physical security is anything that keeps unauthorised people away from the system such as a swipe card or lock on the door leading to a computer room. Logical security is every way the network is configured to prevent unauthorised people from being able to log on, or to prevent them from gaining access to parts of the network they should not see.

VPN access

A **VPN** is a network that extends beyond the premises to offices in other cities or countries. As the VPN uses Internet access to connect to the other sites, security measures are needed. Routers are used at each end of a VPN to connect the sites together, so they need to be configured to encrypt the data and to require a password.

Key terms

Quarantine – moving a virus or infected file to a safe place on the system to prevent it from doing any damage to the rest of the network.

VPN – stands for virtual private network.

Firewall management

The firewall is a barrier to stop viruses from entering the system. Managing the firewall is essential to not only stop viruses and unauthorised entries, but also to recognise attacks on the network from outside.

Firewall attacks can take several forms.

- **Reconnaissance attack:** where an intruder attempts to discover and map the network systems services and vulnerabilities.
- **Access attack:** where the intruder attacks the network in order to retrieve data, gain access or improve their personal access rights.
- **Denial of Service (DoS) attack:** when an attack on your network damages or corrupts the computer system, or denies users access to the networks and

Key term

ACL – stands for access control list.

services. These can be based on packet flooding, using up bandwidth, CPU and memory resources by overloading the system with data traffic.

A firewall is usually managed with a password-protected web interface providing set-up screens in your browser where the firewall can be configured.

Access control lists

Networks use access control lists (**ACLs**) to deny resources to anyone not entitled to them and to allow authorised users to gain access to networked

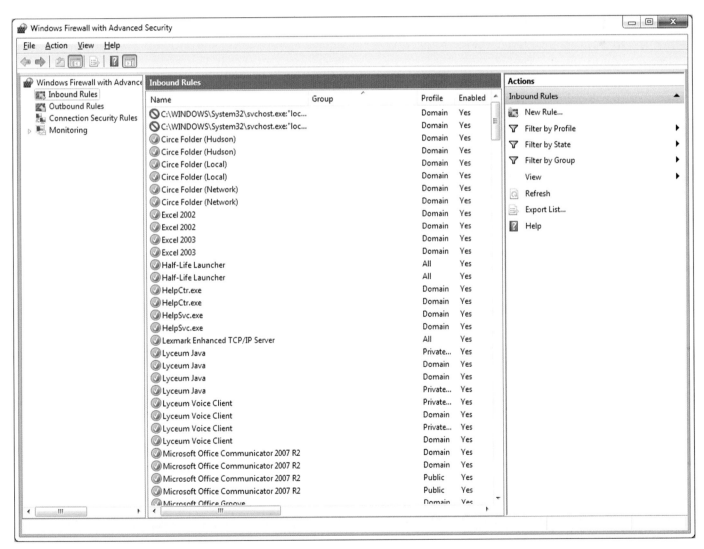

Figure 5.5: The Windows® Firewall Settings

resources, such as a database or printer. ACLs can be used both to prevent unauthorised access and to log those who do have rights and record when they access the resource.

ACLs can also define rights, for example some users might have read-only access to a database so they can see the data, but be prevented from making any changes to it, while other users could have read-write access to the database and therefore be able to make and save changes.

Device hardening

Devices in a network need to be made secure from tampering and made as reliable as possible. This is called device hardening, which could include any of these techniques:

- **patches** and updates released by the manufacturer: these should be applied as soon as possible to protect against any newly discovered security issues
- switch security: this can be enhanced by only allowing specific **MAC addresses** to connect through the switch
- routers – these can use ACLs to block unauthorised access attempts.

Continuous policy review

There needs to be a continuous policy review of how security is dealt with on the network as threats keep evolving. Any other experience gained through running the network should also be acknowledged and used.

Forensic analysis

Real-time monitoring of network traffic requires expensive and unreliable human attention, as well as not being a practical approach to much more than a single workgroup. Network forensics is when all traffic is archived and analysed, a process known as reconstructive traffic analysis, which is a much more practical approach to understanding what data is travelling through the network.

This is usually limited to data collection and packet level inspection. If needed, a network forensics analysis tool (NFAT) can provide a richer view of data collected, so you can inspect traffic further up the **protocol stack**.

User rights

The user rights are defined in the user profile and help to secure the network by restricting the user from accessing any part of the network they have no rights to.

3.6 Security policies and procedures

Security policies and procedures strengthen network security. Policies are the rules that an organisation expects users to follow, such as not opening email attachments from unrecognised sources. Procedures are step-by-step instructions that should be followed, such as configuring a new router. Procedures make sure that the job is done properly and documented.

These policies and procedures should be regularly reviewed to respond to any changes and new experience gained in running the network.

User access and rights

The network manager should periodically review the user access and rights to check that they are still appropriate. Access to any existing resources that the user does not need any more should be removed. Similarly, access to any new network resources that the user would benefit from should be allowed.

Penetration testing

A good aspect of a complete security policy is to subject the network to regular penetration testing. This is when an expert tries to gain unauthorised access to the network. Any breaches thus discovered can then be secured.

Security audits

There should be a regular security audit of the network. This is a formal review of all aspects of the network security and might include some, or all, of the following.

- Defining the scope of the audit with asset lists, that is which assets to include in the audit.

- Creating a threats list of everything that can compromise the network's security.

- Examining any threat history and checking security trends to understand possible future threats.

- Prioritising the assets and their vulnerabilities to develop a security threat response plan.

- Implementing network access controls to security-check any user trying to access network resources, such as by adding a password to confidential data.

- Implementing an intrusion prevention system to strengthen the firewall.

- Implementing identity and access management to control user access to specific assets, so users have to be authenticated.

- Creating backups, checking storage is secure and that restore procedures work.

- Checking email protection, spam filtering and user policies regarding opening unknown attachments.

- Preventing physical intrusions or break-ins to the premises, as well as reducing risks from stolen or lost laptops by encrypting data on them.

A security audit is an excellent opportunity to review and check how secure the network actually is.

Access control list reviews

The firewall and access control list policies need to be reviewed regularly to ensure old equipment, or ex-users, are removed.

Assessment activity 5.3

You are enjoying your job as network operator with a large organisation and have now been asked to document some of the routine network operations in the organisation. This documentation is to be produced as procedure pages for the network handbook guide to operations. You are to produce pages for your network handbook guide demonstrating that you understand tasks 1–3. You should also log all the network management tasks you complete, as described in task 4.

1 **Introduction to networking tools.** Include on these pages the purpose of networking tools, for example HP Openview, Cisco Works or Wireshark, giving examples of two, with screenshots and written descriptions of how the tools can be used. **P2**

2 **Interrogate a network.** Use a networking tool of your choice to find devices in the network and see their status. Take screenshots of these network interrogations for inclusion into the procedure pages for the network handbook guide to operations. Add to these pages written explanations of how to interrogate the devices. **P5**

3 **Regular maintenance.** Produce pages for the network handbook guide, explaining how to do your choice of three of these activities:

- backup and restoring files
- user account creation and deletion
- design and develop login scripts

- virus scanning
- file cleanup
- configuring user accounts
- setting drive mappings
- configuring virus scanning options. **P6**

4 **Keeping records.** For the merit criteria you will need to keep accurate records of all the network management tasks you have carried out. The records will be in a log that you create using a suitable software application. Your log will include dates, times, accurate technical details of the tools and devices you used with any appropriate comments on the tasks. **M3**

Grading tips

- You may choose to describe other networking tools not named in the task. **P2**

- The evidence for interrogating a network should show you have actually done this. **P5**

- Undertaking routine network management tasks must be from your actual hands-on experience. **P6**

- A log for keeping network management tasks records could be a word processor table or spreadsheet which might be completed by hand or typed up. **M3**

PLTS

You can evidence being a **reflective learner** by reviewing your progress, acting on the outcomes and keeping records of network activities.

You will be a **self-manager** when dealing with competing pressures, including personal and work-related demands and dealing with competing pressures while undertaking the routine network management tasks.

Functional skills

You will practise your Functional **ICT** skills when using IT to select, interact with and use IT systems safely and securely for a complex task in non-routine and unfamiliar contexts such as when interrogating networks.

Jo Maddocks
Network Manager

I am responsible for the operation and administration of the network, servers, email and network security systems of a large insurance broker. This is quite a lot to do and would be impossible without my team: an operator and an administrator. The three of us work well together and are proud of our systems.

My duties include administration and maintenance of our web server (hosted externally) and our internal email, database and proxy servers. We configured and set up all our server systems and other network components.

Security is a large part of our role including firewall administration, anti-spam, anti-virus systems and regular setting of new anti-spam policies. We also provide basic operational support for the employee computer systems.

The users work shifts between 8 a.m. and 8 p.m., so the three of us operate a loose rota to maintain a presence during working hours for any unexpected IT problems.

I have a very good working knowledge of Windows Server®, Linux, Exchange Server® and the MS Office® apps. My hands-on hardware experience is good, covering all our networking and computer hardware components.

We are proud of our documentation, especially the user account and device configuration records, as these are regularly used, regularly updated and save us hours of frustrating wasted time.

It's a brilliant job, a lot of pressure at times, but always interesting and varied.

Think about it!

1 What types of servers are used by this organisation? What do they actually do?

2 Can you identify three examples of routine problems that might occur that make the 8 a.m. – 8 p.m. cover essential?

3 What do you think is the least amount of documentation a network needs?

Just checking

1. How is a network operating system different from a PC operating system?
2. Identify four types of server and explain the network role of each.
3. What is meant by an emerging technology?
4. What is network throughput and why would a network manager need to know this?
5. How many types of security threats can you identify and how can they be reduced?
6. What is data logging software?
7. Can you identify and describe two software tools that are available to check performance and traffic in a network?
8. Explain son, father, grandfather rotations for backup tapes.
9. In what ways are login scripts used?
10. What is SNMP?
11. Explain with examples what is meant by a network topology.
12. Identify three advantages and three drawbacks of wireless networks.
13. What are performance variables?
14. In what ways can staff be a danger to the network?
15. How are security policies useful?

edexcel :::

Assignment tips

- You need to describe networking operating systems, devices, protocols and layouts. **P1**
- The purpose of at least two networking tools must be outlined. **P2**
- You can identify any emerging network technologies that you find in your research. **P3**
- There are many functions of network management, so a brief explanation of each should provide enough evidence here. **P4**
- You must interrogate a network yourself to identify the network assets and their configuration. **P5**
- You will need to undertake some routine network management tasks. **P6**
- The potential impacts of emerging network technologies will be structured into the enhanced capabilities they offer, new working methods and the ease of use. **M1**
- You need to explain the goals of fault management by identifying how each of the P4 functions helps to reduce faults or improve performance. **M2**
- A log can be used to keep accurate records of the network management tasks you do. **M3**
- Your justification for including routine performance management activities within a network managers role should focus on the benefits to users from a reliable network. **D1**
- The network security policy for a small organisation needs to include practical ways of keeping the system secure with explanations of how they will do this. **D2**

6 Software design and development

Computer programs can be written to carry out a wide range of tasks, from writing letters to guiding a space rocket. Programs are particularly good for repetitive tasks, since computers can work very fast; they do not become bored or tired and they can do tasks involving calculations with 100 per cent accuracy. However, computers have no in-built intelligence and are incapable of independent thinking – they can only follow the instructions within a program.

Whatever function you want a computer to perform, all you have to do is write the program.

A program is a little like a recipe for cooking a meal. A recipe lists, in detail, the steps you must follow to make the meal. Recipes are written in English, to be understood by humans and assume a level of common sense from the cook.

Computers, on the other hand, do not have common sense and require a very precise set of instructions.

Learning outcomes

After completing this unit you should:

1. know the features of programming languages
2. understand the principles of software design
3. be able to use tools to demonstrate software designs.

Assessment and grading criteria

This table shows you what you must do in order to achieve a pass, merit or distinction grade, and where you can find activities in this book to help you.

To achieve a **pass** grade the evidence must show that you are able to:	To achieve a **merit** grade the evidence must show that, in addition to the pass criteria, you are able to:	To achieve a **distinction** grade the evidence must show that, in addition to the pass and merit criteria, you are able to:
P1 describe the application and limits of procedural, object oriented and event driven programming paradigms **See Assessment activity 6.1, page 167**		
P2 describe the factors influencing choice of programming language **See Assessment activity 6.1, page 167**		
P3 explain sequence, selection and iteration as used in computer programming **See Assessment activity 6.2, page 174**		
P4 outline the benefits of having a variety of data types available to the programmer **See Assessment activity 6.2, page 174**		
P5 explain the role of software design principles and software structures in the IT Systems Development Life Cycle **See Assessment activity 6.3, page 180**	**M1** explain the importance of the quality of code **See Assessment activity 6.3, page 180**	**D1** discuss the factors that can improve the readability of code **See Assessment activity 6.3, page 180**
P6 use appropriate tools to design a solution to a defined requirement **See Assessment activity 6.4, page 188**	**M2** justify the choice of data types and software structures used in a design solution **See Assessment activity 6.4, page 188**	**D2** develop algorithms to represent a design solution **See Assessment activity 6.4, page 188**

How you will be assessed

This unit will be assessed by a number of internal assignments that will be designed and marked by the staff at your centre. It may be subject to sampling by your centre's Lead Internal Verifier or an Edexcel Standards Verifier as part of Edexcel's ongoing quality assurance procedures. The assignments will be designed to allow you to show your understanding of the unit outcomes. These relate to what you should be able to do after completing this unit.

Your tutor will tell you precisely what form your assessments will take, but you could be asked to produce:

- presentations
- handouts
- notes
- worksheets
- teaching notes
- design documentation.

Shafina Roberts, BTEC National IT learner

This is probably one of the most difficult units I did. I had not done any software design before and I found it very hard to grasp some of the concepts. We did this unit alongside the programming unit and I found that quite hard too, but as I learned more about programming it helped with the design unit too.

The part I found most difficult was learning how to use the design tools. I really struggled to understand where to start. Our tutor gave us some help with this and lots of practice helped. I also found you had to think very carefully about how the program would look to the user and then the design became easier to understand.

I also found it difficult to understand about the different programming approaches, as with little programming experience it was difficult for me to see the difference between them.

I can't really say I enjoyed this unit, but it was challenging and I felt it was one of my biggest achievements to obtain a merit grade in it. I will be studying computer science at university next year and I know this unit will help me there as we have to study software development in even greater detail.

Over to you

- **What do you think you will find most challenging about this unit?**
- **Will you also be studying programming?**
- **Which programming language will you be learning?**
- **Can you find out why that language was chosen?**

1. Know the features of programming languages

Boot up!

Programming is the key to everything about IT. Without **programs** a computer is useless, but a program can make a computer do almost anything. While designing and writing programs can be difficult and challenging, it can also be exciting and rewarding. Many people feel a real sense of achievement when they get a complex program working. Programming gives you an opportunity to be creative and it provides virtually limitless scope to further your knowledge.

Like many complex human endeavours, programs need designing. Just as an architect must design a building before work starts on it, so a programmer must create a design.

- Imagine you are an architect about to design a new 'skyscaper'. What sort of things would you need to know before you began your detailed design?
- Are there similar things a programmer would need to know before starting the design for a new software system?

The microprocessor or chip at the heart of a computer can only understand instructions in the form of binary codes (made up of 1s and 0s), but as binary codes are very difficult for humans to understand, all modern programming is done using **symbolic languages** with English-like statements. This section looks at the nature and features of programming languages:

- the different approaches (or paradigms) to writing programs
- the types of language
- the reasons why an organisation might choose one language in preference to another
- how data can be categorised into data types, ready for processing.

1.1 Programming paradigms

Computer programs can be very complex indeed and over the years a number of different approaches have been developed to deal with this complexity and encourage the development of efficient and error-free programs.

- **Procedural programming languages** break up the programming task into a number of procedures (also called sub-routines or functions). Each procedure carries out a specific task and is called from the main program. The procedural approach is relatively easy to understand and is therefore often used when first learning programming. It is also suitable for systems

that are fairly straightforward and don't involve many different interacting sub-systems.

- **Object-orientated programming (OOP)** takes a different approach to the structure of a complex program. OOP was developed in response to the difficulties that were experienced in creating highly complex systems using the procedural approach. With OOP, a program is broken down into **objects** rather than procedures. A more detailed explanation of the OOP approach is given in the section on software structures on page 176. It is quite a difficult concept to grasp, especially for those new to programming.

Key terms

Program – a set of instructions that tells the computer what to do.

Symbolic language – a programming language where the actual CPU instructions are replaced by English-like key words such as 'If', 'Print' or 'Do'.

Objects – different from procedures in that they group program instructions and data together. An object may be either visual or non-visual. A visual object is anything on a form, such as a button. An example of a non-visual object is the PrintDocument object of VB.NET which can be used by a program to produce hardcopy onto paper.

- **Event-driven programming** relates to how the program responds to user input, not to how the program is structured. Therefore event-driven programs can be written using a procedural approach or an OOP approach. Event-driven programming is synonymous with the Windows® User Interface. Windows® programs respond to user input, for example when you click a button or choose a menu option a particular function is carried out. Clicking buttons or choosing menu options are all considered events. Event-driven programming therefore involves writing event procedures which respond to the actions the user takes.

Supporting tools and enviroment

Most programs are written using a piece of software called an integrated development environment (IDE) which includes all the things a programmer needs to write the program with, such as:

- an **editor** which to write the instructions this often provides additional tools such as pop-up help on the instructions being written

- a **complier** which converts the instructions into machine code that the computer can understand

- a **Windows® forms editor** which creates Windows® forms and add all the required controls (buttons, text boxes, check boxes etc.)

- A **debugger** to help identify bugs in the program.

As well as an IDE, some large software development projects use computer aided software engineering (CASE) tools. These are designed to automate various parts of the software development process. For example, CASE software is available to assist in the creation of design diagrams such as structure charts, **DFDs** and **ERMs**. These are looked at in more detail later in this unit.

1.2 Types of language

Over the years, many different programming languages have been developed, each with their own set of features. As well as individual languages, such as Cobol or Visual Basic®, there are also broad categories into which programming languages fall.

- **Visual programming language:** This is designed to work in a Windows® environment. It has features which support the creation of Windows® objects, such as menus, dialog boxes and buttons.

Key terms

DFDs – stands for data flow diagrams.

ERMs – stands for entity relationship models.

HTML – stands for hypertext mark-up language.

IDE – stands for integrated developent environment.

Scripts – small pieces of code which are included in web pages to provide additional functionality and interactivity that cannot be provided by HTML.

- **Mark-up languages:** These are not true programming languages, as they do not contain instructions to control the flow of the program, such as decision structures or loops. Instead, mark-up languages give instructions to control the format and layout of a computer file. The best known mark-up language is **HTML**, which is used to create web pages.

- Where web pages need to carry out programming functions like making decisions, the code for this has to be included within the HTML using **script** languages.

Table 6.1 summarises the different types of languages.

Table 6.1: Types of programming languages

Types	Examples
Procedural languages	Cobol, Basic
Object-oriented	Java
Visual	Visual Basic®
Scripting	JavaScript
Mark-up	HTML

It's worth bearing in mind that these different categories are not necessarily mutually exclusive. Many modern programming languages combine features of the different types. For example, although Visual Basic® was originally thought of as a procedural language, the latest versions have included facilities which allow programs to be written in a way that follows the object-oriented approach – and, of course, Visual Basic® is also a visual programming language.

Activity: Types of languages

1   See if you can find examples of code written in different languages.

2   What differences and similarities can you find between the languages?

1.3 Reasons for choice of language

The choice of which program language to use is often a complex one. A number of different factors will influence the choice and each of these factors will now be considered.

Organisational policy

Some companies (particularly larger ones) have an organisational policy as to what computer hardware and software is to be used. For example, a company might have a policy to use only Microsoft® software because of the level of support that may be provided by such a large software vendor. Another company might have chosen to use Apple® Macintosh® machines, while another might have a policy to use open-source software such as Linux.

Suitability in terms of features and tools

Two questions have to be answered when deciding on the suitability of a programming language.

- Will it work on the platform, that is the hardware?
- Does it have appropriate features to suit the type of applications that have to be written?

Some programming languages were specifically designed for particular types of applications. They have features and tools which support those types of applications. For example, military application software such as missile guidance tends to be written in languages such as Ada, while Windows® programming is well supported by languages such as Microsoft® Visual Basic®. Languages such as Java™ are well suited to programming for the Internet and mobile devices. **PHP** is an open-source, server-side scripting language used to create dynamic web pages and is thus well suited to web server programming.

Some programming languages only work with particular hardware and software. The Visual Basic® programming language, for example, will only work on PC hardware, running the Windows® operating system. Other programming languages, such as Java™, are hardware and software platform independent.

Key term

PHP – a shortened form of PHP Hypertext Preprocessor. The initials come from the earliest version of the program, which was called Personal Home Page Tools.

Availability of trained staff

In a commercial programming environment, the programmers who work for a particular company may already be skilled in using a particular language, so that language may be the natural choice for a new project.

For a project where staff need to be recruited to complete the programming, it should prove easier to recruit staff for a popular language rather than a less widely used one. So, this may also be a factor to be considered when deciding which language to use.

Reliability

Some programming languages have features built into them which help to make the programs more reliable and less likely to crash. The best example of this is the Ada language – it was designed from the outset to include features which make it reliable. Ada is often used for safety-critical systems such as the fly-by-wire control system of the Boeing 777 aircraft.

Development and maintenance costs

Clearly, the cost of developing and maintaining programs is an important consideration when embarking on a software development project. Some languages have a reputation for cutting development costs by making it quick and easy to develop and maintain (update) programs. For example, in the 1980s, report program generator (RPG) was specifically designed to allow the speedy creation of reports.

Expandability

While most of the programs you will write for this unit will only be used by one person at a time, some software systems have to support hundreds or even thousands of simultaneous users. Systems written for interactive websites, for example, may need to support a very large number of users without crashing.

Some languages expand or scale better than others and have features which support large systems. Such languages would be the choice for a project where this is an important consideration. For example, programming languages such as PHP support computer clusters, where a number of high-performance computers can work closely together to support very large number of users.

Activity: Choice of programming language

1 Which programming skills are in the most demand? Take a look at some computing job websites to see what skills appear in job adverts. Visit Hotlinks and click on this unit to get started.

2 Ada and PHP are popular languages, but are not often used for teaching programming. Use the Internet to research the history of these languages. Where does the name Ada come from?

3 What programming language will be used at your college or school for this course? Find out from your tutor why this choice was made. Were any other languages considered? What languages have been used in the past and on other courses? Are there any web development courses or modules at your school or college? If there are, what programming languages do they use? See if you can get some examples of code written in other languages from these courses or modules.

PLTS

The research you will need to do for this assignment task will help show you are an **independent enquirer**.

Functional skills

Writing the materials for this assignment will help develop your Functional Skills in **English**, Writing. If you give the presentation you will prepare for this assignment task it will help develop your Functional Skills in **English**, Speaking and Listening.

Assessment activity 6.1

P1 P2 :BTEC

You are working as an assistant to a trainer who delivers courses on programming. They have asked you to prepare some presentation materials in the form of PowerPoint® slides for an introduction to the course. The presentation material you prepare should cover:

- the factors which influence the choice of programming language for a particular project **P2**
- the typical applications for and limitations of procedural, object-orientated and event-driven programming approaches. **P1**

Grading tips

- Your PowerPoint slides should cover all the aspects of these topics listed in the Unit Content of the specification under Learning Outcomes 1.1 and 1.3. **P2**

- When considering the typical application for different programming approaches you should give some examples of the type of program these approaches should be used to write. **P1**

- When covering the limitations you should explain the likely disadvantages of each approach and what sort of applications they would not be normally used for. **P1**

1.4 Features

All programming languages have a number of common features. These enable the programmer to handle data (through variables), to structure a program (through loops, conditional statements and case statements involving logical operators) and to write the individual lines of code that set up the data and allow input and output to take place.

To help you understand the features that programs have we will look at some simple example programs written using the Visual Basic® Programming language.

Variables

All the data that is input into a program must be stored somewhere. Programs store this data in defined memory areas called variables. Variables are also used as temporary storage areas for data needed during processing and the data output by a program would normally come from program variables as well.

The contents of variables are lost when a program ends. For more permanent storage, programs must save (output) the data to files.

Variables have two important attributes:

- a name is allocated by the programmer to identify the variable within the program.
- a data type defines the sort of data that the variable can store (see page 173).

Naming conventions for variables expect the name to start with a letter and consist of any combination of numbers and letters (but not spaces). A name can be up to 255 characters long, but you cannot use any symbols (except the underscore symbol). You cannot use any of the **reserved words** in a language either.

You could name variables by simply using single letters of the alphabet, such as a, b or c. However, this is not recommended because it gives no clue as to the variable's use. A better approach is to give variables meaningful names such as 'counter' or 'student_age'.

Did you know?

Underscore in variable names such as 'student_age' is used to separate the words and create visually a more meaningful name.

Variables are normally declared, or created, at the beginning of a program. In Visual Basic®, for example, there is a **Dim** instruction, which takes the general form:

```
Dim variable_name As data_type
```

So, to declare a variable called student_age with an integer data type, your instruction would be:

```
Dim student_age As Integer
```

You could declare more variables with additional Dim instructions, but it is more efficient to list variables with the same data type in the same instruction:

```
Dim student_age, counter As Integer
```

Key terms

Reserved word – a word used within a programming language as part of a command, for example PRINT.

Dim – the instruction used in the Visual Basic® programming language to create a variable.

Array – a variable which rather than storing one value can store a series of related values (called elements), rather like a table.

Local and global variables

The 'scope' of a variable is an important concept.

Most programs are split into a number of different sections (usually called procedures, sub-routines or modules, depending on the language). Variables are normally declared within a section and can only be accessed and used within that section, not throughout the whole program. These are known as local variables. You can, however, declare variables which can be accessed and used across all the sections of a program. These are known as global variables.

In Visual Basic®, global variables are declared at the top of the program before all the different sub-routines. Instead of using the Dim key word, the variable name is preceded by 'Public shared':

```
Public Shared Grand_Total as Integer
```

Although there are occasions when you cannot avoid using global variables, they are not considered good practice. Problems can arise with global variables, especially in large and complex systems which are written by a team of programmers. There may be misunderstandings about how the global variables are used and different procedures may use them in different ways.

Arrays

Variables normally only store a single value but, in some situations, it is useful to have a variable that can store a series of related values – using an **array**. For example, suppose a program is required that will calculate the average age among a group of six students. The ages of the students could be stored in six integer variables:

```
Dim age1 as integer
Dim age2 as integer
Dim age3 as integer
...
```

However, a better solution would be to declare a six-element array:

```
Dim Age(5) as integer
```

This creates a six-element array, age(0) through to age(5). Note that arrays are numbered from zero.

Code structures

There are three basic structures which can be used to build a program, as follows.

- **Sequence** is when the program statements are followed one after the other. An example might be doing a calculation or accepting some input from the user.
- **Selection** (or a decision) is when a choice is made based on some criterion and in most programming languages this is implemented using the 'if' instruction.
- **Iteration** (or repetition) is when a section of code is repeated using a loop. The two main types of loop are fixed and conditional loops.

When designing a procedure, a structure diagram can be used to identify which types of structures are required.

Sequence statements

When the program needs to do things like calculations, accepting user input or outputting data, the program instructions are followed in sequence from top to bottom. But in many situations, a program needs to do different things, perhaps because of the input the user has made. In these situations selection is used.

Selection statements

Selection statements allow a choice to be made as to which set of statements are to be carried out next. The choice is made based on a criterion, such as the value of a variable, and this may depend, for example, on an option that the user has selected. In most programming languages, selection is done using the 'If' key word.

Generally, selection constructs take the form:

```
If (condition) then
    statements to be executed if the
    condition is true
else
    statements to be executed if the
    condition is false
end if
```

For example, the following simple *If* statement adds £2.50 postage and packing only if the total order is under £15:

```
If (ordertotal < 15) then
    ordertotal = ordertotal + 2.5
End if
```

The comparison operator < is used, which means 'less than'. A list of the comparison operators you can use is shown in Table 6.2.

Table 6.2: Comparison operators

Operator	Meaning
>	Greater than
<	Less than
=	Equal to
>=	Greater than or equal to
<=	Less than or equal to
<>	Not equal to

In the previous example there is no *Else* section to the statement, but you can use this to select which one of two sets of code statements are executed. This is shown in the next example which adds a discount of 5 per cent if the total order is over £50 or 10 per cent if it is over £100, but no discount for orders of £50 or less.

```
Dim discount As Single = 0
    If (ordertotal >100) Then
            discount = 0.1
    ElseIf (ordertotal >50) Then
            discount = 0.05
    End If
```

Case statements

The *If… Else …* constructs can become quite complex, especially where there are many different conditions to be tested. An alternative to using multiple If statements is to use a *Select case* statement. This takes the form:

```
Select case Variable_used_as_condition
    Case Is Condition
        Statements to be executed if
        condition is true
    Case Is Condition
        Statements to be executed if
        condition is true
    Etc.
End Select
```

The example code shown below gives an extension of the discount example – now there are four different discount levels:

```
Select Case ordertotal
   Case Is >1000
      discount = 0.25
   Case Is >500
      discount = 0.15
   Case Is >100
      discount = 0.1
   Case Is >50
      discount = 0.05
End Select
```

Iteration statements

Iteration is used where instructions need to be repeated either a certain number of times or until some criterion is met.

There are various types of **iteration construct**. The main two are:

- **Repeat – until**, which execute a fixed number of times
- **While – do**, which execute repeatedly until some condition is met.

Repeat – until

In Visual Basic® (and many other programming languages), Repeat – until is implemented using the For statement, which takes the general form:

```
For counter_variable = start_value to
end_value

    Statements to be executed inside
    the loop

Next
```

The counter variable (called counter_variable in the example) is a counter which is set to the start_value at the start of the section of code. The statements inside the section of code are executed and, when the Next statement is reached, the counter_variable is **incremented** and the loop is executed again.

This continues until the value in the counter variable reaches the end value. Then the loop stops and the statement following the next statement is executed.

This example shows how a For loop could be used to create a 4 times table:

```
Dim result As Integer
Dim counter As Integer
For counter = 1 To 12
    result = 4 * counter
    Console.WriteLine("4 times " &
    counter & " is " & result)
Next
Console.ReadLine()
```

While – do

While – do loops, as the name suggests, continue to loop until some condition is met. In Visual Basic®, these loops are implemented using the *Do…Loop Until* statement. Conditional loops can have the condition placed at the end of the loop, in which case they are known as post-check loops, and have the general format:

```
Do
    Statements to be executed inside loop
Loop Until condition
```

Alternatively, they can have the condition at the beginning, in which case they are known as pre-check loops:

```
Do Until condition
    Statements to be executed inside loop
Loop
```

The only difference is that with a post-check loop, the code within the loop is always executed at least once. With a pre-check loop, if the condition is met at the start of the loop, the code within the loop will not be executed at all. Therefore, the choice of which to use depends on the application.

The following piece of code will work out the average of the numbers entered. The user stops entering numbers by inputting an X (note that it must be a capital X):

Key terms

Iteration construct – (also called a loop) a part of a program that is repeated. For example, if you wanted a program that printed out a times table from 1 to 12, the most efficient way to write the program would be with a section of code that repeats 12 times.

Incremented – when 1 is added to a variable, so it 'counts'.

```
Dim numbers As String
Dim total As Integer
Dim counter As Integer = 0
Console.WriteLine("Averages program")
Console.WriteLine("Enter number, X to
exit")
numbers = Console.ReadLine
Do Until (numbers = "X")
   total = total + numbers
   counter = counter + 1
   Console.WriteLine("Enter number, X
   to exit")
   numbers = Console.ReadLine
Loop
Console.WriteLine("Average is " &
total \ counter)
Console.ReadLine()
```

In this example the condition is placed at the beginning of the loop (pre-check) since if the user inputs an X the loop must be exited before the rest of the loop is executed, otherwise an error will result when trying to add the X to the total.

Logical operators

The selection statements used in both *If* statements and in *Do Until* loops can use **logical operators** to combine two or more conditions. The logical operators are shown in Table 6.3.

Table 6.3: Logical operators

Operator	Meaning	Example
AND	Produces true if both sides are true	Age >18 AND Gender = 'F' Will only produce true if BOTH are true (over 18 and female)
OR	Produces true if either side is true	Age >18 OR Gender = 'F' Will produce true if EITHER the age is over 18 OR the gender is female
NOT	Produces the opposite result	NOT(UserInput = 'Y') Will produce false if the user input is 'Y', otherwise it will produce true

Key term

Logical operators – AND, OR and NOT are used to combine conditions together using Boolean logic.

The following example shows how a logical operator can be used in an *If* statement. It is another version of the code used to select the correct discount. In this case, some customers are 'Gold' customers, as they have ordered over a certain amount in the past. Gold customers automatically get the 25 per cent discount no matter how much they order. A variable called 'level' is used to record the fact that a customer is a Gold customer.

```
If (ordertotal >1000 Or level = 'Gold')
Then
    discount = 0.25
ElseIf (ordertotal >500) Then
    discount = 0.05
End If
```

In this example an *Or* logical operator is used to give the 25 per cent discount to any order that is over £1000 or is made by a Gold customer.

Assignment statements

Assignment statements are used to assign values to variables. The equals sign is the assignment operator and the value is assigned from right to left. So, in the following example, a value of 20 is assigned to the variable.

```
myVariable = 20
```

Did you know?

In some languages, the assignment sign is an equals sign preceded by a colon as in var := 0.

Assignments can also be done in combination with mathematical operators. For example:

```
myVariable = 20 + subtotal
```

This will take the value in the variable subtotal, add 20 to it and place the result in myVariable. The full list of mathematical operators is shown in Table 6.4.

Where operators are combined, the order in which they are executed is not left to right. Instead it is based on the order of mathematical precedence (as shown in Table 6.4). For example:

```
myVariable = 10 + 2 * 3
```

In this instruction the answer is not 36 but 16, as the multiplication is done first. Parentheses (brackets) can be used to modify the order – anything in parentheses will be done first:

```
myVariable = (10 + 2) * 3
```

This will produce a result of 36.

Table 6.4: Mathematical operators

Operator	Meaning	Example	Order of precedence
^	Exponentiation (raise to the power of)	2 ^ 3 = 8	1
*	Multiply	3 * 2 = 6	2
/	Division	5 / 2 = 2	3
Mod	Remainder part of division	5 mod 2 = 1	4
+	Add	4 + 5 = 9	5
-	Subtract	3 – 2 = 1	6

Input and output statements

In a visual programming language such as Visual Basic®, input and output are usually done via **controls**. Text boxes, list boxes and buttons are placed on the form or web page that is displayed to the user.

Visual Basic® is an event-driven language, so event procedures (sometimes called sub-routines) are written to respond to user events, such as clicking a button. The procedures can collect values that the user has entered in text boxes by assigning the text property of the text box to a variable. For example:

```
MyText = txtMyInput.text
```

This statement assigns the value entered in a text box called txtMyInput to a variable called MyText.

In a similar way, you can output a value to a text box or label simply by writing the assignment statement the other way around. So, to output text to a label called lblMyLabel, you would use the statement:

```
lblMyLabel.text = "Hello"
```

In this case, a string value has been used (note that it must be in double quotes), but a value contained in a variable could just as easily have been used. For example:

```
lblMyLabel.text = MyText
```

Figure 6.1 shows an example of a simple Visual Basic® form with a label, text box and button.

Key term

Control – an object on a form such as a text box, label or drop-down box. Controls have attributes which decide how they look (such as their colour and font) and behave.

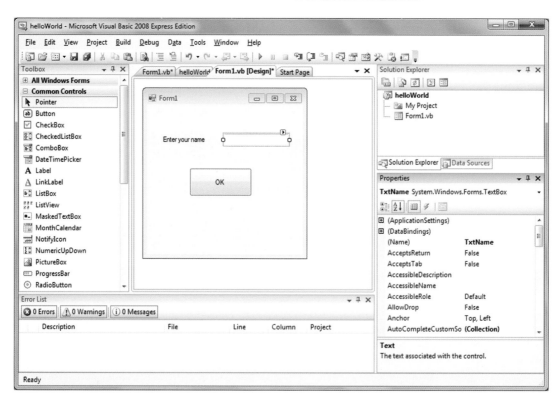

Figure 6.1: A Visual Basic® form

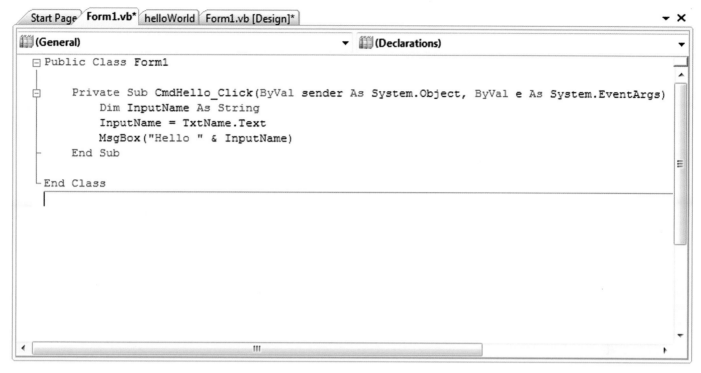

```
Start Page  Form1.vb*  helloWorld  Form1.vb [Design]*                          ▼ ✕

 (General)                                      ▼    (Declarations)                          ▼

 Public Class Form1

     Private Sub CmdHello_Click(ByVal sender As System.Object, ByVal e As System.EventArgs)
         Dim InputName As String
         InputName = TxtName.Text
         MsgBox("Hello " & InputName)
     End Sub

 End Class
```

Figure 6.2: CmdHello button click event procedure

Figure 6.2 shows the event procedure for the CmdHello button on the form.

1.5 Data types

Every variable has a data type. This sets the type of data that will be stored and the range of values that the variable can accept. It can also define how the data will be formatted when displayed. The data types supported by Visual Basic® and the range of data they can accommodate are listed in Table 6.5.

Choosing the right data type for a variable is important. Inappropriate choices could result in excessive amounts of storage space being set aside. If a variable is unable to accommodate the size of value assigned to it, the system will crash.

If a data item needs to be used in more than one part of a program, then it is important that the data type is consistent.

Data that you need to do calculations with must be placed in a numeric data type such as Integer or Single. However, you must ensure that only numeric data gets placed in these variables, as otherwise the program will crash.

Table 6.5: Data types supported by Visual Basic®

Type	Used for	Range of values
Boolean	Values that can be true or false	True or false
Byte	Whole numbers	0 to 255
Integer	Whole numbers	–32,768 to +32,767
Long	Very large whole numbers	Approx. plus or minus 2 billion
Currency	Decimal numbers with 2 digits after the decimal	
Single	Numbers with a decimal part (known as floating point)	Up to 7 significant digits
Double	Large numbers with a decimal part	Up to 14 significant digits
Date	Date and time	
Variant	Any type of data	
String	Any type of text	

Assessment activity 6.2

You have been asked to add to the presentation materials you created for Assessment activity 6.1. These new materials, in the form of PowerPoint® slides, should:

1 explain how sequence, selection and iteration are used when writing programs **P3**

2 explain why different data types are needed in programs and describe the benefits of having a variety of data types available to the programmer. **P4**

Grading tips

- You should include some annotated examples of simple programs which demonstrate how these are implemented. **P3**

- You should explain what different data types are available and give examples of how they are used. You should also explain why the choice of data type for a variable is important and what problems can arise if an unsuitable data type is used. You might also consider why different data types are available for numeric data and what the benefits are of using one type over another, for example why use Integer instead of Long? **P4**

PLTS

The research you will need to do for this assignment task will help show you are an **independent enquirer**.

Functional skills

The work you do on different data types for numeric values will help you develop your Functional Skills in **Mathematics**. Writing the materials for this assignment will help develop your Functional Skills in **English**, Writing. If you give the presentation you will prepare for this assignment task it will help develop your Functional Skills in **English**, Speaking and Listening.

2. Understand the principles of software design

You will need an understanding of the basic features of programming languages before you can start to write a program. Before that, though, you need to consider how to design programs. Writing all but the simplest of programs is a complex process that requires planning. Just as an architect needs to design a new house, the first step in creating software is to produce a detailed design.

Much of the work done at the design stage is done by a systems analyst rather than a programmer. Systems analysts are often people who were previously programmers and who use the experience gained in developing software to help them plan and design how complete systems will work.

2.1 Software development life cycle

Developing a complex piece of software is a process involving a number of steps. Generally these steps are:

- understanding the scope of the project
- identifying requirements
- designing the system
- writing (coding) the programs
- testing the programs work properly
- maintaining the system once it has begun to be used.

Figure 6.3 shows the software development lifecycle represented as a diagram.

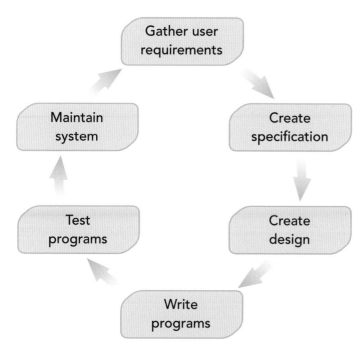

Figure 6.3: The software development lifecycle

Stages

Understanding the scope

The question being asked here is really, 'What will the system do, and what won't it do?' This may sound like an obvious question, but it is an important one to consider. It is also important to decide what is to be included and what is to be left out.

Computers are very powerful machines and there are many facilities you could include in the software you are developing if you had endless time and money. However, resources are likely to be limited. So, in some cases, you may want to decide on the most important features and to develop the first version of the software with those features. You would then put the remaining features on the 'wish list' for future versions.

Identifying requirements and specification

The next step in software development is to obtain a statement of the user requirements. What do they want the program to do? This may also sound like a simple question but, for a number of reasons, it is often difficult to answer.

- The user may not clearly understand what is required or they may not be able to give sufficient detail.

- The user requirements may be stated in terms which relate to their business and which the programmer may not be familiar with. For example, a user in the banking world will tend to state their requirements in banking and financial terms, but the programmer is an expert in programming, not banking.

- The user may not understand what is (and is not) possible when writing the software.

The user requirement may therefore need to be the subject of some discussion and negotiation between the user and the programmer.

There are a number of key questions that need to be asked.

- What are the primary aims of the system you are going to develop?

This is one of the first things that need to be defined and will probably be in terms of the problem that the system is intended to solve or some opportunity it will provide. It is important to clarify this at the start because, sometimes, during the process of developing the software, people can lose track of the original reason for which the software was required.

- How does the current system work?

In many cases, the software to be developed will replace an existing system. It may be a manual system (that is using people rather than computers) or it may be an old computer system that has outlived its usefulness. In any case, it is important to understand the current system thoroughly so that the new software can preserve its essential elements and its good features and avoid the problems from which it now suffers.

- What other systems does it need to interface with?

No system works in isolation. All systems take input, from the user or another computer system. They also produce some kind of output. Part of understanding the system to be developed involves defining these inputs and outputs. At this stage, there is no need to go into great detail – that will come later.

Designing the system

Once the scope and requirements have been defined, you need to consider how the program will achieve what is required. You will need to draw up a design for the program which defines:

- the user interface that will be provided – this might include designs for the screens that users will use to input data and the reports that will be output from the system

- the general structure of the program, including how it will be broken up into procedures and how those procedures will relate to each other
- the detailed design, showing how each of the procedures will carry out their required tasks
- how data will be stored by the system, including the variables that will be used and the file structures required.

A number of techniques can be used to produce this design, some of which are described in the Tools section (see page 183).

Coding the program

Once the design is complete, the task of coding the program can begin. In a large development project, this may involve a number of programmers, each of whom works on a different aspect of the system.

Testing the programs

As each part of the system is completed, it needs to be tested. Testing involves checking that the program works as it should and that all the functions and features of the program work correctly.

Testing is important to ensure the quality of the finished product and to ensure the program does not contain any **bugs**. It is also important to ensure that what has been produced matches the requirement outlined at the start of the project.

Maintaining the system

Once the program has been completed and is in use, the process is not over. Even with careful testing, it would be very unusual for a program not to experience problems when it is used for real. Such problems need to be corrected and there may also be improvements or additions to the program that are required. These issues are dealt with during the maintenance phase of the development cycle.

2.2 Software structures

The structure of a program depends on the type of programming language you are using. Procedural languages split the system into procedures while object-oriented (OO) languages are based on objects.

Key term

Bug – a fault or error in a program which causes it to crash (end unexpectedly) or produce unexpected results.

Functions

Most programming languages have a number of built-in facilities which carry out commonly required tasks for the programmer – these are usually called functions. Visual Basic® has two types of function: the built-in ones which are provided as part of the language and user-defined functions which can be written by the programmer.

An example of a Visual Basic® built-in function is the IsNumeric function. This function is passed a value (in the brackets that follow the function name) and returns a value of true if the value it has been passed is numeric or false if it is not numeric. This function can be very useful in validating values entered by the user to check they are numeric. For example, in the student records system one of the student details that needs to be entered is their age. The following code could be used to ensure that the value entered by the user is numeric:

```
If IsNumeric(txtAge.Text) Then
    age = txtAge.Text
Else
    MsgBox('Age must be numeric')
End If
```

There are of course many other built-in functions – some useful ones are shown in Table 6.6.

Procedures

Procedures have already been mentioned. Visual Basic® programs are mostly made up of event procedures which respond to user events, such as clicking a button. These procedures always start with a line of code which Visual Basic® creates for you, as shown in Figure 6.4.

For more information about the many other functions included in Visual Basic®, use Help.

Table 6.6: Useful functions

Function	Purpose	Example
Format()	Used for formatting values	If variable MyNumber contained 27.5 the following would format it as £27.50: format(MyNumber, '£0.00')
Rnd()	Produces a random number between 0 and 1 (useful for games etc.). Multiply it to get a number in a larger range	MyNumber = 10 * rnd() This will produce a random number between 1 and 10
Left$()	Selects characters from a string starting from the left	If variable MyString contained 'BTEC' the following would produce 'BT': left$(MyString, 2)
Right$()	Selects characters from a string starting from the right	If variable MyString contained 'BTEC' the following would produce 'TEC': right$(MyString, 3)
Lcase$()	Converts a string to lower case	If variable MyString contained 'BTEC' the following would produce 'btec': Lcase$(MyString)
Ucase$()	Converts a string to upper case	If variable MyString contained 'btec' the following would produce 'BTEC' Ucase$(MyString)

In this example, 'cmdHello' is the name of the button that this event procedure responds to. We know it responds to the user clicking the button as it contains the instructions 'Handles cmdCheck.Click'.

Visual Basic® event procedures always end with the instruction 'End Sub'. You must ensure you don't change the starting and ending instructions and that all your code for the event is between them.

Classes and objects

Object orientation involves linking the data and the functions together in the basic OO building block of the object.

Software objects are based on real-world things in the application area that the software is being written for.

- In a library system, the objects might include books, members and loans.
- In a mail order system, the objects might include customers, orders and products.

Objects generally represent either physical things, like customers and books, or conceptual things like an order or a loan.

Closely related to the concept of the object is the **class**. A class is like a template for the objects of that class. For example, in the class cars, objects of that class might be my Renault, the Queen's Rolls Royce and my neighbour's Ford. These are all instances of the class.

Key term

Class – in the OO approach to programming a class is a program building block which provides a template for the creation of objects.

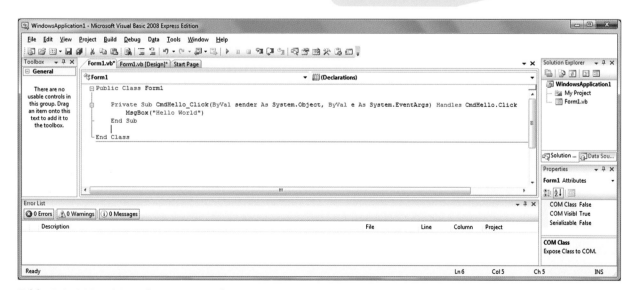

Table 6.4: A Visual Basic® event procedure

Classes have data associated with them, called **attributes**.

- A customer class would have attributes such as name, address, telephone number, etc.
- A book class would have attributes such as title, author, ISBN, publisher, etc.

Classes also have functions, called **methods**.

- A customer class might have a 'change of address' method.
- A book class in a library system might have a 'go on loan' method.

A class defines the attributes and methods and all objects of that class have the same attributes and methods.

Classes can be described by using a class diagram. This lists the name of the class, the attributes and the methods. Imagine a system that keeps track of the marks students have achieved in various assignments. Figure 6.5 shows the class diagram for the Student class. This simple class has just two attributes (name and marks) and three methods (set name, show marks and update marks).

An OO system is made up of objects (created using the class as a template) which work together by one object requesting a service from another object (using the methods of that class). This process of requesting services is known as **message passing**. For example, imagine a Tutor class. An object of the Tutor class might pass a message to the Student class asking it to invoke its showMarks method and the Student object returns the mark.

It is important to understand that the only way in which other objects can gain access to the attributes of a class is by the methods of that class. This is one of the key differences between the earlier approaches

Student
StudentName
StudentMarks
setName
showMarks
updateMarks

Figure 6.5: Class diagram for the Student class

to program design and the OO approach. In earlier methods data is passed between functions. In the OO approach, data is contained within the object and is accessible only by the object's methods. This concept is known as **abstraction of data**. This means that the object's users know nothing about how the data is manipulated inside the object.

Activity: Programming terms

1 List and describe the three main software structures.

2 What are functions? Give an example of how they can be used.

3 Explain what objects, classes and methods are.

Pre-defined code

Many different software systems share similar requirements and it may be that some functions can use procedures or code from previous projects. Using a pre-defined code can save a lot of time as the procedures have already been written and tested.

Readability

Complex software projects will often have standards set which the programmers on the project must follow. This will include things like adding comments to the programming code they write. Comments are ignored by the computer, but make it much easier for other people to read the code. This is important on a large project, particularly during the maintenance phase, when bug fixes or modifications may need to done by someone other than the programmer who originally wrote the code. Even on small software development projects, adding comments to the program instructions

Key terms

Attributes – the data that belongs to the class, i.e. the things that describe the class.

Methods – functions of a class, i.e. the things that the class can do.

Message passing – the technical name for the process by which one class gets another class to do something by calling one of its methods.

Abstraction of data – data within the object is hidden from the object's users.

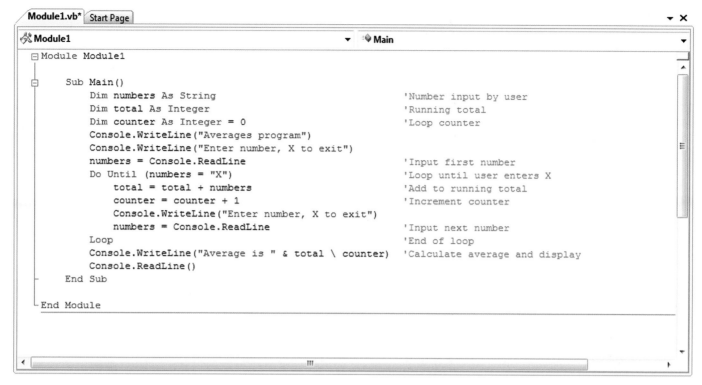

```
Module1.vb*  Start Page                                                    ▼ ✕
Module1                                         ▼   ◆ Main                   ▼
  Module Module1

      Sub Main()
          Dim numbers As String              'Number input by user
          Dim total As Integer               'Running total
          Dim counter As Integer = 0         'Loop counter
          Console.WriteLine("Averages program")
          Console.WriteLine("Enter number, X to exit")
          numbers = Console.ReadLine         'Input first number
          Do Until (numbers = "X")           'Loop until user enters X
              total = total + numbers        'Add to running total
              counter = counter + 1          'Increment counter
              Console.WriteLine("Enter number, X to exit")
              numbers = Console.ReadLine     'Input next number
          Loop                               'End of loop
          Console.WriteLine("Average is " & total \ counter)  'Calculate average and display
          Console.ReadLine()
      End Sub

  End Module
```

Figure 6.6: Program with comments

is regarded as good practice. Figure 6.6 shows an example of a program with comments added. In Visual Basic®, comments must be preceded by a single quotation mark and are coloured green automatically by the editor

Using appropriate names for variables is another example of good practice. Variables can be given names such as 'A' or 'B' or 'Data1'. However, these sorts of names give no clue as to the purpose of the variable. It's a much better idea to use names that describe what the variable is used for, such as StudentName or Unit1Grade (note that variable names cannot contain spaces). Some programmers recommend prefixing the variable name with a code which indicates its data type. So a text variable called StuName (shortened version of StudentName) might be named TxtStuName, while an integer variable called Points might be named IntPoints. This can help prevent the mistake of assigning an incorrect type of data to a variable, such as a text value to a numeric data-type variable.

A final example of good practice which improves readability of code is indenting loop or selection blocks of code, which makes it easier to see where they start and finish. In fact Visual Basic® does this for you.

Quality of code

It takes a long time and a lot of practice to become a proficient programmer and there are many pitfalls in writing programs that you really only learn about with experience. Some attributes of a well-written program are listed below.

- **Reliable and robust:** Although you might imagine users will use the program in the way it was intended, sometimes they may misuse it. For example, users may make a text input where a numeric one is expected. A well-written robust program will be able to cope with such a user error and display an error message rather than crashing. The best way to ensure a program is as robust as possible, is by thoroughly testing it to ensure it works properly and can cope with being used incorrectly.

- **Usability:** The best programs are easy to use and intuitive. Ease of use is a subject of its own (sometimes called HCI – Human Computer Interface), but there are some easy things you can do when designing the user interface to make a program easier to use. Clearly labelled controls (buttons, text boxes etc.), logically arranged controls (that is arranged in the order they are likely to be used) and controls grouped by function all make it easier for the user to figure out how the program is to be used.

- **Portability:** This is the ability of a program to run on different hardware or software platforms. This may be important for some systems. As mentioned earlier some languages, such as Java™, support many different types of hardware.

- **Maintainability:** Every commercial software product needs to be maintained with updates, bug fixes and new features.

There are a number of things that can be done to make software easier to maintain.

These include:

o good, detailed technical documentation describing the design and implementation of the software

o well-written programs – already mentioned are good practices such as adding comments, using meaningful variable names and indenting loop and selection instructions.

Assessment activity 6.3  **BTEC**

Following on from the previous assessment activity, create some additional PowerPoint® presentation materials covering the following topics.

1 Explain where software design and structures fit into the systems development life cycle. **P5**

2 Explain the importance of creating program code which is of high quality. Describe how the code quality can be improved. **P5** **M1**

3 Discuss the ways in which a programmer can make codes easier to read. **D1**

Where possible, include examples of the methods for improving the quality and readability of program code.

Grading tips

- Tasks 2 and 3 are probably best combined rather than being dealt with separately as quality of code and readability are closely linked. **M1** **D1**

- To cover M1 adequately you need to make sure you cover all the quality issues mentioned in the unit content. Remember that for a merit criterion you need to provide more than a descriptive list. You need to explain why the quality issues you list may be important in a particular development project. **M1**

- As with M1 a simple description of how to make a program more easily readable is not sufficient. You need to discuss the issues involved, the benefits and drawbacks of each technique used to improve readability, giving examples of actual code, and explaining what problems may arise if the technique is not used. **D1**

PLTS

The work you do towards criterion D1 will help show that you are a **creative thinker**.

Functional skills

Writing the materials for this assignment will help develop your Functional Skills in **English**, Writing. If you give the presentation you will prepare for this assignment task it will help develop your Functional Skills in **English**, Speaking and Listening.

3. Be able to use tools to demonstrate software designs

3.1 Requirements specification

The requirements specification stage of the development process involves identifying the user requirements, not identifying technical requirements – that comes later in the design stage. As previously mentioned this stage and the design stage are often carried out not by a programmer, but by a system analyst.

Clearly, this stage needs to be undertaken in close consultation with the users and there are various ways in which their requirements can be defined. One way is to ask users to make a list of what they require from the new system. Another is for the systems analyst to interview users to identify what they think needs to be achieved by the new system. It is important for the users to prioritise the list of requirements, as not all may be achievable due to constraints on time or money. The end result of the requirements stage is a document which describes in detail what the user requires. This is usually agreed with the users before work on the design of the system begins.

We will look at the various sections of the requirements specification in turn.

Inputs

The purpose of this section of the requirements specification is to identify the data that will be input to the system. Because it is important that the data that is input is correct, it should be validated. So, the users will need to identify what would be valid and invalid input for each data item. This might be in terms of ranges of acceptable values if the data is numeric or a list of valid text entries. The information about the input data will be used at the design stage to create the data dictionary and DFDs for the system (see page 185). It will also be used much later when testing the system to ensure that the validation works as required.

Outputs

The purpose of this section is to identify the outputs that the users will expect from the system. As with the input, this information will later be used in the creation of the DFDs.

Processing

In this section, the user defines what functions the program will need to have. This should not be thought of as processing in the technical programming sense, but rather the user's explanation of the functions or facilities that the program should have and what they should do from the user's perspective.

User interface

This section outlines the type of user interface required, including any special requirements such as touch screens or special methods of input, for example a bar code scanner. With the user interface being the most obvious point of interaction between the users and the system, the developers may involve the users quite closely in the design of this part of the system, perhaps through the creation of 'prototype' versions of the software so that users can test out the look and feel of the interface.

A number of different tools may be used to define and design the screens that will provide the interface between the system and its users. Storyboards are often used – these are simply drawings that show how the screens will appear on the user's computer at various stages of the interaction.

Did you know?

Storyboards are commonly used in the film and TV industry to design and develop scenes in a drama.

Figure 6.7 shows an example of a storyboard created at the specification stage and the actual form created when the program was written.

Constraints

Every software development project has a limit on the funds and time available to complete the project and this budget is normally set by the sponsors of the

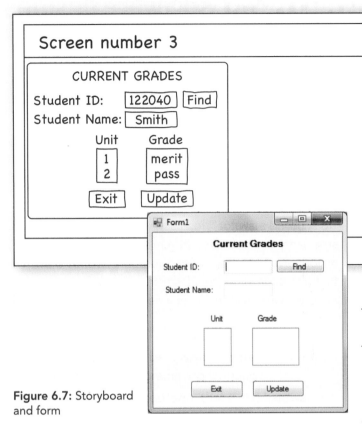

Screen number 3	Designed by: Wendy Smith
CURRENT GRADES Student ID: [122040] [Find] Student Name: [Smith] Unit Grade [1] [merit] [2] [pass] [Exit] [Update]	Used to display and update student grades. User enters Student ID number and presses the 'Find' button. Details for that student are then displayed. • Exit button goes to Main Menu • Update button goes to the Update Grades screen

Figure 6.7: Storyboard and form

project. The requirements specification will need to estimate the cost of completing the project, including the cost of hardware and software, manpower for developing new software and training.

The new development will probably also have cost benefits. These might be tangible cost benefits, such as reduced costs of processing or manpower, increased sales, etc., or they may be intangible benefits such as improved customer service. The systems analyst may have to identify what cost–benefits the project sponsors are expecting and to consider these carefully to see if they are achievable. This section is sometimes known as a cost–benefit analysis.

3.2 Design

Having completed the investigation stage and received the go-ahead from management, developers can move on to the next step – producing a design. The system design provides more detailed information about the internal working of the software. Much of what is done at this stage involves taking what has already been decided at the investigation stage and adding more detail to it. There are a number of things that need to be designed and planned, such as how the program will look to the user, what data the program will need to store and how that data will be processed.

Structure

Where the problem is large and complex, consideration also needs to be given as to how it can be split into manageable sections. The key to deciding how to split up a problem is to choose sections that can be as self-contained as possible. Clearly, when dividing a system into different sections (called modules or procedures), the modules will need to communicate with each other (probably by passing values, often called parameters) to a certain degree. However, this should be kept to a minimum, with each module having a clearly defined purpose and as little interaction with other modules as possible.

Where several programmers are working on the same software development project, dividing the system up into modules is necessary so that each programmer can work on an individual module. Dividing a program into modules also makes the testing easier, because developers can test each module as it is completed rather than having to wait until the whole program is complete.

Table 6.7: A data dictionary

Variable name	Scope (Local or Global)	Data type	Used for
StudentNo	Local	Integer	ID number of student
Name	Local	String	The name of the student
Age	Local	Integer	The age of the student
Course	Local	String	The course the student is on
AddrLine1	Local	String	Address line 1
AddrLine2	Local	String	Address line 2
Town	Local	String	Town
Postcode	Local	String	Postcode

Data and files

Data dictionaries are used to list all of the data items that a program will use. They should include all the relevant information about the variables, including the name of the variable, the data type that will be used, the scope of the variable (local or global) and the procedure the variable is used in. If the program needs to read and write data to files then the structure of the file, or files, will be defined with their own data dictionaries listing the file names, field names, data types, etc. When the software being developed uses a database system, the data dictionary will relate to the Entity Relationship Models (ERMs) that will be drawn up and will include information on primary and foreign keys (for information on ERMs see page 185). An example data dictionary is shown in Table 6.7.

3.3 Tools

Developing programs is a complex process and, over the years, a number of different tools have been developed to model the way a software system will work. Most of the techniques involve creating diagrams, often starting with simple ones and then building up to more complex ones as the understanding of the system develops.

As Visual Basic® is an event-driven system, any system developed with it naturally breaks down into the procedures that run as the various events occur. In simple programs, most of these event procedures are associated with command buttons. Therefore, creating the design for the user interface will often identify the main procedures in the program.

The design tools used are often chosen to match the language that is to be used at the coding stage, but this is not essential. Instead, they can serve to bridge the gap between the original problem and the solution that will, eventually, be coded. The diagrams produced clarify the problem and provide a way of communicating it to all concerned.

Structure diagrams

One tool that can be used to define the steps that are required within a procedure is a **structure diagram**. This defines how the system will be broken down into procedures. It can also be used to model the working of individual procedures by showing how they can be split into decision structures and loops.

Key term

Structure diagram – a simple diagram that shows how a program will be split into procedures.

Case study: Northgate College

Northgate College requires a program that will keep track of students, including their personal details and the course(s) on which they have enrolled. The system needs to provide the following functions:

- enter new students on the system
- search for an individual student
- produce class lists of students by course.

This list is used to create the first simple structure chart, which breaks the system down into the three functions, as shown in Figure 6.8.

Having created one level of structure chart, more detailed structure charts can be created for the individual modules within the system.

The 'Enter new students' module needs to validate the details entered by the user (such as the student's age and postcode) to check they are correct. This

requires a decision structure, because if the details are valid they can be saved, but if they are invalid an error message should be displayed. When drawing a structure chart, a decision structure is shown as a box with a circle in the corner, as in Figure 6.9.

The 'Produce class list' module requires a loop. First the course for which the class list is required must be identified. Then records of the student details on file need to be read off one by one until the end of the file is reached, using a loop. The records of the students who are enrolled on the course in question need to be displayed. Records for students on other courses can be ignored. The structure chart for this module is shown in Figure 6.10. A loop structure is shown as a box with an asterisk (*) in it.

1 Is the box process 'Input class required' (Figure 6.9) all that is required? Does the class number or name need validating? What would happen if the class entered did not exist? Add more detail to this part of the chart.

2 Produce a structure chart of the 'Search for an individual student' process shown in Figure 6.8.

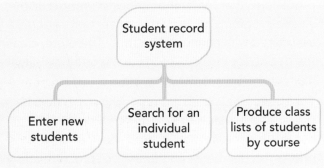

Figure 6.8: Basic structure chart

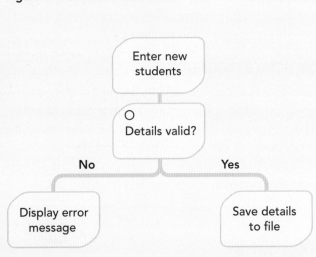

Figure 6.9: Structure chart for the 'Enter new students' module

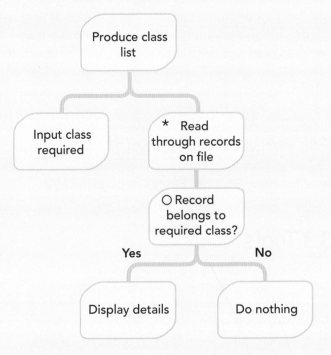

Figure 6.10: Structure chart for the 'Produce class list' module

Case study: External entities

For the Northgate College student records system, the external entities are:

- administration staff who enter student details and enrol them on the courses – input data flow
- teachers who request student lists for their classes – input data flow (to request the particular list) and output data flow (to produce the list).

To draw the high-level data flow diagram (DFD) for this, take a piece of A4 paper and write each of the external entity names inside an ellipse (an oval shape) around the outside of the paper. In the centre of the page draw a single process box, with the name of the system in it. Now add in arrows indicating the data flows that have been identified. With input data flows, the arrow must point into the process box. The output arrows must

point from the process box to the external entity. Each arrow must be labelled with the data flow name.

The complete high-level DFD for the student records system is shown in Figure 6.11.

1 Are there any other external entities, and/or additional data flows in or out of the system, that might exist in a real-life student records system?

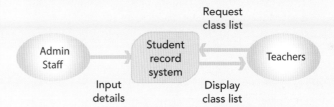

Figure 6.11: High-level DFD for the student records system

DFDs and ERMs

A data flow diagram (DFD) is concerned with how data flows into and out of the system, how it flows between the procedures inside the system and how it is stored inside the system.

Entity relationship models (ERMs) are used to model the relationships that exist between different entities (data items) in the system.

So far the DFD has used external entities, processes and data flows. A new component is needed for the low-level DFD: the data store (see Figure 6.12). This is drawn as an open-ended box and is where data is held or stored in the system. It represents real-world stores of data such as files, lists, tables, etc. When drawing DFDs, only a process can write or read data to, or from, a data store and each data store must be written to and read from at least once.

Both process boxes and data stores are numbered for identification purposes. The one shown in Figure 6.12 is numbered D1.

The same external entities and the same data flows in and out of the external entities should appear in both the low-level and the high-level DFD. If you realise that you have missed out an external entity and/or data flow, you must redraw your high-level DFD.

You may find it helpful to practise drawing DFDs in small groups so you can discuss different ways of drawing the diagrams.

When an analyst has used the DFDs to identify the processes and data stores in the system, the entity relationship models (ERM) can be produced – although in some cases the ERMs are produced first, then the DFD. There is no strict order in producing these diagrams. Often the design evolves over some time with DFDs, ERMs and other diagrams being refined through several versions.

Entities are real-world things (customers, products, books) that need to be represented in the system. Entities have attributes – these are the elements that define a particular entity. Some simple examples are shown in Table 6.8.

Table 6.8: Examples of entities and attributes.

Entity	Possible attributes
Customer	Name Address Credit limit
Product	Description Type Price
Book	Title Publisher Price

D1	Student Details

Figure 6.12: A data store

Case study: Low level DFD

The single process in the high-level DFD of the student records system can be broken into two processes in the low-level DFD (see Figure 6.13).

Finally, a data store is added, along with data flows that write data to the data store and read data from it. The data store is used to hold the student details. The completed low-level DFD is shown in Figure 6.14.

1 Think of a simple application, such as a system for tracking books in your college or school library, then create a high-level and a low-level DFD for the system.

2 Once you have created your DFDs, work in small groups to compare your DFDs. Remember that there is not always one single correct way to draw the DFD for a given system.

Creating DFDs can be quite difficult and requires practice. It may take several attempts to get a DFD right. Following the rules will help, but there is not necessarily just one correct diagram for a particular system.

Although this course only looks at two levels of DFDs, an analyst may go on decomposing the processes in the DFD to show even more detail.

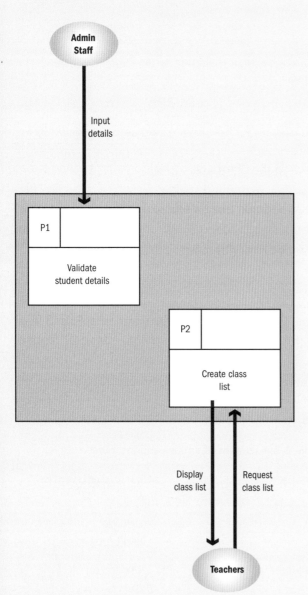

Figure 6.13: Processes added to the low-level DFD

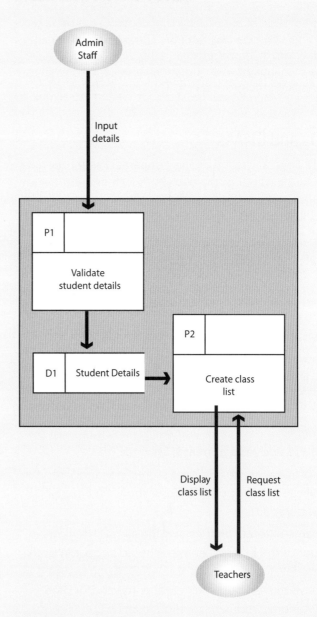

Figure 6.14: Complete DFD

Credit value: 10

7 Organisational systems security

In the management of any networked computer system, IT professionals need to consider every aspect of the system's security to protect the corporate interests of the organisation it supports.

This unit describes threats and methods of securing systems and the impact of threats on various organisations. As you read this, please consider that there are already more threats to your system than are mentioned here, be it at home, college or work.

> **WATCH OUT!**
>
> This unit covers 'hacking technologies'. Carrying out some of the techniques explored in this chapter on a network without the direct permission of the network manager is a criminal offence. See the section on the Computer Misuse Act on page 220.

Learning outcomes

After completing this unit you should be able to:

1. understand the impact of potential threats to IT systems
2. know how organisations can keep systems and data secure
3. understand the organisational issues affecting the security of IT systems.

Assessment and grading criteria

This table shows you what you must do in order to achieve a pass, merit or distinction grade, and where you can find activities in this book to help you.

To achieve a **pass** grade the evidence must show that you are able to:	To achieve a **merit** grade the evidence must show that, in addition to the pass criteria, you are able to:	To achieve a **distinction** grade the evidence must show that, in addition to the pass and merit criteria, you are able to:
P1 explain the impact of different types of threat on an organisation **See Assessment activity 7.1, page 203**	**M1** discuss information security **See Assessment activity 7.1, page 203**	
P2 describe how physical security measures can help keep systems secure **See Assessment activity 7.2, page 216**		
P3 describe how software and network security can keep systems and data secure **See Assessment activity 7.2, page 216**	**M2** explain the operation and use of an encryption technique in ensuring security of transmitted information **See Assessment activity 7.2, page 216**	**D1** discuss different ways of recovering from a disaster **See Assessment activity 7.2, page 216**
P4 explain the policies and guidelines for managing organisational IT security issues **See Assessment activity 7.3, page 224**		
P5 explain how employment contracts can affect security **See Assessment activity 7.3, page 224**		
P6 review the laws related to security and privacy of data **See Assessment activity 7.3, page 224**	**M3** explain the role of ethical decision making in organisational IT security **See Assessment activity 7.3, page 224**	**D2** evaluate the security policies used in an organisation **See Assessment activity 7.3, page 224**

How you will be assessed

This unit will be assessed by a number of internal assignments that will be designed and marked by the staff at your centre. It may be subject to sampling by your centre's Lead Internal Verifier or an Edexcel Standards Verifier as part of Edexcel's ongoing quality assurance procedures. The assignments will be designed to allow you to show your understanding of the unit outcomes. These relate to what you should be able to do after completing this unit.

Your tutor will tell you precisely what form your assessments will take, but you could be asked to produce:

- presentations
- illustrated reports
- leaflets
- case studies.

Mary Roach, BTEC National IT learner

I am not very technical and this sounds like a technical unit – lots of stuff on viruses, hacking, denial of service attacks, as well as really boring legal stuff (who wants to know about the Copyright, Design and Patents Act?)

When I started it, I was fascinated by the challenges facing organisations and impressed by what they have to do to remain legal as well as protect their systems. In fact I must admit, I was intrigued by the different attacks and crimes that take place and very interested in the methods used to detect and prevent them.

When I worked on my assignment, I had the opportunity to investigate how different illegal activities take place and understand some of the methods used. While most of the work was written, it could also be given as a presentation, with many accompanying images, diagrams and charts.

Personally, looking at how local organisations protect their systems has given me a greater understanding of what is happening in the real world. My career in the IT profession will depend on this knowledge. Hopefully I too may become a network security expert.

Over to you

When reading this chapter, ask yourself the following questions:

- **What vulnerabilities are there on the computers at home?**
- **How could I improve my personal practice, to make my use of systems more secure?**
- **What is the best way of securing any system I may use?**
- **In the world around me, where are there examples of different attacks?**

1. Understand the impact of potential threats to IT systems

Watch out, watch out – there be hackers about

In small groups, search the Internet for news stories of companies whose network security has been compromised.

Do a mini-presentation to the rest of your class. Discuss who the company is, what their 'line of business' is and how the security breach is likely to have damaged their reputation.

1.1 Potential threats

The landscape of threats to an organisation, and the IT which supports it, is constantly changing, with new, imaginative and often destructive ideas being developed all the time. This section looks at potential threats and their impact on organisations. These include methods for gaining unauthorised access, damage and destruction of systems and information, information security, e-commerce threats, counterfeit goods and the overall impact of threats on organisations.

Malicious damage

Sadly, the threat of malicious damage (through internal and external causes) to a system is constant. Malicious damage can be caused by an external hacker hacking into and attacking systems or by a disgruntled employee seeking revenge against management for, say, an unsatisfactory pay rise. While there are many security techniques available to limit access, dedicated and devious hackers will always find a way to cause damage. This is covered in more detail in subsection 1.2 on page 195.

Activity: Cyber damage

1 Complete a search on well-known search engines for 'cyber damage'.

2 Find out how many insurance companies now offer cover for this possibility.

Threats related to e-commerce

Since the dramatic increase in the use of e-commerce since 1996, this area has become another battleground in the war against hacking and other criminal activities. This is covered in more detail in section 1.3 on page 199.

Counterfeit goods

The trade and exchange of counterfeit goods has a two-fold impact.

- It affects the creator of the software, game, movie or music as there is a direct loss of potential income.

- It places the recipient in an illegal position where they could endure a heavy fine, be sued for damages and have all their equipment seized.

This is covered in section 1.4 in more detail on page 201.

Technical failure

While networking and computing technology has become increasingly reliable over the last 20 years, the complex nature of the systems being used means that technical failure is still always a risk. The loss of a server, storage devices, or an Internet connection, can cause considerable disruption to any individual worker, as well as to an organisation as a whole.

With our increased dependence on networked technology, with voice-, video- and CCTV-based systems being transmitted across many systems, technical failure can cause commercial damage, as well as compromise the security of the system.

Human errors

Human error is probably the most unpredictable yet most constant cause of security threat in any networked system. Forgetfulness, ignorance, innocence and lack of knowledge can all contribute to systems failure and the increased potential of a security breach.

Forgetting to back up data, to place data in a secure location, to erase a hard drive before a computer is disposed of, or to close a port on a firewall when installed, can all cause serious problems on a networked system.

Ignorance and the lack of appreciation of the need for network and general systems security have been the most common cause of network intrusion and virus infection. With the increase in use of broadband/ADSL connections over the last few years, there has been a noted increase in 'hack attacks' and virus/worm/trojan transmission. (For more on these threats, see pages 196–97.) As a result, firewalls are now common on most operating systems, with many home and commercial users more aware of the issues.

However, many otherwise intelligent and well-informed individuals have succumbed to social engineering and phishing attacks (see page 197). Innocent misunderstandings can lead to the best people being deceived. Avoiding such attacks comes through learning from experience, both good and bad. For many, forgetting once and seeing the effects means it will not happen again.

Activity: Portable data

One area of concern in recent years has been the accidental loss of USB memory, where some civic-minded individual has been pleased to hand it in to a national newspaper. Using your preferred search engine, search for relevant news stories, as well as sites advising on the use of USB memory in organisations.

Theft of equipment

Theft of data and technical property can have a long-lasting impact on an organisation or an individual. Theft can take place both in the 'cyber' sense, as with hacking, or in the physical sense, with data being removed on CD/DVDs or USB memory. Discarded printouts which have not been shredded might be stolen and the theft of computers is also a possibility. Theft of data can have many serious consequences, including long-term commercial damage, a competitor gaining an advantage (even if it is not they who have stolen the data), loss of goodwill with customers, financial ruin through loss of fiscal control, the inability to track current business, loss of employment (often for the employee whose error has allowed the theft to occur) and legal action.

Theft of technical property can have the same impact as the theft of data. Laptops that are used outside the office, as well as external hard drives, can constitute a major risk.

1.2 Malicious damage

Internal and external threats

To appreciate the types of threats posed to any system, you need to identify the different internal and external threats in existence. Unfortunately, you cannot rely on all the people using your network to be entirely trustworthy. Internal threats and external threats may include those shown in Table 7.1.

Table 7.1: Internal and external threats

Internal threats are from within your system	External threats are from outside the network infrastructure
Use of scanners	Virus attacks
Man in the middle attacks	Trojans
Magic disk tactics	Worms
Key logging	Hacking with piggybacking, tunnels and probes
	Forging data
	Phishing and identity theft

Access causing damage

In gaining unauthorised access the software used may cause damage to data or jamming (restricting) resources. Some attacks may have the intent of accessing systems or data without damage and the impact may initially go unnoticed. Whatever the intent, an intrusion always has an impact on the system.

Virus attacks

Virus attacks occur when a rogue code has entered the system. A virus will hide itself inside ordinary executable code and can do the following.

- Be a nuisance, for example opening/closing the CD/DVD door, swapping key responses (£ for @, etc.).

- Self-reproduce, spreading itself from application to application to evade detection and elimination.

- Cause serious damage to data and cause critical damage to the hard drive.

Viruses are concealed by a simple deception. They will embed themselves inside an application, redirecting its commands and code around itself while running as a separate task (see Figure 7.1).

Most virus scanners will detect a virus by opening the file and scanning the code, looking for this type of redirection. Ironically, students who create code in languages such as Pascal, C++ or Java™ can get stuck, because their programming style is treated as suspect by their college's virus scanner.

Many anti-virus applications will create a hash (known as an **MD5**) for each application. If the MD5 changes, this may be treated as a virus attack (or an application update). For more on MD5, see page 207.

Once found, the anti-virus application offers the option to remove or isolate the virus in a quarantine zone (see Figure 7.2).

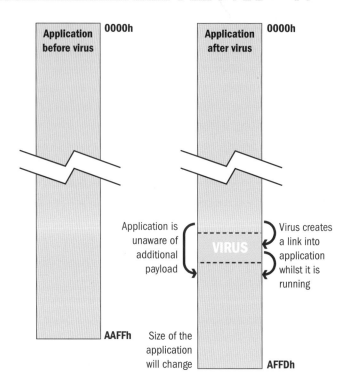

Figure 7.1: How a virus is concealed

Key term

MD5 – an independent code that represents the data inside an application. If the program is altered (by a virus) then the code will change, rendering the application subject to tampering.

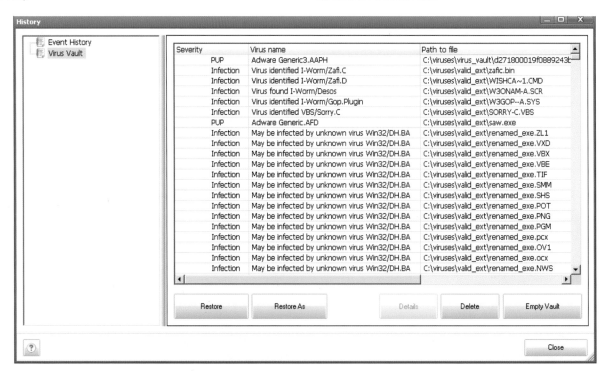

Figure 7.2: A virus quarantine

Trojans

Trojans are stealth applications, which are designed to allow others to access your system. Transported via infected email attachments, infected downloads, infected CD/DVDs, or worms which use vulnerabilities in your operating system, trojans have the potential to cause the most damage. An infamous trojan is Sub-7, which has been used for key logging, pranks, remote attacks (controlling your computer to start the real attack) and distributed **denial of service** attacks (see page 200).

Worms

Worms are self-transporting applications which carry an active payload such as a trojan or a virus. Worms are active or passive. Active worms self-transport without human intervention, while passive worms rely on the user's innocence to transport themselves from one location to another.

Active worms use email, vulnerabilities in your operating system, the web and DNS servers, as well as other alternative 'traffic' systems, to move their payload around a network infrastructure.

While many system weaknesses have been patched up over the years, worms still exist and often exploit the unsuspecting. Many worms are currently attempting to exploit VoIP systems like Skype or chat systems such as Windows® Live Messenger.

Access without damage

Some hackers are very effective at getting into your system without appearing to leave any trace of what they have accomplished. It is therefore essential that you:

- continuously check your system
- ensure all anti-virus systems are up to date
- are able to educate staff on what to be watchful for.

Sadly, you may not discover you have an issue until some considerable time later, when your organisation realises that it has a problem with competitors or customers.

Phishing and identity theft

Phishing and identity theft are relatively recent developments in methods for unauthorised access. The purpose of a phish (pronounced fish!) is to lure you into revealing personal information. It does this by social engineering, that is using something or someone trusted by you. Phishing employs many tactics, which are evolving all the time. For example:

- an email purporting to be from a long-forgotten school friend, looking for contact details – this leads to identity theft
- an email that claims to be from your bank, ISP, etc., asking you to follow a link to their site to update your details – the email looks authentic and when you follow the link, the site looks very much like the site of the bank/ISP, except the protocol is unlikely to be HTTPS and some links on the page may not be operational.

Phishing may also exploit **homographs** and our detailed reading skills by directing us to domain names with similar spellings. (Have you ever mistyped a domain name with surprising results?)

Piggybacking, tunnels and probes

Hacking attacks using piggybacking, tunnels and probes can be formed when network traffic is 'corrupted'.

- **Piggybacking:** This is when a normal, safe communication carries an additional harmful payload of a trojan or covert application.

Key terms

Denial of service – when a service (such as a web server) is sent so much traffic that it slows down to the point of failure, either through the lack of bandwidth or through an increased load for its processor to handle.

Homograph – one of two or more words that have the same spelling, but differ in meaning.

- **Tunnels:** These can be formed via existing communication channels to send alternative data. Common data channels, such as port 80, are used for HTTP. Someone with the necessary level of network expertise could send any data they wish via this port and create a wide range of applications running underneath one innocent communication channel.
- **Probe:** This can use an open, and therefore available, port to start an in-depth analysis of a network or computer system. Once the open hole is found, it will start digging into the system.

Forging data

Forging, or spoofing, data requires knowledge of programming in networking languages such as Java™ (see Figure 7.3), C++ or VB.NET. A hacker could 'hand craft' a **data packet** to force an application or server to give away information, cause a denial of service attack (see page 200) or piggyback/tunnel into a system via an 'acceptable' protocol. The code needed to accomplish this is on the Internet and is openly available on many non-hacking websites.

Key term

Data packet – when data is sent from one computer system to another it is broken down into smaller units of data (the packet).

Hacking

Hacking is a criminal offence covered by the Computer Misuse Act. Hacking may sound a wonderful idea, but is treated by many nations as a criminal offence.

Various law enforcement agencies employ experts with skills to use measures to detect and respond to any cyber criminal activity. It is normally only a matter of time before detection as most computer technologies include mechanisms to uniquely identify the computer being used.

Activity: Hacking the hackers

There has been a number of high profile cases where hackers have been caught and subjected to long terms in prison. Research these cases, the crime committed and the penalty imposed.

```java
import java.io.*;
import java.net.*;
public class forgeData
{
    private static void delay(int duration)
    {
        try{
            new Thread().sleep(duration*1000);
        }
        catch(InterruptedException e)
        {
        }
    }
public static void main(String[] args)
throws IOException
{
    System.out.println('Forge Data');
    Socket echoSocket = null;
PrintWriter out = null;
String host = 'dodgywebsite.org.uk';
        int ping = 100;
        int port = 80;
        String userInput = 'blah!';
try
{
echoSocket = new Socket(host, port);
}
catch (UnknownHostException e)
{
System.err.println('Don't know about
host');
System.exit(1);
}
catch (IOException e)
{
System.err.println('Couldn't get I/O for
the connection');
System.exit(1);
}
out = new PrintWriter(echoSocket.
getOutputStream(), true);
        for (int loop=1;loop<=ping;loop++)
        {
        out.println(userInput);
        System.out.print('!');
        delay(1);
        }
        out.close();
        echoSocket.close();
        System.out.println('');
        System.out.println('.... Finished');
}
```

Figure 7.3: Java™ code to send 'hand-crafted' packets

1.3 Threats related to e-commerce

Website defacement

Website defacement is an incredibly common nuisance attack. It involves a brand of hackers called **crackers** looking for **script** or version vulnerabilities in web servers and website code. Once crackers have found the vulnerability, they can 'edit' the **HTML** and/or the script on the website to display their own version of the site. For example, they might change the website to show:

- sexually explicit or other inappropriate images
- their personal tag to impress other crackers and prove it was them
- political or religious statements, depending on the site attacked
- random statements of a childish nature.

While such attacks are seldom financially motivated, there have been some cases of organised criminals trying to use this technique for their own gain by writing in **meta-refresh** tags to forward victims to their own 'spoofed' site (which comes under the domain of phishing).

Key terms

Cracker – a type of hacker who 'breaks in' to a website to display their own version of the site.

Script – programming code, often short and used as part of another system. The most common web script language is JavaScript.

HTML – stands for hyper text mark-up language

Meta-refresh – an HTML tag which redirects the website visitor to another web page.

Web 2.0 – represents a development in web technology that allows different systems to share data via common methods of data exchange. Many social media resources such as Twitter and Facebook® make extensive use of Web 2.0 technology.

Third party – in the context of retail and e-commerce, this is an additional organisation that is involved in the commercial transaction. It is called a third party because it is additional to the supplier and the customer

---

For an e-commerce system, any form of website defacement is an issue. Apart from the time and income lost as the website is recovered, there is the potential loss of goodwill with customers who may stop trusting the site. They might ask the question *If hackers can change the web page, can they get into my account?*

Control of access to data via third-party suppliers

With the advent of **Web 2.0** the ease with which many organisations can share their data with **third-party** suppliers has increased. While this has always been an issue, as technology progresses, it has become easier.

The challenge lies in particular where data is involved, especially personal data. For example, consider the following:

- Booking a flight. Who else needs to see this information?
- Taking a holiday. Which other organisations is the holiday company required to share this information with?
- Your education. Who does your centre need to share your information with?

For organisations who need to provide data to third-party suppliers, the exchange is regulated by a binding legal contract, clearly defining what will be given, how it will be used and how long it may be retained.

This data relationship is controlled by the Data Protection Act 1998 (see page 221) and has to be recorded and managed by the data owner. Even a data item as seemingly trivial as your birthdate needs to be carefully managed, as this is a key resource for those interested in identity theft.

Some e-commerce sites use third-party suppliers to enhance the services they offer. Instead of directly stocking and selling the service or product, they act as an agent (or outlet) for the third-party supplier. This approach is common on sites such as eBay™ and Amazon. eBay™ offers its services to private retailers who set up an 'eBay shop'™. Amazon cannot feasibly stock all the products and services it offers and so extends its portfolio by acting as a go-between for many other sites (see Figure 7.4 on page 200).

The principal weakness of working with third-party suppliers is the threat to the commercial security of an organisation, as well as the personal security of the customer because of the need to exchange personal information in the transaction.

eBay™ overcame the financial transaction issue by creating the PayPal system, which acts as a level of obscurity in hiding the financial information of the third-party supplier and the customer from each other. Amazon approaches the problem by taking the income directly and then sending the supplier an agreed fee.

The risk remains when sending the goods, as the third-party supplier has to obtain the address details of the customer. This allows the supplier to collect customer details which, in turn, increases their customer base and potentially enables them to set up shop alone.

An additional issue is the matter of trust. While e-commerce sites work with third-party suppliers, they ensure that the exchange of data, especially financial data, is carefully managed. Some third-party retailers never deliver on their goods, which has an adverse impact on the good name of the e-commerce site. To combat this, eBay™ and Amazon manage a fraud and complaints section to remove any rogue suppliers

Denial of service attacks

There have been many distributed denial of service attacks over the years, with worms being devised to leave trojans that will send traffic from multiple devices. While firewalls can be configured to prevent most uninvited traffic from entering the system, traffic can be 'crafted' to evade many systems as well as

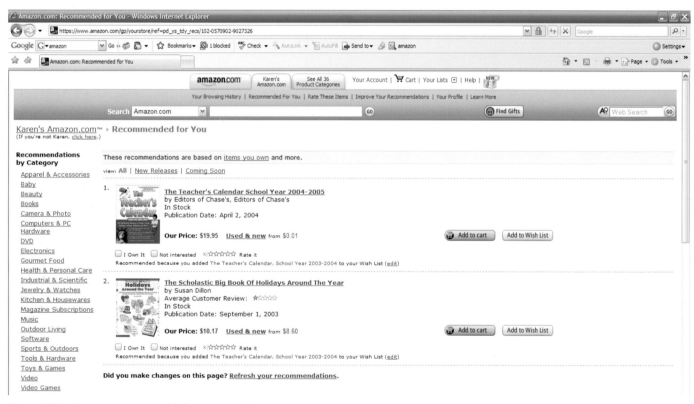

Figure 7.4: Amazon acts as a third-party supplier

flood a firewall and cause problems at the entry point to the system.

For an e-commerce system, any denial of service is a denial of income. While the denial of service attack may only last for a few minutes, with the loss of service and the recovery time, an organisation stands to lose a considerable amount of income.

Activity: E-commerce attacks

1   What examples of e-commerce attacks can you find in the media?
2   Try to find out how the organisations involved combated these attacks.

Activity: Threat analysis

1   What are the various types of threats to organisations, systems and data?
2   What is the impact of these threats?
3   What are the most common threats?
4   How can the risk of threats be reduced?

1.4 Counterfeit goods

As described on page 194, the trade and exchange of counterfeit goods has a two-fold impact, which puts various products at risk and puts recipients in an illegal position because of the distribution mechanisms used by counterfeiters.

Products at risk

With the technology to duplicate all media formats using a computer system readily available, pirates can create a comprehensive collection of illicit media, placing many products at risk.

Software and games can be easily copied using CD/DVD duplication software, and software now exists to create images of the CD/DVD and load these as a virtual CD/DVD drive. With DVD cloning software, any commercial DVD movie can be easily 'ripped' from its original media, and many versions can be created, including compressed versions for **MP4** devices.

With the many available music formats and media players, creating files of favourite songs and albums has been commonplace for over ten years.

Distribution mechanisms

Distribution of pirated media is rife – as soon as one system is closed, another appears. The first system to offer this service was Napster, which has been famously pursued through the legal system by the music industry and now offers a fully legitimate service.

Napster, like its many clones, used a peer-based file sharing system, with each member keeping a collection of their favourite music in a folder. This is then distributed via the peer software which advertises what you have to a central server.

Since Napster, there have been many peer systems, with the current popular system being BitTorrent™.

Illegally downloading any software or media is an offence which may result in a heavy fine, litigation (being sued) and the loss of your computer system. Because of the way networked technology operates, each data packet sent and received has to have the destination **IP address**. This means that network professionals with suitable technical knowledge can identify where the download is heading and work with the music, film or software industries to prove who is downloading what and when.

Key terms

MP4 – a coding format for highly compressed movies to be played on portable media players.

IP address – (in full, Internet Protocol Address), this is a unique number that identifies a particular computer on the Internet.

1.5 Organisational impact

Already, in describing each area of unauthorised access, you have seen how they might impact on an organisation or an individual. To summarise, an organisation may suffer the impact in a variety of ways. A potential loss of service for the customer, or to the Internet, can impede the organisation's ability to operate. There may be loss of business or income through the loss of essential data. In the long term, increased costs are caused by the replacement technology and the need for increased insurance. It is likely that the increased cost will be passed on to the customer. Damage is also caused by the potentially poor public and commercial image that can result if aunauthorised access is uncovered.

1.6 Information security

Wherever data is stored, the overall security of the data must be controlled. This area is covered by three principles: confidentiality, integrity and availability.

Confidentiality

In managing the confidentiality of information, the system manager has to consider these points:

- Who can see the information?
- Who can update the information?
- For how long is the information to be stored?
- How often must the information be reviewed for currency?

- What information can be stored?
- What systems are available to store the information?

Regularly reviewing who can access this confidential information and what information is stored is essential. Systems storing personal information such as bank details, credit records or medical records must be accurate and managed in a confidential manner.

Integrity and completeness of data

The integrity and therefore completeness of data is critical. Having incorrect data on any matter can cause considerable personal as well as commercial damage. The wrong information on a medical record, credit report or police system can cause an individual considerable distress, as well as possibly lead to legal action.

Checking the data is correct may involve asking appropriate people to review the information. In the case of customer or personnel details, asking the customer or colleague to check the data is correct and up to date enhances the integrity of the data stored.

Access to data

Who can access what data and when, controls the overall availability of data. It is important to review regularly who has access to data and when they have access, because:

- those who have access may no longer need it
- access may be driven by a legal protocol, for example a credit report may be requested by a lender only when someone applies for credit.

This is managed by the creation of different user rights and levels of password access, which is discussed in further detail later in this unit.

This issue is also discussed in *Unit 9: Computer networks* and *Unit 10: Communication technologies.*

2. Know how organisations can keep systems and data secure

The previous section of this unit investigated many of the attacks, scams and issues which impact on the systems security of any organisation or individual.

Preventing a security incursion, like the attacks themselves, is a constantly evolving process. The security measures described in this section are a sample of those in use and are an introduction to what you may have to manage in the IT industry.

2.1 Physical security

While no one would wish to live in a society with a 'Big Brother' figure watching every move, it is natural for people to desire the assurance that the working environment and all systems are safe.

The system may be secured with the latest anti-virus system and firewall technology, but this will be useless

if anyone can 'pop' into the server room and copy all the critical data to a USB memory stick.

In the management of a secure system, these features should be present: lock and key security; equipment identification; CCTV; intrusion detection systems; staff and visitor identification; access control (sign in/out) systems; security personnel; cable and communication shielding; port lockdown.

Lock and key security

There is a need to secure mobile devices such as laptops. If you look closely at a laptop, you will see on many a small slot, into which you can fit a padlocked chain. Fitting a chain ensures mobile technology is not so mobile while you are not using it.

How can organisations keep systems and data secure?

Key term

Lock and key security – when essential systems are held in rooms and buildings which are secured under lock and key.

Many **lock and key security** systems in buildings operate on a master/sub-master system. There are a series of keys for individual doors, groups of doors and for the whole building. The network manager may have a sub-master key for all of the server and communication rooms.

When keys are issued to employees, most organisations keep a journal of who has what key and what access it offers.

Household and car keys can be reproduced at high-street key cutters. However, the lock and key systems used by many organisations are unique, often with only one set for the building in question.

Digital keypads may reduce the cost of the reproduction of keys and can be reprogrammed at regular intervals, but these cannot prevent access by observation – when the key code is observed – or by colleagues passing on the code to others.

While having a high-quality lock and key system is essential, it has no value if the surrounding environment is vulnerable. Unauthorised access can be gained through unlocked windows (even on upper floors), via unmanned side doors, through walls (most interior walls are plaster, which is not difficult to penetrate), over ceilings (in a building with suspended ceilings, security is an issue) or by damaging the door and/or breaking the lock.

With technology the same applies – leaving cables exposed or wireless networks insecure may be an open invitation, allowing unauthorised access to your system. Shielding cables, as well as removing them from exposure, will deter all but the ardent thief.

So, lock and key security relies on the quality of the environment it is supporting. In some critical areas, it may be necessary for the walls, doors, windows and ceiling space to be reinforced and possibly alarmed.

Visitor passes

Most medium to large organisations maintain a system of staff and visitor identification – your college may have a system which identifies staff, students and visitors. This system offers immediate authority for those who should be there to challenge unknown people's rights to be there.

In many environments, identification only has value if the culture supports it – there is no point issuing identification cards if no one wears them. Many organisations use the identification card as a method of entry, with security and reception personnel checking identification on entry. Many identification

Why are digital keypads insecure security systems?

card systems are used in combination with access control systems (see next section starting on page 207), where the identification card also acts a key.

With current technology, the identification card can form part of the personnel database. Together, with photographic identification from a personnel record, many organisations also use a colour-coding system on their cards to indicate, for example if you are a contractor; which department, site or partner company you work for; the level of access allowed; the floor(s) you may access; your position in the company.

Visitor cards are by their nature temporary and indicate that the visitor has limited access rights. Most organisations have a policy of escorting all visitors from entry (sign in) to exit (sign out).

Sign in/out systems

These are a variation on lock and key systems and are often used in conjunction with staff and visitor identification systems. Instead of using keys to access areas of a building, the system relies on personnel using swipe cards or dongles as keys. There are several advantages of access control systems.

- The system can log personnel entering and exiting buildings (which means they can also be used to monitor the time-keeping and attendance of employees).
- Each key can be programmed, which means personnel can be allowed/denied access to any area on a 'door by door' level.
- Records can be maintained on who has used what door, with secure and critical areas open to scrutiny.
- When an employee leaves the organisation, if they do not return their key, it can be disabled.
- The keys can be reprogrammed when an employee changes role within the organisation.

Most swipe cards and dongle systems contain no information, only a unique ID (like a MAC address on a network card). The access information is kept on a central server which manages the access control system. Naturally, if these keys fall into the wrong hands, before anyone becomes aware of this, they can be used to gain access. To overcome this, some systems work in partnership with CCTV, or key code systems, which record who has entered the area, as well as creating a secondary security mechanism.

What are the advantages of access control systems?

Key term

Biometrics – the implementation of technology to use biological information about ourselves as a method of unique identification. It comes from the ancient Greek *bios*, meaning life and *metron*, meaning measure.

Biometrics

The technology of **biometrics** is constantly being developed and refined. Common technologies in current use are fingerprint recognition, retinal scans and voice recognition.

Retinal scans

The retina is the rear of the eye and, like a fingerprint, everyone's has a biologically unique configuration. Unlike fingerprints, which can be changed (as the skin can be cut or burned), retinal scans rely on the biological fact that it is almost impossible to change the retina without considerable damage (so it is unlikely that anyone would let someone tamper with their eyeball) and the retina remains the same from birth, acting as a constant and reliable method of identification.

Retinal scans take about two seconds to complete, but require very close proximity between the eyeball and the scanner – so glasses and contact lenses have to be removed.

Fingerprint recognition

This form of biometrics has been used in crime detection over the last 100 years and no two prints have yet been found to be identical. Our fingers secrete a fine watery solution from the ridges, which allows detection and fingerprint scanners to operate. Some scanners use a rapid laser to detect the ridges in our fingers. Others have an electro-statically sensitive pad which detects the current formed by the small quantities of water in our fingerprint.

Fingerprint scanners are often used along with other forms of identification. For example, international travel requires a passport, visa and, in some countries, additional recognition using fingerprint identification from more than one finger.

Case study: Biometrics

A well-known resort and theme park uses biometric fingerprint scanners to prevent fraudulent sharing of multi-day passes among visiting families.

1 What is the cost implication of using such a system and what impracticalities may be involved?
2 What are the benefits to the resort?
3 What are the potential legal implications?

Iris scanning

Another eye feature which is unique is the iris. Unlike retinal scanning, iris scanning can be accomplished when the recipient is wearing glasses or contact lenses. Like the retina, the chances of the iris changing are incredibly remote, allowing for a reliable source of biometric information. Iris scanning is already in use at some international destinations and may increase in popularity through time.

Activity: Retinal/iris scans

1 With the consent of your classmates, look closely at each other's eyes with a pen light and notice the differences.
2 There is a well-known recent science fiction film that shows iris scanning in use. Do you know which it is? If not, use the Internet to find out.

Voice recognition

Voice recognition as a method of biometric access control has considerable limitations because voices can change in different circumstances. For example, when we are stressed, excited, tired or ill (say with a

throat infection) and, more importantly, as we age (for example, the inability of young men to control their voices during puberty).

Voice-based security systems can also be 'circumvented' by a mobile phone on speaker mode or a voice recording. This means the voice recognition system has to be used in addition to other access control systems (such as CCTV, swipe cards and dongles). In many other situations, however, voice recognition has improved considerably. It has an important role in speech to text systems for people with disabilities and in handheld games consoles.

Other biometric technologies

Other biometric systems are being developed and deployed. Facial recognition systems, for example, have been developed which can be used to scan groups of people via live CCTV footage. Alongside facial recognition systems, technology has now been developed to identify individuals who may be behaving in a suspicious manner by their actions and posture.

Cable shielding

Any data which is transmitted using electromagnetic or radio transmission is open to being remotely monitored. The signal travelling along a copper data cable emits a magnetic field, which can be analysed to discover what data is travelling along the line. This may seem the stuff of fiction, but the technology does exist to access data covertly. Only data sent via fiber optic cable cannot be 'tapped into' without considerable effort and possible damage. Some cable systems are shielded, partly to protect the cable from external magnetic interference (power sources, etc.), but also to dampen the external noise generated by the cable.

Wireless systems are by their nature less secure and so a system which uses Wireless Encryption Protocol (WEP) encryption has been developed (see page 207). To maintain total trust, the devices which can join a wireless system need to be pre-configured, so that the wireless system does not allow just any device to join the system.

Activity: Biometrics

1 What biometric systems have you encountered?
2 How do you think biometric systems will evolve?

Activity: Stop and think

1 What physical security techniques should be employed to protect a computer system?

2 Biometrics has many advantages. What are the weaknesses?

3 What software security techniques improve network security?

2.2 Software and network security

To combat intrusion and subversion of a networked computer system and commonplace accidental damage to data and resources, all IT systems need to employ an extensive range of security and data management techniques and technologies. The following examples are covered in this section: **encryption** techniques, call back, **handshaking**, diskless networks, the backup and restoration of data and redundancy, audit logs, firewall configuration and management, virus management and control, VPNs (virtual private networks), intrusion detection systems and traffic control technologies, passwords, levels of access to data and software updating.

Key terms

Encryption – a method of converting normal information such as text, images and media into a format which is unintelligible unless you are in possession of the key that is the basis of the conversion.

Handshaking – a process where two communication devices continuously agree a method of data communication.

RSA – stands for the last name initials of the mathematicians who patented the principle for public/private key encryption using prime numbers, i.e. Ron Rivest, Adi Shamir and Len Adleman.

Public/private keys – keys that are mathematically related. The public key can be widely distributed and is used to encrypt data. The private key only can decrypt the data and is kept secret. It is not technically practical to derive the private key from the public key.

Prime number – a number that can only be divided by itself and 1. This means that by no matter what number you try to divide this number, it will never return a whole value. Prime numbers are mathematically interesting as no one has yet managed to predict the next prime number – they appear to follow no pattern. This property is invaluable in network security.

Encryption

Many simple ciphers exist, such as the Caesar cipher, which relies on a simple key of changing one letter with the letter a fixed number of places down the alphabet. So, using a shift of four places, A becomes E, B becomes F, etc.

Ciphers such as data encryption standard (DES) use a key which is 56 bits in length. Using simple mathematics, this means there are 2^{56} (72,057,594,037,927,936) possible combinations. With the increasing power of computers, this cipher is now obsolete, as it is possible to crack the cipher in a short time.

RSA encryption uses a **public/private key** exchange – the security certificate issued by a website is a common example. The certificate is a public key part of the exchange and a private key is also created. The private key is based on a 1024-bit value (2^{1024} which is 1.797693134862315907729305190789e+308 – the e means you move the decimal point to the right by 308 digits) and is a **prime number**.

For many secure WAN connections, routing protocols exchange their updates using a MD5 hash. This is a formula that provides the result of a complex calculation based on a large dataset, with the hash being the result from each calculation. This is used across common communication systems to ensure that no one attempts to add unauthorised equipment to the system, as well as by anti-virus systems to check if an application has been changed by the insertion of a virus. For more on Secure WAN connections, see *Unit 9: Computer networks*, page 266.

For wireless systems, wireless equivalence protocol (WEP) is used to encrypt the connection between the client (you) and the Wireless Access Point. It allows all members of a wireless system to share a common private key which is used to encrypt all the data transmitted. The wireless device cannot join the system, unless the WEP key is directly entered into the wireless settings for the mobile device.

Two WEP key standards are in use, offering 64-bit (18,446,744,073,709,551,616) and 128-bit (3.40282366920938463463374607431 77e+38) keys.

As WEP keys are in binary, they can be entered in hexadecimal, as this has a direct mathematical relationship and is a more understandable format.

Call back

Call back is used on dial-up systems where remote workers or network administrators can dial into a network or a network device and it will call them back. The call back number is pre-configured, which means that the user cannot connect from any location, only a trusted, registered line.

While dial-up systems using modems (see *Unit 10: Communication technologies* page 320) may seem out of date, many remote areas and developing regions still use this reliable technology. Modems are still used as a backup connection to gain direct access into the network router in the case of major failure of the main incoming line (which may be caused, for example, by a hacker attack).

Handshaking

On WAN (wide area network) systems, data may be sent across a medium which is not trusted (a public communications line). To improve the trust, each device completes a challenge – which may be random and carries a remote username and password – to establish the identity of the opposite device. This is known as CHAP – challenge handshake authentication protocol.

Diskless networks

One of the greatest risks of data being stolen is caused by the ability to easily transfer data from a computer to a mobile storage device.

In diskless networks, workstations do not have CD/DVD drives, USB ports (or Windows® is prevented from recognising new USB devices) or floppy disk drives. In most cases of diskless networking, the BIOS must also be configured and secured to prevent more astute individuals from adding new devices.

Some systems also prevent local hard drive access, either by applying local restrictions so the user cannot view, add or remove files, or by having no local hard drive, with the workstation booting from a remote location into memory, using terminal services technology. Various versions exist, including Remote Desktop with Windows XP® and Vista®; Virtual Network

Computing (VNC), which can be used on a diverse range of systems; Linux® X-Windows, which offers similar facilities.

As technology is improving and cloud computing is evolving (see the activity *Cloud bursting* below), many systems now use virtual machines to create diskless networks. A virtual machine is an application that emulates the behaviour of your computer systems with popular versions including VMWare® and VirtualBox. By using this technology, a computer desktop can be 'delivered' to your local system, via a client application or a web browser. The virtual machine is then locked down and secured for the remote system and will be inaccessible to the user. This removes any security concerns about the local system, with which there is no interaction.

Activity: Cloud bursting

Using your preferred search engine, do some research on cloud computing and how it is being used, as well as popular virtual machine technologies available to enable this to happen.

Use of backups

The use of backups and the restoration of data are critical in ensuring that data is safe and secure. Having a centrally managed backup system, where all the data is safely copied in case of system failure, with everyone following the same standards, is essential.

Backing up and restoring disks and data are considered to be the vital work of a network administrator. Depending on the size, type and nature of the organisation, it is expected that the network administrator completes at least one backup per day. Some systems employ **incremental backups**, while others use **differential backups**.

Effective backup relies on defining the quantity of data that requires backing up and the frequency of backups, deciding on an appropriate backup storage medium and storing a copy of the backup data off-site.

Some organisations complete a backup every eight hours as the data is undergoing continuous change. It is normal for most companies to complete an overnight backup and, once a week, take a copy to another location (off-site).

To ensure **redundancy**, most server systems storage is managed by **RAID**. The benefits of RAID are that if one hard drive fails the system can be rebuilt from the existing images or the system can continue while a new hard drive is installed.

Systems such as RAID and **mirroring** provide companies with quicker recovery times. RAID allows data to be recovered from 'duplicated' hard drives. Mirroring requires a second, duplicate server to be in operation at the same time as the primary server.

Key terms

Incremental backup – involves storing only changed data since the last backup of any type.

Differential backup – involves storing only changed data since the last full backup.

Redundancy – a term in computing meaning duplication of information

RAID – stands for redundant array of independent disks. It is used as a live backup mechanism with multiple hard disks maintaining multiple images of the data.

Mirroring – a backup server that 'mirrors' the processes and actions of the primary server. If the primary server fails, the backup server can take over without any downtime because it has mirrored the content of the primary server.

Audit logs

Audit logs are used to keep a record of network and database activity, recording who has done what, where they did it and when. The audit log may contain a simple reference to the service accessed along with the system identity of the user.

The majority of database and network activities will go unnoticed, but the purpose of the audit log is:

* to maintain a detailed record of how any system has been used
* on recognition of an issue, enable system administrators to track the possible cause (or infringement)
* to work with monitoring systems to enable alarms to be placed on a system, alerting system administrators to potentially suspicious activity.

Syslog is one of the most common systems in use to maintain simple, auditable records of system activity across a networked system. The syslog server stores all access records for the network administrator to review as appropriate as can be seen in Figure 7.5, a Syslog record list.

Firewall configurations

Most simple firewall systems in use at home are automatic and seldom require user intervention and configuration. For a commercial environment, firewall configuration is essential to ensure the efficient and effective transit of data.

As the purpose of a firewall is to block unwanted traffic from entering the network, configuration must be done with care. In many systems where traffic has to enter to reach servers (such as email or

```
2006-12-30   17:32:35      192.168.1.101      www.hellochristmas.co.uk
2006-12-30   17:32:38      192.168.1.101      images.shopping.msn.co.uk
2006-12-30   17:32:39      192.168.1.101      www.maketheworldabetterplace.com
2006-12-30   17:33:30      192.168.1.101      www.downloadwindowsupdate.com
2006-12-30   17:33:36      192.168.1.101      update.microsoft.com
2006-12-30   17:54:53      192.168.1.99       www.googleadservices.com
2006-12-30   17:54:53      192.168.1.99       www.orient-express.com
2006-12-30   17:54:55      192.168.1.99       orient-express.lbwa.verio.net
2006-12-30   17:54:56      192.168.1.99       oe.nucleus.co.uk
2006-12-30   17:59:16      192.168.1.99       download.windsupdate.com
2006-12-30   18:53:13      192.168.1.100      rad.msn.com
2006-12-30   08:53:02      192.168.1.99       photos.apple.com
2006-12-30   08:53:04      192.168.1.99       ax.phobos.apple.com.edgesuite.net
```

Figure 7.5: Example of what a Syslog record list may look like

web servers), two or more firewalls may be installed to offer zones of security. This allows different security levels depending on the direction of traffic – data intended for externally accessible devices is managed differently to data for internal devices.

Many systems will not allow internal traffic to exit the system unless it has been sent from a computer and user that has been 'authenticated' using the internal directory system. Therefore, if the traffic is coming from a computer that is not logged in, then the traffic will not exit.

Many firewalls work in conjunction with network address translation (NAT) systems, with the internal devices all hidden behind one (or a small number of) external IP address.

There are 65536 UDP ports and 65536 TCP ports, as well as ICMP, IP and other protocol traffic.

How to… Check your firewall settings

1 Typically with Windows® you can find a resource by many avenues. The easiest way to find the Windows Firewall is to open the Control Panel (under system and security).

2 Select the advanced settings option (to the left).

3 You can change either the inbound (from outside) or outbound (to the outside) rules.

4 You may consider adding a new rule.

WATCH OUT!

Be very careful to find out what ports you may open, as you do not want to open up your network to attack.

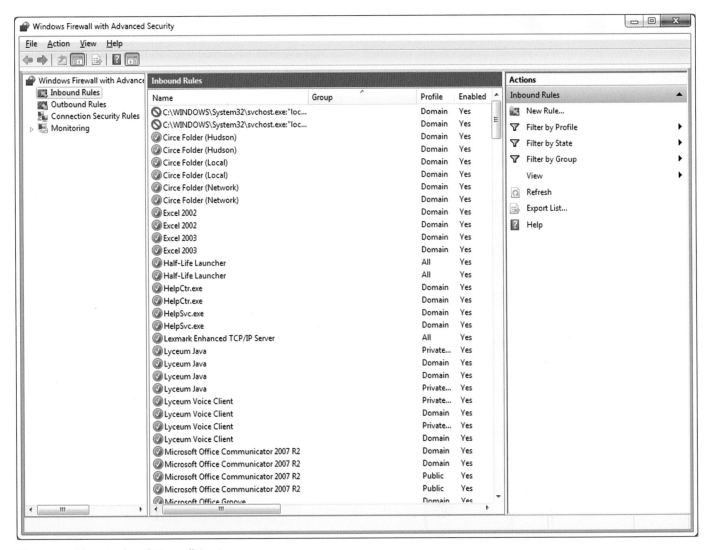

Figure 7.6 The Windows® Firewall Settings

Virus checking software

In the home environment, virus checking software comes in many shapes and sizes, from those which only cover viruses, trojans and worms to comprehensive integrated security suites that interact with a firewall and the operating system to maintain the welfare of the system.

All virus checking systems are only as good as the databases (called dictionaries) they maintain on the latest attacks. So, it is essential to ensure that the anti-virus software downloads the latest virus **definitions** daily.

Anti-virus software always runs in the background of any system. On your computer you may see its icon in the system tray. The anti-virus software will scan each file as it is being opened for any 'fingerprints' which match the virus definitions. It will also attempt to identify any 'suspicious' activity from a program while it is running.

Corporate anti-virus systems must be deployed centrally, as well as on each local computer system. Many medium to large organisations will:

- have a server which downloads the latest virus definitions and distributes them to each computer daily

- monitor all incoming and outgoing traffic for potential threats; this may be via the router, proxy server or firewall

- monitor all incoming and outgoing email traffic for potential threats; it will look at all attachments

- use the anti-virus application in partnership with local computer administrative policies to prevent the local system from running unacceptable software (a tactic used to stop employees using well-known hacking software and games by finding the MD5 hash for each application).

To download and install the software, visit the AVG website (a link to this website has been made available at Hotlinks).

For anti-virus applications, a **heuristic** analysis suggests there may be a virus infection inside a file – it does not declare absolutely there is an infection.

How to... Install free anti-virus software

Running a computer without anti-virus software installed is a recipe for disaster, so don't do it. AVG offer their anti-virus software in a free version, which will:

- update its anti-virus definitions daily

- run a comprehensive scan of your entire system on demand, or scheduled daily

- check all running programs

- check all emails, incoming and outgoing

- check for 'script' attacks from websites

- carry out a heuristic analysis.

Key terms

Definition – in the context of an anti-virus application, this is a rule explaining which applications are not trusted.

Heuristic – in computer science this is a method of arriving at a good solution that works, rather than a perfect solution.

Heuristic analysis is used to discover new viruses or when a virus has managed to replicate itself in a unique manner.

Computer systems cannot run with anti-virus software only – they must also run with anti-spyware tools. Spyware deploys many tactics used by worms, viruses and trojans and often comes as part of a welcomed application (like a free download or website you have visited).

The primary risk from spyware is the information it will send out about your activities – the sites you have visited and possibly the keystrokes used.

Available to download for Windows XP® and part of the Vista® suite of operating systems is Windows Defender®, which is designed to replace the Microsoft® Anti-Spyware application and monitor your system continuously.

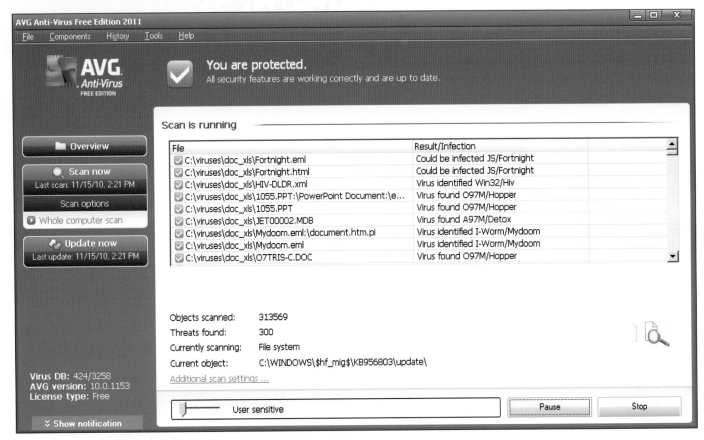

Figure 7.7 A comprehensive virus scan

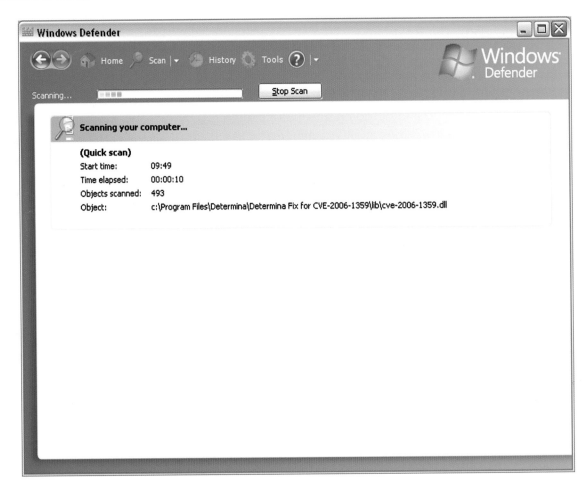

Figure 7.8 Windows
Defender® in action

Use of VPNs

The use of virtual private networks (VPNs) allows organisations to communicate from site to site across a public system (like the Internet) via a tunnel, which is an agreed route for all encrypted traffic. Many home workers can connect directly to the corporate network via local VPN tunnels.

Therefore, VPNs create a trusted connection on a system which is not trusted.

There are many protocols and methods used in the management of VPNs. The primary purpose of these is to prevent snooping (**packet sniffing**) and fraudulent authentication.

Intrusion detection systems

Intrusion detection systems go beyond the role of the firewall and will monitor traffic for undesirable manipulations from hackers and the tools they may use.

Some systems are passive, which means they will record the attempts for the network administrator to decide what is to be done. Others are reactive (called intrusion prevention systems) – on identifying an intrusion attempt, the system will reconfigure the firewall to block the intrusion.

Traffic control is accomplished on many networks by the use of access-control lists and routing protocols.

- **Access-control lists (ACLs)** may be applied to routers and servers alike. They can be used to create traffic-based permit or deny rules for whole networks, individual devices or a specified range of devices.

- **Routing protocols** enable routers to make decisions about which way and to whom network traffic can be sent.

Some ACLs can be used in a temporal (time-based) context, allowing or denying access to networks at certain times.

While many different systems use ACLs, the common rule may look like the one shown in Table 7.2.

Key term

Packet sniffing – looking for data on the network, by listening to network traffic on your connection.

Table 7.2: An access list to allow one network to access a small collection of web servers, but prevent web access by any other system

access-list 101	Permit	TCP	192.168.0.0	0.0.0.255	172.16.10.16	0.0.0.15	eq 80
This is the rule which has a unique number	Can be permit or deny	This could be TCP, UDP or IP	This identifies the source network, device or range of devices	This is a wildcard mask*	This identifies the source network, device or range of devices	This is a wildcard mask*	This is equal to TCP port 80 for HTTP traffic

Rules are in lists (or collections) and are executed in order. When a rule with a condition matching the incoming or outgoing traffic is met, the rule is executed. If you have a 'deny FTP' before a 'permit FTP', then FTP traffic will never be allowed.

ACLs have a default 'deny all' rule at the end. If you only write permits, all other traffic is automatically denied, which is a subtle and useful security feature.

* Wildcard masks are used as matching rules and are: binary 0 = must match, binary 1 = does not care.

Passwords

The management of passwords is essential. This tried and tested authentication technique is still the most commonly used in all areas of organisational systems security. To ensure that passwords are suitable and secure, many organisations adopt a policy that will encourage common practice. In an example policy, users must:

- not write down their password
- change their password periodically, from 90 days (three months) to as little as every seven days
- use a **strong password** with eight or more characters
- choose a password which is nonsense, to evade casual attempts at social engineering while remaining memorable.

Many systems will log failed attempts when users forget their password, with their username being locked out after three failed attempts. The hapless user then has to visit the network manager to explain why the password has been forgotten and to provide suitable proof of identity. (In some cases, it may have been an unauthorised user who tried to enter the system using the legitimate user's identity.)

How to... Think of a nonsense password

Picking the name of a family member, pop star, football team or town you were born in is susceptible to discovery through social engineering.

Trying to devise a word which has no meaning, but can be easily remembered is also a challenge. Lewis Carroll managed to create a whole new vocabulary with considerable skill in his poem 'The Jabberwocky' (Jabberwocky is one example of a nonsense word).

Try mixing nouns (names) and adjectives (something which modifies a noun). For example:

Adjective	Noun
Red	Chicken
Atomic	Snail
Hyper	Cucumber
Micro	Titan

Key term

Strong password – uses letters (upper- and lower-case), numbers and symbols, e.g. Jac0b_$m1th instead of jacobsmith.

Levels of access to data

All centrally managed network systems, servers and many client-based operating systems offer control over the levels of access to data. This may be accomplished by controlling a user's access to files, directories (folders) and data.

- **Read privilege** allows the user to see selected information.
- **Write privilege** allows the user to change selected information.
- **Execute privilege** allows the user to create new files, folders or data sets.

These privileges may be issued via a user group, as a direct privilege or as part of a domain a user belongs to. The level of privilege may also roam with the user as they use a range of systems or may be specific to one computer system.

Membership of user groups (see Figure 7.9) and the privileges offered to each employee must be reviewed at regular intervals. It is essential that someone who no longer needs access to certain files, or data, has their privilege level amended.

Software updating

Ensuring that software updating takes place guarantees the system is safe from possible faults and vulnerabilities. For many applications, the update process is automatic, removing the need for the user to worry about how up to date their system is.

Operating systems, such as Windows®, use automatic updating (see Figure 7.10) to maintain the security and quality of the operating system. Linux® systems use the apt-get tool, which accomplishes a similar function.

Figure 7.9: Members of a user group

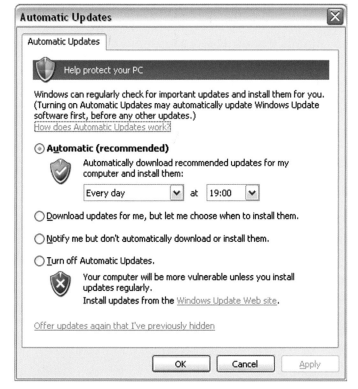

Figure 7.10: Automatic updates for the Windows® operating system

Disaster recovery

Ensuring that you are able to recover from any system loss, during the running of a commercial system is of critical importance. Having a disaster recovery policy and ensuring you can recover at least the data, may save the day.

Backup systems

Having a mirror image of the data (and the servers) enables systems upon failure to switch to the alternate system. Also, with many backup systems, having extra systems as a mirror image, means that you can distribute the demand across multiple systems.

Whole system replacement

This is to be avoided at all cost. If this happens you have either not planned very well or have experienced a disaster of unforeseen proportions. Many organisations will have a contract with a 'dark site' provider who, on system failure, will hire their remote services as a duplicate of your system.

Tiers of recovery

Depending on the issue, there are seven tiers of disaster recovery, depending on how an organisation has planned their disaster recovery.

Tier 0: No off-site data – Possibly no recovery
If you work for a company with this level of recovery, get out, the data is unsafe, one power surge and that's the end.

Tier 1: Data backup with no dark site.

Here the backups are taken, but there is no replacement location if the system fails.

Tier 2: Data backup with a dark site.

Copies of the data are taken and there is a centre available to transfer data control to.

Tier 3: Electronic vaulting.

Mirrored copies of the system state are continuously maintained.

Tier 4: Point-in-time copies.

Remote copies of the data are the same as local data.

Tier 5: Transaction integrity.

The system ensures both copies are in tune with each other.

Tier 6: Zero or near-Zero data loss

For very fast systems, where a sudden fault, could result in some minor 'transactional' (while being transferred) data loss.

Tier 7: Highly automated, business-integrated solution

Now the system will do all the thinking for you.

Activity: Security check

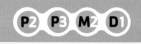

1 Check what security is on your home computer, assess the threats and complete a comprehensive audit of your system.

2 Use your audit to improve security as you proceed.

Assessment activity 7.2

P2 P3 M2 D1 **BTEC**

Spanners R Us provides next-day delivery for all types of spanners required for the networking industry. After a major power outage had a serious impact on the income of the organisation, and which was in turn exploited by an offshore team of hackers, the management has sacked their Information Security Manager and has promptly promoted you into the position.

Fortunately the management board understand spanners, not network security, so time is on your side. You have to offer them a visual way of understanding systems security and disaster recovery.

Create a poster, which will be the thrust of your message, it must include:

- what physical security measures can help keep systems secure **P2**

- how software and network security can keep systems and data secure. **P3 M2 D1**

Grading tips

- Keep it visual, and keep the explanations, discussion and descriptions short and to the point. **P2 P3**

- You need to explain the operation of an encryption technique and how this is used. **M2**

- To achieve a distinction you need to discuss different ways of recovering from a disaster using a poster/diagram showing clearly how this could be accomplished. As the verb 'discuss' is used, you can include short 'paragraphs' as callouts on the poster/diagram. You could make your presentation using PowerPoint®, YouTube or AudioBoo. **D1**

PLTS

You can demonstrate your skills as a **creative thinker** by creating a poster that effectively explains the physical security measures, software and network security that help keep IT systems secure.

Functional skills

You can demonstrate your Functional **English** skills by creating a poster using short callout paragraphs.

3. Understand the organisational issues affecting the security of IT systems

Ensuring the security of IT systems is essential. Security measures have an impact on organisations, as well as individuals, and in many instances are covered by legislation.

3.1 Security policies and guidelines

Many organisations will agree, maintain and operate a range of policies in the management of security in their organisation's IT environment. The purpose of these policies is to ensure that all employees, departments, suppliers and customers adhere to a common principle which will ensure their welfare, as well as that of the system, and the data held.

Common policies agreed by most organisations include:

- budget setting
- disaster recovery
- predetermined updates and reviews of security procedures and scheduling of security audits
- codes of conduct, including email usage, Internet usage and software acquisition and installation
- how surveillance and monitoring may occur
- risk management.

Disaster recovery policies

A disaster recovery policy details what actions are to be taken in the event of a human-based, or natural disaster, which may befall an organisation. Disasters may include:

- natural disasters
- fire
- power failure
- terrorist attacks
- organised or deliberate disruptions
- system and/or equipment failures
- human error
- computer viruses
- legal issues
- worker strikes
- loss of key personnel.

The disaster recovery policy may include procedures for data relocation, use of alternative sites, the hiring of additional personnel and equipment and will be supported by appropriate levels of insurance to fund the immediate aftermath and recovery process.

Updating security procedures and scheduling security audits

Predetermined updates and reviews of security procedures need to be carried out on a periodic basis. A security review is only as good as the knowledge acquired at that time. It is essential to check security policies for currency and to compare the policy against current knowledge and new threats. While security and computer systems need regular updating, the update may have an impact on established systems. Often updates need to be tested before a planned roll out occurs.

Security audits of physical and networked systems also need to take place at regular intervals. These are often done without informing the employees of the organisation to prove the authentic effectiveness of the systems.

In network management, an audit of database and network logs may occur, with detailed analysis to look for recurring issues, which may represent an existing threat. This audit is often combined with penetration testing, simulating a hacker or a denial of service attack to establish the validity of existing systems.

While breaking into a building may seem an extreme way of testing physical security, some organisations will employ covert personnel to attempt to circumvent their physical security systems.

Codes of conduct

Many employees, contractors, customers and suppliers may use your organisation's systems. To allow them complete freedom is inadvisable. Creating codes of conduct which are signed by the individuals, who need access to your system, places the legal responsibility on them

A verbal assurance from an employee (and therefore user of the system) that they will 'behave' is not quite enough assurance for most employers and systems managers. Instead, employees are expected to sign, agree and adhere to a variety of policies (see Table 7.3), each of which ensures that the system users will abide by rules that suit the organisation and its security needs.

Surveillance and monitoring policies

Placing a CCTV, or covert surveillance camera, in any organisation may cause considerable distress among the workforce and could be the prelude to union action. How surveillance and monitoring may occur has to be clearly defined and agreed with employees, including describing the reasons for using surveillance, where it will be used and the type of surveillance equipment.

Risk management

Risk management involves the measurement and prediction of possible issues, together with a strategy for dealing with each risk if it arises. Depending on the severity and the type of threat, an organisation may elect to:

- tolerate the risk and 'ride the storm', for example a change in the economic climate or a competitor attempting to undermine the product

- treat the risk by investing in an upgrade or an alternative approach
- terminate the risk by attacking it head on, stopping the hacker or the virus
- transfer the risk by adapting the approach of the organisation.

Budget setting

Annual budget setting and the management of finances, to ensure organisational systems security is maintained at an acceptable level, are essential. Effective security is not free and requires continual investment to maintain control. In budgeting annually for organisational systems security, you may need to consider:

- the replacement cost of redundant equipment and software versions
- the cost of each audit
- the training of staff
- software licensing
- the procurement of external consultation and support
- staff wages relating to organisational systems security.

Table 7.3: Security policies to be agreed by employees

Policy type	What the policy covers
Email usage policy	Governs what subjects are unacceptable in the sending of emails. Often the policy will define the acceptable size of attachments to be sent, the types of attachments and how to manage the mailbox contents. Gives details of unacceptable activities such as stalking, harassment, spamming and the deliberate exchange of corporate information to external parties. Many email usage policies will declare the network management's right to monitor all emails.
Internet usage policy	Details which sites cannot be visited and what cannot be downloaded. Like the email policy, the network management normally declare their right to monitor network traffic.
Software acquisition and installation policy	The purpose of a software acquisition and installation policy is to prevent personal and unlicensed software from being installed on the system, as well as ensuring that there is no duplication of software – this prevents compatibility issues, as well as the transmission of worms, viruses and trojans.
User area usage policy	In systems with a large number of users (such as your educational centre), storage space is at a premium. To ensure that copyright is not infringed and that decency is maintained, many organisations will define what users cannot store, as well as the limit you may have on your user area. Naturally, storage needs will vary according to role, for example software developers may need more space when working on a complex application.
Account management policy	An account management policy operates at two levels, and will define: • the responsibilities of the network management in maintaining a level of service • the responsibilities of the user to ensure that their password is current and that they do not share their details with anyone else.

Even at times where the national (or international) economic climate is restrictive, any reduction in investment in organisational system security could in the longer term have a commercially damaging impact on an organisation.

3.2 Employment contracts and security

Hiring policy

When recruiting new employees or promoting existing personnel, organisations need to establish a positive hiring policy which does not conflict with national employment law. It is essential to look at the background of the employee, their previous employment record and criminal record to check their references and to set an assessment task.

Many organisations have a probationary period for new personnel and, in some cases, when internally promoting staff. This enables the organisation to carefully establish trust with the new recruit and allow them responsibility one stage at a time. It is foolish to give the new recruit full access to all systems straight away before they have proved their trustworthiness.

Separation of duties

To ensure that there is not complete reliance on one individual to maintain the overall systems security of the organisation, a separation of duties is often established. This involves having many team members who each have one critical duty to manage and a deputy who is also experienced in that area to cover in the case of absence or departure.

The same can be said for the way the system is understood, with no one individual having full knowledge of the entire system or understanding of how each individual element is configured. Therefore the firewall expert will have no knowledge of the VPN system and the chief security officer may have an overview of the entire system, but not have detailed knowledge of the rules of each component.

Ensuring compliance including disciplinary procedures

While organisational systems security is paramount, infringement by any employee or business partner has to be dealt with in a fair, confidential and legally acceptable manner, ensuring compliance with established disciplinary and investigation procedures.

There is always the possibility that the suspected employee might not be the one who has caused the infringement, so to falsely accuse someone could lead to a very damaging legal action. If an infringement has occurred, appropriate steps may include:

- suspension (with pay) of the employee involved
- an independent party recruited to investigate the matter fairly and impartially
- the immediate involvement of the police if it appears to be a criminal matter.

An employee's contract and job description gives a clear definition of their roles and responsibilities, as well as the penalties that may occur if they are in breach of their contractual terms.

Training and communication with staff as to their responsibilities

While ignorance is no defence in law, it is reasonable to expect any employer to ensure that staff receive necessary training, as well as maintaining regular communication with staff to ensure they are aware of their responsibilities.

Assessment activity 7.3

P4 **P5** **P6** **M3** **D2**   **BTEC**

Following the interview in Assessment activity 7.1, please create a small website (you may consider using a wiki or Google site), based on your academic centre. In this web resource, you must:

- explain any policies and/or guidelines used for managing IT security issues (hint: did you sign anything at enrolment?) **P4**
- evaluate the effectiveness of these policies **D2**
- explain how someone's employment contract would affect the security of a system, in an educational centre or a bank for example **P5**
- review the laws relating to security and privacy of data. **P6** **M3** **D2**

Grading tips

- You must explain the role of ethical decision making in organisational IT security. The verb 'explain' requires an overview/description of the principle that would help another individual understand. **M3**

- You must evaluate the security policies used in an organisation. Evaluation requires you to make a critical judgement on a given fact, often evaluation can be based on speed, size, cost, effectiveness or even fairness. **D2**

- Both the merit and distinction criteria can be accomplished using either a report or a presentation. The presentation could be delivered using PowerPoint®, a website or a short YouTube video.

PLTS

You can demonstrate your skills as a **creative thinker** by creating a website based on your academic centre.

Functional skills

You can demonstrate you Functional **ICT** skills by creating a website based on your academic centre.

Mary Chang
Systems specialist

I work with a team of system security specialists as part of a large financial institution. We support the daily operation of the network and work closely with desktop support, as well as the network managers. Our role is to ensure the system runs without any complications and to protect it from internal and external threats

Occasionally we are called in to resolve issues, completing forensic investigations when required and possibly working with human resources and/or law enforcement. As new systems and applications are used by the organisation, we are tasked with planning how to support these and ensure their secure operation

A typical day

There is no typical day, as I have a dual role. I have many routine administrative tasks – checking network traffic, system performance and behaviour, looking for any potential anomalies. I also work on the implementation of new technologies, understanding the risks they may bring to my organisation.

We occasionally have security or communication issues. As the network is the lifeblood of the organisation's ability to do business, we have to respond promptly and often create and communicate a secure solution while we establish the cause.

Best things about the job

Apart from providing me with new technical challenges, I find that in systems security, as is true for many IT professions, you are always learning about new threats and how they may operate. As new applications and devices come onto the market, we are always looking at how we could implement them on our network without causing the system any problems.

Think about it!

1 What have you covered in this chapter, to give you a technical understanding of Mary's job? Write a list and discuss this with others.

2 What additional skills would you need to develop for this career to become a reality? Work in a small group and create a list.

Just checking

1. What are common internal threats to a system?
2. How is a trojan transmitted?
3. Why is disaster recovery important in maintaining system security?
4. How could data be stolen?
5. Why is the integrity of data of critical importance?
6. What techniques are used to physically identify equipment?
7. What mathematic principle is used for RSA encryption?
8. What are the two WEP standards?
9. The execute privilege offers what access rights?
10. Which law covers copyright?

Assignment tips

- While this is a theory unit, much of the theory is 'fun'. When doing your assignments use the mindset of a hacker or rogue employee and look at how your work would be affected by one of these individuals.

- Use plenty of diagrams. While a picture is not always worth a thousand words, with supporting text explaining what is required you may find you achieve a merit.

- Evaluation requires supporting evidence. This can be accomplished using tables, presentations or complex (structured) diagrams.

8 E-commerce

E-commerce has provided the most exciting shift in business in recent history and not only changed the way business is done, but also the way customers shop. There are now more opportunities to do business, for established businesses and those new to the market. Even a sole trader can sell internationally through an e-commerce site.

Shoppers can now make purchases from anywhere they can access the Internet and do it 24 hours a day. The ability of shoppers to shop from home, in the middle of the night and easily search for the cheapest price has needed a dramatic response from business in order to survive in these changing times.

In this unit you will investigate the different types of e-commerce and their benefits and drawbacks. Also you will look at how e-commerce businesses can stay on the right side of the law and protect them themselves from security threats. You will then explore the effect this change in business has had on society as a whole. Using all your new knowledge, you will finally develop an e-commerce strategy for a new business.

This unit is very useful if you are considering a career in e-commerce – but is also interesting to everyone who shops online.

Learning outcomes

After completing this unit you should:

1. know the technologies required for an e-commerce system
2. understand the impact of e-commerce on organisations
3. understand the effects of e-commerce on society
4. be able to plan e-commerce strategies.

Assessment and grading criteria

This table shows you what you must do in order to achieve a pass, merit or distinction grade, and where you can find activities in this book to help you.

To achieve a **pass** grade the evidence must show that you are able to:	To achieve a **merit** grade the evidence must show that, in addition to the pass criteria, you are able to:	To achieve a **distinction** grade the evidence must show that, in addition to the pass and merit criteria, you are able to:
P1 describe the technologies required for e-commerce **See Assessment activity 8.1, page 236**		
P2 explain the impact of introducing an e-commerce system to an organisation **See Assessment activity 8.2, page 248**	**M1** recommend methods to promote an e-commerce system **See Assessment activity 8.2, page 248**	**D1** evaluate the use of e-commerce in a 'brick and click' organisation **See Assessment activity 8.2, page 248**
P3 explain the potential risks to an organisation of committing to an e-commerce system **See Assessment activity 8.2, page 248**	**M2** discuss how security issues in e-commerce can be overcome **See Assessment activity 8.2, page 248**	
P4 review the regulations governing e-commerce **See Assessment activity 8.2, page 248**		
P5 examine the social implications of e-commerce on society **See Assessment activity 8.3, page 256**		**D2** compare different payment systems used by e-commerce systems **See Assessment activity 8.3, page 256**
P6 plan an e-commerce strategy **See Assessment activity 8.4, page 260**	**M3** design an interface for an e-commerce business **See Assessment activity 8.4, page 260**	

How you will be assessed

This unit will be assessed by a number of internal assignments that will be designed and marked by the staff at your centre. It may be subject to sampling by your centre's Lead Internal Verifier or an Edexcel Standards Verifier as part of Edexcel's ongoing quality assurance procedures. The assignments will be designed to allow you to show your understanding of the unit outcomes. These relate to what you should be able to do after completing this unit.

Your tutor will tell you precisely what form your assessments will take, but you could be asked to produce:

- presentations
- short reports
- leaflets and booklets
- your own e-commerce strategy.

Saria Vijey, BTEC National IT learner

I really enjoyed doing this unit. I enjoy shopping online and now I have a better understanding so I can do it safely. Also I would like to work in web design in the future and this unit gave me a really deep insight into e-commerce.

In this unit I had to create three projects. The first looked at e-commerce from a business perspective. I enjoyed learning about the laws which sites have to conform to and learning about my rights as a customer.

The second project examined e-commerce from the viewpoint of a customer and also looked at the impact it had had on society as a whole. We had some lively debates in class about the benefits and drawbacks of e-commerce, but I made sure my coursework was objective and balanced.

In the final project, I first of all created a podcast reviewing some existing e-commerce sites. Then I devised my own strategy for an existing business. I chose my local sports centre and investigated how they could sell their own branded sports equipment. It was fascinating to bring together all of the things we had been learning about to produce my own strategy and I felt as though I had really understood the essence of e-commerce. Being able to compare and evaluate specific features, then implement these into my strategy helped me achieve my distinction.

Over to you

- **Which business might you choose to create an e-commerce strategy? Is there a local business you are familiar with which does not yet sell online?**
- **What impact do you think e-commerce has made on society? What affect has it had on your life?**
- **What aspirations do you have after completing this course?**

1. Know the technologies required for an e-commerce system

Start up

Bricks and clicks

With the introduction of e-commerce, a range of terminology has evolved to describe the new trading patterns – in particular, to distinguish between traditional retailing and online trading.

- Create a mind map for each of these types of business: '**bricks**', '**clicks**' or '**bricks and clicks**'. Write down as many businesses as possible that fit into each category.
- Examine your three mind maps. What patterns, if any, can you identify?

Key terms

'**Bricks**' – any organisation that trades solely using traditional methods. It may have a presence online, perhaps a static website giving the business's contact details, but does not do any business over the Internet.

'**Clicks**' – any organisation that trades solely online. It has no physical presence for trading and all business is carried out over the Internet.

'**Bricks and clicks**' – any organisation that trades using both traditional and online methods. It may have been a 'bricks' organisation originally and developed the business to run online as well or it may have set up both businesses simultaneously.

Web server – a server that distributes web pages on to the Internet.

Browser – the software that allows the user to view the web page.

Cache – a store on a computer hard drive of all the web resources visited by a user. If the user accesses a cached page which has not been updated since the last download, the cached version will be displayed.

1.1 Technologies

The advent of e-commerce in business was made possible by the introduction of technology such as the Internet and credit cards and this technology continues to improve. Using a combination of web hardware and software, e-commerce not only gives more functionality to a business, but also improves effectiveness. In addition, now that a great number

of customers have access to high speed Internet connections, such as broadband, it is even more important that e-commerce is efficient. If a site is slow, a customer is likely to choose to shop elsewhere.

Hardware and software

As with all computer systems, e-commerce consists of a collaboration of hardware and software (see Figure 8.1). The software of both the web developer and the user need to be considered.

Web servers

A **web server** holds the live copy of the web page which can be seen by anyone who has access to the Internet.

Browsers

Browsers are installed on a user's computer and convert the data received via the modem into a visual web page.

There are several types of browser available. For Microsoft® Windows® the most common is Microsoft® Internet Explorer®, which comes free with the operating system (see Figure 8.2). Others that are becoming more popular are Mozilla Firefox® and Opera™. The most popular for Apple® products is Safari®.

When a user first loads a browser, they will be taken to the home page that is set in their browser options. This setting can be changed so a browser automatically opens on your chosen website. This could be the main page of your ISP, a search engine such as Google™ or, for a business, the organisation's home page.

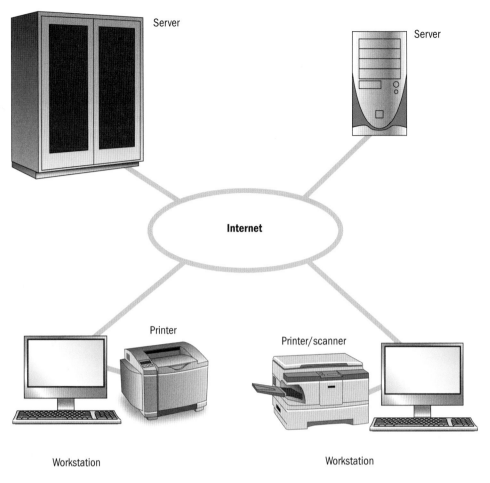

Browsers store viewed web pages in a **cache** so they can be reloaded quickly if viewed again. This allows you to view previous pages using the back button. When you are viewing previous pages, browsers also give an option to reload pages using the forward button. In addition, they provide a history list of frequently, and recently, visited sites to allow you to return to them quickly.

Most browsers have a Favorites or Bookmarks list – these are sites that the user has chosen to add to the list, either websites that they accessed frequently or ones they know they will want to return to in the future. At any time, the user can access this list and select a website. A target of web design is to encourage users to bookmark the site, which usually means they will visit again, hopefully regularly.

Figure 8.1 How the Internet is connected together

Figure 8.2: Example of a web browser. Other web browsers include Mozilla Firefox®, Google Chrome™, Opera™ and Safari®.

By using a cache and the Favorites or Bookmarks list, the user can access sites with a single click.

Browsers provide a visual interpretation of **HTML** and other web languages. HTML is the generic language in which all web pages are written and understood by all browsers. Web pages are linked together by hyperlinks, which can be presented as menus, buttons or images. Hyperlinks direct the browser to load a different page, allowing a user to move around the massive selection of web pages on the Internet.

> ### Did you know?
>
> In 2010 the European Commission forced Microsoft® to provide a Browser Choice statement to inform users of Internet Explorer® that other browsers were available. This is because most PCs are sold with Internet Explorer® being the default browser and there is concern over lack of choice for the customer and monopolisation (one company taking over the market).

Server software

There are several web server software applications, such as Internet Information Services (IIS), which comes bundled with modern versions of the Windows® operating system and Apache HTTP Server. In addition, there is software which makes uploading web pages to the web server easier. This process is called FTP, as it uses the file transfer protocol (FTP). Programs such as CuteFTP are designed to make uploading more user friendly.

Web authoring tools

Web authoring tools make it possible for more people to create web pages because they simplify the process and make it less technical. This means that creating and uploading websites on to the Internet is no longer solely the territory of IT experts. There has recently been much debate as to whether this has helped or hindered the Internet, as the quality of content on the Internet has come into question. Suggestions have been made to 'clean up' the Internet, although how that would be carried out is a very difficult question. One response has been to begin to develop Web 2.0, also known as www2. This is a 'new' Internet which has the aim of sharing resources and promoting online collaboration between users.

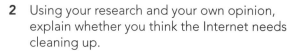

> ### Activity: Safety first
>
> 1 Research Web 2.0 and make notes.
>
> 2 Using your research and your own opinion, explain whether you think the Internet needs cleaning up.

All web authoring tools provide the basic facilities to create a web page and upload it to a web server. The two leading web design tools are Microsoft Expression Web®, which is part of the Microsoft Office® 2007 suite, and Adobe® Dreamweaver®. Both have a huge range of tools for web design, **wysiwyg** interfaces and include additional features such as templates and cascading style sheets (CSS).

Database systems

E-commerce websites usually have a database back-end storing the catalogue of products, customer records and other business information. This database should link to the website seamlessly so that the user is unaware of it.

Some organisations outsource the creation of their website, but retain control of the content of the database. This means that if any changes need to be made, such as price changes, only the database needs amending and the organisation can do this themselves.

Applications such as Oracle®, or languages such as **MySQL**™, can be used to create the database.

Networking

This section focuses on the methods used to connect computers together to create the network. It looks at how individual computers are identified so data can be sent to the correct place, the methods of data transfer across such a massive network and the naming of websites.

> ### Key terms
>
> **HTML** – stands for hypertext mark-up language. All web pages are controlled and structured using HTML, even if they use other languages as well.
>
> **Wysiwyg** – stands for 'what you see is what you get'. In web design programs, it means what you see in design view is the same as if it was published on the internet.
>
> **MySQL**™ – a language for creating online databases. it uses an SQL base, which is the language behind most databases.

TCP/IP addresses, ports and protocols

TCP/IP is a **protocol** that is used when transferring data across a network.

If computers do not use the same protocol, it becomes impossible for them to understand the data transmitted between them. This is similar to humans who speak different languages – unless they agree to speak a common language, they will not be able to understand each other.

To make sure the data reaches the right location on a network, each computer is given a unique number, called an **IP address**. It is a set of four numbers, each from 0 to 255. For example, 145.2.78.255 would address a specific computer on a network. The Internet is a large global network and works in the same way as a **WAN** (wide area network).

Ports connect protocols and IP addresses together. Each computer has several ports for data to pass through – they are virtual so they cannot be seen. Ports are like doors – each has a number to identify it and it can be open or closed. There are some default ports, for example port 25 is usually for email and port 80 is usually for the Internet, although these can be changed. For a web server, it is good practice to close all ports that are not being used otherwise hackers can take advantage of open ports to get into the system.

Domain names

Every website has an IP address, relating to the server which hosts it. For example, if you were to type 72.14.207.99 into the address bar of a browser, the page for www.google.com should appear. Smaller sites will always use the same IP address. However, large sites like Google have several, because they have many web servers.

Businesses would struggle to entice many customers to their e-commerce sites if the customers had to remember the IP address, so domain names were invented. Each IP address **resolves** to a domain name e.g. 72.14.207.99 resolves to google.com. A domain name is only the core part of the name (google) and the extension (.com).

HTTP and **www** are protocols which tell the computer that the data is a web page. This makes sure that the computer interprets the data in the right way. There are several extensions available (see Figure 8.3).

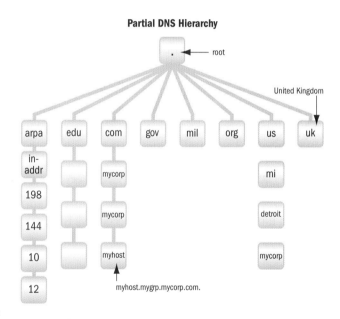

Figure 8.3: URL extensions

Each website can be contacted by its universal resource locator (URL) (see Figure 8.4). For example, if www.google.com is entered into the address bar in a browser, Google's website should open at its home page. A URL is any website address, for example www.google.com/about/contact/ would also be a URL. However, the domain name is still just google.com.

Figure 8.4: URL sections

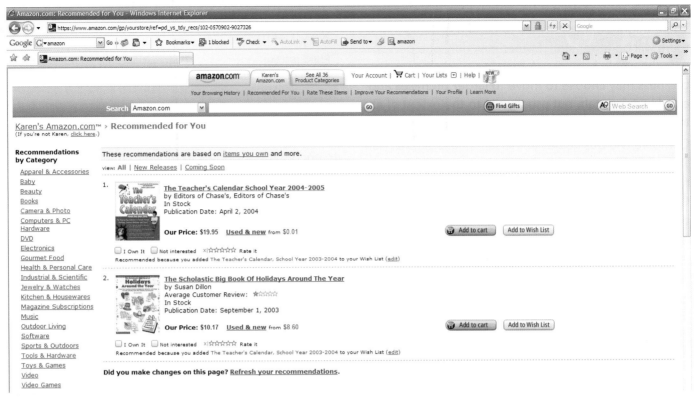

Figure 8.5: A personalised web page from Amazon

Alternative income sources

Once a business has an e-commerce facility, additional sources of income become available to it. For example, an e-commerce site could have **pay-per-click advertising**. This may navigate the customer away from the site, but each click on the advert would still gain money for the business (see the section on banners and pop-ups, page 241).

2.2 Drawbacks

Although e-commerce is a tremendous opportunity for businesses, there are also downsides which need to be explored.

Consumer trust

The most difficult issue that online businesses face is customer confidence.

> **Key term**
>
> **Pay-per-click advertising** – where a website hosts an advert and benefits by earning money every time a user clicks the advert.

Case study: Consumer trust

Mrs Jones has heard reports in the news about identity theft and has never purchased items online before. She does not believe suppliers will keep her financial details private or deliver the products requested so she will not purchase from them. She has also heard that e-commerce sites will personalise her online experience, for example making suggestions of products she may like based on what she has previously purchased. She has had a similar experience of this with store loyalty cards and finds it annoying.

1 Research the Internet to find out which stores offer loyalty cards. Conduct a survey to find out what people think about these loyalty card schemes. Present your findings to others in your group.

2 Conduct a survey of people who buy through sites such as Amazon. How do they feel about the personalisation of the site, based on information gleaned about them?

Lack of human contact

Some customers are deterred from purchasing online because they cannot speak to anyone from the business. They find this impersonal and prefer instead to shop in traditional stores.

Customers are also wary of buying clothes online because they are unable to try them on before they buy.

Delivery issues

When going to a traditional shop, customers have the option to take their purchases home immediately. When shopping online, they have to wait until the purchases are delivered.

Case study: Delivery issues

Mr Mahmood has never shopped online. He worries about the cost of postage and packaging and whether the goods will be delivered on time or even at all.

1   What reassurance can you offer Mr Mahmood that his worries are unfounded?

2   If Mr Mahmood does make a purchase online and the goods do not turn up, what can he do?

International legislation

When selling online, businesses are subject not just to legislation in the country of origin, but also to the laws in the countries where the customers live.

Legislation for e-commerce is a very complex area, one that is still being defined. For example, in the UK, you have to be 18 to buy alcohol, but in the United States you must be over 21 in all states. However, it would be quite possible for a business based in the UK to sell a case of wine over the Internet to a customer aged 18 in the United States. Which law should be followed, UK or US?

Product description problems

Some customers worry that what is described on the e-commerce site might not accurately reflect the

Activity: Legislation

1   Research the Internet to find out what laws exist regarding the sale of alcohol to minors in a number of countries. At what age does a person reach majority in these countries? Present your findings as a table.

2   Choose another product for which you think there may be legislation affecting its sale or movement between countries. Research the Internet to find out what legislation exists in the UK and one other country.

real product. This is especially difficult for colours, as different computer systems may display colours slightly differently. The quality of the original picture of the product shown on the website is another factor. E-commerce sites can exaggerate their descriptions of products, which may put some people off buying online.

Security issues

Perhaps the biggest worry for customers is that their financial details will not be safe – that the business will use them in some unauthorised way or security may be insufficient, resulting in their identity being stolen by criminals (see the section on identity theft, page 244).

2.3 Promotion

A business which uses e-commerce to trade online must also advertise. Several traditional methods can be used, such as billboards, television adverts and direct mailshots. However, the Internet provides its own advertising opportunities.

Effective use of search engines

If you wanted to find something on the Internet, how would you do it? If you did not know the address of the website, your first thought might be to use a search engine such as Google, AskJeeves or Yahoo. Because of this, e-commerce businesses want to be listed as highly as possible on the search engine results page, so that they are one of the first addresses that users see when doing a search (see Figure 8.6).

Highest search result

Sponsored links

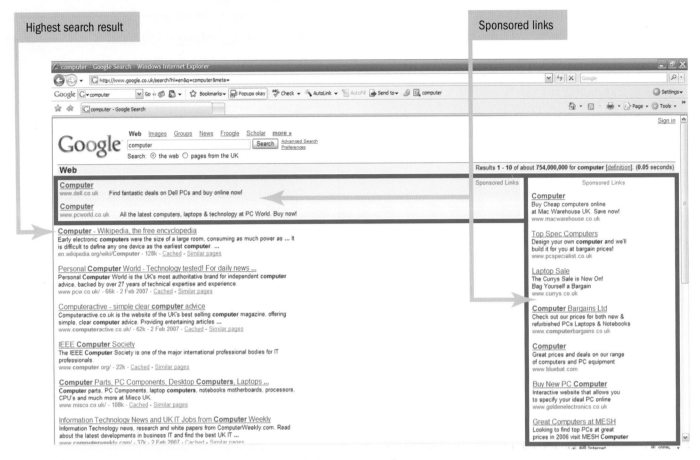

Figure 8.6: Companies that appear top in a search are likely to get more business

When a search engine carries out a search on the word(s) keyed in, it does not literally search the whole Internet. Instead, enormous databases are used to store information about all the websites of which the search engine is already aware and it is this database that is searched. To build up and maintain this database, search engines use **spiders** to trawl the Internet.

The spiders examine each web page encountered and send information back to be stored in the database. To ensure these spiders list the web page correctly, the web developer can include **meta tags** in the coding for the web page. These can include a description and/or keywords for the web page. For example:

<meta name='description' content='Board No More – board games from around the world'>

<meta name='keywords' content='board games, dice, Cluedo, Monopoly, chess'>

If meta tags are not present, the spiders will read the content of the page and make a best guess as to what it

Key terms

Spider – a bot (a program that runs on a computer 24/7, automating mundane tasks for the user) which examines websites on behalf of search engines.

Meta tags – words that are put into the HTML code of the web page, but are not displayed on the screen.

Did you know?

Spamdexxing is sometimes used to try to give a website priority in a search list. This can be repeating a phrase over and over on a site (usually unrelated to the site's actual content), in the hope that a search engine's spider will pick up on it, consider it important and move it higher in a search list. Alternatively, it can be using unconnected meta tags, such as the names of other popular businesses, to try to move up the list.

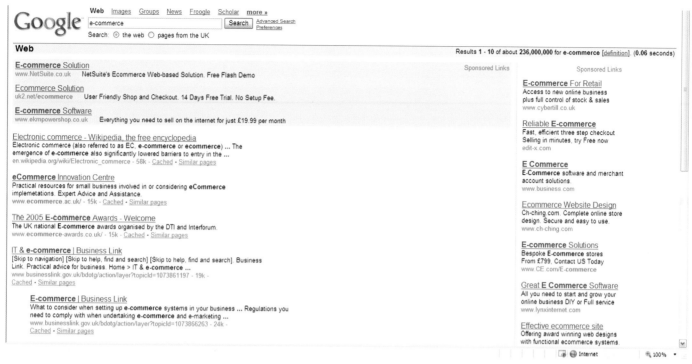

Figure 8.7 Sponsored links have been paid for to be listed highly

is about. This can result in the page being listed very low in searches, so it is important the meta tags are effective.

With the huge increase of the number of web pages, however, it is no longer sufficient to rely on meta tags. Businesses often pay a search engine to ensure they are listed highly in a related search. These are called sponsored links (see Figure 8.7).

Newsgroups and forums

Newsgroups normally use Usenet, a distributed bulletin board system. Newsgroups are separated into very specific topics and there is one for practically every subject. Generally they are text-based only.

Forums are mostly attached to websites and discuss the topic of the site. For example, IMDb (The Internet Movie Database) is a website about films and has a large forum where users can discuss each individual film on the website.

Typically, forums are not just text-based. They also allow for graphics, including **avatars** and signatures.

Because they are usually used by people with a particular interest, newsgroups and forums can be used to advertise to specifically targeted groups of people. For example, a website selling computer games may advertise on a gaming forum.

Banners and pop-ups

With pay-per-click advertising, adverts designed by a business are put on to other websites. The host website benefits by earning money every time a user clicks the advert, for example £0.02 per click – 100,000 clicks per week would earn £2000 for having the advert on the site. This may seem like a huge number of clicks, but it is a very tempting opportunity for a lot of websites. The pay-per-click adverts are often banners,

Key terms

Newsgroups – a method of posting messages to other Internet users.

Forums – web pages where users can post messages to other users.

Avatar – an image used to represent a user online. This could be an image of the user, something that interests them or something completely random.

Figure 8.8: Examples of banner adverts online

either across the top of the website or in sidebars (see Figure 8.8).

Pop-up adverts open in a new browser window and can be irritating for the user.

Recently, there has been a rise in centre-screen Flash adverts – the animation activates as soon as the website loads. Often, these will be designed to blend in with the host site and, due to the time and expense of creating them, are usually only used by large businesses.

Spam

Spam is the Internet equivalent of a direct mailshot. A business can use its own registered customer list (or buy a mailshot list) and then send an advert out in an email to all the people on the list. In this way the business targets their message straight to the customer. However, there are also disreputable people using spam and now it is seen as a nuisance that email users unfortunately have to accept as an Internet hazard.

Key term

Spam – the term used for junk email.

Spam has also been used to send unsavoury adverts and attached viruses. A number of email services, such as Hotmail and Gmail, have spam filters which are designed to stop these types of emails reaching the user's inbox. Some businesses have set up filters so that spam is immediately deleted as soon as it arrives in the email server, so their employees are not troubled by it.

Site names

Businesses try to use memorable domain names so that customers will remember them and return to visit their sites. While short domain names are generally preferable, there are some such as www.iwantoneofthose.com which have proved that longer ones can also be unforgettable.

Did you know?

Typosquatting is a form of cybersquatting (see page 234), where domain names are purchased that are similar to the names of real sites or businesses, relying on customers mistyping the name. Therefore when buying a domain name it is important to think of how it could easily be misspelled and buy these addresses as well.

Direct marketing

Businesses wanting to advertise straight to the customer often use direct marketing. This method involves sending emails to existing or potential customers. When a customer registers on the website their email address will be captured in a database, which can be used to generate a list of the email addresses of existing customers. The email addresses of potential customers can be purchased from agencies that operate purely for direct marketing services.

By using direct marketing, businesses can target their marketing precisely. Sometimes, it is also combined with tracking a customer's purchases and tailoring the advertising. For example, if a customer buys science fiction DVDs, they may receive a direct marketing email advertising a new *Star Trek*™ box set.

Direct marketing is sometimes considered to be spam (the electronic equivalent of junk mail). It is a matter of perception – if it is unwanted and a nuisance, it is spam. But if the recipient is interested in the content of the direct marketing email, then it is not.

Effective user interfaces

The user interface is one of the most important parts of an e-commerce site. There is no point having the most amazing coding and database behind a website if the user interface is unusable. There are several usability paradigms for a good user interface, as discussed on page 257.

Establishing customer loyalty in a virtual environment

Due to the lack of human contact and the underlying mistrust a number of customers still have of e-commerce, it can be more difficult to ensure customer loyalty to an e-commerce site than to a traditional retail business.

Loyalty can be encouraged, however, by personalising web pages (see pages 237–38), ensuring customer confidence in the site's security and always delivering on promises.

2.4 Security

Any business that operates online is at risk from Internet threats and so security is vital to successful operation. Identity theft can make customers the victims of serious fraud and damage caused by viruses can close companies down. Businesses need to be able to prove that customers' personal details, such as credit card numbers, will be safe. If this is done well, it can reassure potential customers and widen the potential market.

Prevention of hacking

E-commerce sites need to prevent **hacking** so that the running of their business is undisturbed and, more importantly, their customers' details are not stolen.

Specialist software can be used to look at all the ports on a computer and see which are open and which are closed. If a port is open and not being used, that gives a hacker a way in. Therefore, the best way to deter hackers is to make sure unused ports (see page 233) are closed by the firewall (see page 244).

Viruses

'Virus' has become a catch-all term to describe any malicious computer program that can cause an unwanted result when run. There are three main types: viruses, **worms** and **trojans**.

Key terms

Hacking – when someone attempts to enter a computer system with the aim of stealing data, damaging the system or just to show that they can.

Virus – a manmade program or piece of code that causes an unexpected, usually negative, event and is self-replicating. It is often disguised as a game or image with a clever marketing title, such as officeparty.jpg, and attached to an email or a download file.

Worm – a virus that resides in the active memory of a computer and duplicates itself. It may send copies of itself to other computers, such as through email or Internet Relay Chat (IRC).

Trojan – a malicious program that pretends to be a benign application, but purposely does something the user does not expect. Trojans are technically not viruses since they do not replicate, but can be just as destructive. If left in a computer system, provides 'back door' access to the hard drive and data.

To try to prevent virus infections, anti-virus software must be installed on the web server and all of an e-commerce business's computers. Not only must it be installed, but it also must be updated regularly, ideally every day. New viruses are developed all the time and anti-virus software must have the latest defences to provide the best protection possible. All computer users must be wary of email attachments, downloading files, floppy disks and any unsolicited communication.

See *Unit 7: Organisational systems security* for more on viruses.

Activity: Viruses

1 Research further into recent viruses and the effects they had on businesses and the public. Make notes for future reference.

2 Categorise each of the viruses as virus, worm or trojan.

Did you know?

Computer viruses do not just appear – they have to be written and then released 'into the wild'. They are usually created for two reasons: to cause disruption or to steal data (such as credit card details). Some of the worst viruses have included Melissa, ILOVEYOU, Nimda, MyDoom and the Storm Worm. Try looking these up on the Internet to find out more about the damage they caused.

Identity theft

Identity theft is a new form of crime that has had a recent upsurge and has been highlighted in the media.

Identity theft involves a thief who has stolen the personal details of their victim and uses them to apply for services such as credit cards, loans and mortgages under the guise of their victim. This crime is difficult to detect if the thief has a great deal of information about the victim. The crime is often detected when the victim receives correspondence requesting payment for the thief's spending. Tracing the thief is also difficult, although possible by following the paper trail of all the correspondence received.

The type of customer details stored by e-commerce businesses provides enough information to

commit identity theft, so it is very important that all e-commerce businesses protect their customers' data with every method possible, as described below.

Firewall impact on site performance

A **firewall** builds a protective virtual barrier around a computer or a network of computers so that only authorised programs can access the data. It sets up a gateway and only allows authorised traffic through the gateway. Incoming data is inspected and only allowed through if it is legitimate. This is done by the opening and closing of ports (see page 233). If ports are left open, a 'back door' becomes available for hackers to enter the system.

When a user views a website that has passed through a firewall, they might not see all of the features on the site. This is because the security policies on the firewall can be set to block certain types of scripts running on the user's computer. This is done to prevent viruses and hackers attacking the system. When a security policy is decided for a firewall, the administrator must balance the need for high security with the possibility of losing functionality from websites.

Secure sockets layer

Secure sockets layer (SSL) is a cryptographic protocol that provides secure communication on the Internet. It provides endpoint authentication, meaning that both the server and the client need to be identified and confirm that they are who they say they are. This is done by **public key encryption** and **certificate-based authentication**.

Key terms

Identity theft – occurs when a victim's details are stolen and someone else pretends to be him or her, for example applying for financial products and making purchases.

Firewall – a piece of software that protects the system from unauthorised access. This is especially important for web servers.

Public key encryption – a method of coding information so that only the people with the right key at both ends of the communication can decode it.

Certificate-based authentication – a method of cryptography which prevents data being read by unauthorised parties.

Key terms

HTTPS – stands for secure hypertext transfer protocol.

Encryption – a method of encoding that is difficult to decipher by unauthorised parties. It uses prime numbers. The higher the prime number, the stronger the encryption.

HTTPS

HTTPS is the protocol usually used by websites on the Internet. HTTPS is a secure version of the protocol, which uses **encryption** to protect the data entered on the site. This protocol is usually used when customers are entering their payment details.

RSA certificates

RSA certificates are a method of coding information so that the people at either end are identified by a digital certificate, coupled with a digital signature. These can confirm the identity of the sender or recipient.

Strong passwords

It is vital for all computer users to use strong passwords. This is especially important for web servers and other e-commerce systems.

A strong password should have:

- both letters and numbers
- both capitals and lowercase
- symbols such as * or #
- more than eight characters.

Hackers can take advantage of weak passwords, especially those which are easy to guess. If a password is personal to the user, for example a pet's name, it will not take too much effort for a hacker to guess it. Software programs, called password crackers, can run through many possible combinations of characters and test whether each one is the chosen password. The stronger the password, the longer this software will take to work it out, and the more likely hackers will be to go on to try a different website. They are not likely to spend time working their way into a well-protected site.

Alternative authentication methods

A new authentication method that is slowly becoming more popular is the use of digital signatures. These are the electronic equivalent of the traditional signatures that have been used for hundreds of years as a personal authentication method.

A digital signature allows someone to authenticate a document over the Internet. For example, a customer setting up a direct debit payment would traditionally need to wait for the paperwork to be posted to them, sign it, then return it. Now digital signatures can be used to authenticate the documents immediately anywhere in the world. This benefits both the customers and businesses.

Case study: Tines (Part 2)

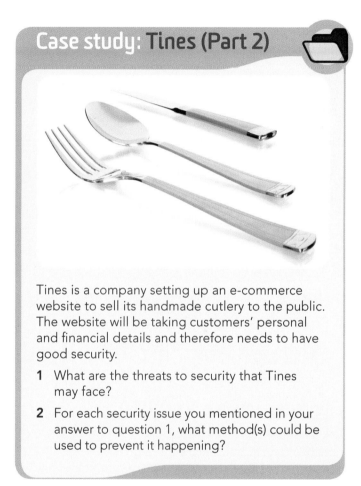

Tines is a company setting up an e-commerce website to sell its handmade cutlery to the public. The website will be taking customers' personal and financial details and therefore needs to have good security.

1 What are the threats to security that Tines may face?

2 For each security issue you mentioned in your answer to question 1, what method(s) could be used to prevent it happening?

2.5 Legislation

E-commerce is regulated by laws and guidelines. These aim to ensure that sites operate effectively and that online trading is fair and lawful. These laws protect both the business and the consumer. All the legislation discussed in this section relates to the UK only.

Data Protection Act (1998)

The Data Protection Act (1998) was designed to protect sensitive data held in databases. It was originally passed in 1984, with an update in 1998 which was brought into effect in 2000. It is upheld by the Information Commissioner. Every business that stores data electronically, for example, information about customers, must register and state the data that they plan to hold.

There are eight principles in the Act (see Figure 8.9).

The data subject is the person to whom the data refers. Under the Act, the data subject has several specific rights, including:

- the right to compensation for unauthorised disclosure of data
- the right to compensation for unauthorised inaccurate data
- the right to access data and apply for verification or erasure where it is inaccurate
- the right to compensation for unauthorised access, loss or destruction.

1 Data must be stored fairly and legally.

2 Data must be obtained for limited and clearly declared purposes.

3 Data must be adequate, relevant and not excessive.

4 Data must be accurate and maintained as such.

5 Data must not be kept any longer than necessary.

6 Data must be processed in accordance with the data subject's rights.

7 Data must be kept secure.

8 Data must not be transferred to any other country without adequate protection.

Figure 8.9: The eight principles of the Data Protection Act

Activity: Data Protection Act

Visit the website of the Information Commissioner's Office by going to Hotlinks. Find more information on each principle of the Data Protection Act and make notes.

1 What might an e-commerce site do that would contravene the rules of the Data Protection Act?

2 What would happen if they did?

Computer Misuse Act (1990)

The Data Protection Act was designed to protect sensitive data stored on computers, but there was no legislation to prosecute those who hacked or attacked computer systems with viruses. Towards the end of the 1980s, with the increase of computer use, it was becoming necessary to legislate against these serious problems.

The Computer Misuse Act (1990) introduced three new offences:

- unauthorised access to computer programs or data
- unauthorised access with the intent to commit further offences
- unauthorised modification of computer material (for example programs or data).

The Act makes a distinction between **computer misuse** and **computer abuse**.

Key terms

Computer misuse – an illegal act involving a computer.

Computer abuse – a legal, but unethical act, involving a computer.

Activity: Computer Misuse Act

Visit the website of the Information Commissioner's Office by going to Hotlinks. Find more information on each offence defined by the Computer Misuse Act and make notes.

1 What might an e-commerce site do that would contravene the rules of the Computer Misuse Act?

2 What would happen if they did?

Consumer Credit Act 1974

Customers paying by credit card are protected by the Consumer Credit Act for payments up to £25,000. So, if a payment cannot be made by the customer, the business will still receive the money from the bank and can therefore confidently send out the products purchased.

The Act also guarantees a cooling-off period during which customers can change their mind about a purchase – for mail order goods the cooling-off period is 14 days. This is good for the customer, but can be disadvantageous to a company as it means that, even after a purchase has been completed, there is the possibility of the customer asking for a refund.

Trading Standards

The Trading Standards Institute works with consumers and businesses to maintain fair trading. It is part of local government and ensures that legislation is enforced, such as the:

- Trade Descriptions Act (1968)
- Consumer Protection Act (1987)
- Price Marking Order (2004).

The Trading Standards Institute also deals with issues such as counterfeit goods, the sale of alcohol and tobacco to underage persons and the exploitation of vulnerable consumers from scams and doorstep crime. E-commerce websites must clearly describe their products. This is especially important because customers can only see pictures of the products before purchasing, not the items themselves.

Freedom of Information Act (2000)

This Act gives the public the 'right to know'. The public can request information about public bodies, such as the government, and legal entities, such as businesses. (See *Unit 7: Organisational systems security*, page 221.)

Copyright legislation

The Copyright, Designs and Patents Act (1988) protects all works such as music, art, writing and

programming code once it is tangible, which means in a fixed form. As the Internet has grown, the question of whether websites are subject to protection under copyright has often been discussed. It is now accepted that a website becomes tangible once it is coded and saved on to storage media, especially if the source code is also printed. Websites are therefore protected by copyright.

E-commerce regulations

The Electronic Commerce Regulations (2002) specified several rights to ensure fair trading through e-commerce sites, including:

- the business should provide information about itself such as its name, its geographic location and a method of contact
- communications cannot be sent unless the sender is easily identifiable and that any offer or promotion is unambiguous
- when an order is placed, the business must acknowledge the receipt of the order by electronic means without delay
- allowing a customer to correct misplaced orders, such as typing in 100 instead of 10.

Assessment activity 8.2

In Assessment activity 8.1 (on page 236) you began a presentation for Cuckoo, a small business selling clocks and watches which is thinking about starting to trade online. They have asked you to help the company decide if this is a good idea and, if so, how to go about it.

Continue your presentation called 'Why E-commerce?' which will explain the key points of the issue.

1a Explain the benefits of e-commerce for a business, referring to Cuckoo. **P2**

1b Explain the risks of e-commerce for a business, referring to Cuckoo. **P3**

To accompany your presentation, create three leaflets to provide Cuckoo with information about promotion, security and legislation.

2 Describe the methods available to promote an e-commerce business and recommend which Cuckoo should utilise. **M1**

3 Discuss the security issues affecting an e-commerce business and how Cuckoo could overcome these. **M2**

4a Describe each of the major pieces of legislation to which all e-commerce businesses must adhere. **P4**

4b For each piece of legislation described in 4a, explain how it would affect Cuckoo if they were to begin trading online. **P4**

5 Write a short report to evaluate the use of e-commerce by Cuckoo, currently just a 'bricks' organisation, but hoping to become a 'bricks and clicks' business.

5a Carry out further research, finding information from reliable sources to explain this terminology with examples. **D1**

5b Analyse the 'click' part of business and discuss the key features of their potential use of e-commerce. **D1**

5c Explain the advantages an e-commerce site will give over and above Cuckoo's traditional shop presence. **D1**

5d Explain the disadvantages an e-commerce site may bring to Cuckoo. **D1**

5e Make your recommendations for Cuckoo based on your findings. **D1**

Note: You are advised to research wherever possible and use correctly referenced sources.

Grading tips

- When discussing benefits and drawbacks, ensure you stay objective and give a balanced account of both. **P2** **P3**
- Discuss all types of promotion and, when recommending promotion for Cuckoo, take into account the types of customers they are trying to attract. **M1**
- When talking about security issues, remember that every e-commerce is at risk from all sorts of threats and no type of protection is 100 per cent safe, but businesses should try to protect their sites as much as possible. **M2**
- Searching on the internet is a good place to start. Make sure you select reliable websites and only focus on UK law, as laws in other countries are different. Consider government websites such as www.ico.gov.uk for the Information Commissioner and www.direct.gov.uk, the website of the UK government. **P4**
- Consider the practical applications and consequences of each law, analysing them one part at a time. For example, you could look at each principle of the Data Protection Act one at a time and think about how conforming would affect the business. Would they need to have certain business practices? Would they need to purchase security hardware and software such as firewalls or anti-virus? Will they need to train their employees? **P4**
- Use reliable sources on the Internet to investigate the terminology of 'bricks and clicks'. **D1**
- Remember when explaining advantages and disadvantages for distinction criteria you should include some analysis and comparison. **D1**
- Think through your recommendations carefully as this will demonstrate your level of understanding of the topics and if you can apply them to a business. You will be doing more of this in Assessment activity 8.4. **D1**

PLTS

By carrying out further research using the Internet you can demonstrate you are an **independent enquirer**.

Functional skills

You can provide evidence for your Functional **ICT** skills in Developing, Presenting and Communicating Information by combining your research to produce informative documents.

3.   Understand the effects of e-commerce on society

3.1 E-commerce entities

There are several types of e-commerce entities, for example manufacturers and retailers, including organisations set up just to trade on the Internet called e-tailers. Some e-commerce sites are consumer led or primarily offer information or a service, for example financial services. A variety of types are considered here.

E-tailers

E-tailers are businesses that source products from suppliers and sell them purely online, such as Amazon and ebuyer.co.uk. Some of these organisations wouldn't have existed without e-commerce. There is a minimal need for warehousing if orders are shipped directly from the supplier to the customer, with the website providing an intermediary service. This is one of several reasons why overheads can be lower. However, as prices must be relentlessly competitive, profit margins can be low. Therefore these businesses must operate at maximum cost-effectiveness. Another reason for lower overheads is that e-tailers do not need shop space, therefore reducing costs of lighting, heating and other utilities. They often employ fewer staff, resulting in lower salary costs.

A relatively recent development in online selling has been the inclusion of second-hand products. For example, Amazon provides both new and used books, games and other goods. This development has been encouraged by eBay™, which specialises in customers using the website to sell their own items.

Case study: Amazon

Amazon, originally called Cadabra, was launched by Jeff Bezos in 1995. It was set up during the dotcom boom of the 1990s with an unusual business model – it did not expect to make a profit until after at least four years of business. While other dotcom businesses grew rapidly, Amazon slowly built strong foundations. Finally, at the end of its fourth year, it made a $2.5 million profit. In 2005, it made a profit of $359 million and in 2006, $190 million.

Amazon is most famous for selling books, but the company also sells a wide range of products from CDs to small kitchen appliances, such as coffee machines. Sales in books from traditional stores have reduced recently and Amazon has often been blamed for 'stealing' their sales.

Amazon provides an enhanced experience for its customers. For example, when a customer logs in they see a personalised page with suggestions of products they might like. Amazon does not just provide the products, but includes customer reviews, detailed product descriptions and other information to help customers to select the right product for them.

There are facilities to create a wish list and a wedding list. Customers create a list of products that they would like and pass this on to family and friends to let them know what to buy for a wedding gift or other occasion such as a birthday.

For more information, visit the Amazon site, especially the About Amazon and Help sections. Go to Hotlinks and click on this unit.

1   What sort of e-commerce entity is Amazon?

2   Why has Amazon become a very successful business? How has the company gained and retained its customers' loyalty?

3   How have the lower start-up and running costs of e-commerce affected Amazon?

4   What impact has Amazon had on traditional book stores?

5   To what extent do you think it is Amazon's responsibility to consider traditional book stores?

6   What other factors could explain the decline in book sales?

Manufacturers

Some businesses manufacture products themselves and sell them purely online, such as Dell™. It is not possible to purchase a Dell™ computer from a traditional shop such as PC World. However, they do have physical offices in Bracknell, Berkshire, employing over 1500 staff and running a huge call centre. Manufacturers also buy through e-commerce as well as sell. Dell™ publishes a newsletter which is posted out to all existing customers in the hope that they may upgrade. Dell™ also uses direct marketing online by emailing adverts at least once a week to existing customers.

Manufacturers like Dell™ can afford to sell their products at lower prices and have more dramatic special offers, because they do not need to pay for retail premises or for as many sales staff to sell the products. They can also provide a much more personalised product, because the computer systems can be made on demand. For example, when purchasing a Dell™ computer (see Figure 8.10),

customers select every component from a range. This means they receive a more precise product to fulfil their requirements. As they are making choices for the product, a running total is calculated so the customers are always aware of how their decisions are affecting the total price. At any point during the selection process, the order can be cancelled or restarted. Once all selections are made and the product is completely chosen, the customer can then click to process the order and pay online.

Existing retailers

Some businesses that exist already in the traditional marketplace with branches all over the country have now converted to selling online as well. This 'bricks and clicks' approach can allow companies to enjoy the best of both worlds. However, it is an expensive process as the business has to be able to keep financing the traditional store and also pay for the initial outlay and maintenance of the new online business. If done

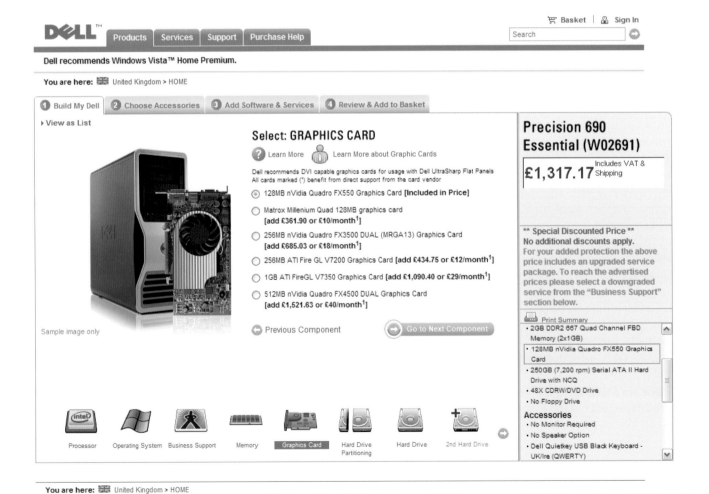

Figure 8.10: Dell™ purchasing screen halfway through the process

Key term

Niche market – a small, specialised section of the buying public that is likely to be interested in a certain type of product or service.

proficiently, the profit from the e-commerce branch of the business should offset the costs and therefore the business's profits should increase.

Moving from 'bricks' to 'bricks and clicks' can often only be done by larger, more stable businesses as it can be too risky a strategy for many smaller businesses. However, some small businesses do manage to make the transition from purely traditional to combining traditional and online successfully, usually if they have a unique product for a **niche market**. An example is New Zealand Nature Company, which specialises in silk and sheepskin products and sells worldwide and focuses on a target market of sailors and people who take part in outdoor activities.

Consumer-led e-commerce entities

One interesting development of the Internet is the emergence of consumer-led sites, such as eBay™, where the public can buy and sell their own items through an auctioning system.

Case study: Tesco

Tesco is a UK-based international supermarket chain. The core retail area is groceries, but Tesco has expanded into other retail areas such as clothing and household goods, as well as finance, insurance and telecommunications. It is the largest retailer in the UK and the third largest worldwide.

Tesco was founded in 1919 at the end of World War I by Jack Cohen, who operated as a one-man trader in London's East End. At that time, food was scarce and Jack bought damaged goods from other businesses and resold them – he learned the skill of knowing what was in a tin by just shaking it. The first Tesco store was opened in 1929 in Edgeware, London. From these small beginnings, Tesco has gone from strength to strength, with an annual profit of over £3 billion in 2006.

Tesco took advantage of new technology very quickly and began trading on the Internet in 1994. In 2003, Tesco's Chief Executive Officer, John Browett, received an award for the innovative systems which supported Tesco's e-commerce site.

When purchasing online, customers select the products and quantities they want and are given a running total so they know exactly what they will pay, although discounts are only taken off the final bill. Then, a two-hour delivery slot can be booked. The information is sent to the most local store where, on the appropriate day and time, the products are packed and delivered to the customer's house. If any products could not be included in the delivery, a substitute may be included or an apology will be made at the door. The customer signs to confirm they have received their goods.

As Tesco moves into more areas and becomes a bigger organisation, it has been criticised for trying to create a monopoly (which means it would become the only business providing these products).

For more information visit the Tesco website, especially the Talking Tesco section go to Hotlinks.

1   What sort of e-commerce entity is Tesco?

2   How has Tesco managed the transition from 'bricks' to 'bricks and clicks'?

3   How has Tesco taken advantage of 24/7 global trading on the Internet?

4   What impact has Tesco had on retailing in the UK?

Why not write a report about the advantages and disadvantages of e-Commerce compared with traditional forms of commerce?

Many sites provide a wealth of information and, although there are opportunities to make a purchase, this is not in the forefront of the minds of most visitors to these sites. Many travel sites offer tickets, but to support this they also provide details of services and may offer to help the visitor to plan a journey. For example, the National Rail Enquiries website mainly provides information to train travellers, but also allows them to purchase train tickets.

Many organisations, such as the BBC and the daily newspapers, have websites that are a rich source of information on current affairs, as well as providing learning opportunities and the option to buy products.

The *Daily Telegraph*, for example, ran a series of articles on novel writing and provided a message board for interested people to post their comments and their answers to writing exercises set in the weekly articles. A business aim of this project was to use the Internet to increase sales of the newspaper.

Links to the websites mentioned in this section have been made available at Hotlinks.

Service providers

Not all organisations have a product that can be sent to you through the post. Some, such as easyJet and Lastminute.com, provide a service rather than selling a product. Both specialise in the leisure and transport industry. easyJet provides low-cost air travel and Lastminute.com specialises in selling services at very short notice, for example, flights and holidays close to the time of departure.

Links to the websites mentioned in this section have been made available at Hotlinks.

Financial e-commerce entities

Some service providers focus on financial services online. For example, Esure sells insurance and Egg is a purely online bank.

Online banking is an area which has had a huge hurdle to surmount – trust is much more of an issue with a service such as a bank than a retail business – but it has become an increasingly popular alternative to traditional banking companies. The main reason for this is that online banking services offer especially competitive rates due to the lower overheads and running costs.

Insurance is another service that can be sold online and a new business has developed from this – searching a number of businesses for the best deal, such as Confused.com. To use this service, a customer inputs their details for the type of insurance they want and Confused.com searches all registered insurance brokers for the best quote on those specific details. This service is free for customers to use and a number of companies have signed up to be part of it, in the hope that it will increase the number of people applying to buy insurance from them.

Links to the websites mentioned in this section have been made available at Hotlinks.

3.2 Social implications

The e-commerce revolution has changed business practices around the world and traditional retailers have had to learn how best to operate in the new faceless global market. One area where established brands have had an advantage is in trust and existing customer relationships. Customers need to trust the e-commerce site and see the advantages of buying through them.

Changing customer perspective

The main issue with e-commerce is the customer's perception of online trading. Scare stories in the media (see Figure 8.11) warn potential customers about identity theft, items not being delivered and other reasons not to trust buying online.

A site should attract more customers if it promises:

- value – not just offering lower prices than high street stores, but also products that are not available elsewhere
- service – the majority of websites offer a 24-hour delivery time for a small additional cost

Figure 8.11: Newspaper scare stories about e-commerce

- ease – open 24/7 and accessible from home, e-commerce is relatively effortless for the customer; customers may find it is easier to locate products using a website's search facilities rather than searching in a physical store
- security – there are a number of ways to protect customers and websites should ensure that they adopt these to reassure their customers.

Activity: Customer perspective

1   Conduct a survey with people of different ages. What is their opinion of e-commerce? Do they trust it? Collect relevant data and make notes for future reference.

2   Present your findings graphically to your group, showing any trends that relate to age.

Economic and social impact due to speed of changes

With the rise of e-commerce threatening traditional businesses, there is an issue for people who do not have Internet access. More remote are Internet users who can only use dial-up (56K), as broadband is not available where they live. For these people, e-commerce is not always an effective alternative to traditional shopping. In addition, families on low incomes may not be able to afford to buy a computer, or pay a monthly subscription for Internet access or broadband, meaning that they cannot benefit from the lower prices of e-commerce. This is called the social divide.

'Bricks and clicks' organisations

By bringing together the high street and the virtual world, 'bricks and clicks' organisations are changing the face of shopping. Whereas in the times before e-commerce people had to go physically to the high street to buy the products they wanted, they can now buy these products from their own home, with all the inherent benefits and drawbacks discussed below. It has resulted in changes to the way business is done, to patterns of customer behaviour and to the businesses which exist in our high streets. It could be argued that the introduction and rise in popularity of e-commerce has been the single most radical change to business in the last century.

Benefits for customers

Remote shopping means that customers do not need to leave their house in order to make their purchases. This is a valuable feature for e-commerce customers who live in remote places or find it difficult to travel to their local towns or shopping centres, such as those who do not drive. It also allows people who are housebound access to a huge variety of goods and services. Where they may have previously had to rely on other people to do their shopping, they are now empowered to shop for themselves online, giving them independence.

By being able to buy products and services 24/7, customers can access the sites, browse and buy at any time. This especially benefits people whose jobs do not fit into the normal routine and allow them to get to high street shops during normal times or at weekends, such as shift workers and those in public services, such as nurses, firefighters and police officers.

A popular benefit is that online stores can usually offer goods at a lower price than can be found on the high street, as they do not have to pay for rent, utilities and staff for the physical store. Although customers need to pay for postage and packing, which can sometimes be high, in general purchasing from e-commerce sites is often cheaper than the high street.

Being able to search for products can be of huge advantage, especially if looking for products in a hurry. The facility to search for a particular product then find the lowest price (or sort the findings by other categories such as customer reviews) is provided by a number of sites, including Google, and can be invaluable to customers.

Drawbacks for customers

One of the toughest hurdles that e-commerce businesses have to overcome is to prove that they can be trusted. Customers can be fearful of inputting their personal and financial details into a website, worried that they may not receive the goods they have purchased or they may be the victim of identity theft.

Buying a product without being able to inspect it can also be a deterrent to customers purchasing online. This is less of a problem with standard products, such as electrical goods, but with items which are more individual, such as clothes and food, customers often prefer to see the product in real life before paying for it.

When ordering online, the customer must rely on a delivery service to receive the product, whether this is through the post or a specialist delivery service. They must depend on the service to bring the item on time and without being damaged.

Impact on customers

It is often said that 'the world is getting smaller', and this is mainly due to the advance of technology. Communication is easier and contact can be made with anyone anywhere in the world in seconds. By trading online, businesses open themselves up to the global marketplace. Previously, it might have taken months, even years, to break into foreign or niche markets. E-commerce has allowed instant penetration into all marketplaces.

In contrast, there are challenges that accompany the increase of e-commerce that are advantages for customers while being drawbacks to smaller businesses. For example, as discussed above (see page 237) traditional booksellers are facing huge competition from online booksellers such as Amazon. As pure e-commerce businesses can offer the same products as traditional stores at lower prices, as well as offering other benefits, traditional stores must change their methods of business and advertising to remain competitive and profitable.

E-commerce and high street employment

As more businesses begin to trade online, there is an effect on employment opportunities. As traditional stores close, workers cannot gain employment in a similar field. E-commerce favours those with IT training. Additionally, as e-commerce businesses can be run from small locations, shop rent prices may fall due to fewer businesses buying or renting store premises or warehousing. These issues could have a significant effect on the economy.

3.3 Payment systems

In the early days of e-commerce, online transactions were not possible. Customers could pay by a cheque sent in the post, but this could mean a long delay – waiting for the cheque to be delivered and then to be cleared by the banks before the goods would be dispatched. The other method was credit card, but this would involve either telephoning or emailing the credit card details. Customers were worried about sending

Why are traditional booksellers facing competition from online booksellers?

their financial details by email, especially as security was not as good then as it is now. Credit card details would be split over several emails, but if one email was not received or arrived in the wrong order, the payment would not go through.

Nowadays, there are several instantaneous payment systems available. Improved technology, such as SSL and HTTPS (see page 245), has also allowed websites to provide better security to reassure customers.

Electronic cheques work in a similar way to paper cheques, although they are instigated digitally. The customer asks their bank to make a payment to a creditor or vendor and the bank can either pay this immediately, if they can accept electronic payment, or produce a paper cheque for the company if they cannot.

When taking payment from a credit card, businesses are protected because the bank will provide the money and invoice the customer. So, the business will always be paid with this type of transaction, whether or not

the customer can pay their credit card bill. However, as e-commerce becomes more popular and there are more potential customers, businesses have to accept more payment methods, such as debit cards, as not everyone has a credit card. It must be remembered that this is an area where some customers are worried about the safety of their personal financial details and the possibility of someone else being able to access their account and steal their money.

There has recently been an upsurge in digital methods of payment. PayPal is currently the most popular. A user 'uploads' money into the PayPal account from a bank account using a digital transfer. That money can then be used to make a safe, instant payment. A number of customers feel happier using this method, as they are not inputting their bank card details into a variety of websites, just the PayPal site. Another similar method available in the UK is NoChex. However, unlike PayPal, NoChex only accepts bank accounts with debit cards.

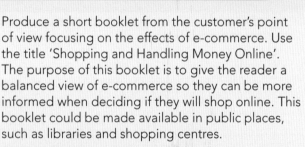

How does payment by credit cards protect businesses financially?

Activity: Payment methods

1 Look at several e-commerce sites. What payment methods does each take? Present your findings in a table.

2 Is there a correlation between the size or type of a website and the amount of payment methods it takes? Make notes for future reference. Present your findings graphically.

When making payments online, several details from a card are necessary, including the CV2 security number from the back, which was originally introduced just for e-commerce transactions.

Splash Plastic was devised by PrePay Technologies Ltd, a UK company. This card can be 'loaded' with money at shops such as the Co-op, Post Offices or straight from a bank account. It can then be used instead of a credit or debit card to make online purchases. As this payment method became more popular, in March 2006, a new card was introduced called 360money Splash Plastic. This new card has the Maestro® symbol, which means it is accepted in more places. It is available for people aged ten and older (parental consent is needed for under-fourteens) and it can be loaded with a maximum of £1000.

Assessment activity 8.3

 BTEC

Produce a short booklet from the customer's point of view focusing on the effects of e-commerce. Use the title 'Shopping and Handling Money Online'. The purpose of this booklet is to give the reader a balanced view of e-commerce so they can be more informed when deciding if they will shop online. This booklet could be made available in public places, such as libraries and shopping centres.

1a Describe the benefits of shopping online, from the customer's perspective. **P5**

1b Describe the drawbacks of shopping online, from the customer's perspective. **P5**

1c Explain the issues of the social divide in relation to e-commerce. **P5**

2 Select several different payment systems and compare them objectively, their good and less good points, from the customer's perspective. **D2**

Note: You are advised to research wherever possible and use correctly referenced sources.

Grading tips

- Make sure you look at the issues from the customer's perspective, rather than the business's perspective as you did in Assessment activities 8.1 and 8.2. Remember that this booklet's aim is to give the reader the facts objectively, without giving your opinion on whether online shopping is good or bad. **P5**

- When selecting the payment systems to compare, make sure they are 'different'. For example, debit card and credit card are the same type of payment system. Similarly, PayPal and NoChex are the same type. Remember that you are comparing them, rather than describing them. You may wish to use tables to present your comparisons clearly. **D2**

PLTS

You can show that you are a **reflective learner** by thinking about real-life situations and examining issues from different people's points of view.

Functional skills

Your Functional **ICT** skills in Developing, Presenting and Communicating Information can be evidenced by presenting your information appropriately for your audience.

4.   Be able to plan e-commerce strategies

4.1 E-commerce strategy

An e-commerce strategy encapsulates all the decisions which need to be made when setting up an e-commerce site. As it is documented, it fixes the ideas, which is especially useful if several people are involved, it can cement the decisions so there is no disagreement. It can also be given to any external agencies, if they being used to create any part, so they can clearly see what is needed.

4.2 Structure

It is important to consider the structure of the website and of each page within it. At all times customer considerations should come first, making sure they will enjoy their experience of using the site, find it easy to navigate and use and hopefully make purchases,

perhaps also returning again to buy more products and advertising your site by word of mouth to their family and friends.

Customer interface

The customer interface is the first point of contact the user will have with the online business. If visitors are not able to use it easily, it is very likely they will shop elsewhere.

Usability issues such as those listed below must be considered when designing an interface (see Figure 8.12).

- Who are the users?
- What do the users already know?
- What do the users want or need to do?
- What is the general background of the users?
- What context is it to be used in?
- What is to be done by the computer?
- What is to be done by the user?

For customers to buy products from e-commerce sites, they must register by entering their personal details). This usually involves giving full name, date of birth, address and sometimes financial details such as credit card numbers, ready to be used if the customer makes a purchase.

E-commerce businesses can use this data to personalise a website (see pages 237–38).

This can also be used to store a user's purchasing details so they do not have to retype this every time they wish to buy a product. A **cookie** is stored on the user's

Figure 8.12: What do you think of the Pearson Education Limited website?

computer so when the website is downloaded into the browser or the user logs in to a web page, the cookie is recognised and the customer's information is inserted into their personalised web page. This could be a problem as it makes purchasing from such sites very quick and easy and could encourage irresponsible spending.

When buying products online, some customers worry about the delay between paying for goods ordered and receiving those goods. Will the goods arrive? When will they arrive? To allay these fears, some e-commerce businesses provide customers with the facility to see where their order is in the delivery chain (see Figure 8.14).

For example, a customer may log on and use the order number to view a particular order and see that the order is being processed. Later, the customer may see that the order has been dispatched and that the products are due for delivery the next day. This reassures customers who might otherwise be contacting the business, worried that they have not yet received their goods.

E-commerce sites also take advantage of flexibility to win over customers. Rather than being tied to the house all day, awaiting a package, many sites allow e-shoppers to have their orders dispatched to an alternative address or addresses.

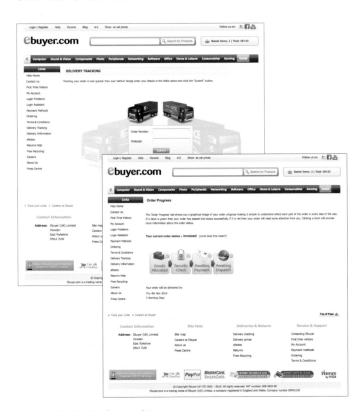

Figure 8.13: Order tracking pages

Image

E-commerce site designers must pay careful attention to their company's image, or brand reputation. With the emergence of a vocal community of bloggers, Tweeters, and other social media users, it is very easy for one bad customer experience to go viral and be seen around the world.

Many companies have keyword alerts set up for any mention of their brand online, so that the PR department is aware of a potential loss of reputation – and can act to resolve it – before the situation goes critical.

But protecting the company image can also be handled badly and the news media is full of stories of company employees getting into trouble for insulting customers via an official Facebook® page or Twitter feed.

Style

An e-commerce site is an extension of a business, no matter whether it trades in a traditional store or purely online. Most businesses will have a logo and a colour scheme, possibly a standard design or specialised font. A customer should be able to look at an e-commerce site and recognise it as being part of the business as a whole. This can instill confidence in the customer – if they can trust the business, they can trust its e-commerce site.

Activity: House style

Look at several e-commerce sites with which you are familiar from the high street, such as Asda or HMV. Do their e-commerce sites reflect the style of their traditional stores?

4.3 Hosting

When setting up an e-commerce site, there are two issues of hosting which need to be decided – who will host it and which ISP to use.

Who will host?

If the site is to be hosted in-house, the business has to make sure its staff has the skills required to design a professional-looking, fully functioning website. This may mean employing another member of staff, or several, depending on the size of the site and the desired functionality. Keeping it in-house should result in lower costs, but businesses can fall into the trap of giving responsibility to employees who lack the necessary design or technical skills, resulting in amateurish websites that do not instill confidence in customers.

Subcontracting means the business will pay another company to create the website. It depends on the deal as to how much is done by the subcontractor – it could be just the design, then the site is handed over to the company to maintain. Sometimes the subcontractor has full control long term. Although the latter option can be expensive and there can be communication issues between business and subcontractor – for example over design elements, with each having a different idea of how something should look – it is likely to result in a more professional website with more reliable functionality than using in-house resources.

A decision also has to be made as to the location of the web server. Will it be secure and safe in the business? Can the business afford to buy their own server or is it better to rent a server, or part of a server, from a professional service?

Which ISP?

Secondly, the business needs to decide which ISP they will use. They need to decide whether they change their existing one and choose the type of Internet connection they want. If they have been using a low-speed broadband line, they may need to purchase a bigger line, perhaps a dedicated line that gives them continuous guaranteed access at all times.

4.4 Promotion

Marketing is a vital part of e-commerce. There is no point in creating a wonderful website and selling amazing products if no one knows your business exists. Promotion is the way to attract the attention of potential customers.

Decide how you are going to advertise the site. There are many different methods, ranging from simple, cheap options such as including the address on business stationery and leaflets, to advertising on television and radio, bus banners or roadside billboards.

Search engines are key to promoting an e-commerce site and you need to decide how you are going to make best use of them. Will you use meta tags (see page 240), which are just included in the pages, or go to the extent of paying for primary positioning?

Also consider making use of message boards and chat rooms. Guerrilla marketing is a powerful tactic if done well, but if not done carefully it can backfire. Watch boards and chat rooms and mention your site when it is relevant. Related to this is viral marketing, which works like word of mouth advertising. It might be by doing something outlandish or mysterious to get people talking, something interesting which people will forward in an email or another approach which draws attention.

4.5 Costs

An important part of an e-commerce strategy is identifying the costs. Whether they are specific prices or just isolating where the business will need to spend money, it is very useful for the practical implementation of the strategy.

The costs which should be considered include the following.

- **Set-up:** The hardware, software and networking elements will all need to be paid for. Will you hire them or buy them for the business? Will you use an outside agency or internal skills to build and develop the website? Will you lease the equipment to set up the site?

- **Maintenance:** Once it is built, the website still needs a lot of work, most of it weekly or even daily, as products and other business elements need to be updated. Will this be done in-house or by an outside agency?

- **Security:** How many security features will you have? What effect will they have on the running of your site? How will you tell your customers that you are protecting the safety of their data and financial information to reassure them?

- **Advertising:** Consider the cost of printing, such as leaflets or posters, of adverts on television or radio, in magazines or newspapers, or paying for search engine listings.

- **Delivery strategy:** How will customers receive the goods they have bought online? How much will delivery cost or will it be free? Will couriers be used or the postal service? Might charges increase for next day delivery? Can the items be tracked and, if so, will that be through the e-commerce site or the delivery company?

- **Staff training**: How much training will your staff need – what are their skill levels at the moment? How much access will they have to the site and what level of permission will they have, for example will they be allowed to make changes? Will the training be done in-house, by an external company who made the site (if one has been used) or an external training organisation who specialise in training adults in IT?

4.6 Security

What measures will you take to protect your business and your customers' details? They have to have to have faith in your business as e-commerce relies on trust – trust that you will protect their details and deliver the goods.

What steps will you take for fraud protection, hackers and viruses?

Assessment activity 8.4

Before developing your own e-commerce strategy, you should review existing e-commerce sites so you are better informed.

1 Select three very different e-commerce sites and create a review for each. You may present this as a print magazine article or a podcast. Focus on the interfaces of the sites, including:

- ease of use
- display of products
- personal details entry
- payment. **P6**

Note: You do not need to make a purchase from any site to complete this task.

2 Create your own strategy for an e-commerce site in the form of a report, entitled 'Name of Business – an e-commerce strategy'. Choose a real-world business for whom you can create a strategy, preferably one currently not selling online.

Include:

- promotion of the site
- any costs involved (actual figures are not required)
- security measures
- site hosting and other technical details
- any other information you feel is relevant. **P6**

3 Design an interface for your chosen business's e-commerce site. This may be done by hand or on computer, using a suitable program. The interface should be of the site's home page and should demonstrate all the key features of a e-commerce site. If required, include designs for other pages. **M3**

Note: You are advised to research wherever possible and use correctly referenced sources.

Grading tips

- When selecting e-commerce websites to compare, make sure they are varied. Consider the products they are selling, the customers they are trying to attract, the key features they have included and the style of the website. **P6**

- Select your real-world business wisely. This may be a large national or international business, a local business, a charity, a business which provides a service – you should be able to find some interesting opportunities for your analysis. **P6**

- Remember that when designing websites you must find a balance between aesthetics and technical. Make sure your website will have all the functionality it needs, that it is easy to use by the customer, but also attractive and pleasing to the eye. Consider any logos or colours that your chosen business may use as standard – an e-commerce website is an extension of a business and therefore should look like part of that business's brand. **M3**

PLTS

Show you are an **independent enquirer** by carrying out additional research perhaps by looking at good and bad examples of website.

Use your **creative thinking** skills when coming up with your own original e-commerce strategy.

Functional skills

Evidence for your **ICT** skills could be created when designing your interface as you use ICT in complex and non-routine tasks.

House style

House style is a set of design decisions which create a visual identity for a business. For example, it may include a distinctive logo, a colour scheme, choice of fonts and layout. Some businesses purposefully use their house style so their traditional and online businesses are instantly recognisable as part of the same organisation, whereas some businesses aim to create a different identity on the web. Consider the designs of the following e-commerce sites.

1. HMV

The similarity between HMV's high street store and e-commerce website is striking. They use the same font, in lowercase, and same simple colour scheme: pink and black. They have chosen to tightly join the identities of their online and offline businesses.

Go to Hotlinks to visit the HMV website.

Due to the threat of digital music and iTunes, HMV have had to use a strong brand identity, along with other techniques, to maintain a strong position in the market.

2. PC World

Go to Hotlinks to visit the PC World website. Notice how the website and store are similar, but different. They use the same colour scheme of red, yellow and purple, but the combinations of colour are different, producing quite dissimilar logos. Also, if you look closely, especially at the C in PC you will notice the names of the business are in different fonts.

3. Marks and Spencer

This business has chosen to have different online and offline branding. The high-street store uses the full name of the business, whereas the e-commerce site has shortened it to M&S. In addition, it is called 'Your M&S'. Go to Hotlinks to visit the Your M&S website. The aim of the branding on the website is to personalise the shopping experience, making it distinct from the traditional store by instilling the idea that when shopping online Marks and Spencer will tailor itself to you, become 'your' store. Whereas the store reflects its more traditional, dignified position on the high street as one of the longest-running retailers in the UK.

Think about it!

1 Why is a house style important?

2 Why have these three businesses used their house style differently across their high street and online businesses?

3 Do you think house style affects customers' behaviour? Justify your answer.

4 Find some more examples of different ways businesses have used their house style online and offline. Interview people of different ages who shop online and ask them whether the image and style of the high stores and websites affects their potential to look at the products and make a purchase.

Just checking

1. Define the terms 'bricks', 'bricks and clicks' and 'clicks' businesses. Give examples for each.
2. Identify five pieces of legislation which affect e-commerce websites and their primary purposes.
3. Name three advantages and three disadvantages to a business using e-commerce.
4. Name three advantages and three disadvantages to a customer using e-commerce.
5. How can an e-commerce site be positioned higher up a list by a search engine?
6. Describe three methods of promoting a website, other than search engine optimisation.
7. List the hardware, software and networking technologies needed to create and upload an e-commerce site to the internet.
8. State three threats to the security of an e-commerce website and suitable measures which can be taken for protection.
9. Describe three different payment systems and compare their advantages and disadvantages.
10. What are the key features which need to be considered when designing an e-commerce website interface?

edexcel :::

Assignment tips

- Although you are completing separate projects, each one does link into the other. So keep safe any research you do for a project, as you will likely need to refer to it again.
- When you find a useful website, make sure it is reliable. Note down the address so you can return to it again. Also, copy the text you wish to use in a document, as websites can change and the information may disappear when you next access it.
- When choosing your business in the final project to create your e-commerce strategy, pick something interesting as you will do better work with a business that appeals to you or is challenging and unusal.

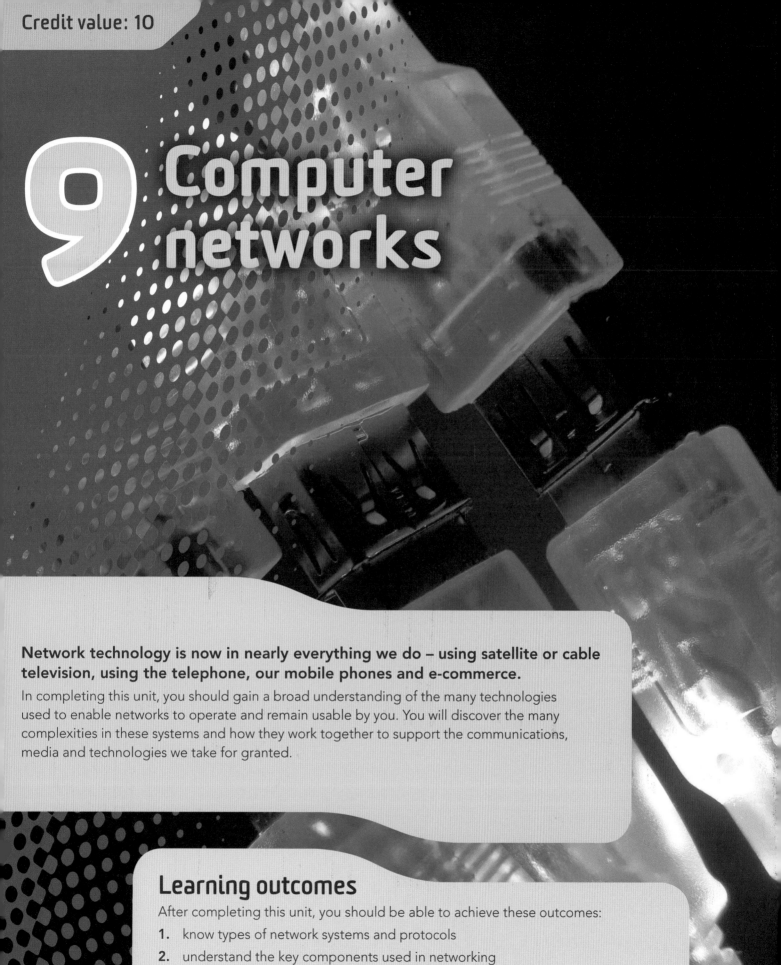

9 Computer networks

Network technology is now in nearly everything we do – using satellite or cable television, using the telephone, our mobile phones and e-commerce.

In completing this unit, you should gain a broad understanding of the many technologies used to enable networks to operate and remain usable by you. You will discover the many complexities in these systems and how they work together to support the communications, media and technologies we take for granted.

Learning outcomes

After completing this unit, you should be able to achieve these outcomes:

1. know types of network systems and protocols
2. understand the key components used in networking
3. know the services provided by network systems
4. be able to make networked systems secure.

Assessment and grading criteria

This table shows you what you must do in order to achieve a pass, merit or distinction grade, and where you can find activities in this book to help you.

To achieve a **pass** grade the evidence must show that you are able to:	To achieve a **merit** grade the evidence must show that, in addition to the pass criteria, you are able to:	To achieve a **distinction** grade the evidence must show that, in addition to the pass and merit criteria, you are able to:
P1 describe the types of networks available and how they relate to particular network standards and protocols **See Assessment activity 9.1, page 273**	**M1** compare the benefits and disadvantages of peer-to-peer network and client/server networks **See Assessment activity 9.1, page 273**	
P2 describe why different network standards and protocols are necessary **See Assessment activity 9.1, page 273**		
P3 explain the key components required for client workstations to connect to a network and access network resources **See Assessment activity 9.2, page 281**	**M2** design a networked solution to meet a particular situation with specific requirements **See Assessment activity 9.2, page 281**	**D1** justify the design and choice of components used in a particular networked solution **See Assessment activity 9.2, page 281**
P4 explain the function of interconnection devices **See Assessment activity 9.2, page 281**		
P5 describe typical services provided by networks **See Assessment activity 9.3, page 291**		**D2** evaluate typical services available from a network operating system directory service **See Assessment activity 9.3, page 291**
P6 make a networked system secure **See Assessment activity 9.4, page 298**	**M3** report on the business risks of insecure networks and how they can be minimised **See Assessment activity 9.4, page 298**	

How you will be assessed

This unit will be assessed by a number of internal assignments that will be designed and marked by the staff at your centre. It may be subject to sampling by your centre's Lead Internal Verifier or as an Edexcel Standards Verifier as part of Edexcel's ongoing quality assurance procedures. The assignments will be designed to allow you to show your understanding of the unit outcomes. These relate to what you should be able to do after completing this unit.

Your tutor will tell you precisely what form your assessments will take, but you could be asked to produce:

- reports
- presentations
- observation report
- network diagram
- posters
- blog
- witness statement.

James York, BTEC National IT learner

I have not done any networking before. My friends tell me that networking is difficult and I will struggle with all of the technologies involved.

When I started the unit, I was fascinated by the different types of network systems in use. In fact, I would have to admit that I was impressed by how large and also how small networks can be. My Bluetooth® mobile phone can run its own network infrastructure based on the same technology as the entire Internet!

When I worked on my assignment, I had the opportunity to investigate the different types of network infrastructures and how they are used by individuals as well as organisations such as my school.

Personally, looking at how networks operate and how I could implement a secure system gave me the confidence to explore further networking as a skill and how this may enhance my career.

Over to you

When reading this chapter, ask yourself the following questions.

- How could you accomplish the networking described on a handheld device such as an iPad or a mobile phone?
- What technology is required to accomplish this at home?
- Does my home network support this? If so, how?
- In the world around me, where are there examples of this type of system?

1. Know types of network systems and protocols

Start up

Topology of a network

In small groups, working with pens and a large sheet of paper:

- search the Internet for different network systems (they may be called topologies)
- draw each one and discuss as a group and in a class session how they may operate.

Explore in the discussion how modern commerce and communication could manage without the Internet.

For networks to communicate locally, as well over considerable distances, different systems operate to ensure effective communication connecting smart phones and servers as well as public and private networks to each other.

1.1 Types of network

This section considers the many different types of networks, their **topologies** and access methods.

LANs

The definition of a **LAN** (local area network) has become increasingly vague over the last ten years. At one time, it was understood to mean a system of interconnected computers at one location, such as your school or college. Now, with faster technology and the ability to use LAN devices over greater distances, LANs can span many sites within a town or city, depending on who is using the system.

You may have a wireless router at home – this will allow between five and ten wireless devices and at least four devices connected by cable to share a broadband or ADSL connection.

A LAN can be as small as two computers, connected with one cable, and is only limited by the size of the organisation.

Larger LANs are carefully managed to ensure that network communication is transmitted efficiently. Devices such as switches and routers are used to extend the number of computers connected. The network infrastructure is divided into separate subnetworks to ensure a greater level of control.

Key terms

Topology – the structure or layout of the communications network.

LAN – stands for local area network.

WAN – stands for wide area network.

WANs and WAN technologies

A **WAN** (wide area network) is a complex network system, comprising interconnected LANs. A WAN could be two LANs connected to each other over distance (for example the head office of an organisation and the production facility) or it could be many networks in a large organisation.

Your school or college is a member of a WAN infrastructure provided by your local education authority or joint academic network (JANET).

The Internet is also a WAN, although unlike most WANs, which are privately managed by an individual organisation, the Internet is a network of interconnected WANs with the LANs connected at the edge of the system. It enables commercial organisations, academic centres, governmental organisations, telecommunications companies and you, the private user, to communicate via one common system.

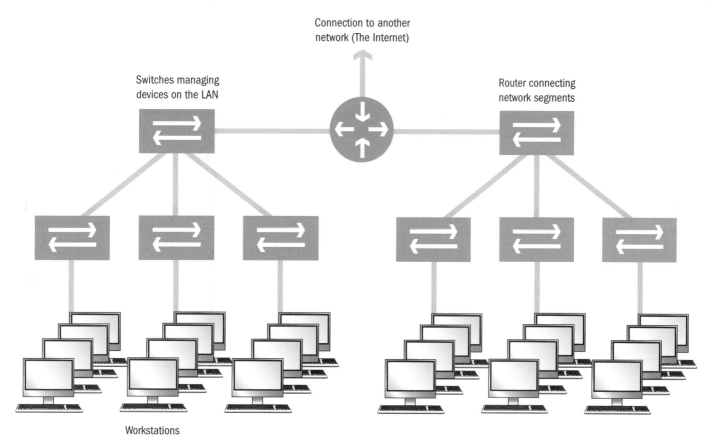

Figure 9.1: A LAN infrastructure

Depending on the location and who is offering the WAN connection, there are many WAN technologies that you may encounter, including **frame relay**, **ATM** and **MPLS** systems.

Frame relay is used at the core of the WAN, where all traffic is directed from system to system. Frame relay is a **packet-switched** network structure and can be configured to enable multiple systems to communicate on the same structure without any direct communication. This is accomplished by ensuring that every connection in the frame relay system is connected in a mesh (see Figure 9.2) and configuring the equipment to create the logical structure required for the customer.

Key terms

Frame relay – a packet-switched network structure. It can be configured to enable multiple systems to communicate on the same structure without any direct communication.

ATM – stands for asynchronous transfer mode.

MPLS – stands for multi-protocol labelled switching.

Packet switching – a mechanism which sends network traffic in small manageable data units across the system.

Frame relay can monitor the amount of traffic on the system – if the system gets too busy it can be configured to ensure the system does not overload. This is very useful for telecommunications and video, as these types of system do not cope with delays on the system – when there are delays, voice communications sound terrible and videos keep stopping and starting.

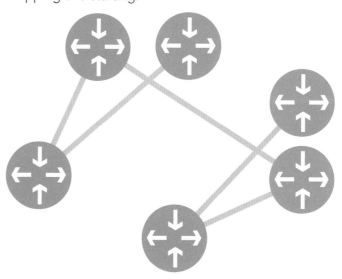

Figure 9.2: Frame relay

ATM (asynchronous transfer mode) has many similarities to frame relay as a WAN-based packet-switched network system. Its principal difference is the size of the packets sent. In ATM, the packets are called cells and the data size is considerably smaller than most systems. This offers the advantage of speed, reliability and reduction in jitter (staggered loss of data), which affects voice communication systems, such as Skype™.

MPLS (multi-protocol labelled switching) is the most recent successor of frame relay and ATM technologies. ATM and frame relay are systems, which operate at layer 2 of the **OSI** (open system interconnection) model only (see Unit 10, Table 10.2, page 314). In contrast, MPLS is designed to cooperate with routing protocols at layer 3 of the OSI model. Routing protocols are used to enable networks to communicate with each other and ensure that the structure can adapt to changes such as the loss of connections, changes in bandwidth or preferred routes. For MPLS, this ensures that the central WAN structure is highly adaptable when working with the routing protocol to spot changes in the network, follow the network structure and work with corporate or customer needs.

PAN

A **PAN** (personal area network) is any system using **Bluetooth®** within 10 metres. Therefore any Bluetooth® phone connected to a Bluetooth printer, headset, hifi, car stereo is part of a PAN structure. A PAN can be used to exchange data, as well as synchronise devices.

The most common use of a PAN is Bluetooth® audio, where a simple device (a headset) is paired with your phone.

Topologies

In the conventional development and operation of a network infrastructure, each system has a physical topology as well as a possible logical topology.

Unit 10 explores this subject in detail – please refer to Table 10.13 on page 330.

Network access methods

A network is a highly competitive environment. For a device to send data, it must find an open **time slice**. **Token ring** networks solve this problem by each device

on the system waiting its turn (as in the game pass the parcel) to communicate fairly. When a device has received the token, it can send data. The problem arises when there are **big talkers** on the system that need more network time.

Ethernet overcomes the big talker problem with a best effort solution. Each device on the system can send data as and when it sees fit. The problem with this occurs when two devices contest for the same service. Figure 9.3 shows how, when two devices send data across the same line at the same time, a collision occurs. Each device has to wait and resend, where another collision may occur, in which case the devices have to wait and then resend the data – and so on.

To overcome the collision issue, Ethernet has a solution called **CSMA/CD**. CSMA/CD is commonly referred to as the backoff algorithm and is applied by all devices on the system. Unless the network is too busy, the re-attempt is normally successful.

CSMA/CA is a variation of CSMA/CD, which is based on the detection of the signal before any data is sent. CSMA/CA is used in wireless systems. With more homes using wireless, collision is increasingly becoming an issue as each network contends for a channel on the network.

Key terms

OSI – stands for open system interconnection.

PAN – stands for personal area network.

Bluetooth® – a network structure that enables devices such as phones and headphones to interconnect with other systems.

Time slice – when a portion of device/system time is allocated to a given task.

Token ring – a circular network structure, where every device has a fair 'turn' to communicate.

Big talker – the term used for a network device that communicates more than the others, normally a server.

CSMA/CD – stands for carrier sense multiple access/collision detection. It is a method employed by Ethernet to detect continuous collisions of network data.

CSMA/CA – stands for carrier sense multiple access/collision avoidance. A variation of CSMA/CD, to avoid continuous collisions of network data.

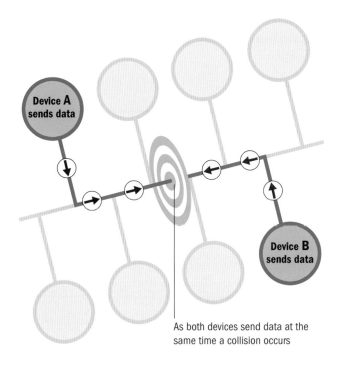

As both devices send data at the same time a collision occurs

Figure 9.3: A collision

Network models

The OSI (open system interconnection) model is a logical ideology that describes network communication between different network devices. The OSI model is a concept that is often used as a tool to describe networking. The benefit of the OSI model is that it makes no difference if you are on a Windows®-based system at home and the website you are visiting is on a Linux® platform – it ensures that all devices concerned in this communication act equally and effectively.

The OSI model is represented by seven layers, with 7 at the top (nearer the user, who is considered to be layer 8 by some experts) and 1 at the bottom for the communication medium (the data leaving the computer).

See the full OSI model in Unit 10, Table 10.2 on page 314.

The **TCP/IP** (transmission control protocol/Internet protocol) model applies the same principles as the OSI model, using four layers instead of seven. Whilst this is still an abstract concept, unlike the OSI model it has a direct relationship to the TCP/IP protocol suite used to manage Internet communication.

Key term

TCP/IP – stands for transmission control protocol/Internet protocol. It is a complex suite of protocols which operate on four layers to enable LANs and WANs to intercommunicate.

Activity: Creating a WAN for Widgets

Widgets R Us, the global widget manufacturer, requires a business needs analysis of its system and has hired you as a consultant to report on:

1   the best WAN structure to support its regional offices in Europe

2   how broadband/ADSL will support managers who work from home

3   how the OSI model affects the choice of equipment purchased

4   why Ethernet is preferable to token ring based networks.

1.2 Network protocols and standards

For any device on a network to communicate, the system and each device must use a range of protocols. This ensures that the communication is consistent and reliable; each protocol is used for a different purpose depending on what data is to be transmitted.

TCP/IP

Internet development was based on the standards of the TCP/IP four-layer model and gained popularity because of its various protocols.

For more on TCP/IP model layers see Table 10.4 on page 316 of Unit 10.

The TCP/IP protocol suite has an extensive range of protocols in common use on a LAN, as shown in Table 9.1.

Table 9.1: Common TCP/IP protocols

OSI layers		Common TCP/IP protocols			
7	Application	FTP	HTTP	POP3	SMTP
6	Presentation				
5	Session	DNS			
4	Transport	TCP	UDP		
3	Network	IP	ICMP	DHCP	
2	Data Link	ARP	RARP		
1	Physical				

Key terms

FTP – stands for file transfer protocol. It is used for file exchange and storage.

HTTP – stands for hypertext transfer protocol. It is used for the distribution of web pages.

POP3 – stands for post office protocol version 3. It is used to collect mail from an ISP.

SMTP – stands for simple mail transfer protocol. It is used for sending emails.

DNS – stands for domain name system. It is used to match easy-to-remember domains typed in by the user, such as www.bbc.co.uk, to IP addresses like 82.165.26.58 (which are not so easy to remember).

UDP – stands for user datagram protocol and is used for connectionless systems.

ICMP – stands for Internet control messaging protocol. It is used by a variety of management applications, including Ping, to test communication.

DHCP – stands for dynamic host configuration protocol. It is used to issue IP addresses to devices as they log into a network.

ARP – stands for address resolution protocol.

RARP – stands for reverse address resolution protocol and is used to match IP addresses to MAC addresses on a computer.

FDDI – stands for fiber-distributed data interface

UDP (user datagram protocol) is part of the TCP/IP protocol suite – the suite in simplified terms operates in two parts. TCP is connection-oriented, so that each communication, such as a download, is managed in groups of packets (called windows). If any packet in any group is lost, the group is resent. UDP is connectionless, used for Internet streaming, such as

your favourite Internet radio station. If a packet is lost, there is no resend, as the sound of your music will sound strange.

AppleTalk®

AppleTalk® (devised by Apple® for the Mac OS® system in the early 1980s) is a historical protocol suite that has lost the battle against the more dominant TCP/IP protocol suite. Some old systems may still have to use this protocol for legacy reasons, normally when there is an application or device which requires the use of the older protocol.

LAN standards

The IEEE (Institute of Electrical and Electronic Engineers) maintains the LAN standards for communication at layer 2 of the OSI model. These are defined as 802.2, 802.3 and 802.5.

- **IEEE 802.2:** Manages Ethernet data packets (called frames) and the link to the upper and lower layers of the OSI model (called the logical link control).

- **IEEE 802.3:** The definition of the MAC addressing on a network card and data collision detection over a variety of different speeds and media.

- **IEEE 802.5:** Manages token passing over a ring topology.

FDDI (fiber-distributed data interface) is a LAN standard using fiber optic technology to extend the distance of a LAN to over 200 kilometres (120 miles). It enables LANs to operate over considerable distances. FDDI uses two connections to enable traffic to travel in both directions. This enables greater speed and efficiency but also adds to the complexity of the system.

Wireless technologies

Beyond the technologies you may use at home, with your laptop or smart phone, the range of wireless technologies available in networking is a diverse field and always enjoying new development. At the time of writing, a well-known car manufacturer was teaming up with a computer supplier to provide in-car WiFi, enabling a range of Internet-based devices to work in a car. The time may come when online gaming is not constrained to home-based systems.

The 802.11 wireless standards are wide-ranging and vary internationally. The common standards in use are a, b, g and n. You may see these listed on manufacturers' material as 802.11n, etc. From a standards perspective, the higher the letter, the faster it may be and it will be compatible with all the lower letters.

- 802.11a works up to 120 metres outside, but there is a higher-powered variant that will run up to 5000 metres. It can run up to 54 Mbps (**mega bits** per second).
- 802.11b works up to 140 metres outside. It can run up to 11 Mbps.
- 802.11g works up to 140 metres outside. It can run up to 54 Mbps.
- 802.11n works up to 250 metres outside. It can run up to 150 Mbps.

WiFi is not the only wireless technology. Bluetooth® and **3G** both use high-frequency radio, and **infrared** uses light.

Bluetooth®, using the same microwave wireless technology as WiFi, is a unification of many standards. Depending on the device you are using, you will find that it can be used for PAN (personal area network) as well as for wider distances.

- Class 1 Bluetooth® can communicate (in optimal conditions) over a distance of up to 100 metres.
- Class 2 Bluetooth®, used by most mobile phones, can communicate over a distance of up to 10 metres.
- Class 3 Bluetooth®, used by hands-free devices (your Bluetooth headset), can communicate over a distance of up to 1 metre.

All devices can work with each other – it is the range that differs. A class 1 Bluetooth® **dongle**, will work with a class 3 headset, so long as it is within the range of the class 3 device.

3G is an extension of mobile telecommunications standards. The 3G standards were created to ensure broadband speeds via mobile Internet on the mobile phone system.

3G speeds are not standardised, so it depends on your provider. If you are stationary (that is not walking) in a city, you can expect at least 2 Mbps from your connection, which is enough to stream video.

The **4G** standards have already been ratified and 4G will soon be more common. Offering higher speeds than its 3G counterpart there is nominal agreement

Key terms

Mega bit – an 'optimal' measurement of data transferred (in the case of wireless). 1 bit is a single binary 0 or 1; a kilobit is 1000 0s or 1s transmitted per second, therefore a megabit is 1,000,000 0s or 1s being transmitted per second (abbreviated as Mbps).

Infrared – a legacy technology that is still used on some mobile devices to connect them to printers or to exchange data. It uses light at the lower end of the light spectrum, and technology similar to that used by some games consoles and all television remote controls. A mobile device's infrared transmitter can be placed next to a receiver on some printers for a connection. Infrared has been superseded by both Bluetooth® and WiFi, with most devices able to print and share files by these means without the need for a 'line of sight connection'.

Dongle – normally a USB device that can be connected to your computer to offer extra services, such as Internet access.

3G – Third Generation of mobile phone technology, includes broadband services.

4G – Fourth Generation of mobile phone technology, includes high speed broadband services.

that data rates could be at least 10 Mbps and reach 300, equivalent to the wired LAN in most schools and colleges.

As you will have noticed with the wireless standards, the distances covered can be considerable, with 802.11n having a range of 250 metres. Indoors it is likely to only work for a third of the distance, being reliable for about 75 metres. This is the same for all 802.11 wireless technologies. What are the main reasons for this sudden drop?

- Interference – from wires or electrical devices (called radio-frequency interference). If your family has a microwave oven, for example, it is a high-powered ultra-high frequency device and when running may affect communication.
- Absorption and reflection from the fabric of the building. Any metal cladding, pipe work and frames will divert the wireless radio signal. Some building materials (such as concrete) will absorb the radio signal.

How has Bluetooth® helped with the development of wireless technologies?

With other mobile technologies the same principles apply. For 3G the quality of signal depends on physical location, terrain as well as distance from a **base station**. Therefore if you are in a hilly location and on the move in a car or train, your signal will not be as good as if you are sitting in a cafe in the centre of a large city.

Unit 10: Communication technologies explores wireless technologies in great detail, including 802.11a, b, g and n; infrared; Bluetooth®; and the various factors which affect the range and speed of wireless technologies.

Key terms

Base station – a wireless device, used to give wireless network connectivity to other wireless devices.

Domain – a group of networked computers and devices that are treated as a unit and have the same communications address.

1.3 Application layer protocols

When you use the Internet or email, different protocols are used to transfer the data; these are commonly referred to as application layer protocols. Common examples of application layer protocols include:

- **HTTP** (hypertext transfer or transport protocol), used to send websites via a webserver and receive your web pages via your Internet browser
- **FTP** (file transfer protocol), used in partnership with web servers to upload large files and share files
- **SMTP** (simple mail transfer protocol), one among many different mail exchange protocols, used to send mail
- **DNS** (**domain** name system), used to map an IP (Internet protocol) address such as 150.75.50.25 to a domain like www.teraknor.co.uk
- **DHCP** (dynamic host configuration protocol), used by devices such as your home router to automatically issue TCP/IP network address information to your computer when it is switched on and joins the network.

Assessment activity 9.1

1 With the permission of your tutor and technical support staff, take a detailed look at your study centre's network, and create a short video in the style of YouTube that describes the types of networks available and how they relate to network standards and protocols. **P1**

In your video it would be good to answer the following questions in order to describe why different network standards are necessary. **P2**

  - Why TCP/IP is used on this, and any network.
  - The benefit of a WAN standard.
  - The benefit of a LAN standard.
  - What protocols are used on WAN.
  - What protocols are used on a LAN.

Note: You may consider the Internet to be an example of a WAN for this assessment task.

2 Create a further short video comparing the benefits and disadvantages of peer-to-peer networks and client–server networks. **M1**

Grading tips

  - To meet both pass criteria, you *must* address all five points above. **P1 P2**

  - To meet the merit criterion, you should create a poster to advertise your YouTube-style video and create a visual comparison of peer-to-peer and client–server networks. **M1**

PLTS

You can demonstrate your skills as an **independent enquirer** by researching network standards and protocols.

Functional skills

You can demonstrate your Functional **ICT** skills by creating a short video on networks.

2.   Understand the key components used in networking

2.1 Key components

A network is not simply the infrastructure and protocols that move the data around the system. The network offers many services, with specialist devices accessing and supporting the network.

The key components of a network are:

  - network devices
  - interconnection devices
  - connectors and cabling
  - software.

These are discussed in detail below.

2. 2 Network devices

Workstations

The workstation is the most commonly found device on a network infrastructure, whatever the size. The sole purpose of a network is to enable the user to access its wide range of services via a workstation.

In the last ten years the term workstation has changed its definition, as new technologies are blurring what can be used on a network infrastructure. In its purest form, a workstation is a computer (or terminal) which enables you to access the network and the services it

An example of a more obscure workstation!

offers. Now, a workstation can also be a mobile phone; a PDA, Blackberry® or any specialist handheld device; a Nintendo® Gameboy™ or PSP (PlayStation® Portable); a laptop computer or a net book; a television set-top box; an Internet telephone; a microwave oven (yes, no joking, an Internet-enabled microwave has been released).

Servers

A server is a specialist computer system that is designed to offer a dedicated service to other workstations (and other servers) on a network. Some of the server types you may encounter are:

- web servers for the distribution of data, communication and e-commerce

- email communication servers

- servers for the management of shared printing services, to centralise control, reduce printer investment and output costs for an organisation

- servers for the central management and storage of files and data

- security servers with the use of a proxy (go-between) or firewall (access control)

- network addressing servers, including DNS and DHCP

- chat, discussion and conference servers

- game clan management servers.

To operate, most servers need to have a better hardware specification than an ordinary desktop computer system. It is considered normal for most servers to have more memory (which now may be in excess of 2 GB), a large hard drive system (which may be in a **RAID** array to cope with any failures) and multi-processor motherboards, to cope with the greater demands.

Network interface cards

To use the services of the network, the workstation will use a network interface card (**NIC**) and an operating system (which may be XP®, Vista® or Linux®, or may be a dedicated operating system like those found in some mobile and smart phones) to communicate with the network and the protocols in operation.

Key terms

RAID – stands for redundant array of independent disks. It is used as a live backup mechanism with multiple hard disks maintaining multiple images of the data.

NIC – stands for network interface card, part of the workstation hardware that allows connection to a network.

The NIC's sole purpose is to provide a workstation with network connectivity. The type of NIC will vary with the network topology and media type in use:

- UTP network cards automatically detect the network speed, for example as 10 Mbps, 100 Mbps and 1000 Mbps
- wireless adapters for 802.11a, b, g or n systems, used in a range of technologies
- Bluetooth transceivers, used for close-range communication
- fiber-optic network cards, used for high-speed communication, such as servers on a corporate network
- external network adapters (which can be plugged in via USB) like a 3G dongle, which can be for personal use
- on board (on motherboard) network adapters, used on the majority of home, server and desktop systems
- Pre-eXecution Environment (PXE), where a computer can be booted remotely on receipt of a given signal packet, send for systems where the devices require a managed startup or in a controlled roll-out of an update during hours of darkness
- Wake-on-LAN, very similar to PXE, used on many systems, including Ethernet and WiFi.

2.3 Interconnection devices

To enable our computers and networks to communicate with each other, a wide range of interconnection devices are used according to the communication system and whether it is a WAN or LAN connection.

Equipment

Routers

A router is an inter-networking device, enabling different networks to connect to each other. At home you have a basic router allowing your home devices to connect to the Internet. This device in its default configuration could allow 254 devices to connect to the Internet.

Routers are managed by a range of routing protocols. These share information between the routers on their connections. This enables routers to make decisions about which direction they are going to send your Internet traffic, which is very important as the system has to consider the bandwidth of the communication, as well as the quality of the connection.

Using this technology makes the system highly adaptable. If a interconnecting router decides to fail, routing protocols can replot an alternate route. This is happening all of the time on the Internet.

Switches

Bridges and switches are closely related. The bridge is a simple technology formerly used in networking. Its purpose was to separate segments of a network and reduce the number of network broadcasts. The bridge has enjoyed a minor renaissance – some commercial VoIP (voice over Internet protocol) phones have internal bridges so a PC can be connected to the phone and the phone to the single outlet on the wall.

A switch is a complex array of bridges, which has developed as networking technology becomes more complex. The switch increases the speed of communication as it creates unique mini-networks (circuits).

Wireless access points

Devices can connect together on a peer or ad-hoc basis as well as look for a wireless access point which will control and direct traffic, often to a cabled network infrastructure.

For more information on wireless access points, see Unit 10, page 308.

Activity: What ever happened to ...?

Technology such as the modem appears to have 'died a natural (technological) death', but has it?

In a group, explore areas in networking and communication technology where the modem is still used. Furthermore, explore explanations on how this technology works and the speeds that it offers.

2.4 Connectors and cabling

To ensure successful communication different networks use different **media** to ensure connection takes place.

> ### Key term
>
> **Media** – the material used in communication. This could be wireless, fiber or copper.

Leased lines and dedicated lines

Telecommunications organisations and Internet service providers (ISP) offering network services to corporate and private customers will offer two levels of service.

- **Leased line**: This is where the customer leases time, bandwidth or download capacity. It is similar to home broadband/ADSL and will be on a system shared with other customers.
- **Dedicated line**: Here the customer pays for total ownership of the communication on this line. While more expensive, the service is potentially limitless and is more secure as there are no other customers on this system.

Media types

Unit 10: Communications technologies explores media types and transmission systems in detail, including the connectors and cabling for STP and UTP, Category 5, coaxial, fiber optic, wireless and microwave and satellite links.

How have fiber-optic cables helped to make communication better?

Wireless networks

Wireless networks rely on high-frequency radio transmissions, normally limited to a range of no more than 100 metres. Wireless networks are susceptible to noise, which can be caused by metal-framed buildings as well as any powerful unshielded electrical equipment. Wireless networks tend to suffer from external interference and can have considerable limitations.

A successful wireless network must have many wireless access points, all offering overlapping coverage to ensure the mobile device (your laptop, mobile phone or PDA) has continuous coverage.

Mobile technology

Mobile technology, such as satellite data transmission and reception, has been used for some considerable time as a method of core high-speed data transmission between countries. For the user, or smaller business, this facility is becoming more accessible as costs reduce. Satellite transmission is reliant on atmospheric conditions, as well as line-of-sight communication with the satellite, but communication with a satellite in a geostationary orbit can increase the distance around the globe a network can reach.

Satellite communications rely on the satellite being in a geosynchronous orbit, with receiving stations being positioned to communicate with these satellites. In the UK, due to our latitude (position in relation to the equator), dishes used for satellite communication have to point to a position low on the horizon towards the south. Major international satellite communications follow this, with the Goonhilly satellite station being in Cornwall, the UK's southern-most county.

Wireless devices are microwave-based and operate in similar bands on the electro-magnetic spectrum, with microwave being on the upper end of the radio wave frequencies. These communication systems are used in WiFi and 3G, which has been described in the previous section of this unit.

Cable connection standards

Standards such as 10Base-T are used to define the signalling, communication rules and speed of a cabled system. The standards defined by the IEEE do not specify the exact length of cable (as there are multiple fiber and copper systems which differ in distance) but rather the rule base used to ensure quality of communication (see Table 9.2).

Table 9.2: IEEE cable standards

IEEE Standard	Description
802.3	10Base5 10 megabit over thick coaxial
802.3a	10Base2 10 megabit over thin coaxial (often described as 'thinnet')
802.3b	10Broad36, transmission over a coaxial cable TV system
802.3e	1Base5 or StarLAN, the first standard using RJ45s on a phone system, this only transmitted at 1 megabit over unshielded twisted pair
802.3i	**10Base-T** 10 megabit over twisted pair
802.3j	10Base-F 10 megabit over fiber optic
802.3u	100Base-TX, 100Base-T4, 100Base-FX Fast Ethernet at 100 megabit
802.3z	1000Base-X gigabit Ethernet over fiber optic
802.3ab	1000Base-T gigabit Ethernet over twisted pair
802.3ae	10 gigabit Ethernet over fiber optic; 10GBase-SR, 10GBase-LR, 10GBase-ER, 10GBase-SW, 10GBase-LW, 10GBase-EW
802.3af	Power over Ethernet – while not a definition of speed, VoIP phones and wireless access points could be powered via the same cables carrying the data; reduces the cost of the network, along with the flexibility of the devices on the system
802.3ak	10GBase-CX4 10 gigabit Ethernet over twin-coaxial cable
802.3an	10GBase-T 10 gigabit Ethernet over unshielded twisted pair
802.3aq	10GBase-LRM 10 gigabit Ethernet over multimode fibre, which is used on many LANS

2.5 Software

A networking infrastructure is purposeless unless there is software using, maintaining and managing the system. In the normal use of a network infrastructure you may encounter a network operating system, a virus checker on servers and workstations, firewalls (either dedicated or software based) and email **clients** and **servers**.

Network operating systems

Network operating systems offer two defined structures: peer-to-peer and client–server.

Peer-to-peer

A peer-to-peer network is an infrastructure which ensures that all devices on the system are treated as equals sharing a wide range of network services between each other. There is no centre to a **peer** system, but some devices may offer greater services than others. This ensures that users of many different computers systems can join a simple network infrastructure.

Peer networks are found in many situations. Four common examples are:

* a private network created at home to share an Internet connection

* some network gaming clans (teams who play network games together)

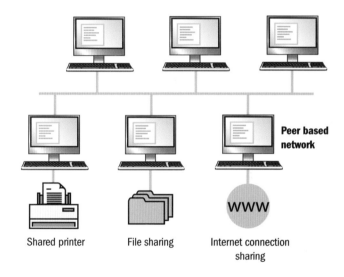

Figure 9.4: Peer-to-peer networks

Peer based network

Shared printer   File sharing   Internet connection sharing

Key terms

10Base-T – the 10 represents the bandwidth in Mbps (megabits per second), the Base is for a baseband signal and the T represents twisted pair cables.

Peer – someone (or something) which is an equal to yourself or others (for example your friend is a peer).

Client – a person or a system which receives a service from another individual or system (for example when you go to McDonald's to order a meal you are a client receiving a service).

Server – a device or an individual offering a service to one or many clients (for example the person behind the counter at McDonald's).

- a small network in a company with fewer than ten computers
- file- and resource-sharing systems like BitTorrent, which are applications designed to ensure that file sharing occurs.

The principal advantage of peer-to-peer systems is their technological simplicity – they are easy to install, operate and manage. But their ability to scale (grow larger) is restricted – it is accepted in the networking industry that 20 workstations is the reasonable maximum and 40 is pushing your luck!

File-sharing systems overcome the issues of scale by providing your computer with a client which reports your files to a server which manages the peer connections.

All operating systems since the early 1990s have offered a peer-based element. It is now possible to create peer connections with all operating systems.

Client–server

As opposed to the peer-to-peer system, a client–server system has central control and management, which allows a considerably larger number of devices to become part of the system.

Examples of client–server systems are wide-ranging and diverse. Some examples include:

- web server being accessed by many clients (the client being the web browser)
- many online gaming systems
- the file server at work or your centre of learning which is accessed via Windows Explorer®
- MSM, Skype™ and other chat/communication systems
- web radio, with the client being, for example Windows® Media Player, Winamp or RealPlayer.

To operate, a client–server system must have different operating systems and computers for the client and the server. As a rule of thumb, the client can be implemented on most standard operating systems. It can be very small in software terms but must allow network or Internet access. It can run on a lower-specification computer system.

The server must run on a network operating system (or one which supports multiple connections and processes). It may need a system with a higher-specification computer (multiple processors, more memory, larger hard drives, etc.) and it needs a better-quality network/Internet connection as it will be busier.

Virus checker

It is essential to ensure that your virus checker is current. As you are reading this paragraph, a new **virus**, **worm** or **trojan** will have been released which may affect your computer system.

The terms virus, worm and trojan are often simplistic, as most attacks will be hybrids of two or more of them. (For more on viruses, worms and trojans, see *Unit 7: Organisational systems security*.)

Key terms

Virus – a malicious file which, when inserted into your system, will cause some form of damage. An additional feature of viruses is their ability to reproduce.

Worm – a program that can move itself around a computer network and leave a payload, which may be a virus or trojan.

Trojan – a malicious program that pretends to be a benign application, but purposely does something the user does not expect. Trojans are technically not viruses since they do not replicate, but can be just as destructive. If left in a computer system, provides 'back door' access to the hard drive and data.

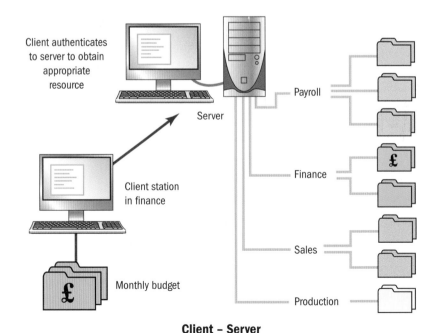

Client authenticates to server to obtain appropriate resource

Server

Client station in finance

Monthly budget

Payroll

Finance

Sales

Production

Client – Server

Figure 9.5: Client–server systems

Activity: Installing anti-virus software

1 Visit the AVG® website (you can access this by using Hotlinks), where you can download a free and updateable anti-virus application called AVG® Anti-Virus Free.

2 With the permission of your tutor, install this application and ensure you are connected to the Internet to update the anti-virus database. Run a comprehensive scan of your hard drive and any other storage devices.

Firewalls

Firewalls, either dedicated or software-based, are essential for all networks and network devices. The best implementation of a firewall is to:

- ensure you are running one on your workstation – the Windows XP® or Vista® internal software firewall is suitable for this
- ensure you are also running one on the edge of your network – this may be an external hardware firewall running as part of the wireless/wired ADSL/ broadband router at home
- have a firewall at the edge of each network segment of a corporate network to ensure multiple layers of security.

Firewalls filter traffic using TCP and UCP ports at layer 4 of the OSI model (see Table 10.2 on page 314 of Unit 10). In principle all ports are blocked and a network administrator will open only those that are needed – a very small number of the 65535 ports available on a computer (0 is not available).

Strong firewalls use 'reflective' rules – this means that traffic is only allowed in if a device, or application, on the inside of the firewall has originated the network conversation. To test if your firewall is secure, use the Nmap application which can be obtained by visiting Hotlinks.

Email client

Email client and server systems have been operational since the early 1970s. Email uses protocols such as SMTP (simple mail transfer protocol), IMAP (Internet message access protocol) and POP3 (post office protocol version 3).

```
Client: HELLO teraknor.co.uk
Server: 250 Hello teraknor.co.uk
Client: MAIL FROM:webmaster@teraknor.co.uk
Server: 250 Ok
Client: RCPT TO:student@teraknor.co.uk
Server: 250 Ok
Client: DATA
Server: 354 End data with<CR><LF>.<CR><LF>
Client: Subject: test message
Client: From: webmaster@teraknor.co.uk
Client: To: student@teraknor.co.uk
Client:
Client: Hello,
Client:
Server: 250 Ok: queued as 23296
Client: QUIT
Server: 221 Bye
```

Figure 9.6: An email SMTP command conversation

To send an email requires SMTP. To receive (or pull) an email requires POP3. SMTP is a 'plaintext' language, which can be typed in via applications such as telnet or HyperTerminal. Figure 9.6 gives an example of an SMTP command conversation when sending an email.

Email has contributed to the boom and popularity of the Internet. The popularity of email has enabled organisations, workers and educators to become more flexible in their communication, with location and time zones becoming irrelevant. Email can be accessed via many systems, with websites, mobile phones and television set top boxes all offering this service.

2.6 Commercial systems

Software

Examples of network operating systems are various versions of Linux, Novell Netware (now Linux® Powered via SuSe), Apple® X Server Snow Leopard®, Windows® 2003 and 2008 and IBM iSeries™ OS.

Desktop systems such as Windows Vista®, Windows® 7, Linux® and Mac OS® X Snow Leopard® can offer this resource, but in a more limited format as they are not specifically designed for the task.

A network operating system is multifaceted and serves many purposes for many organisations. Unlike the client operating system you are used to (for example Windows XP® or Vista®), the network operating system will reside on a dedicated computer system.

The network operating system manages the server that provides a network service accessed by many other computers and users on the network. The services offered by network operating systems are wide and varied – common services include:

- web servers, to provide e-commerce and information portals

- file servers to share common resources

- database servers which manage large quantities of information

- print servers, to manage access to network printers, which are used by many users

- domain name servers (DNS), which keep a log of all web addresses and IP addresses, so you can find your favourite website no matter where it is on the planet

- firewalls, which control corporate security and protect entire systems from unwanted intrusion

- proxy servers, which regulate access for many devices to the Internet

- content management systems, which will control what websites users may visit

- dynamic host configuration protocol (DHCP) servers, used by many organisations and Internet service providers (ISPs) to ensure your computer has an address which will enable your computer to access the network or Internet

- mail servers to manage email.

All of these services are available using Windows® 2003/2008. Linux® and Unix® also offer these services according to the needs of a particular organisation, allowing network managers to configure them to specific requirements.

Activity: Setting up a small server

Setting up a simple server is not difficult. In fact, you can run one from your own home computer, without placing any unreasonable demands on your computer system. In the Linux® community there is a movement for 'small = good', so you can find operating systems that will run in less than 50 MB of storage (small enough to fit on a small memory stick).

1 Visit the Teraknor website (you can access this by going to Hotlinks), where you can download a free copy of DSL, which is a small version of the Linux® operation system. The readme file includes instructions on how to start the operating system while you are running Windows® (it uses a simple PC emulator).

2 Follow the instructions included and you can set up a simple web server using this system.

Assessment activity 9.2

You have been asked to design a network for an office relocation of a successful mobile phone applications development software house.

The solution must have suitable technology to support a wired LAN, as well as a secure connection to the Internet. The system is to be in two different business units on a trading estate, with three different networks.

- One network must support over 25 iPhone®/iPad™ developers.
- The second network will support at least 10 Blackberry® developers (there are also five Android developers in their team).
- The third network will be for the central financial and strategic management, with at least 10 devices.
- While each system will be a conventional wired LAN, it must also support wireless access for a range of mobile devices.
- Each system is connected to a core router, which will provide the access to the Internet.
- In addition, on the core system, there will be an infrastructure server and a file storage server.

1 Explain the key components required for client workstations to connect to a network and access network resources. **P3 M2 D1**

2 Explain the function of interconnection devices. **P4**

Grading tips

- You may use a PowerPoint® presentation to support all explanations and your design/justification.
- To achieve a pass you must complete all the bullet points listed. **P3 P4**
- To achieve a merit grade, you must design a networked solution to meet the situation described above with the specific requirements. You may use any relevant design application. **M2**
- For the given problem you must justify the design and choice of components used in a particular networked solution. You should explain the benefits and disadvantages of each design and choice of components. **D1**

PLTS

You can demonstrate your skills as a **creative thinker** by designing a networked solution to meet the situation described.

Functional skills

You can demonstrate your Functional **ICT** skills by creating a PowerPoint® presentation to explain the network you have designed.

---

3. Know the services provided by network systems

On the top of the network infrastructure, networked systems provide a variety of services which enable you, the user, to interact with other users, systems and applications. The services covered in this section are directory services, telecommunication services, file services and application services.

3.1 Directory services

When a network has only ten devices, or fewer, it is easy to remember the IP address or the device name

for a printer or file server on the system. But what happens when the system grows?

When a network increases beyond ten devices there needs to be a way of managing user's **rights** on the network and ensuring that each device is easy to identify.

Key term

Rights – in computing, this relates to those systems and services you are allowed to access.

To offer comprehensive directory services, a network operating system must offer:

- domain control (which may also be called 'active directory' or 'directory services')
- account management for groups and users
- **authentication** management.

Domain control

On a networked system a domain is either:

- a system that is provided by major networking operating systems that provides control over computers, servers and services, or
- an Internet system that consists of a set of network addresses. This type of domain is organised in levels. The top level identifies the geographic location or the purpose of the domain (for example, the nation that the domain covers or a category such as 'commercial'). The second level identifies a unique place within the top level domain and is equivalent to a unique IP address on the Internet.

In Windows®, each domain is managed by a **domain controller**. To support this, the system requires additional domain controllers to ensure resilience (to act as a backup if the main domain controller fails).

Users may authenticate (log in) to the domain controller to obtain access to the network's services. If the domain controller is too busy or the server has failed, then the user can continue their work by authenticating to additional domain

controllers. A large system will have multiple domain controllers to ensure that all users can always access the system.

The domain controller is a complex database with details of all users' accounts, all servers and services, printers, files system and permissions, backup systems, any specialist services and the addressing scheme. This is called the active directory (as the directory is constantly being changed). At regular intervals the domain controller will send an update of this database to all additional domain controllers. This allows all users seamless access to the system. (See Figure 9.7.)

If any of the servers are switched off or are unavailable for a considerable period of time (for example while repairs take place), an engineer has to ensure that the latest image of the database has been loaded onto the server. Otherwise the system becomes fragmented and users may not be able to gain access to system resources.

Servers that are part of the domain, but do not provide access to the directory, are member servers. They rely on the domain controllers to manage access to their resources. A common example of this is an Internet proxy server. This server is the gateway to a shared Internet connection – not all users may be allowed to use this service, so the domain controllers will manage access according to directory permissions.

A simple network system will have one domain controller and may have one additional

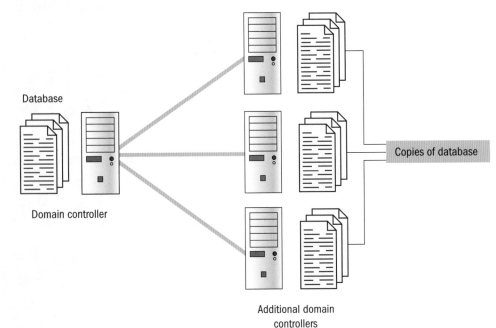

Database

Domain controller

Copies of database

Additional domain controllers

Figure 9.7: Domain controllers

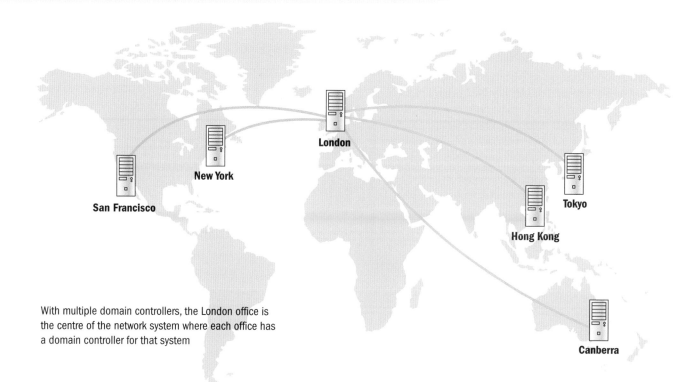

With multiple domain controllers, the London office is the centre of the network system where each office has a domain controller for that system

Figure 9.8: Multiple domain controllers in a large organisation

supporting domain controller. This will work for a small to medium enterprise that is situated on one site. Large organisations will have multiple domains according to region, department or business need. Figure 9.8 shows how multiple domain controllers can operate in a tree structure across the world to manage the network.

A team of network administrators often manages the database. The database allows a hierarchy of management – this means that there are administrators who can control the whole system, as well as local administrators who only have responsibility for part of the database.

Each domain is named according to the infrastructure of the organisation and the network administrator will issue names using a common sense principle. Figure 9.9 shows the likely domain names for the company Widgets R Us, which has offices in Seattle, San Francisco and Madrid. The office at each site has three departments: finance, production and sales.

The advantages of using a directory services structure are:

- each section can be managed according to a specific business need
- localised management means that the system can adapt without the management of the whole network being too cumbersome

- local management also allows part of the system to be backed up and restored separately – any failure will have only a local impact
- new branches of an organisation may be added at any time – the network does not have to be redesigned to adapt to a changing business climate.

```
\\WidgetsRUs

The domain entry for each location:

\\WidgetsRUs\Seattle

\\WidgetsRUs\San_Francisco

\\WidgetsRUs\Madrid

The domain entry for each department:

\\WidgetsRUs\Seattle\finance

\\WidgetsRUs\Seattle\sales

\\WidgetsRUs\Seattle\production

\\WidgetsRUs\San_Francisco\finance

\\WidgetsRUs\San_Francisco\sales

\\WidgetsRUs\San_Francisco\production

\\WidgetsRUs\Madrid\finance

\\WidgetsRUs\Madrid\sales

\\WidgetsRUs\Madrid\production
```

Figure 9.9: An example of domain naming

The Internet and the majority of network infrastructures use a domain management system called the DNS. This is based on the **UNIX®** domain system. The domain name architecture is managed in a tree structure by **registrars**. The organisation InterNIC controls the allocation of Internet addresses. They manage a group of local registrars who in turn manage a range of domains.

Key terms

UNIX® – a centralised server operating system from the 1970s.

Registrar – an organisation that manages Internet domain names.

The web address of www.yourcollege.ac.uk is therefore managed by:

- InterNIC, who manage all Internet addresses
- Nominet, who manage all .uk addresses
- JANET (Joint Academic Network), who manage all .ac and .gov addresses
- your college, who manage their own domain (yourcollege) and any subordinate domains (www).

(You can access the InterNIC, Nominet and JANET websites by going to Hotlinks.)

InterNIC controls all address naming conventions to the right-hand site of the Internet address. Once you have control of your own domain it is your choice, for example the following names are allowed:

- www.yourcollege.ac.uk for the web server
- mail.yourcollege.ac.uk for the mail server
- technology.yourcollege.ac.uk for the technology campus
- cappuccino.yourcollege.ac.uk for the online coffee machine!

Each network that connects to the Internet must have a DNS server. This server contains a database (like active directory or DNS) of all Internet domains. This database will map the Internet address to an OSI model layer 3 IP address. For example:

- www.yourcollege.ac.uk could map to 80.10.55.1
- mail.yourcollege.ac.uk could map to 80.10.55.2
- technology.yourcollege.ac.uk could map to 80.10.55.3
- cappuccino.yourcollege.ac.uk could map to 80.10.55.4

Like an active directory, the DNS needs to have a primary and secondary domain controller (called servers in DNS terminology). Figure 9.10 shows that you can find an example of a DNS system on your home computer.

The Internet is an ever-growing system, where all domain servers point to a controlling server higher up the domain tree, each leading to the core server run by InterNIC. Therefore, all domain servers point to each other in a mesh structure, where any update that takes place on the Internet (a new domain name) is distributed from one domain server to another up the tree until it reaches the core and then it is distributed to all systems across the Internet.

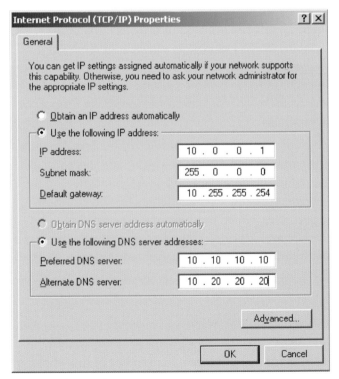

Figure 9.10: DNS system

For your college, the domain structure will be:

- all computers in your college will point to the network domain server

- your college's domain server will point to the .ac domain server at JANET

- JANET's domain server will point to Nominet's domain server

- Nominet's domain server points to the InterNIC core server.

Domains with Windows® 2000/2003 and Linux® are based on the UNIX® DNS. If you create a network at home, you can point your DNS server to the service provided by your ISP, where the Internet allows for further connections at the edge. If you purchase and register a domain name, it may take up to five hours for the registration to propagate to all DNS servers on the Internet.

Account management

With the directory structure intact, each network administrator has to ensure that there is appropriate account management for groups and users.

User groups

Networked systems with domains will allow personnel within a company to be managed by associating them with a variety of user groups. Each group may provide the user with access to different resources, such as files, directories, printers or servers. User groups can also be associated with the allocation of privileges: some users may only have read access, while other users have read and write access.

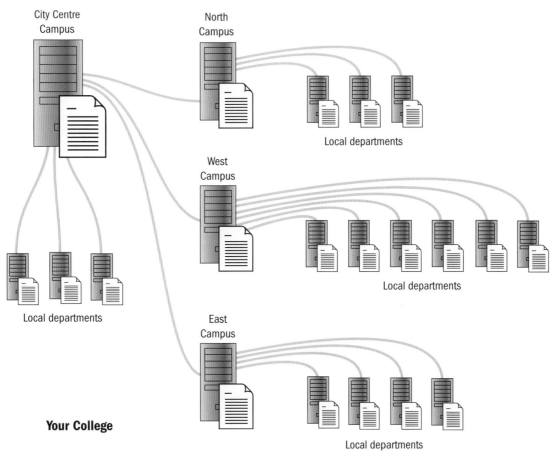

Figure 9.11: A networked system

The advantage of user groups is that a company employee can be mobile (moving from computer to computer, or from site to site) and their network privileges follow them.

User accounts

In order to visualise user accounts, you are a user on the network at your centre, as are your tutor and the network technician. With current technology, devices such as other servers, printers and workstations are also allocated 'user' privileges and are treated in a similar fashion. Each of you will have an account on the network directory, which will contain a variety of important information:

- personal details
- login or account name (for example you are Jacob Smith and your account is jsmith01)
- your password (encrypted of course)
- a date for when you need to be reminded to change your password
- groups that you are a member of
- directories and files that you have access to, along with your rights to those files
- servers and printers that you may access
- times that you may (or may not) be able to login
- computers that you can or cannot use (newer systems can lock a user to a range of computers based on their IP address)
- websites you may or may not be able to access
- email address (for example jacobsmith01@yourcollege.ac.uk).

User accounts are added to the directory as and when people join an organisation. Your centre may create a large number of accounts in September when the new academic year starts. You also need to be aware that user accounts can be removed or suspended from the system. You may have experienced this if your centre has a policy of disabling user accounts for misuse of the network.

Activity: Check your understanding

1. What is a user group?
2. Give at least five pieces of information contained in a user account.

Authentication management

Combining domains, groups and users, the networked system can implement comprehensive authentication management. This is used to ensure that only those who are allowed to use the system have access to it.

Authentication management occurs at many levels and is not simply focused on the user. Some examples of where authentication takes place follow.

Internet e-commerce and secure web pages

For secure web pages, authentication involves the use of **SSL**. This requires a website to issue a security certificate, which is checked by the browser as part of the exchange. The certificate is the **public key** part of the exchange and a private key is also created. The **private key** is based on a 1024-bit value (2^{1024} which is 1.7976931348623159077729305190789e+308 – the e means you move the decimal point to the right by 308 digits) and is a **prime number**. This is commonly referred to as **RSA encryption**.

Key terms

SSL – stands for secure sockets layer. It requires a website to issue a security certificate.

Public/private keys – keys that are mathematically related. The public key can be widely distributed and is used to encrypt data. The private key only can decrypt the data and is kept secret. It is not technically practical to derive the private key from the public key.

Prime number – a number that can only be divided by itself and 1. This means that no matter what number you try to divide this number by, it will never return a whole value. Prime numbers are mathematically interesting as no one has yet managed to predict the next prime number – they appear to follow no pattern. This property is invaluable in network security.

RSA – stands for the last-name initials of the mathematicians who patented the principle for public/private key encryption using prime numbers, ie Ron Rivest, Adi Shamir and Len Adleman.

Secure WAN connections

For secure WAN connections, routers use authentication methods such as CHAP (challenge handshake application protocol) or exchange updates using a MD5 hash (message digest) – this is a formula which provides the result of a complex calculation based on a large data set, with the hash being the common key result from each calculation. This is used across common communication systems to ensure that no one attempts to add unauthorised equipment to join the system.

Devices such as routers, servers, switches and proxies

To manage many devices can be an issue for network administrators, as this requires the creation and management of a large number of usernames and passwords. To coordinate this task, many systems have centralised authentication servers, known as TACACS+ (terminal access controller access-control system) or RADIUS (remote authentication dial in user service).

Wireless systems

For wireless systems, wireless equivalence protocol (WEP) allows all members of a wireless system to share a common private key. The wireless device cannot join the system unless the WEP key is directly entered into the wireless settings for the mobile device.

3.2 Telecommunication services

The primary use of the Internet is as a means of communicating with other people. As such, it is becoming increasingly prevalent in our lives. This section will look at the many technologies in use on the Internet and how they have enabled low-cost and effective communication to take place.

Communication

Common and popular methods of communication include email, Internet relay chat (IRC), Voice over Internet Protocol (VoIP), short message service (SMS) and discussion boards. We will look at these in more detail in this subsection.

Email has been explored earlier in this unit (see page 279).

IRC is an older term for the various forms of chat used by many on the Internet. Popular chat services include Windows Live™ Messenger, Yahoo!® Messenger and Skype™.

Chat operates using a server which acts as a relay for all conversations. Each member logs in and allows (or refuses) other users to create private conversations. Chat can be one to one, or many to many, depending on the type of conversation taking place.

Many of the chat systems available also offer application sharing, video conferencing and remote assistance tools. These features enable professionals from many geographic locations to work together and offer each other support.

VoIP usage is rapidly increasing, with Skype™, SIP (session initiation protocol) and H.323-based telecommunication systems across the Internet (see Figure 9.12 on page 288). Skype™ is a proprietary service, which means that the technology used by Skype™ to communicate with other Skype™ systems is incompatible with any other VoIP technology – this is considered to be a downside to Skype™ by many people.

All Skype™ conversations are secure, and are relayed via the many Skype™ hosts, as well as central servers. You can now easily obtain a personal number for Skype™, which means that landlines can phone your computer. Alternatively you can use Skype™ to buy credit to telephone mobile phones and landlines in almost any country – this is a considerable benefit for people involved in international travel and business. Skype™ is free for Internet-only conversations. You can find out more about Skype™ by going to Hotlinks).

Many alternative systems exist using SIP and H.323 as these are **open source**, allowing organisations to work together to create common communication systems. A popular server which can be used on Windows® and Linux® is Trixbox®. This can be connected to traditional phone systems, as well as a conventional networked system and can be used to control communication between them.

> ### Key term
> **Open source** – software code (or related technologies) which are free and open to anyone to use or improve.

Trixbox® works like any client-server system, offering telephone communication to as many users as there is server power to handle them. For example, an old 700 MHz PC with Trixbox® would be able to manage 20 phones, while a modern server with a 4 GHz multi-process system would be able to manage 200+ phones.

Trixbox® is free and can be obtained from the Trixbox® website. Many clients are also available for free download, for example X-Lite from CounterPath.

Figure 9.12: Skype™

(For both of these websites, go to Hotlinks.)

With VoIP and web interaction, many system offer free or versatile SMS solutions. For example, those who have already installed Skype™ can use their SMS tool (at a small cost) to send SMS to any mobile phone and tag the return number with their mobile phone number (see Figure 9.13).

SMS can also be sent via many websites and mobile phone providers may also offer this service to customers. Independent, free or low-cost providers offer web servers with SMS capability.

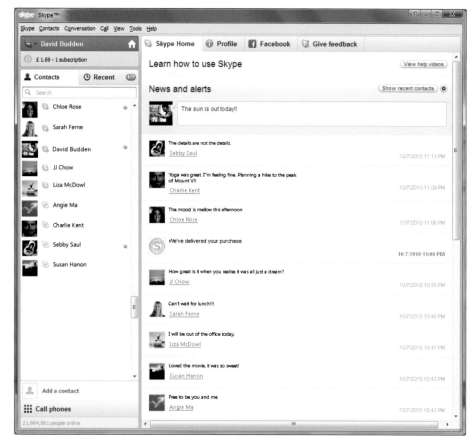

Figure 9.13: Skype™

Discussion boards, news groups and bulletin boards are among the earliest methods of common communication and information sharing. Email clients are able to manage bulletin board services via the news group feature.

Remote access

As mobile devices have evolved, it is possible to access your primary computer system remotely via small graphical user interface (GUI) applications such as Microsoft® Terminal Services, Remote Desktop and virtual network computing (VNC). These allow a limited system to use Internet technology to access a fully enabled system.

Social networking on web browsers, as well as mobiles (smart phones, netbooks), is now being used as a remote communication resource. The Web 2.0 domain allows multiple data feeds and software application programming interfaces (APIs) to be interconnected. Therefore the ability to remotely access different communication formats, media threads and data services is becoming easier.

3.3 File services

File transfer and file sharing

Networked systems allow users to share files, from documents to media files and applications. This functionality has been a feature of the Internet and networked systems since the early 1970s with UUCP (Unix® to Unix® CoPy). Many systems exist to enable file transfer and file sharing.

- FTP is the file transfer protocol for dedicated servers and clients. Internet Explorer can be used to access a FTP site. Many Internet domains have FTP. Anonymous FTP exists to enable the open sharing of files without the need to create usernames or passwords.

- Peer-to-peer systems use file-sharing applications such as BitTorrent™, Kazaa and Blubster™ to enable common storage for all users.

- Windows Messenger® and other chat applications allow users to send each other files direct.

- HTTP websites allow the download (and also upload) of files.

- Email can be used to send files as attachments.

Figure 9.14: File transfer using Windows Live™ Messenger

While broadband/ADSL technology has increased the speed at which files can be downloaded, moving large quantities of data can still be time-consuming. Also the transfer of multiple files can be cumbersome. To overcome this, files are often collected together and compressed.

Depending on the operating system, files can be compressed as ZIP, TAR (Tape ARchive), JAR (Java™ ARchive) or RAR (Roshal ARchive) files. Windows Vista® and 7 support file compression and Office 2010® compresses all documents automatically.

File sharing can also be accomplished with many operating systems, where a user or network administrator can enable a folder (or collection of folders) to be accessible.

In Windows®, to share a folder is simple. Find the folder you wish to be shared, right click on the folder icon and select the Sharing and Security option. Decide on the name of the share and if the other users are allowed to alter the files (in which case, you are enabling write and execute file privileges instead of read only). On your local computer, the shared folder will have an open hand icon. Across the network, you will be able to find the folder via the My Network Places icon.

Figure 9.15: Folder sharing

At the time of writing, there has been considerable debate about file sharing and a Digital Economy Act became law in 2010. For more time than many are aware, service providers have been able to 'shape' and 'track' traffic from illegal downloads. The new law will mean that anyone caught illegally downloading material will be subject to a three-strikes-and-out (no Internet connection) penalty.

3.4 Application services

There are many applications used on networked systems, from servers to printing, from storage to email.

Application software

Many servers on a networked system are purpose specific. Within large organisations, servers are installed to offer single services to their customers or employees.

Database servers

Database servers normally run in the background, managing large quantities of data. Applications run from web servers, or clients to access, and manage this large data set. Common systems include Microsoft® SQL® and Oracle® 9i.

Web servers

Web servers were originally designed to act as information-sharing tools. Although this original purpose has not changed, the level and complexity of the information and applications available from web servers has extended their use to become the most common type of server in current use.

Web servers can be used for e-commerce and trade tools, email portals, chat and discussion boards, educational environments, gaming systems, VoIP management portals, device management and configuration portals, CCTV portals, video and entertainment systems and web radio relays and servers.

Proxy servers

As mentioned earlier in this unit (page 282), proxy servers manage Internet access on a large networked system. Proxy servers enable network administrators to time-control users' access to the Internet; log and record when, where and on whose computer users have visited the Internet; control who can and cannot visit the Internet; control what websites users can and cannot see; keep a local cache of some popular sites, to speed up local access, as well as reduce Internet traffic (this has some weaknesses, as some sites are continuously updated).

Shared resources

Printing is still considered a costly resource. Even though the cost of printers has reduced dramatically over the last 20 years, a network administrator still needs to consider:

- the cost of printers for hundreds of users
- the replacement cost of printers, as they are subject to wear and tear
- the cost of toner or ink per printer (this is also based on use)
- the cost of paper
- the need to reduce waste and encourage limits on printing to reduce the ecological impact of paper use.

Print servers can manage many printers simultaneously. This enables control over how much a user can print and who can print to which printer, for example to avoid everyone printing to the same printer.

Standard modern office printer.

Storage space

Many of you will have a network drive (storage space) on your college network. This is a small part of a larger storage (file server) system held at your study centre. Protocols, such as FTP, deal in the large-scale storage and transfer of data from remote servers.

With FTP you could easily configure your home computer with suitable free software to act as remote storage space and enable you to have continuous access to your work from anywhere.

Voice over Internet Protocol (VoIP)

As mentioned earlier in this unit, VoIP has been a developing technology with many interesting servers and services available. With the competition between Skype™ and open source systems it is likely that the many different systems will continue to co-exist, but will be developed so that each will have a 'gateway' allowing that system to work with others.

Mobile working

Mobile working has given the Internet and related technologies their greatest push. As commerce becomes increasingly international, being able to work with customers irrespective of location offers considerable benefits. Laptops, smart phones and netbooks offer professionals the chance to take their office with them when they are on the move. Many hotels, coffee bars and airports now offer wireless Internet access.

Authentication

As discussed earlier in this unit, user authentication (checking you are who you say you are) is a feature of many networked application services. With computer crime being a constant risk, every system you encounter will have a system to check your identity and prevent misuse. Software authentication may take place by ensuring you have exchanged a 'trust' certificate; checking a password and username; using a key personal identifier, such as your mother's maiden name.

Hardware authentication systems tend to work in partnership with software systems and may include chip and pin; biometrics (fingerprint and retinal scanners); dongles (specially programmed USB sticks); cards inside selected computers. Using such a device adds an additional layer of application security, as the device has to be security compliant as well as the user.

Assessment activity 9.3   P5 D2   BTEC

Following your design work for Assessment activity 9.2, take a look at what services you would consider offering the same mobile phone application software house.

1 Consider how their business operations would benefit from them.

2 Describe the typical services provided by networks. **P5**

Grading tips

- You may use a PowerPoint® presentation or use a YouTube-style talking head video to address this task.

- To achieve a distinction, you are required to evaluate the typical services available from a network operating system directory service in the context of a mobile phone app software firm. **D2**

PLTS

You can demonstrate your skills as a **creative thinker** by providing a solution to meet the situation described.

Functional skills

You can demonstrate your Functional **ICT** skills by creating a PowerPoint® presentation to explain the solution you have provided.

4. Be able to make networked systems secure

Network security is now an everyday part of our lives, at home, work and college and when out shopping. Ensuring that the networks we all use are secured is paramount. Apart from the issues surrounding personal data, the impact of network failure or a system being compromised could be financially costly.

4.1 Securing a system

Managing your systems security is paramount. As a network administrator you must ensure that:

- all security software is up to date
- firewalls are checked regularly
- privileges (who has what and why) are checked
- no business decision will compromise the network and vice versa.

Any data which is compromised or accessed without authority is open to abuse and can lead to fraud, corruption and compromise. To ensure data and networked systems are secure, many technologies and techniques are employed.

Working in the IT profession in the management of a network you may encounter:

- authorisation techniques
- permissions and access control lists
- backup and restoration of data
- encryption
- biometrics
- vetting and control of personnel
- CCTV
- lock and key.

Passwords

The management of the network requires that there are systems and procedures in place to ensure standards and common practices in the use and control of the network password policies.

Many organisations will not openly reveal their password policies. It is considered common practice on networked systems that all users must:

- not write down their password
- change their password periodically, from 90 days (three months) to as little as every seven days.

- use a **strong password** with eight or more characters.
- sign an agreement before they are issued their first username, which binds them to corporate policy and requires them to acknowledge laws such as the Computer Misuse Act and the Data Protection Act.

Key term

Strong password – a password that uses letters (upper- and lower-case), numbers and symbols, e.g. Jac0b_$m1th instead of jacobsmith.

Creating a strong password is not a complicated science. Most of us can do it, the trick is to pick a word that you will remember, but no one else will know (so brothers, sisters, parents and football teams are out of the question).

If you have a common eight character word, you can make it strong, lets say your word is

- somerset
- You can add a capital letter, in an unusual place. soMerset
- Then you can convert one of the characters to a number: 5oMerset
- and also convert one of the characters to a symbol of choice: 5oMer$et

You will recognise this and you can probably remember it, but to others, and to many hacking tools used to crack passwords, it becomes hard work.

Many systems will log failed attempts when users forget their password, with their username being locked out after three failed attempts.

Authorisation permissions and access control lists

As described on page 286, networked systems use many authentication techniques, ranging from the exchange of certificates, secure WAN links and WEP encryption of wireless systems, to password control and strong usernames.

In authorising a user, the system must be assured that the person using the system is the person to whom the authority has been issued. Ensuring that fraudulent use does not take place is critical, as it often leads to financial loss or damage to commercial reputations.

- To authorise a user, checks need to be made before they join the system. Creation of an online account with a bank, insurer or credit broker is dependent on this. Often such systems will check the user's place on the electoral roll; send an email to which the user must reply within a time limit; ask for a phone number, which an operator will use to contact the user; book an appointment at a local branch of the business for a face-to-face meeting to which the user must bring along a passport and additional identification documents; check the user's credit history; confirm previous addresses.

- In a corporate setting, authorising a user follows a similar pattern. Network management will not issue a network username unless the person has been employed by the company; the supporting line manager has made a suitable application for permissions; the details of the terms of the individual's contract have been submitted, with details of contract expiration if they are working for the organisation on a short-term basis; a contract (commonly called an acceptable use policy) has been signed by the individual, indicating their acknowledgement of the terms under which they can use the networked system.

- When a username is issued on any networked system, specific permissions are allocated. Personnel are seldom given complete authority over the entire system unless they are the network manager. Permissions issued for a user may define where their home drive is located; the storage capacity they may use; times they may access the system; locations they may access the system from (which allows some professionals to work from home); areas with read-only permissions; areas with read and write permissions; printers, servers and databases they may access; groups they may belong to; whether they can grant local permissions to other users (some systems have the concept of a super user); websites they can and cannot visit.

An access control list (ACL) is a tool used in network traffic management and may be applied to routers and servers alike. ACLs can be used to create permit or deny rules for networks, devices or a specific range of devices based on specific traffic.

ACLs are applied to firewalls and can be used in a temporal (time-based) context, allowing or denying access to networks at certain times. While many different systems use ACLs, the common rule may look like the one shown in Table 7.2 (see *Unit 7: Organisational systems security*, page 213).

Backing up and restoring

The backup and restoration of data is a critical factor in all networked systems in order to maintain the management and reliability of the system. Having a centrally managed backup, where all the data is safely copied in case of system failure and with everyone following the same standards, is essential. Many organisations have fallen into the trap of not managing local backups using the same standards or frequency, so when there is a system failure the site loses essential data. Another common error is to have differing levels of support, which means that many employees are missing out on potentially essential assistance.

Backing up and restoring disks and data are considered to be a critical role of a network administrator. Depending on the size, type and nature of the organisation, it is expected that the network administrator completes at least one backup per day. Some systems employ **incremental backups**, while others use **differential backups**.

Key terms

Incremental backup – involves storing only changed data since the last backup of any type.

Differential backup – involves storing only changed data since the last full backup.

When considering the backup requirements of a system, you must identify the exact quantity of data that requires backing up, the appropriate media that needs to be used in the backup process, the frequency of backups and where a copy of the data needs to be stored off-site.

While it is desirable to back up and recover all information on the network, there is data that is not critical to the running of the organisation, such as system logs, applications that can be re-installed, etc. You need to ensure that the media (tape, network storage server, DVD-RW or CD-RW) can hold the required volume of information and the frequency of backups take place according to the changeability of the data.

Some organisations complete a backup every eight hours, as the data is undergoing continuous change. It is normal for most companies to complete an overnight backup, where once a week a copy is taken to another location (off-site).

The backup disaster recovery procedure is based on what is critical to the running of the system and is based on the following considerations:

- how quickly data that has been deleted or altered can be recovered
- how effectively a 'downed' server can be restarted
- how soon a damaged or stolen server can be replaced and the data accessed.

On most server systems the storage is managed by RAID (see *Unit 7: Organisational system security*, page 209). Currently there are nine different RAID systems. The benefits of using RAID are that if one hard drive fails the system can be rebuilt from the existing images or the system can continue while a new hard drive is installed.

The amount spent on backup and recovery will be based on the critical nature of the network in respect to the main business of a company. For example, an office cleaning company may be able to manage for 48 hours without their computers, whereas a City bank could be struggling after five minutes of computer loss.

Encrypting

Encryption has already been explored in this unit (see page 286). The main characteristics of data encryption are obscuring the data in transit and ensuring the sender and receiver trust each other in the process of sending the data.

Other methods of securing data

Biometrics

Biometrics is still evolving as a method of secure authentication, although the technology already exists.

> **Key term**
>
> **Biometrics** – the use of methods of authentication based on unique physical characteristics, such as fingerprints, retinal and iris scans and signatures.

Limitations are based on cost and reliability. Some PDAs and USB dongles have single finger scanners, while advanced systems use retinal scanners.

With the changes in airport security, you may have been on a long-haul flight to a country, where you were required to offer a forefinger scan from each hand as a method of tracking your entry and exit from the country.

Vetting and control of personnel

An essential part of maintaining the security of systems is the initial vetting of personnel. Vetting involves checking the background and personality profile of someone who will enter a position of trust and is crucial for personnel who will be involved in using or managing systems with highly sensitive data.

Once permissions have been issued, it is also prudent to check continually whether the individual still needs them. For example, the project they were working on may have ended, so they may no longer need the same level of permissions.

CCTV

In the popular press, much is made of the increasing CCTV culture of the UK (and many other nations). While we are all entitled to our view in this matter, for the management of network security it offers an additional advantage. The use of CCTV in key locations can:

- monitor access to server and communications rooms
- allow an independent check of the identity of personnel
- limit the potential for theft
- authenticate that the person at a computer is the authorised user.

Lock and key security

Lock and key security has been with us for hundreds of years and is still a proven technique in maintaining the overall security of many computer systems. The technology may have advanced, with swipe cards, proximity dongles and chip and pin systems all in use.

A security manager can work in partnership with the network management to control physical access to sensitive resources. They can control who has access to what, where and when, as well as keep a record of all personnel entering and exiting some areas.

Firewalls

As discussed on page 279 of this unit, firewalls control access to the network by opening only the TCP or UDP ports that are needed for network traffic. Most firewalls will prevent incoming traffic unless it was requested by a device on the inside of the network.

With many firewall systems, you may also find **intrusion detection systems**. Some of these are passive and simply warn the network manager of a possible incursion, while others are active and can be configured to disable the offending data stream.

With applications such as Snort®, Aircrack-ng® and Wireshark (formerly Ethereal), it is easy to create a **span port** on a network switch and attach a PC to monitor the traffic for the entire system. This is surprisingly efficient and can be used to trap many users' illegitimate activities.

Software protection

Software protection using anti-virus software is of considerable importance. Prevalent since the late 1980s, viruses have caused considerable havoc and continue to do so.

Ensuring you have a current anti-virus application is of immense importance. Ensuring it maintains its virus definitions (database of viruses and their identifying features) is possibly more important. It could be argued that an out-of-date anti-virus application is almost as useless as having none at all.

All anti-virus vendors strive to ensure their definitions are up to date, working with a range of international experts to review each new development, indentify risk and establish if it is a virus or a **false positive**.

4.2 Business risks

The majority of networks support business. Business in this context may mean a trader on the Internet, a large corporation, your college (as its business purpose is to provide your education), a government department, a charity or a sole worker using their computer at home.

A networked system has many advantages, but with many organisations now dependent on their network and its connection to the Internet for the majority of their business functions, the network is considered to be a primary risk to business. If this fails, or any part of the system is unavailable, it is likely to cause considerable loss of service and therefore loss of commercial business and eventually loss of income. If a single server fails, it may not appear initially to be a major issue, but if it handles customer financial transactions, the impact can be both immediate and far reaching.

For many companies the loss of Internet connectivity or the use of **primary networked services** may have many adverse effects, including:

- loss of essential income from customers
- inability to carry out core business
- loss of essential, irreplaceable data
- loss of goodwill with trading partners and suppliers.

Key terms

Intrusion detection system – used to monitor network traffic and analyse if an incursion has taken place.

Span port – a port on to which all the data on the network is copied.

False positive – when something is a positive result, but is not the cause you are looking for. For example, if someone wins the long distance race, you would think they are the fastest, until you discover all the other contenders had been injured on the way.

Primary networked services – when this is the only connection you have to the Internet.

Data integrity

Data integrity is vital for any business and means the quality of the data you hold. As such, data integrity can relate to data accuracy or to data security. The loss of confidentiality, or the inaccuracy of data, are both examples of compromised data integrity. If your tax records become publically available and they are also wrong, you individually are open to identity theft, as well as the taxation service now being mistrusted on how effectively they execute your income tax.

Inevitably, any loss of service, loss of confidentiality, inaccuracy of data or poor data integrity will affect an organisation's reputation.

Costs will immediately increase as the organisation involved has to pay to:

- resolve the issue
- repair their public image
- suffer the loss of income
- support the legal damages that may occur
- ensure the issue does not recur

See *Unit 7: Organisational systems security*, page 191 for further information on this topic.

Activity: Are you hooked?

In a small group or whole class session, discuss your dependence on Internet technology.

- What could you do without the Internet?
- What services are now only available (easily) on the Internet?

Increased costs

Unless an organisation relocates, or acquires a new site, it is uncommon for a network to be built from scratch. To ensure the network is viable it has to be maintained and each year of operation brings new costs and new opportunities.

When managing any system, a network manager has to consider the cost of ensuring that:

- the size of the system increases in line with the size of organisational growth
- there is enough bandwidth on inter-network WAN connections
- there is enough bandwidth on the Internet connection
- the core network devices can handle all the services required of the network
- the servers are fit for purpose.

Responsibilities

Because of the security risks involved in running networks, the administrators of many large network systems are responsible for ensuring that resilience is part of their infrastructure. They do this by:

- carrying out regular backups of critical data
- using multiple connections to the Internet and other networked locations
- using multiple systems, such as routers, to ensure that if one fails another will take its place automatically
- load balancing data on more than one server, to ensure that the system will cope if one server fails or in times of increased load, such as the pre-Christmas rush on e-commerce sites.

Security issues

Malware

As the technology of networks advances, with more users being able to access them from a wider range of locations, the problem of **malware** has become an increasing problem, including viruses, trojans, worms, **phishing** and **spam** scams. (Definitions of virus, worm and trojan can be found on page 278.)

Key terms

Malware – a hostile, intrusive or annoying piece of software or program code.

Phishing – involves criminals sending out fraudulent emails that claim to be from a legitimate company, with the aim of obtaining the recipients' personal details and committing identity theft.

Spam – unsolicited bulk email used for advertising purposes.

Phishing is a mailing technique, usually used to deceive individuals into revealing their bank password and login details or parting with their money for dubious deals. Some phish emails will direct you to a phoney website that looks the real website, for example a bank's website. Even if you do not fall for the deception and do not enter your details, visiting the site could enable the site's web server to download a trojan. As you click on the hyperlink in the email, you will have activated a server-side script which could cause you many problems.

Most spam sent today is a form of low-level advertising, often for dubious medical or commercial offers. As with phishing, avoid clicking on links to any sites or opening attachments, as it is very likely the web server will attempt to download a trojan.

Spyware is a type of malware that may have been downloaded willingly by the user. The information collected by spyware can range from the sites visited by the user to, more dangerously, the passwords and usernames they use.

In some contexts spyware is used as a tool to enable commercial organisations to direct their marketing and product development, while others use spyware to commit fraud.

Some free applications come with 'legitimate' spyware, using the creators of the spyware to sponsor the development of their applications.

There are some excellent free anti-spyware applications available, but be careful as some of these may themselves be a form of spyware. Microsoft® have released Windows Defender® as part of Vista®, with free downloads for older versions of Windows®.

Adware is not normally considered malicious, just annoying. Many free applications (often referred to as shareware) are supported by the fees generated from the advertising that is included in the application as a banner or a separate window.

Many adware systems, such as Gator, Gain and HotBar, will impose advertising on you even when you are not using the offending application. Some adware systems, especially ones downloaded from

Key terms

Spyware – collects information about a user's various activities without their consent and reports it back to a central server.

Adware – an application (often free) that when installed comes with adverts, either via your browser or in the application itself.

dubious sites, border on the spyware and malware category and are considered problematic.

Levels of security risk

As discussed earlier in this unit, protecting your computer with anti-virus software is essential. (See the activity on page 279 which describes how to download a free anti-virus application.)

Each virus, worm, trojan, spam or phishing email will carry a different level of risk – in most cases those which cause the greatest damage entail the greatest risk. If a worm or trojan is involved, it can be safely assumed the risk is high, as someone is looking to gain access to your computer system.

Organisations such as McAfee® profile each new malware they learn of and monitor its effect across the world. McAfee® categorise each malware according to the level of threat, using the following categories: High-Outbreak, High, Medium-On Watch, Medium, Low Profiled and Low. Visit the McAfee® website to discover the current malware issues by going to Hotlinks.

Assessment activity 9.4

1 This is a practical activity which takes place in your classroom.

- Set a password.
- Set an access control rule, which may be a simple change to a local firewall (opening port 21:FTP).
- Back up some data and restore it.
- Set a screensaver password.
- Look at lock/key security.
- Install an anti-virus application. **P6**

2 Complete a review of your centre's network, reporting on the business risks, which must include:

- the impact of loss of service
- the impact of loss of business or income
- potential increased costs
- the impact of loss of confidentiality
- the impact of compromised data integrity
- the impact of potential security issues caused by a viral infection. **M3**

Grading tips

- For the merit criteria you may wish to use a PowerPoint® presentation or a YouTube video. The verb report suggests that you simply give information on the facts request. **M3**

PLTS

You can show your skills as a **self-manager** by setting up the security on your computer and reviewing your centre's network for IT security risks.

Functional skills

You can demonstrate your Functional **ICT** skills by creating a PowerPoint® presentation to present your review of your centre's IT security risks.

Pradeep Modi
Network engineer

I work with a team of network engineers and security specialists as part of a large corporation. We support the daily operation of the network. Occasionally we are called in to resolve issues.

Our role is to ensure the system runs without any complications and protect it from internal and external threats. As new systems and applications are used by the organisation, we are tasked with planning how to support these and ensure their efficient (and safe) operation.

A typical day

I don't have a typical day. There are many routine administrative tasks, backing up data, checking the integrity of the backups and organising safe/secure offsite storage. We support a large workforce that uses the network and its connection to the Internet for many different reasons.

We will occasionally have hardware or communication issues. As the network is the lifeblood of the organisation's ability to do business, we have to respond promptly, communicate the solution and often create a workaround while we establish the cause.

Best things about the job

Apart from having new technical challenges, which give me plenty to think about, I find that in networking, as for many IT professions, you are always learning about new technologies and how they may operate. As new applications and devices come onto the market, we are always looking at how we could implement them on our network without causing the system any problems.

Think about it!

1 What have you covered in this chapter, to give you a technical understanding of Pradeep's job? Write a list and discuss this with others.

2 What additional skills would you need to develop for this career to become a reality? Work in a small group and create a list.

Just checking

1. What is the difference between a LAN and a WAN?
2. What is a PAN?
3. What role does network software carry out on a network?
4. What do CSMA/CD and CSMA/CA stand for?
5. What does RAID stand for and what is it used for?
6. What four pieces of information are needed when configuring the NIC?
7. What are SMTP, IMAP and POP3?
8. Give three examples of network operating systems.
9. What are ZIP, TAR, JAR and RAR files?
10. What is a proxy server and what is it used for?

Assignment tips

- Use plenty of diagrams. While a picture is not always worth a thousand words, with supporting text explaining what is required you may find you achieve a merit.
- There are many practical opportunities in this unit. Make sure you take the time to explore them.
- Evaluation requires supporting evidence. This can be accomplished with tables, presentations or complex (structured) diagrams.

Credit value: 10

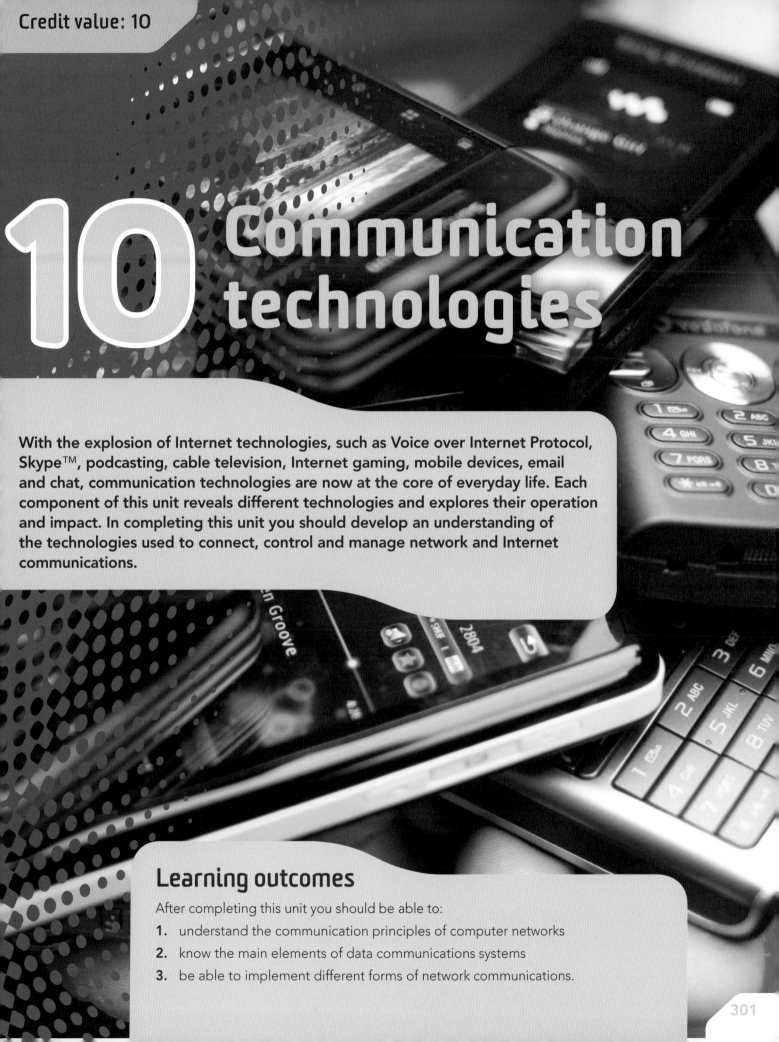

10 Communication technologies

With the explosion of Internet technologies, such as Voice over Internet Protocol, Skype™, podcasting, cable television, Internet gaming, mobile devices, email and chat, communication technologies are now at the core of everyday life. Each component of this unit reveals different technologies and explores their operation and impact. In completing this unit you should develop an understanding of the technologies used to connect, control and manage network and Internet communications.

Learning outcomes

After completing this unit you should be able to:

1. understand the communication principles of computer networks
2. know the main elements of data communications systems
3. be able to implement different forms of network communications.

Assessment and grading criteria

This table shows you what you must do in order to achieve a pass, merit or distinction grade, and where you can find activities in this book to help you.

To achieve a **pass** grade the evidence must show that you are able to:	To achieve a **merit** grade the evidence must show that, in addition to the pass criteria, you are able to:	To achieve a **distinction** grade the evidence must show that, in addition to the pass and merit criteria, you are able to:
P1 explain how networks communicate **See Assessment activity 10.1, page 319**		
P2 identify communication protocols and models **See Assessment activity 10.1, page 319**	**M1** explain why communication protocols are important **See Assessment activity 10.1, page 319**	**D1** compare the OSI seven-layer model and the TCP/IP model **See Assessment activity 10.1, page 319**
P3 identify different types of communication devices **See Assessment activity 10.2, page 337**		
P4 describe what data elements are and why they are important **See Assessment activity 10.2, page 337**		
P5 describe the principles of signal theory **See Assessment activity 10.2, page 337**		
P6 describe different transmission methods used **See Assessment activity 10.2, page 337**	**M2** explain why particular transmission methods are chosen in particular situations **See Assessment activity 10.2, page 337**	**D2** compare the effectiveness of different transmission methods **See Assessment activity 10.2, page 337**
P7 create direct network communication between two users **See Assessment activity 10.3, page 342**	**M3** assess the effectiveness of data transfer over wired and wireless networks **See Assessment activity 10.3, page 342**	
P8 set up interconnection devices for direct communication **See Assessment activity 10.3, page 342**		

How you will be assessed

This unit will be assessed by a number of internal assignments that will be designed and marked by the staff at your centre. It may be subject to sampling by your centre's Lead Internal Verifier or an Edexcel Standards Verifier as part of Edexcel's ongoing quality assurance procedures. The assignments will be designed to allow you to show your understanding of the unit outcomes. These relate to what you should be able to do after completing this unit.

Your tutor will tell you precisely what form your assessments will take, but you could be asked to produce:

- written reports
- documented discussions
- PowerPoint® presentations and notes.

Jacob Cole, BTEC National IT learner

I am not very mathematical and there seems to be a great deal of technology that is driven by the sort of maths I struggled with at school.

After getting started, a great deal seemed very straightforward. The technologies are fascinating and it is amazing how they manage to transmit data over so many systems at such high speed.

The hands-on work was incredibly enjoyable. I did not realise that I could get these systems talking to each other.

The assignment was a combination of practical work, as well as written work. I found the work done in the classroom made the written work easier to produce.

Personally, seeing how the technology on the Internet and my mobile phone works is amazing. So much is going on in the moment I am sending an email. Professionally I can see how this knowledge will support many careers in IT, as web developers, systems support engineers and programmers need to know what is happening when data is being sent.

Over to you

- How could you accomplish the networking described on a handheld device such as an iPad™ or a mobile phone?
- What technology is required to accomplish this at home?
- Could I develop my hands-on skills in this area?

1. Understand the communication principles of computer networks

Networked systems have become increasingly complex over the last 30 years. This section describes many of the common systems used to implement and manage a computer-based network.

1.1 Computer networks

Types of network

In networking, the type of network is defined by its geographic reach. The term **LAN** (local area network) normally describes a system contained on one site and running as a self-contained network with a connection to a **WAN** (wide area network) or the Internet. The term WAN usually describes a distance-based system which may connect many sites or organisations.

With networking speeds always increasing, these terms have become blurred. With current technology a LAN may be spread across many locations and WANs may be international in nature. Some LANs and WANs use secure connections across the Internet to maintain their communication, for example a home user can connect to a corporate WAN or LAN and become part of the system.

Some regions have a **MAN** (metropolitan area network) so that organisations with a common goal can share data and services. MANs are often found in local authorities, education and finance (for example, the City of London).

Bluetooth has defined a different type of network strucure with the **PAN** (personal area network) connection of laptop and mobile devices.

Network topologies

Each LAN, WAN or MAN requires a structure – this is called its topology. Common **topologies** include bus, ring, star, tree (or hierarchical) and mesh – see Table 10.1.

Some are **logical topologies** – this means the design does not reflect the actual system. An excellent example of this is the star topology. To have a central point of failure is a considerable risk and this is overcome by having a switched network which interconnects using the bus topology (see Figure 10.1). Therefore, a network can have multiple connections in a tree, or extended star, using the bus infrastructure on the switches. A specialist **protocol**, **STP** (spanning tree protocol), will configure the switches to stop loops occurring and watch for any lost devices or connections on the system.

Key terms

LAN – stands for local area network.

WAN – wide area network. It is a large network, usually covering more than one geographical location and often crossing countries and continents.

MAN – metropolitan area network (MAN) is a network connecting LANs in an area that might be small as a campus or as large as a city. A MAN could use wireless, or leased circuits, to allow the system to communicate.

PAN – stands for personal area network.

Topology – the layout of devices in a network.

Logical topology – how data actually transfers in a network, as opposed to the physical topology. For example, some networks are physically laid out in a star configuration, but they operate logically as bus or ring networks.

Protocol – a common method of communication and information exchange, following a set of rules.

STP – stands for spanning tree protocol.

Table 10.1: Common topologies of networks

Topology	Operation	Advantages	Disadvantages
Bus	A historical system centred around one cable which runs as a core. The term 'bus' comes from the language used in describing the system bus on the motherboard. In modern networking the bus is still in use, but condensed to the circuitry of a network switch.	It is easy to add new devices to the bus.	If cut or dislocated, one half of the system will be unable to communicate to the other.
Ring	Like the children's party game 'pass the parcel', the ring network works on an equal share, where everyone gets to communicate in turn.	Easy to manage and everyone has equal share of the bandwidth.	Limited security as everyone can see the traffic of others. Is not ideal if the system has big talkers like file servers.
Star	With a central core to the system, all the nodes (components) of the network are directly connected.	Easy to add new nodes. If one node fails then the network is not affected.	If the core of the system (the hub) fails then the whole network will fail.
Tree (or hierarcical)	A centrally controlled and managed system where the network can be designed to reflect an organisation structure from HQ to region to each branch office. (It is worth noting that the hierarchical network is a logical hybrid of the star.)	Easy to add more components.	Like the star if the centre fails, the whole system fails.
Mesh	This system enjoys multiple redundancies, where there are multiple connections and multiple routes for the data. The Internet is a large-scale version of the mesh network structure.	If more than one line fails, a node can continue to communicate.	The management of this is very complicated as it involves circular routes, split trees and repeated information.

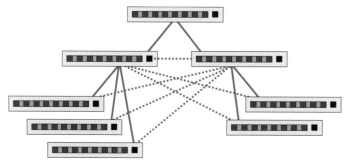

Figure 10.1: Star and bus topologies combined

Activity: Can you man a pan?

1   What type of network is each of the following: LAN, WAN, MAN, PAN?

2   What is a topology?

3   Give five examples of topologies, how they work and the advantages and disadvantages of each.

Network services

When transferring data across distances, across a WAN, via broadband or through wireless, a variety of network services have to be used. Common examples include packet-switched, circuit-switched, multiplexed, ADSL, broadband and WAP.

Packet switching

There are many packet-switched WANs in operation. Popular examples include multi-protocol label switching (MPLS), asynchronous transfer mode (ATM) and frame relay.

Packet switching is a mechanism which sends network traffic in small manageable data units across the system. It operates by ensuring that there is a group of **routers** or WAN switches interconnected, all communicating which connections are active and the speed and reliability of each connection.

A packet-switched system can direct the traffic via a variety of routes (like the mesh topology). These can be logical permanent virtual circuits **PVCs** defined by the communications expert. One system, or one connection, may contain many PVCs, each oblivious to the communication of the other. Large telecommunications providers use this technology to separate the traffic of their different customers, even though they may be using the same lines across part of the network (see Figure 10.2).

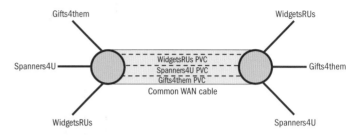

Figure10.2: PVCs across the same line

Key terms

Router – a device which connects networks and makes traffic forwarding decisions based on information learned via its connections or a routing protocol.

PVC – stands for permanent virtual circuit.

To identify each PVC, different technologies use mapping or labelling techniques. This equates to each device having an identity set for each connection and directed to the connection across the system. The physical WAN topology will then differ from the logical network topology created with the PVCs (see Figure 10.3).

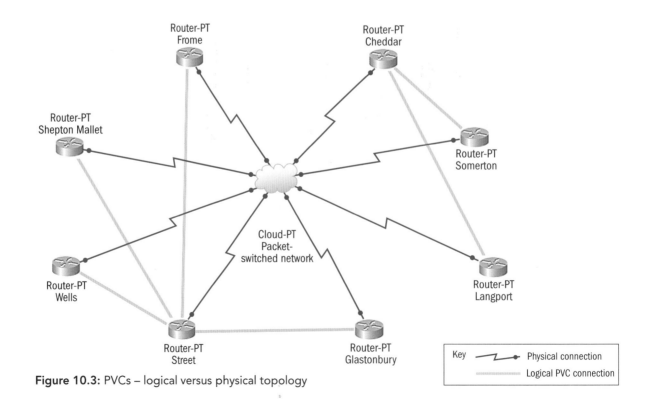

Figure 10.3: PVCs – logical versus physical topology

Circuit switching

Older circuit-switched systems like **ISDN** (integrated services digital network) create a physical wired circuit during the period of communication. This is not necessarily logical or adaptive, as the communications line has to be in place for this to happen. For historical reasons, there are still some ISDN services in use, where broadband and/or ADSL have not yet reached the location. As the reach of higher **bandwidth** services extends, we will see a further demise of the service.

ISDN was the first solution to attempt to bypass limitations set by the public telephone system to data transmission in the 1980s. ISDN is different from a public telephone line in several respects – it has the capacity to have a separate channel for data, the capability to send voice and data simultaneously and can be used for 'other signals'.

An ISDN line can be provided in one of two ways.

- BRI (basic rate interface) is used for connections to remote sites, or customers such as small business or home users.

- PRI (primary rate interface) is the core circuit-switched system for medium to large organisations to connect their BRI-based sites.

Each interface is divided into channels.

- A BRI can have two 64K B channels, each of which can carry voice or data and one 16K D channel for control signals. So, you could have one voice line and one data line on a shared connection, or you could have a data line of up to 128K.

- A PRI can have up to 30 B channels of 64K and one D channel of 64K. This allows for up to 30 voice lines or data lines. If all the data lines were in use, then the PRI would have a data carrying capacity of over 1.9 megabits.

With multiplexed communication across a WAN, multiple communications have to use the same single channel (or communications line). Multiplexed communication is managed by a **MUX**, which rapidly switches from one communication to another. Unlike packet-switched networks, the MUX is part of a complex circuit-switched system which allows more than one circuit to occur on the same line (see Figure 10.4).

ADSL

ADSL (asymmetric digital subscriber line) is a technology for transmitting digital information at higher speeds on existing phone lines to homes and businesses.

ADSL can provide a continuous connection. It is asymmetric (having no balance or symmetry) – it uses most of the transmission line to transmit downstream to the user and only a small part to receive information from the user. ADSL simultaneously accommodates analogue (voice) information on the same communications line. Some systems will transmit from 512 Kbps to 10 Mbps down to the user. Also, on some business ADSL systems, the company can purchase a specific 'upload' bandwidth so that they can maintain successful two-way communications with other sites or with their web server.

Key terms

ISDN – is a digital telephone line that shares voice and data communications.

Bandwidth – the measure of how much data can be sent across a given communication method per second. It is almost impossible to use the full bandwidth of any system.

MUX – stands for multiplexer. A multiplexer is an electronic device that selects one of many analog or digital signals and sends the input into a single line, therefore allowing many signals to share one device.

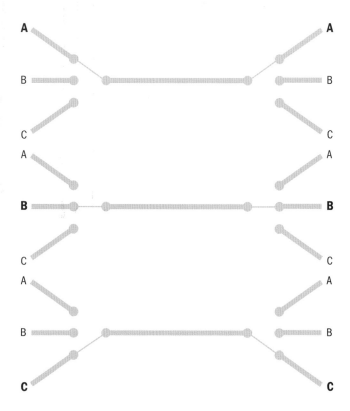

Figure 10.4: The operation of a MUX

ADSL is designed to exploit the one-way nature of most web-based communication in which large amounts of data (web pages, etc.) are downloaded and only a small amount of control information is ever returned.

ADSL relies on the local telephone exchange being enabled for ADSL. It is also distance-to-speed limited where a modern exchange can serve homes and businesses in a two kilometre radius. RADSL (remote ADSL) has been developed to serve wider communities and is currently available in some phone exchanges in the UK.

Broadband

Broadband is a general heading for a variety of technologies which include ADSL. For some ISPs, broadband is provided by sharing a range of frequencies unused by other services.

Cable TV providers offer the best example of broadband. The local cable junction which is fed into the subscriber's home offers three services – phone communication, TV and high-speed Internet. This is accomplished by multiplexing the frequencies at a core location.

WAP

WAP (wireless access point) offers a hive communications medium where each device is part of a larger 'communication colony' for LAN and WAN systems. With the positioning of WAPs in crossed-over fields of influence, a mesh can be created (see Figure 10.5), which ensures the roaming device always has communication and provides a method of increasing bandwidth by sharing multiple communication channels.

Activity: In the distance

1 Define these terms: packet switching, circuit switching and router.

2 What do these acronyms stand for: PVC, BRI, PRI, MUX, ADSL, RADSL, WAP?

Network software

The network operating system **NOS** often resides on a server. The purpose of the NOS is to provide controlled access to common services on a network. Examples of NOS products include the current Microsoft® Windows® range, Linux®, Unix® and the IBM® System I platform.

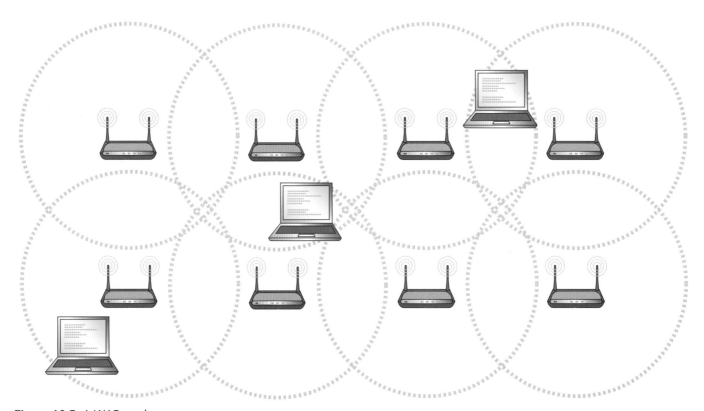

Figure 10.5: A WAP mesh

A NOS is normally on a specialist computer platform with greater processor, storage, communications bandwidth and memory to handle the task. A NOS may offer a variety of services such as printer control and management, access privileges for services and files, file management, database management, web servers, **proxy** and content management systems for Internet access, email servers, directory and **domain** control (for large systems and the Internet), Messenger® and chat relay and voice traffic relay.

In the world of open-source and licence-free technologies, with some research it is possible to convert a home computer into a server and effectively turn ordinary client-based operating systems such as Windows® 7 or Vista® into a NOS.

Key terms

NOS – stands for network operating system.

Proxy – a person or system which acts as a go-between.

Domain – a group of networked computers and devices that are treated as a unit and have the same communications address.

Network connection software

Network connection software is often referred to as a client – the software allows a system to access the services provided by a NOS and the server it is managing. The client will vary according to the service offered, such as in the examples below.

- Printer control and management clients are part of the printer wizards in Windows XP® and previous Windows® operating systems.
- Access privileges for services and files will be controlled centrally by the server and will be based on the login used to start the operating system profile.
- File management is accessed by Windows Explorer® or FTP (file transfer protocol) clients.
- Web servers are available via Internet Explorer® or Firefox®.
- Proxy and content management systems for Internet access will be invisible to the user and will be contacted by Internet Explorer® or Firefox®.
- Email servers can be accessed via a web-based client or using applications such as Outlook®.
- Messenger® and chat relay are available via GAIM, Windows Live® Messenger (see Figure 10.6), etc.
- Voice traffic relay is available via the Skype™ client.

Figure 10.6: Windows Live® Messenger client

Access methods

On a LAN, devices cannot communicate whenever they feel like it. To ensure order, an **access control method** controls who has the 'next turn' for network communication. Token ring networks make each device on the system wait its turn as in the party game pass the parcel. Problems arise when there are **big talkers** on the system that need more network time.

Ethernet overcomes this problem with a best-effort solution – each device on the system can send data as and when it sees fit. The problem with this solution

Key terms

Access control method – a system used to control which devices may use and access the network communication system.

Big talker – the term used for a network device that communicates more than the others, normally a server.

occurs when two devices contest for the same service and a collision occurs (see Figure 10.7).

Each device has to wait and resend. If another collision occurs the devices have to wait and then resend the data – and so on. To overcome the collision issue, Ethernet has a solution called **CSMA/CD** (carrier sense multiple access/collision detection) which works by following five steps.

1 Checks if the local data line has any traffic on it (the power level will be higher).

2 If there is no traffic, then send data.

3 Wait for the recipient to send an acknowledgement.

4 If no acknowledgement, wait for a random period of time.

5 Go back to step 1 and resend data.

CSMA/CD is commonly referred to as the backoff algorithm and is applied by all devices on the system. Unless the network is too busy, the reattempt is normally successful.

CSMA/CA (collision avoidance) on LAN systems is a less common variation of CSMA/CD. It is based on the

detection of the signal before any data is sent. CSMA/CA is used in 802.15 (which is known as Wireless PANs or Bluetooth). It is used to stop Bluetooth devices contending with existing communications. It would be useful if you were sending a MP3 ring tone to a classmate and someone else with a Bluetooth-enabled mobile phone wandered by and unwittingly disrupted the transfer.

Activity: Access methods

1 Define the following: NOS, proxy, domain, PAN.

2 What types of service might be provided by the NOS?

3 What is a big talker? How does CSMA/CD solve the problem caused by big talkers?

4 What are the five steps followed in CSMA/CD?

Key terms

CSMA/CD – stands for carrier sense multiple access/collision detection. It is a method employed by Ethernet to detect and avoid continuous collisions of network data.

CSMA/CA – stands for carrier sense multiple access/collision detection collision avoidance. A variation of CSMA/CD, to avoid continuous collisions of network data.

1.2 Network components

In a network infrastructure, two devices form the 'fabric' of the network – servers and workstations. These are connected to the network via different network cards.

Servers

Servers offer many different services on a network. Each system is different and these are examples of common uses.

- Servers offer printer control and management, regulating who can print to what printer and in some cases how much they can print.

- With directory and domain control, servers manage a user's levels of access and can control their privileges for networked services and files.

- File management is achieved by ensuring the data is backed up – this involves placing files somewhere where they can be accessed by specific users or groups of users.

- Database management is achieved by controlling the integrity of the data and how the information is accessed.

- Web servers are both information services and 'retail outlets'.

- Servers used to manage common proxy and content management systems for Internet access can prevent certain users from accessing inappropriate website material.

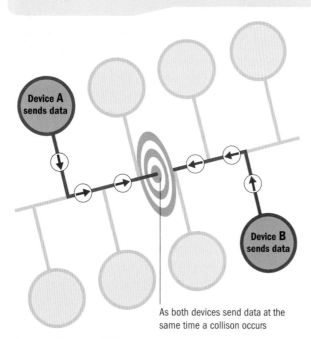

As both devices send data at the same time a collison occurs

Figure 10.7: A collision

- Email servers, Messenger® and chat relay enable communication between users and customers.
- Voice traffic relay, a relatively recent development, is used to direct and manage voice communication across a network that has many users.
- Virtualisation servers, hosting a range of servers or remote workstations using one platform.

Workstations

The definition of a workstation has become more ambiguous over the last ten years. At one time, the term described a personal computer or terminal with access to a network. Since then, technology has advanced considerably. Nowadays, a workstation is considered to be any device which accesses services offered by the network, for example:

- a personal PC, with Windows® or a similar operating system accessing the Internet at home or the network at school/college through regular phone links
- a laptop, at home, work, school/college on a regular phone link, or roaming on a wireless system like those provided at an airport or in some fast food outlets
- a mobile device (such as your phone) anywhere with wireless roaming facilities
- some set-top boxes for cable and satellite TV, which act as clients, especially when you select on-demand TV.

Network cards

To enable workstations and servers to connect to a network infrastructure, they need a network card. For smaller devices, this may be a chip hidden on the main circuit board.

The type of network interface used depends on the communication medium available: wireless interfaces are used for Bluetooth as well as conventional wireless; for a standard Ethernet LAN, the network interface is via an **RJ**45 connector (see page 335). A **3G dongle**

is as much a network card as a conversional Ethernet adaptor, only the method of data transmission changes.

Some network cards are specialised in the speed of service they offer with 10Mbps, 100Mbps and 1000+Mbps autodetecting cards (or chips) available.

Some specialist systems have fiber optic network cards or cards for token ring systems.

1.3 Interconnection devices

The fabric of a network is managed by a range of complex communications devices. Each has a purpose in enabling access and connectivity to the network infrastructure. This section explains more about these devices, including hubs and repeaters, switches and bridges, routers, gateways and wireless devices.

Switches and bridges

Bridges and switches are closely related. The bridge is a simple technology formerly used in networking. Its purpose was to separate segments of a network and reduce the number of network broadcasts. The bridge has enjoyed a minor renaissance – some commercial **VoIP** (Voice over Internet Protocol) phones have internal bridges so a PC can be connected to the phone and the phone to the single outlet on the wall.

> **Key term**
>
> **VoIP** – stands for Voice over Internet Protocol. It is the method used to allow voice telecommunications to take place over a computer data network.

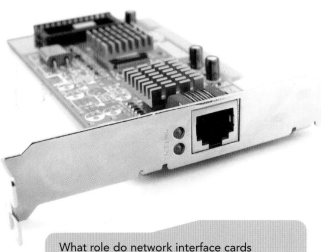

> **Key terms**
>
> **RJ** – stands for registered jack. This is an American term for the type of plug used on a connector that has been recognised by a standards organisation.
>
> **3G dongle** – normally a USB device that can be connected to your computer to offer extra services, such as Internet access.

What role do network interface cards perform?

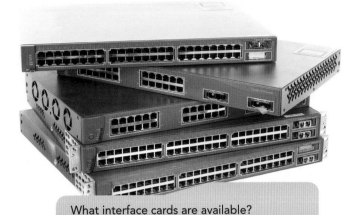

What interface cards are available?

A switch is a complex array of bridges which has developed as networking technology becomes more complex. The switch increases the speed of communication as it creates unique mini-networks (circuits).

Switches can be implemented on a LAN to:

- increase the speed of the connection – most network systems are 100 megabit or 1000 megabit to the computer: you can purchase specialised or auto-sensing switches that will remotely detect the speed of the NIC

- aid control and security of the network via managed switches that can be divided into **VLANs**

- control some large systems, which require a core switch to manage all the other switches on the system.

Switches come in a variety of specifications – you can purchase very small switches with four **ports** up to commercial switches with 96 ports.

The switch creates virtual circuits between each device communicating on the system, thus increasing bandwidth, improving security and reducing collisions. This is achieved by the switch storing in memory the **MAC** (media access control) address of all devices attached to each port. This allows the forwarding decisions to be made, as each MAC has to be unique. (For more about the MAC address, see page 328.)

Key terms

VLAN – stands for virtual local area network. It is a method used to divide a LAN into smaller logical structures.

Port – a technical term for a socket or connection.

MAC – stands for media access control.

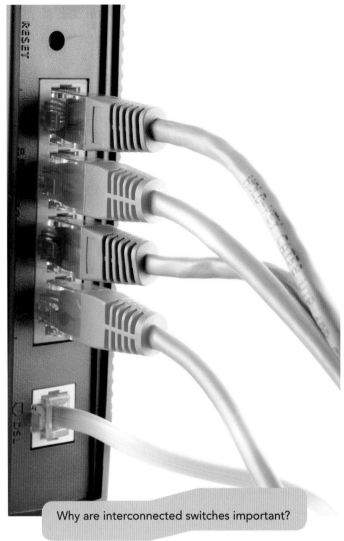

Why are interconnected switches important?

Routers

A router is actually a 'bridge with attitude'. Instead of connecting LAN segments the router will connect multiple networks, that is WANs. A router is a device which connects your network to the Internet, connects your network to a greater WAN, forwards traffic coming into the networks and directs outgoing traffic.

A corporation may have many switches, but only one router. So this device has to be efficient in order to move a considerable quantity of network traffic. Routers are often combined with other systems – they can provide access control and firewalls, and manage connections between different sections of a company LAN.

To operate, most routers have to be programmed and joined to a WAN using a routing protocol. The routing protocol is a limited form of artificial intelligence as it learns what devices are connected in the WAN infrastructure (see Figure 10.8).

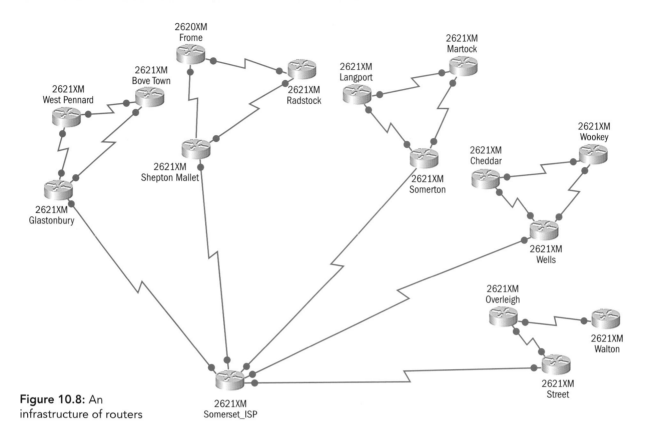

Figure 10.8: An infrastructure of routers

Gateways

A gateway is a device on a network which acts as an entrance point to another network. This is often referred to as the **default gateway** or the 'way out'; naturally, this is also the way in. A gateway may be a router, a switch with routing capabilities, a firewall and/or a proxy server.

A suitably advanced network will have multiple default gateways, each available if any fail. This is derived from a routing technology called HSRP (hot standby routing protocol) as shown in Figure 10.9.

Figure 10.9: HSRP for managing default gateways

> **Key term**
>
> **Default gateway** – a device, which may be a router or switch, which will enable your device to connect to another network, such as the Internet.

Wireless devices

Like access points, these devices are also hubs but with a different technology and differing sensibility. Devices can be connected together on a peer or ad hoc basis. There may also be a hub (WAP) to control and direct traffic, often to a cabled network infrastructure.

Figure 10.10: WAPs

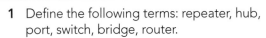

Activity: Topologies

1 Compare the different topologies and describe the advantages each offers.

2 Visit a well-known networking retailer's website and complete a price comparison for all the different devices. Explain why some devices are 'better' than others and how they may enhance the network at your centre.

3 Can you explain:
   a) why different topologies exist?
   b) why there are differing standards of ISDN?
   c) the purpose of a router?
   d) how a server supports a network?

Activity: Interconnecting devices

1 Define the following terms: repeater, hub, port, switch, bridge, router.

2 What is a VLAN?

3 What is a gateway and a default gateway?

1.4 Models

Protocols offer different methods of communication between devices on a networked system. To ensure that the communication devices operate fairly and in a controlled fashion, models are used to describe the controls in place. One of the most commonly used

Table 10.2: The OSI model

Layer	OSI role	Component
7	Application	Used for applications such as email and web browsers, this layer has many protocols associated with its operation.
6	Presentation	This layer is responsible for the organisation of the data into a format that humans can use. There are as many presentation layer entities as there are media types. Common examples include: • ASCII (American Standard Code for Information Interchange), which is the plain text used for HTML (web page) documents • SWF (shockwave format), used in all flash media on web sites • Doc, for word documents • Jpg (Joint Photographic Engineers Group) for images • MP3 (Multimedia Players Engineers Group, format 3) for audio media.
5	Session	This allows you to have multiple browser, chat and email windows open simultaneously without any conflicts in the data transmitted.
4	Transport	Devices such as firewalls and layer 4 switches operate at this layer. The traffic providing security and prioritisation is controlled here. This is essential when VoIP (Voice over Internet Protocol) operates as it needs to have the greater share of any bandwidth. Protocols such as TCP and UDP exist at this layer. Each network communication channel is called a port.
3	Network	The logical address for the server or work station is managed on this layer. The most common protocol in use is TCP/IP, where a dotted decimal IP address is allocated to the network card (e.g. 10.189.12.3). Routing takes place at this layer and is completed by routers and specialist layer 3 switches.
2	Data link	On a LAN the data link layer has a physical address (a MAC address) which is used to identify each device (normally hard-wired into a chip on the network card). Some WANs have a similar addressing scheme, which is simpler. At the data link layer you will find network cards and Ethernet switches, as well as specialist WAN connections.
1	Physical	This is principally the media, cables or wireless layer. It concentrates on the transmission and encoding of the bits of data (010101010111). A wireless access point operates at this level but uses layer 2 to maintain control.

models is the OSI model. The TCP/IP protocol suite also has a model, with many similarities to OSI.

In commercial practice, OSI is often used for teaching – TCP/IP is used to describe Internet communication in a practical context. Other systems have their own variations and models, but will follow very similar principles. The TCP/IP model is explained in more detail below and is compared to the OSI model.

The OSI model

The OSI (open systems interconnection) model is a logical ideology which describes network communication between network devices. Because of the variety of manufacturers and technologies, the ISO (International Organization for Standards) agreed the OSI model to ensure that differing computer systems could communicate effectively with each other.

The benefit of the OSI model is that it makes no difference if you are on a Windows®-based system at home and the website you are visiting is on a Linux® platform – it ensures that all devices concerned in this communication act equally and effectively.

The OSI model (Table 10.2) is represented by seven layers, with 7 being the top (nearer the user, who is considered to be layer 8 by some experts) and 1 at the bottom for the communication medium (the data leaving the computer).

Activity: Open systems

1   What does the acronym OSI stand for?
2   What is the OSI model used for?
3   What are the seven levels of the OSI model?

TCP/IP model

The development of the Internet was based on the standards of the TCP/IP four-layer model and gained

Table 10.3: OSI and TCP/IP models

Layer	OSI model		TCP/IP model	
7	Application	Application layers	Application	Protocols
6	Presentation			
5	Session			
4	Transport	Data flow layers	Transport	
3	Network		Internet	Internet
2	Data link		Data flow (or network access layer)	
1	Physical			

credibility because of its various protocols (see Table 10.4 on page 316). While the OSI model is not generally used to build networks, it is often used as a guide for those who need to understand network communication.

The OSI and TCP/IP models are similar in that both use layers to distinguish tasks. They also have very similar transport and network layers. Networking professionals need to know both models and their differences.

The TCP/IP protocol suite has an extensive range of protocols working at each layer of the OSI model (and the TCP/IP model). See Table 10.5 on page 316.

- FTP (file transfer protocol) is used for file exchange and storage.
- Telnet is used for remote access and control of servers and networking equipment, such as routers.
- HTTP (hyper, text transfer protocol) is used for the distribution of web pages.
- HTTPS (hypertext transfer protocol secure) is used in credit card and other secure web transactions.
- POP3 (post office protocol version 3) is used to collect email from an ISP.
- SMTP (simple mail transfer protocol) is used for sending emails.
- TFTP (trivial file transfer protocol) is used by network devices to back up critical data, simply and quickly.
- DNS (domain name system) is used to match easy-to-remember domains, such as www.bbc.co.uk, to IP addresses like 82.165.26.58 (which are not so easy to remember).
- TCP (transmission control protocol) is used for connection-oriented systems.
- UDP (user datagram protocol) is used for connectionless systems.
- IP (Internet protocol) is used to identify a computer and all devices on a network.
- ICMP (Internet control messaging protocol) is used by a variety of management applications, including Ping, to test communication.
- EIGRP (extended interior gateway routing protocol), OSPF (open shortest path first), RIP (router information protocol) and BGP (border gateway protocol) are all used by routers to manage communication and connectivity between different

network infrastructures.

- HSRP (hot standby routing protocol) enables a LAN to have multiple default gateways for extra reliability.
- DHCP (dynamic host configuration protocol) is used to issue IP addresses to devices during the login

process for a network.

- ARP (address resolution protocol) and RARP (reverse address resolution protocol) are used to match IP addresses to MAC addresses on a computer.

Table 10.4: TCP/IP model layers

4. Application layer

In TCP/IP the application layer also includes the OSI presentation layer and session layer. This includes all of the processes that involve user interaction. The application determines the presentation of the data and controls the session (which is true for the Windows® operating system). In TCP/IP, the terms 'socket' and 'port' are used to describe the communications route.

Protocols

3. Transport layer

In TCP/IP there are two transport layer protocols. The transmission control protocol (TCP) guarantees that information is received as it was sent. The user datagram protocol (UDP) performs no end-to-end reliability checks (see page 329).

2. Internet layer

Internet

The Internet Protocol (IP) is the TCP/IP network layer. Because of the inter-networking emphasis of TCP/IP this is commonly referred to as the Internet layer. All upper and lower layer communications travel through IP as they are passed through the TCP/IP protocol suite.

1. Data flow (or) network access layer

In TCP/IP the data link layer and physical layer are normally grouped together. TCP/IP makes use of existing data link and physical layer technologies rather than defining its own. This ensures TCP/IP is adaptable and can work across a multitude of differing systems.

Table 10.5: Some TCP/IP protocols

OSI layers		Some TCP/IP protocols						
7	Application	FTP	Telnet	HTTP	POP3	SMTP	HTTPS	TFTP
6	Presentation							
5	Session	DNS						
4	Transport	TCP	UDP					
3	Network	IP	ICMP	EIGRP	OSPF	BGP	RIP	HSRP	DHCP
2	Data link	ARP	RARP					
1	Physical							

Activity: TCP not IP?

1   What are the four layers of the TCP/IP model?

2   Give ten examples of TCP/IP protocols. What does each acronym stand for and what is each protocol used for?

Activity: Protocols and models

1   Compare the OSI and TCP/IP models. What advantages do each offer and how are they implemented at your centre?

2   Many protocols are mentioned in this section, the majority of which will be used in your centre's network. Carry out a survey of protocol use at your centre and establish which are the most commonly used.

3   Thinking points:

    a) Why do the TCP/IP and OSI models exist?

    b) Why are there differing standards in networking and what are their benefits?

    c) What is the purpose of the TCP/IP suite individual protocols?

1.5 Protocols

Communication protocols

As we have seen, for systems to communicate physically and to ensure information is successfully atransferred, a communications protocol standard has to be agreed.

Standards

The **IEEE** (Institute of Electrical and Electronic Engineers) regulates the standards agreed for different communications systems to operate (see Table 10.6). By acting as the regulator, it ensures that everyone creates a system that will communicate with other systems.

Key term

IEEE – stands for Institute of Electrical and Electronic Engineers.

The Infrared Data Association (IrDA) defines the standards for PAN communication with infrared receivers and transmitters. IrDA standards follow the principles set by the OSI model.

The lowest levels of control ensure the physical layer with range of 0.2–1 metres, angle of +-15°, speed

Table 10.6: IEEE standards

802.1	Higher layer LAN protocols	Used for LAN control, such as MAC security, VLANs and the spanning tree protocol.
802.2	Logical link control	Defines if a system is connectionless or connection oriented.
802.3	Ethernet	A collection of standards which define the operation of Ethernet across multiple systems.
802.5	Token ring	Defines the operation of token ring networks.
802.11	Wireless LAN (Wi-Fi certification)	Defines the 802.11a, b, g and n standards, each definition looks at distance and speed.
802.15	Wireless PAN	Definition for low power short range networking devices. ZigBee® is a standard being developed at the time of publication for devices requiring lower processing payloads than that demanded of Bluetooth.
802.15.1	Bluetooth certification	
802.15.4	ZigBee certification	
802.16	Broadband wireless access (WiMAX certification)	Definition of a standard for mesh.
802.16e	(Mobile) broadband wireless access	
802.17	Resilient packet ring	Used for fibre optic communication systems.

of 2.4 Kbps to 16 Mbps, modulation (how the signal is sent) and the infrared window. The data link or access control establishes the discovery of potential communication partners, a reliable connection in both directions and the negotiation of device roles.

Cellular radio enables mobile phone technology: the UK and other developed regions have a 'cellular' coverage of base stations to ensure continuous mobile telecommunications. In the UK, however, cellular coverage is not complete, with remote areas lacking mobile communications for some networks (see Figure 10.11).

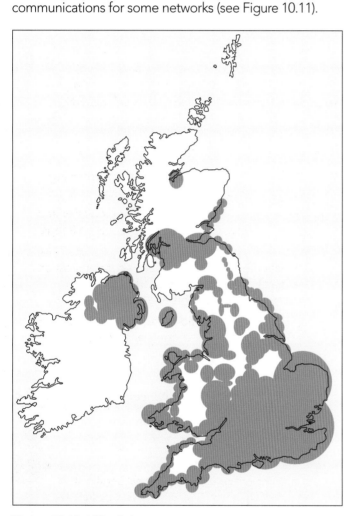

Figure 10.11: UK cellular coverage

GSM is the set of standards used to define how communication is managed on a cellular radio network. GSM technologies are described according to their generation (see Table 10.7), with most phones in current use being 2G (2nd generation) or later.

Key term

GSM – stands for global system for mobile communications.

Table 10.7: Development of GSM technologies

0G	The first cellular communications systems date from the 1980s.
1G	The first common analogue phones were in use from the mid-1980s to no later than 1998. 1G was used as the method for communication, but was insecure and subject to hijacking and listening scandals.
2G	This first digital standard used less power than its analogue counterpart and led the way for smaller phones. It suffered issues around distance from base stations which was not a primary concern for its analogue counterpart.
2.5G	Was a revision which allowed data exchange, such as WAP for mobile phone web pages via WML (wireless mark-up language) and the downloading of ring tones.
3G	Provides the ability to communicate via voice and data simultaneously and has the bandwidth capacity to offer mobiles video phone services. In the transfer of data, 3G uses UMTS (universal mobile telecommunications system) as a standard to ensure different phones on different networks and in different regions are all compatible in the transfer of data.
4G	At the time of writing, 4G was being rolled out in some Scandinavian nations, with the UK and others soon to adopt. The speed promised ranges from 10 Mbps to 300 Mbps. Making mobile data communication comparable with the level of service found in the average LAN structure.

Wireless security protocols

One of the greatest issues with wireless networks is wireless security, or the lack of it. The standards for wireless systems dictates that, when a user first plugs in a WAP and connects using a wireless network card, there must be no security to ensure connectivity.

This means that many home and commercial wireless networks are insecure, thus enabling others to steal bandwidth or snoop on the system.

Many standards for wireless security are designed to overcome this problem. Protocols such as **WEP** (wired equivalent privacy) ensure that the devices exchange a common key, which is set by the user, and encrypt every packet sent via this key. WEP is available in two forms: the 64-bit version has a 10 hexadecimal digit key; the 128-bit version has a 26 hexadecimal digit key.

The wireless connection on a computer, PDA or laptop will also need to be configured for WEP.

Key term

WEP – stands for wired equivalent privacy.

Activity: Title

1 What is a protocol?
2 Which types of standards are defined by the following: IEEE, IrDA, GSM and TCP/IP?
3 What is WEP?

Assessment activity 10.1

P1 P2 M1 D1   **BTEC**

For a mobile phone to make a 3G connection, to send email to your college tutor it requires the application and implementation of a range of different technologies.

1 Create a poster that:
   • explains how your mobile phone gets the email to your tutor's desktop computer **P1**
   • indentifies common communication protocols and models **P2**
   • explains why each communication protocol identified is important. **M1**
2 Compare the TCP/IP and OSI models. You could show the data flow passing through at either end. **D1**

Grading tips

• Demonstrate your understanding by showing the flow of data through different systems. **P1**
• You should consider the size of your poster and the fact that it could be presented as an image or a PDF document. **P1 P2**
• Explain the importance of each communication protocol using arrows and callouts on your poster, in order to achieve a merit grade. **M1**
• To achieve a distinction grade, you will need to outline the different models and compare their features and uses. **D1**

PLTS

You can demonstrate your skills as an **independent enquirer** by researching the knowledge needed to create your poster on communication technologies.

Functional skills

You can demonstrate your Functional **English** skills through writing the information for your poster.

2. Know the main elements of data communications systems

Many technologies provide Internet communication. To use a computer at home or work requires a complex interconnection of equipment, technologies and systems which often remain invisible to the user. The same is true for mobile devices, such as mobile phones, that are Internet enabled.

2.1 Communication devices

To access the Internet and use a network to communicate with others (such as your learning centre or a mobile phone service provider), the technology uses data terminal equipment (DTE) and data circuit-terminating equipment (DCE).

Wired devices

Data terminal equipment (DTE)

DTE is a historical term for the device at the end of the line – this could be a mobile phone, a **modem** within a computer, the cable modem, 3G technology, Bluetooth® or a network card.

> ## Key term
>
> **Modem** – combination and abbreviation of two words: modulator + demodulator. Modulation and demodulation are processes used to convert the computer's digital signal to the method used to transmit the data (such as a phone line) and then back again.

There are different types of DTE according to the communication method used. With Bluetooth®, size and range are important issues, while with mobile phones, quality and bandwidth are more important. Modems and network cards exist in many formats and are configured for a wide range of transmission speeds.

Each system could include DTE devices such as:

- a computer with a network card
- a netbook with a wireless adapter
- a netbook with a 3G dongle
- an iPhone that is 3G-enabled.

Data circuit-terminating equipment

Data circuit-terminating (DCE) works together with DTE. A DTE connects to the Internet or network service offered by the DCE. DCE is network equipment which controls communication. Many examples exist, including:

- the wireless router in your home, to which you connect your laptop or other devices
- the switch in a communications room at work or college, which connects all the classroom computers to the LAN (local area network) and the Internet
- the Bluetooth® dongle on your PC, used to synchronise your mobile device
- equipment at the other end of the broadband service which is connected to your cable modem
- equipment at the other end of your mobile phone providers system, to connect your 3G device
- a central router which connects many other local routers in a WAN (wide area network).

Wireless devices

Over the last ten years, mobile communications have become commonplace, with wireless devices such as third and fourth generation (3G, 3.5G 3.75G and 4G) cellular phones, wireless PDAs and wireless laptops or netbooks being used by many people.

The use of mobile communications has also been accelerated by the blurring of technology boundaries with many mobile devices such as iPhones in common use. Devices like these have greater processing power than computers of, at least, eight years ago and communicate on a greater bandwidth than the early broadband services.

Wireless networks use the 802.11 standard (see page 333), which defines the speed and range of the network communication. The mobile phone network is an interconnection of base stations throughout this country and internationally that allows subscribers to communicate via a low bandwidth voice system. Data services are continuously improving for mobile devices, with greater quality video and audio services as well as faster download speeds for data.

The older **GPRS** (general packet radio service) is still in use, as in areas of limited 3G coverage your mobile device can switch to this system. GPRS is the 2G mobile data service and can transmit 54 to 114 Kilobits (which are similar speeds to the highest speeds of the even older modems). While GPRS is by no means ideal for video data, it is still very usable for text-based communication such as email.

Key term

GPRS – stands for general packet radio service.

Give an example of when GPRS is particularly useful.

Activity: Communications principles

1 Explain these terms: DTE, DCE, modem.
2 Give five examples of DTEs.
3 Give five examples of DCEs.
4 What is bandwidth?

2.2 Signal theory

This section looks at how data is sent across a network from one computer system to another. All computers communicate using a variety of media (light, radio, electrical and microwave). The principles used are based on electronics and physics.

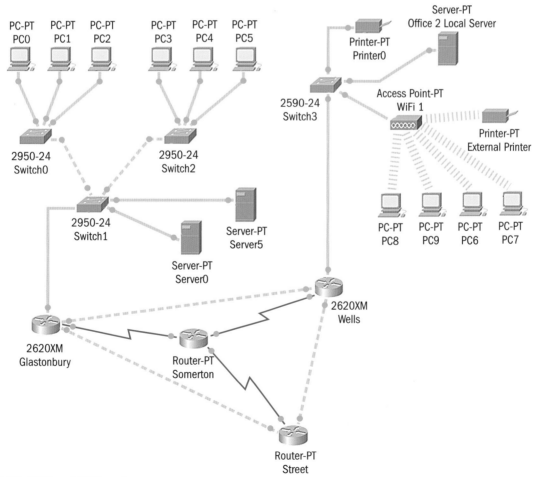

Figure 10.12: DCE and DTE equipment

Digital signalling methods

Figure 10.12 on page 321 shows the properties of a data transmission being sent from one computer system to another.

The sine wave has two properties of interest: amplitude and frequency.

A represents amplitude or strength of the signal, and can be explained simply as volume or loudness. The higher the amplitude of the signal, the louder and stronger it is – the lower the amplitude, the quieter and weaker it becomes. With any transmission, higher amplitude signals will travel greater distances.

For different systems, amplitude has different meanings, as follows.

- Radio and microwave both use the same method of transmission: radio waves. For all radio waves, the amplitude of the waveform is measured in metric terms (metres or millimetres).
- All cables rely on electrical current, the strength of which is measured in volts. The current in a normal data cable will be +/– 5V – any higher a voltage may damage the sensitive computer equipment. A telephone cable can carry up to +/– 50V. The range of the signal switches from positive voltage to negative voltage and is referred to as AC (alternating current).
- With light, the brighter the light source, the stronger the signal. Most fiber optic cables use infrared or laser-generated light; the difference between these two light sources affects the distance the signal can travel and the speed of the line.

F represents the frequency of the signal. The frequency is the rise and fall of the waveform from zero to bottom, then to the top and back to zero (shaped like a rollercoaster ride). This is called a cycle and is measured in hertz (Hz). A low frequency signal has a small number of cycles per second; a higher frequency signal can have billions of cycles per second (such as GHz or MHz).

How to... Create a sine wave

1. Creating a sine wave without a signal generator can be a challenge. Using Excel®, create a sine wave using the chart wizard.

2. In cell A1 enter [0.1]; in cell A2 enter [=A1+0.1] and drag the cell down to row 100.

3. In cell B2 enter [=SIN(A1)] and also drag down to row 100.

4. Select all of column B and start the chart wizard, using the line chart to create a sine wave.

5. What happens if you multiply the contents of the cells in column B?

Representing data electronically

Based on the technology used for a sine wave, data is transmitted as a square (or digital) wave. All computers use binary in which each bit of information is represented as 0 (zero) for the off state and 1 (one) for the on state. The binary is organised in chains of bits, called bytes or words according to the system that is going to use it. For example, 01001100 is a single byte that represents the decimal value of 76 or the **ASCII** value of 'v'.

Key term

ASCII – stands for American standard code for information interchange. It is the format for storing letters, numbers and symbols in documents.

Sending data from one computer to another is called encoding and various formats exist according to the system used (wireless, fibre or electrical cable). Common formats are Manchester encoding or Huffman coding.

Encoding is not a new concept – it is more than 160 years since Samuel Morse developed Morse code to be used on the new electric telegraph (see Table 10.8).

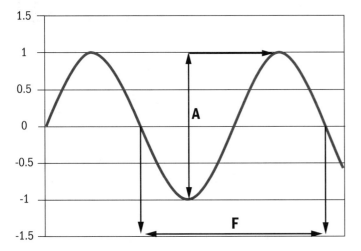

Figure 10.13: The sinusoidal waveform of a sine wave

He created a system of combinations of two signals (a short pulse called a dot and a long pulse called a dash), similar to the binary zero and one. This system was invented so that a telegraph operator could key messages in any language at a relatively fast speed.

Table 10.8: Morse code, which is still used by enthusiasts

Letter	Morse	Letter	Morse	Digit	Morse
A	.-	N	-.	0	-----
B	-...	O	---	1	.----
C	-.-.	P	.--.	2	..---
D	-..	Q	--.-	3	...--
E	.	R	.-.	4	....-
F	..-.	S	...	5	.....
G	--.	T	-	6	-....
H	....	U	..-	7	--...
I	..	V	...-	8	---..
J	.---	W	.--	9	----.
K	-.-	X	-..-		
L	.-..	Y	-.--		
M	--	Z	--..		

Encoding that is used to send data across a computer network is based on a digital 'square' wave, which is an adaptation of the sine wave shown in Figure 10.13.

In order to avoid data being lost or the computer system being confused (which would cause an error), there are two simple rules when sending data:

1 All binary zeros (off) are sent at high amplitude so that there is no confusion with the 'power off' of no signal being sent. This is like the Morse code dash.

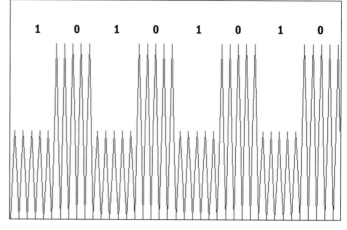

Figure 10.14: A square wave

2 All binary ones (on) are sent at a mid-range amplitude to contrast with the rule for the binary zero. This is like the Morse code dot.

Figure 10.14 shows that the frequency of the signal is fixed (although this value will vary according to the speed of the transmission medium), but the amplitude is varied and based on a zero or a one coming through the line.

To ensure data is successfully transmitted, an agreed common method is used for sending the data, one that can be managed by all computer systems. Representing data electronically, computers use bits, bytes and data packet structures.

A byte is the unit of storage made from 8 bits. A bit has 2^8 (i.e. 256) possible combinations. Units of storage in computer systems operate in powers of 2 because binary has two states (0 and 1).

Did you know?

A bit is the smallest unit of information and is represented as a binary digit (1 or 0).

Table 10.9: Relative sizes of bytes, kilobytes, megabytes, gigabytes and terabytes

kilobyte	megabyte	gigabyte	terabyte
2^{10} bytes	2^{10} kilobytes	2^{10} megabytes	2^{10} gigabytes
1024 bytes	1024 kilobytes	1,048,576 megabytes	1,048,576 gigabytes
	1,048,576 bytes	1,073,741,824 kilobytes	1,073,741,824 megabytes
		1,099,511,627,776 bytes	1,099,511,627,776 kilobytes
			1,125,899,906,842,624 bytes

Activity: Lots of little bits

1 Define bit and byte.

2 What does the acronym ASCII stand for and what is it used for?

3 What are the relative sizes of a kilobyte, a megabyte, a gigabyte and a terabyte?

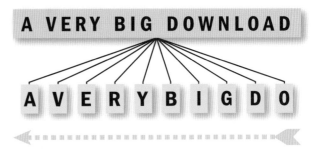

Figure 10.16: Packets

Because transmission media can be unreliable, transmitting or downloading a file which is over 5 or 6 kilobytes in size is also unreliable. To make data transmission more reliable, a large quantity of data is divided into smaller packets. These can easily be re-sent if the data is found to be damaged.

Different methods are used for structuring packets. Each packet normally has information to identify it and its content, for example:

* the number of the packet in a sequence of packets
* the address of the computer or network to which it is being sent
* the address of the computer or network it has come from.

As well as whatever data the packet contains, there are also start and stop bits to indicate the start and end of the packet.

Synchronous and asynchronous transmission

On a network, synchronous transmission and asynchronous transmission are the methods used to regulate the sending of data. For two devices to communicate there needs to be a signal which synchronises the transmission on receipt of data; this is called the clocking signal. When both devices send and receive the same clocking signal, they are able to communicate in tandem and successfully transfer data.

The DCE in a networked system normally sends the clocking (or synchronising) signal. This may be a router, WAP or switch. The clock rate is a bit rate set by the network administrator on some systems but may be automatic on others.

Asynchronous means 'without clocking' and is used to refer to systems which will communicate one way on demand. Examples include computer to printer communication, and computer to keyboard and mouse. While this type of transmission may be local to a computer, the technology used is the same for a network connection.

```
SanFrancisco(config-if)#
SanFrancisco(config-if)#int s0/0
SanFrancisco(config-if)#clock rate 56000
SanFrancisco(config-if)#
```

Figure 10.17 Setting a clock rate

Error correction and detection

Error correction and detection are managed by techniques such as **parity** checking and the cyclic redundancy check.

In the transmission of data across networks, it is important to check the integrity (quality) of data, as error, failure and interference are always likely. To do this, the data is sent with a small **checksum**.

Figure 10.15: A download

Key terms

Parity – equality, for example equal amounts, equal status or equal value.

Checksum – a unique mathematical value obtained from a simple calculation taken on the data.

Figure 10.18 shows how interference can corrupt data. If no parity checking takes place, the computer receiving the data is unaware that the data received is now erroneous, so it will still process the data, possibly causing a serious error (Figure 10.18a).

To prevent this type of problem, parity checking is applied: all the binary 1s are counted. If there is an even number of bits set as on, then a binary 1 is used as the checksum. If there are an odd number of bits set as on, then a binary 0 is used as the checksum (Figure 10.18b).

Parity checking is very simple and involves the counting of odd or even numbers of binary digits (called odd and even parity). However, it is also susceptible to error (Figure 10.18c).

Parity checking is normally applied to small groups of data, or to every byte, where the system can afford the memory overhead of checking every byte. However, most systems are 'best effort' systems and economics dictate that it is ideal to apply one check to a packet of data up to 1514 bytes in size – Ethernet frames (see page 328) provide a good example of this.

The solution used in LANs is called the cyclic redundancy check (CRC). This is a formula that is applied by using a **polynomial**.

The computer that receives the data looks at the **co-efficient** and completes the same calculation. If the receiving computer calculates the same result of 18108, then the data packet is accepted; otherwise, it is rejected.

The probability of a different set of data giving the same polynomial with the same co-efficient is incredibly low, so this error checking mechanism is extremely reliable.

Key terms

Polynomial – the result of a series of smaller formulae all with the same co-efficient.

Co-efficient – a co-related value, which is any number.

Activity: Having a degree of parity

1 Define parity checking and the cyclic redundancy check.

2 What is a checksum?

3 Define polynomial and co-efficient.

0	1	1	0	0	1	1	0	The signal being sent has suffered from interference caused by a nearby power source.

was sent down the line but when it reached the other end it became

0	1	1	0	1	1	1	0	

Figure 10.18a: Data corruption

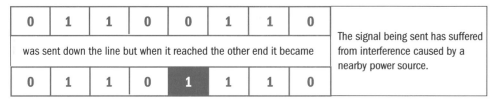

0	1	1	0	0	1	1	0	1	You can see that an extra binary digit is now applied to the transmission.

Data is sent (remember we still have the same problem where interference caused by a nearby power source).

0	1	1	0	1	1	1	0	1	As the check sum is different from what was expected then ERROR RESEND!!!!!!!
Total number of binary 1s = 5. Assuming even parity, with an odd number the check sum should ba a 0.								0	

Figure 10.18b: Checksum applied

0	1	1	0	0	1	1	0	1	The data is still suffering from interference but this time two bits of data are corrupted.

Data is sent (there is still the same problem of interference caused by a nearby power source).

1	1	1	0	1	1	1	0	1	The data has passed the parity check, yet is corrupt!!!!
Total number of binary 1s = 6. Assuming even parity, with an even number, a 1 is expected as the check sum.								1	

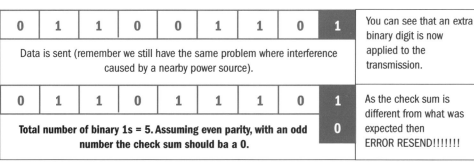

Figure 10.18c: Issues with parity checking

Table 10.10: A simplified example of a CRC

A data packet being sent from one computer to another									
Data	Byte 1	Byte 2	Byte 3	Byte 4	Byte 5	Byte 6	Byte 7	Byte 8	The co-efficient is **2**, which is the first half of the CRC.
	21	34	56	34	34	43	12	4	
Formulae with same co-efficient	$2*21^2$	$2*34^2$	$2*56^2$	$2*34^2$	$2*34^2$	$2*43^2$	$2*12^2$	$2*4^2$	
Result	882	2312	6272	2312	2312	3698	288	32	The polynomial (**18108**) is the second half of the CRC.

The polynomial is the addition of all the above results which equals **18108**.
Therefore **2:18108** is sent with the packet of data.

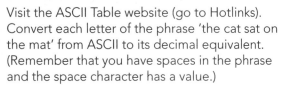

Activity: Cyclic redundancy check

Visit the ASCII Table website (go to Hotlinks). Convert each letter of the phrase 'the cat sat on the mat' from ASCII to its decimal equivalent. (Remember that you have spaces in the phrase and the space character has a value.)

Take the result and then create a CRC where each value can be computed with the formula 4*ASCII where 4 is the co-efficient used to create the polynomial.

Bandwidth limitation and noise

Bandwidth limitation and noise have a considerable impact on the quality of the data being transmitted. In many cases, the quality requirement and volume of the data being downloaded is now greater than some systems can handle. With lower bandwidth systems like wireless networks, there are limits on how much data can be successfully sent at any given moment.

For bandwidth sensitive services such as VoIP and Video on Demand, the central network technology has to be configured to ensure that these services have priority over any email or chat traffic.

This means that sensitive traffic will always be sent, ensuring no delays or loss in transmission. Less sensitive traffic may be stored (queued) until there is an ideal opportunity to send this data. This happens in terms of microseconds on a network device, so the user will notice this happening when chatting using Facebook® or watching a video across a network.

Noise is any external or internal interference that has an effect on the quality of the data being sent. External noise may be caused by electrical equipment or local physical features. Internal noise is often caused by poor-quality cabling or connections.

- Wireless networks rely on high-frequency radio transmissions, which are normally limited to a range of no more than 100 metres. Noise can be caused by metal-framed buildings (causing reflection and acting like a Faraday cage), as well as any powerful unshielded electrical equipment. Wireless networks tend to suffer from external interference.

- Copper cabling, as used for most data networks, is limited to a range of 100 metres for data networks. This is very susceptible to noise from external power sources, even something as simple as a power cable run. Also, with the electro-magnetic nature of the cables and the fact that many cables are run together, the cables have to be twisted to reduce internal noise (called crosstalk) and the connectors have to be 'terminated' professionally to improve the quality of the communication. Otherwise, internal reflection and crosstalk can occur, which add to the noise. In practice, both unshielded and shielded twisted pair cable are used.

- Fiber optic networks are a self-contained method of transmitting data using light. Except on low-quality connections, there is only a small chance of internal interference and no risk of external interference.

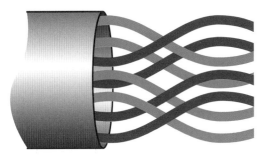

Figure 10.19: Copper cable (unshielded twisted pair)

Activity: A little noisy

1   What is VoIP?

2   What is noise in the context of data transmission? What effect does it have on the data?

Channel types

The transmission of data is also reliant on the channel type, that is the medium used to transmit the data across considerable distances. Wireless, fiber and copper have distance limitations. The following common communications channels are in frequent use.

- **Telephone links:** Often referred to as POTS (pretty old telephone system), these are still used in developing nations and remote parts of the UK, as well as a backup method for accessing core networking equipment in case of a primary communications failure.

- **Microwave:** Transmissions sent by Bluetooth and wireless networks are defined as microwave as they operate on the 2.4 GHz band of the electro-magnetic spectrum. High-powered microwave transmission is still used in line of sight communications for high-speed network communications in large cities.

- **Radio transmission:** At higher frequencies, radio transmission is used by a wide range of services to exchange data. Services such as the police, ambulance and fire use radio transmission to communicate critical information.

- **Satellite:** Satellites have been used as a method for high-speed data transmission between countries for some considerable time. This facility is becoming more accessible to the individual user and small business as costs drop. Satellite transmission is reliant on atmospheric conditions as well as line of sight communication with the satellite. However, communication with a satellite in a geo-stationary orbit can increase the distance around the globe that a network can reach.

- **ADSL (asymmetric digital subscriber service)** and **broadband:** These services are an extension of the type of technology used in a network at work or college. ADSL and broadband use an unbalanced bandwidth to improve performance. You may be able to download at a rate of 2 Mbps, but your upload speed is likely to be one-tenth of this. ADSL accesses unused bandwidth on telecommunications systems and is limited to a two-kilometre reach from the telephone company relay. Newer ADSL technologies are extending this range.

Data compression

Data compression is required on low bandwidth services to improve the rate of data transmission. Compression of applications, games, images, videos and audio also still takes place, for example the JPEG image is a compression format.

There are many formats used on different systems. A common format used in data transmission and compression of files is Huffman coding.

Huffman coding applies a binary sequence to characters (letters of the alphabet, digits and symbols) according to how often they are used. Therefore, if a letter is used more than others, it is given a small sequence. If a letter is uncommon, it is given a longer sequence (see Table 10.11). Huffman coding thus allows data compression in the transmission of information from one system to another.

Huffman coding requires a small overhead in the use of processor resources for the sending and receiving devices.

Table 10.11 Huffman coding, based on the English language

E	0
A	1
I	10
O	11
U	100
S	101
T	110
D	111
....	....
X	11010

And so on, with character such as 1234567890, !"£$%^&*()\{\}[]@~'#,.<>?/

2.3 Data elements

To transmit a packet of data from one network device to another requires that the data is constructed into a set of data elements; the principle is based on the theoretical OSI model, which was explored earlier (see page 314).

Checksums

CRC (cyclic redundancy check)

As described on page 325, the cyclic redundancy check is a method used for error correction and detection in the transmission of data across any network system. The check bits are appended to the packet when it is sent by the computer.

Encapsulation

Frames

Independent of the communication method, a frame is the data sent from one device to another. A large download will not be transferred as one item, but will be divided into smaller units, and the frame is based on the WAN or LAN technology used. A common type of frame is the Ethernet frame, which is used on all LANs, and comprises seven elements (see Figure 10.20).

- In the preamble, the start bits are used to identify an oncoming valid frame of data from any background noise on the cable.

- The SFD (start frame delimiter) is the 8-bit value marking the end of the preamble. The SFD is always 101010112.

- The destination MAC address is a unique 48-bit physical identifier hardcoded into a computer's network card; most network devices also have one. It identifies the device to which the data is being sent.

- The source MAC address, similar to the destination MAC address, identifies the device from which the data is being transmitted (see Figure 10.21).

- The EtherType declares what higher-level packet is being transported in the Ethernet frame. Each type has an identifier in hexadecimal which is recognised by the receiving system. Common identifiers include: 0x0800 Internet Protocol version 4 (IPv4); 0x0806 Address Resolution Protocol (ARP); 0x86DD Internet Protocol version 6 (IPv6).

- Payload is the term used to describe the data that is being sent.

- The FCS (frame check sequence) contains space for the CRC.

Table 10.12: Data elements and their relationship to each other

OSI layer	Data element	Data being transmitted			
4	Data gram using the UDP or TCP protocols	Sequence number			
3	Packet of data being sent	Sequence number	IP (or logical) addresses		
2	Frame, transmitted across a WAN or LAN	Sequence number	IP (or logical) addresses	MAC address for an Ethernet LAN, interface identifier for a WAN connection	
1	Start and stop bits as well as a check sum	Sequence number	IP (or logical) addresses	MAC address for an Ethernet LAN, interface identifier for a WAN connection	Polynomial from cyclic redundancy check

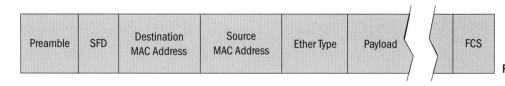

Figure 10.20: The Ethernet frame

Packets

A packet of data can be a collection of frames and it is normally sent by protocols such as IP. Unlike an Ethernet frame, which is limited to 1518 bytes, a packet can be up to 65536 bytes in size (64 kilobytes).

When sent across an Ethernet LAN, the packet will be broken down into smaller frames. A frame may contain the payload from multiple packets. Each packet has a header, payload and trailer (see Figure 10.22).

IP is now offered in two versions: versions 4 and 6. Version 4 systems can handle up to 4,294,967,296 devices, whereas version 6 systems can manage over 340,282,366,920,938,463,463,374,607,431,770,000,000 devices.

An IP packet will contain the following bits of information:

- 4 bits indicate whether it is an IP version 4 or an IP version 6 packet
- 4 bits describe the header size (as this can vary)
- 8 bits are used for quality of service – this is used to prioritise traffic such as voice or video over email
- 16 bits describe the size of the entire packet

- 16 bits have identification numbers if the packet has been divided across many Ethernet frames
- 3 bits contain an identifier to indicate whether this packet is part of a divided packet
- 13 bits contain the order of packets to which this one belongs
- 8 bits are used to record the time to live; in networking, packets are sent through many devices and each one will increase the time to live – then, if the number is too high, the packet is lost and is therefore discarded
- 8 bits contain the protocol being sent such as: TCP, UDP, ICMP, etc.
- 16 bits contain a checksum
- 32 bits contain the source IP address
- 32 bits contain the destination IP address.

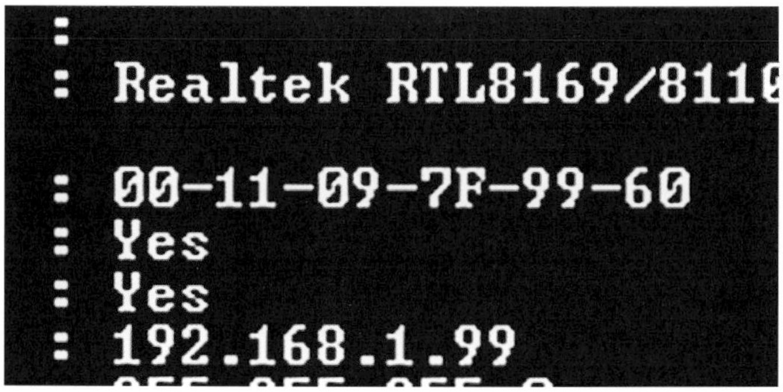

Datagrams

A datagram is the less reliable counterpart of the packet. Packets are sent via **TCP** and IP, which is designed to ensure the data reaches its destination. A datagram, however, is sent via **UDP** and IP, and this is designed to be 'best effort' – it does not matter whether the packet successfully reaches its destination (see Figure 10.23).

Figure 10.21: The computer's MAC address

Key terms

TCP – stands for transmission control protocol. It is used for the transfer of data which is connection-oriented and must be sent via a reliable system.

UDP – stands for user datagram protocol. It is used on connectionless systems; this means that the data may travel different routes and reliability is not a primary concern.

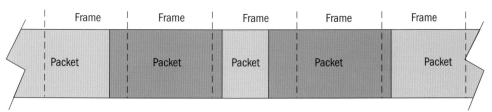

Figure 10.22: Packets and frames

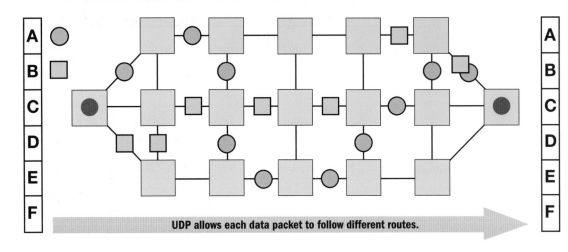

UDP allows each data packet to follow different routes.

Figure 10.23: UDP

Addresses

All networking systems use addresses. Like the postal system, it is an essential mechanism used in ensuring the data is sent to the correct destination. Table 10.13 shows the two principal types of addresses already mentioned in this unit.

Sequence numbers

When packets and datagrams are sent, they form part of a larger set of data. To ensure the data is 'reassembled' in the correct order, each packet or datagram requires an identifier, known as a sequence number.

Consider an image being downloaded from a website. If the packets arrive in the wrong order, because some are re-sent while others travel down a faster route, the result may be a very confusing image. The sequence number ensures that the data will be reassembled exactly as it was sent.

Table 10.13: Types of addresses

Type	Description	Example
Physical address	Can be hard-coded into a device like a network card or configured on WAN connection	MAC address
Logical address	Is configured by the network administrator or issued by a server and may follow a scheme	IP address

Table 10.14: Sequence number and offset

Sequence number	Packet size
0	1340
1341	1290
2632	999
3631	etc.

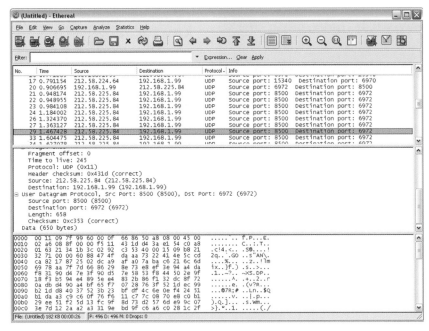

Figure 10.24: UDP data stream

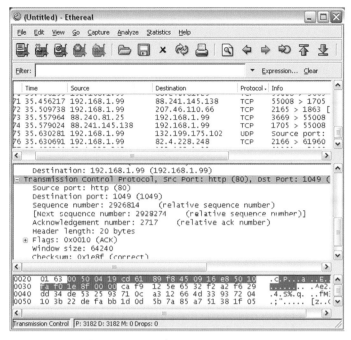

Figure 10.25: Sequence numbers

The sequence number is an 'offset in bytes' based on the size of the packet or datagram being sent. Figure 10.25 shows a download from a website. As each packet is added, the offset moves by 1 and the sequence number increases.

Activity: In sequence

1   Define frame, packet and datagram.

2   What are the seven elements of the Ethernet frame?

3   Define TCP and UDP.

4   What is a sequence number used for?

2.4 Electronic communication

Methods of electronic communication

When network devices communicate with each other, they use a variety of communications techniques.

Simplex, duplex and half-duplex transmission

In many systems, there are three common methods of electronic communication used: simplex, half-duplex and duplex.

- **Simplex:** One-way communication, with no response allowed. FM radio and keyboards are prime examples of simplex communication.

- **Half duplex**: Two-way communication, but only one device can transmit at a time. Most Ethernet and wireless systems use half-duplex to maximise the bandwidth. They use synchronisation and signaling to control whose turn it is to transmit.

- **Full duplex:** Also two-way communication, but both devices can communicate simultaneously. More advanced Ethernet systems use full duplex and will only work on compatible devices. This is accomplished by the fact that most network cables are groups of eight cables and some are unused by most systems.

Parallel transmission

Parallel transmission is a rapidly diminishing technology. While it was designed to transfer data in tandem (each bit on a separate line), it was limited by distance and speed – 3 to 4.5 metres was the maximum reach.

Parallel has been superseded by **USB** (universal serial bus) among other systems. USB operates at 4 megabits per second (and higher). Each USB port on your PC can be cabled to manage up to 128 devices and so some users choose to install a USB hub.

Key term

USB – stands for universal serial bus.

USB offers power to some devices as well as the ability to connect a wide range of devices. Typically you can expect to connect storage devices, cameras, printers, scanners, keyboards, mice, joysticks and external network devices. In fact, the range of devices that can be connected is almost endless.

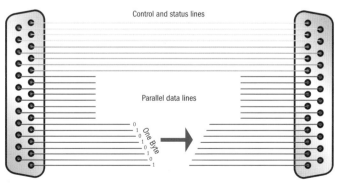

Figure 10.26: Parallel communication

331

Universal serial transmission

While USB has superseded parallel communications, this is not necessarily the case with the **serial RS-232** (or EIA/TIA-232) standard. Some manufacturers have started removing serial interfaces from their PC motherboards, but since all network devices require a serial connection to configure them at an advanced level, this is of some concern to their customers.

Key term

Serial RS-232 – an older standard used to connect mice, modems and external devices.

The RS-232 standard uses synchronous as well as asynchronous communication and it is used on DCE as well as DTE devices. 25-pin, 9-pin and 8-pin connectors can be used for RS-232, each pin having a specific purpose. These are commonly identified as shown in Table 10.15.

Infrared, Bluetooth® and WiFi

Infrared interfaces and communication are used by mobile phones, PDAs, printers and laptops as a method of local peer communication. Bluetooth® has, for many systems, superseded infrared, due to its improved speed and lack of line of sight limitations.

Figure 10.27: USB

A serial connection

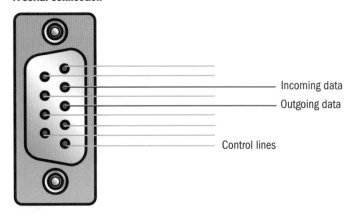

— Incoming data
— Outgoing data

— Control lines

Figure 10.28: A serial connector

Table 10.15: RS-232 standard

Transmitted Data (TxD)	Data sent from DTE to DCE
Received Data (RxD)	Data sent from DCE to DTE.
Request To Send (RTS)	Is it ok to transmit?
Clear To Send (CTS)	It is ok to send.
Data Terminal Ready (DTR)	I am online and ready.
Data Set Ready (DSR)	This connection is active.
Carrier Detect (CD)	Is there a signal?
Ring Indicator (RI	Used on older telephone systems (a modem would need this)

Activity: Serial episode

1 What are simplex, duplex and half-duplex transmission?
2 What is a USB?
3 What is the serial RS-232 standard?

Infrared is on the electromagnetic spectrum, slightly below visible light. For two devices to communicate with each other, they needed to have direct line of sight of each communication port (which was often on the side of the device).

Bluetooth® is available in many systems. It uses an ultra high-frequency spread spectrum signal (this means that the wavelength is over 2.4 GHz). Bluetooth® uses a range of frequencies and techniques to send the data. The purpose of Bluetooth® is to create mobile short-range networking for all small devices. So far, several benefits of Bluetooth® have been identified.

- The inclusion of Bluetooth® in mobile phones allows pictures and files to be sent from one individual to another on a one-to-one basis.

- Laptop computers can be connected to a small personal area network.

- It is possible to connect a PDA to a computer or a mobile phone without any cables or installation of additional software.

- Most Bluetooth® systems operate at a range of 10 metres; a Bluetooth® **transceiver** can be used to increase the range to 100 metres.

WiFi comprises wireless network cards and access points. These devices operate by radio transmission and use the IEEE (Institute of Electrical and Electronics Engineers) 802.11 standard (as listed on page 320), which is closely associated with Ethernet LAN technology. IEEE 802.11 has a set of four specifications in the family: 802.11, 802.11a, 802.11b and 802.11g. Each operates at a different frequency and speed:

- 802.11 and 802.11a operate at speeds up to 6 megabits per second

- 802.11b is the version commonly used for wireless networking at home, school, college or in small enterprises – it can operate at up to 11 megabits per second.

- 802.11g operates in the 2.4 GHz range like Bluetooth but, with greater power, can offer up to 54 megabits per second.

- 802.11n operates in the 2.4 GHz range like Bluetooth but, with greater power, can offer up to from 54 to 600 (theoretical) megabits per second.

Wireless adapters use spread spectrum and narrowband transmission techniques.

- Spread spectrum uses a range of frequencies and techniques.

- Narrowband sends a signal over a limited frequency range.

Common practice is for an organisation that is managing a LAN to offer a wireless network infrastructure, which:

- serves to increase the range of the network into unreachable areas where it may be too costly or impractical to run a cable

- allows users to connect to the system with a laptop or PDA without being tied to a wall socket

- creates portable network centres that can be taken anywhere, hence the popularity of public wireless hotspots.

The implementation of a wireless network is based on geographic coverage. So, the area covered by the radio signal generated by the devices on the system has to be considered. Figure 10.29 gives an example of wireless coverage.

Wireless networking requires two pieces of networking equipment:

- A wireless adapter is a network card that, instead of connecting to a copper cable, will send a radio transmission. Computers with wireless adapters can communicate directly with each other on a **peer** basis.

- The wireless access point (WAP), also called a wireless bridge, is essentially a network hub. This is connected by a copper or fibre cable to the main network. The purpose of a WAP is to share and distribute network communications.

3G enables someone who is stationary in an area of good reception to enjoy a data rate of 2 **Mbps**. Mobile (sitting in a car), the data rate drops to 300 **Kbps** in a good reception area. Whilst reception dependent, the rates can be higher, with some providers offering 4 Mbps and even 7.2 Mbps. This data rate allows graphical browsing and video exchange from the lowest rate onwards.

Key terms

Transceiver – both a transmitter and a receiver, a device which may therefore act as a communications relay.

Peer – someone (or something) which is an equal to yourself or others (e.g. your friend is a peer). Peer devices are devices which have equal 'rights' on a networked system.

Mbps – mega (million) bits per second.

Kbps – kilo (thousand) bits per second.

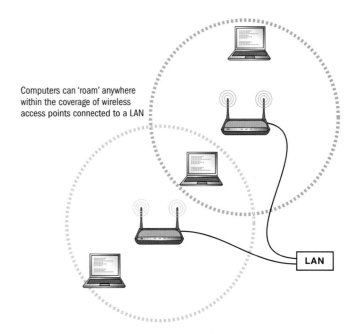

Computers can 'roam' anywhere within the coverage of wireless access points connected to a LAN

LAN

Figure 10.29: Wireless coverage

Wireless network technology uses spread spectrum radio transmission to gain the maximum bandwidth from the radio frequencies available. A spread spectrum signal is automatically varied, which gives the transmission four advantages.

1 If there is interference on one frequency, the data can be successfully sent on another frequency.

2 The data can be shared across many frequencies.

3 The system can adapt if there is more than one communication taking place.

4 There is scope for multiple stations to operate in the same location.

Activity: Mobile networking

1 Describe the properties of infrared interfaces, Bluetooth and WiFi.

2 Define the following terms: transceiver, wireless adapter, WAP.

2.5 Transmission

A transmission medium is the technology used to carry the signal from one device to another across the network. The choice of media depends on cost, quality, speed and the range of data travel.

Methods

Coaxial cabling

Coaxial is an older method of cabling networks. Although it was the networking medium of choice during the late 1980s and early 1990s, it was rapidly replaced by **UTP** (unshielded twisted pair). However, it has always had a place with terrestrial TV (in rooftop aerials) and, more recently, coaxial cabling has made a comeback with home broadband services.

Key term

UTP – stands for unshielded twisted pair.

Coaxial is so named because it has a copper core surrounded by a plastic sheath and then another copper braid (see Figure 10.30). The inner cable is used to transmit the data and the outer cable (usually an interlaced braid of copper wires) is used as a ground (connects to earth).

The advantages of coaxial cable are:

- it can run up to 185 metres before the signal becomes weak and unreliable
- it can handle high bandwidth signals, such as multiple video channels (i.e. television)
- it is flexible and reliable.

The disadvantages are:

- it is susceptible to external interference and noise
- it is costly to install, as the higher-quality cable costs more to produce
- it is less adaptable than its UTP counterpart.

UTP and STP

UTP is the most popular cable type in use on academic and commercial networks throughout the world. UTP and STP originated during a change in phone technology in the 1980s and have endured many revisions. UTP and STP are still in use for several reasons: they are low cost in comparison to fiber optic

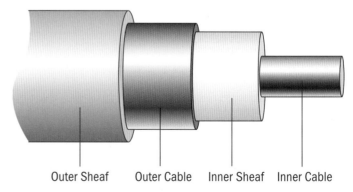

Outer Sheaf   Outer Cable   Inner Sheaf   Inner Cable

Figure 10.30: A coaxial cable

and coaxial cabling; they are versatile and can be adapted to many uses; they can adapt to changing speeds and standards.

UTP comes in a long roll that contains eight cables inside one jacket; these cables come as coloured pairs (see Figure 10.31).

- Orange
- Orange with a white stripe
- Green
- Green with a white stripe
- Blue
- Blue with a white stripe
- Brown
- Brown with a white stripe

Each cable generates a small magnetic field which will create interference for the neighbouring cables. Each pair is twisted around each other to reduce an effect called cancellation, which occurs because of the close proximity of the cables – hence the term twisted pair. Four pairs are used.

UTP is susceptible to external interference and noise. With no protection, external sources such as power supplies or cables can also corrupt the data sent along the media. To overcome this, the more expensive STP cable can be used. It operates on the same principles as UTP, but has an extra foil wrapping around the cables for protection.

UTP is rated in categories – current LAN standards include categories 5, 5e, 6 and 7. Categories 1, 2, 3 and 4 (these included coaxial) are no longer used for LANs and are found solely in the domain of WAN technology (as WANs often use slower connections between buildings). Each category (see Table 10.16) is related to the quality of the cable, its connectors and the speed at which data can be sent reliably.

Table 10.16: Categories of UTP

Category	Maximum data rate	Usual application
1	Less than 1 Mbps	Voice cabling ISDN (integrated services digital network)
2	4 Mbps	IBM token ring networks
3	16 Mbps	The original category for coaxial cable on Ethernet systems
4	20 Mbps	Short-lived
5	10 Mbps	Still in use on small office, home office networks as well as older legacy networks
5e	100 Mbps 1000 Mbps	Ideal LAN cabling standard – will handle a guaranteed 1000 Mbps in ideal cabling circumstances
6	1000 Mbps	Higher-quality termination (wiring) allows this cable to manage continuous higher data rates
7	1000 Mbps and above	

With category 6 and 7 cables, all the termination (wiring) is done within the factory or with specialist equipment. Category 5e cabling is normally terminated with an RJ45 plug (see Figure 10.32) or socket and can easily be done in class with low-cost equipment.

Fiber optic cabling

Both coaxial and UTP reply on the transmission of data using electrical pulses down a copper cable. Fiber optic cables use light to transmit the data so can achieve greater speeds and distances than their copper counterparts.

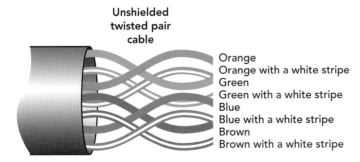

Unshielded twisted pair cable

Orange
Orange with a white stripe
Green
Green with a white stripe
Blue
Blue with a white stripe
Brown
Brown with a white stripe

Figure 10.31: Unshielded twisted pair cable

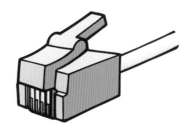

Figure 10.32: An RJ45 connector

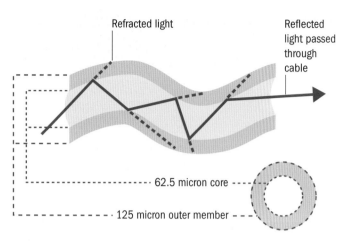

Figure 10.33: Reflection inside a fiber optic cable

There are two types of cable in common use: **single-mode**, which is 8 **microns** in diameter, and **multi-mode**, which is 125 microns in diameter (with an inner core of 62.5 microns).

Key term

Micron – a thousandth of a millimetre.

Figure 10.34 shows an example of a multi-mode fiber optic cable. The light source is a light emitting diode (LED), which sends frequent pulses of light down the cable (no pulse equals a digital 0, a pulse equals a digital 1). The light will travel around the cable based on the different densities of the medium it is travelling through. As it reaches the denser material, most of the light will be reflected and will continue its path down the cable. Some of the light will be refracted (absorbed) into the denser outer coating.

Overall this allows the light to travel up to three kilometres before it becomes too weak. On a LAN, normally the cable is run less than 285 metres, guaranteeing a signal that can carry data of one gigabit per second.

Single-mode fiber optic cable (see Figure 10.34) is thinner (8 microns) and uses a Class 3 laser to send the data. The smaller diameter reduces the angle of reflection and therefore minimises refraction and

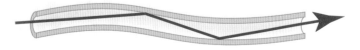

Single-mode fiber offers less refraction

Figure 10.34: Single-mode fiber optic cable

Activity: Bits and pieces

1 List the types of cabling available. Give the advantages and disadvantages of each.
2 Define these terms: Mbps, RJ, micron.

loss. A Class 3 laser is dangerous and is outside of the visible light spectrum. If you accidentally look into a Class 3 enabled fiber optic cable, you will not see any light but will burn the cells at the back of your eye. This will cause a permanent blind spot in your vision.

The fiber optic cable is surrounded by Kevlar® fiber, an ultra strong resin that is used in the manufacture of bullet-proof clothing. This gives the cable strength – important when bending to fit into cable ducts.

Fiber optic cable is more costly than its copper counterparts; the termination of the cable has to be done under exacting and clean conditions.

Infrared, radio, microwave and satellite communications

Infrared, as mentioned on page 332, is a technology which uses line of sight communication between PDAs, mobile phones and laptops. The limitation of this technology is proximity and speed, with an accepted maximum of 4 Mbps.

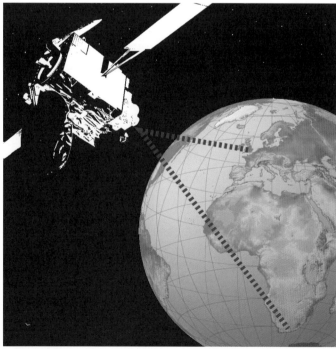

Figure 10.35: Satellite communication between the UK and South Africa

Radio and microwave operate in similar bands on the electro-magnetic spectrum, with microwave being at the upper end of the radio wave frequencies. These communication systems are used in Bluetooth® and WiFi (see page 332).

Satellite communications rely on the satellite being in a geosynchronous orbit, with receiving stations being positioned to communicate with these satellites. In the UK, due to our latitude (position in relation to the equator), dishes used for satellite communication have to point to a position low on the horizon towards the south. Major international satellite communications follow this rule, with the Goonhilly Satellite Earth Station being located in Cornwall, the most southerly county (which was positioned for communication with Japan).

Activity: Communication for mobile workers

1   Identify what key communication technologies exist to enable a worker with a laptop to move from office to office and communicate with others.

2   If a worker wants to work from home, what technologies are available and how do they operate?

3   The worker is dropped in the middle of an uninhabited region and has suitable power from the 4 x 4 they are driving to power communication devices. What technologies exist to enable communication with others via the worker's laptop?

4   Can you answer the following?
   a)   Why are data checking systems such as parity and CRC used?
   b)   Which is the best communication medium for a LAN?
   c)   What communication media are used for long distance communication?

Assessment activity 10.2

 (P3) (P4) (P5) (P6) (M2) (D2)   **BTEC**

This Assessment activity has a direct link with assessment from Unit 9. Your centre may offer you an activity which connects the two units.

1   Create a poster on data transmission, taking the concept from the Assessment activity 10.1, looking at how a 3G mobile would communicate with a desktop computer on a corporate network.

In the flow of data included in the poster:

- show three different network devices **P3**

- describe what data elements are (checksum, encapsulation, addresses, sequence numbers) and emphasise their importance (again use callouts or arrows) **P4**

- show, in the end-to-end communication, a signal (sinewave) and describe each of the principles **P5**

- show and describe the different transmission methods and briefly explain why they are being used in this end-to-end communication. **P6 M2**

2   Add a chart (a table) giving a comparison of the effectiveness (speed, reliability) of each transmission method). **D2**

Grading tips

- This poster may be produced as an image or a PDF document. **P3 P4 P5 P6**

- Think carefully about how you frame the explanation for M2, it needs to be brief but accurate and technically correct. **M2**

- Think carefully about the table, what columns are necessary and what information you need to include in order to make a reasoned comparison. **D2**

PLTS

You can demonstrate your skills as an **independent enquirer** by researching the knowledge needed to create your poster on communication technologies.

Functional skills

You can demonstrate your Functional **English** skills through writing the information for your poster.

3. Be able to implement different forms of network communications

3.1 Internet communication

With the scale of the Internet constantly expanding, different technologies and protocols have to be employed to enable access across our planet and potentially beyond.

Internet communications rely on TCP/IP to operate (see page 315). The Internet is a massive network of interconnected networks and can continuously grow because of its ability to allow new systems to connect to the edge of the existing Internet.

The Internet is not one single technology, but a heterogeneous (all mixed together) combination of technologies. During daily use of the Internet, a user probably only experiences around one-tenth of the technology in use.

Internet terminology

The term worldwide web (www) describes the interconnection of web servers and search engines via HTML (hypertext mark-up language). The single anchor tag creates a hyperlink from one page to another on a website. It can also create a link from one website to another. For example:

```
<a href='http://www.teraknor.co.uk'>Please Visit Me</a>
```

To transfer a web page, a web server uses HTTP and HTTPS. These protocols deal with the delivery of a web page (called a 'get') and the submission of data from web page forms (called a 'put').

FTP (file transfer protocol) does very much as its name suggests. Basic file and data transfer can be accomplished using HTTP, but for large collections of files, uploading websites and common information exchange FTP is still the preferred technology.

Internet Explorer can be used as an FTP client. There are many applications such as CuteFTP which offer more complex services.

SMTP (simple mail transfer protocol) is a language used to transfer email from a client to a mail server; this is often the protocol exploited by Internet worms and junk email scams.

SMTP is a 'command language' which can be used within other programming languages such as Java. The code shown in Figure 10.36 could be used to send an email if the name of the mail server is correct.

URL

The **URL** (uniform resource locator) is a popular synonym (similar term or word) for the **URI** (uniform resource identifier). The URI can be dissected into six sections as shown in Figure 10.37.

Internet technologies and services

The Internet and worldwide web are used for an immense range of technologies and services including wikis, which are online encyclopedias, guides and information services (for example Wikipedia), blogs (short for web logs) and the video equivalent vlogs (see the VlogMap Community website).

Video conferencing can be easily accomplished with a low cost webcam. Software providing this service is

Key terms

URL – stands for uniform resource locator, popular synonym for URI.

URI – stands for uniform resource identifier.

```java
import java.io.*;
import java.net.*;
public class SMTP
{
public static void main(String[] args) throws IOException
{
Socket echoSocket = null;
PrintWriter out = null;
        String host = "mail.mycollege.ac.uk";
try
{
echoSocket = new Socket(host, 25);
out = new PrintWriter(echoSocket.getOutputStream(), true);
}
catch (UnknownHostException e)
{
System.err.println("Don't know about host");
System.exit(1);
}
catch (IOException e)
{
System.err.println("Couldn't get I/O for the connection");
System.exit(1);
}
        String userInput = "";
        userInput="helo";out.println(userInput);
        userInput="mail from: me@mycollege.ac.uk";out.println(userInput);
        userInput="rcpt to: webmaster@mycollege.ac.uk";out.println(userInput);
        userInput="data";out.println(userInput);
        userInput=" Too Much Too Little Too Late";out.println(userInput);
        userInput="";out.println(userInput);
        userInput=".";out.println(userInput);
        userInput="";out.println(userInput);
        out.close();
        echoSocket.close();
}
}
```

Figure 10.36: Javascript incorporating SMTP code

http://	www.teraknor.co.uk	:8080	/genres/startrek	?series=DS9
scheme	host	port	path	query

1. **Scheme,** is the protocol used such as ftp or http
2. **Host,** the DNS (domain name system) entry for the website you wish to visit
3. **Port,** the TCP or UDP channel you wish to transfer the data (8080 is often used by proxy servers)

4. **Path,** the directory and subdirectory used to store the web page or service
5. **Query,** a web form entry set of information sent to the web server
6. **Fragment,** additional information sent to the web server

Figure 10.37: Dissection of the URI

now freely available, with Windows Live Messenger® and Skype™ offering competing alternatives. These applications offer direct communication via voice, video and text (chat).

Email offers long-term storage of conversations as well as the exchange of files, information and ideas. Together with the Internet, email is one of the main causes of improved global communication, mainly because it is not dependent on time barriers. Although email now seems indispensable, it has only become commonly used in the last ten years.

3.2 System requirements

When setting up a computer system for Internet communication, you need to consider the different technologies available:

- wired systems, like UTP network cards or fibre connections
- mobile systems such as Bluetooth® or Wireless for an Internet connection
- hardware with the specification of the computer system, mobile device or laptop as well as the specification of the network card (type and speed) and the communication media type (fibre, wired or wireless)
- the communication services you intend to use, such as email, video, voice, chat or Internet gaming
- software such as Internet Explorer®, Google™ Chrome, Opera or Mozilla Firefox® for web access, as well as the operating system to use on the computer system, such as Windows 7®, Linux® or Mac OSX®.

Activity: Web technology

1. What are URL and URI?
2. Give an example of a URL and name each section of the URL.
3. Define these terms: wiki, blog and vlog.

How to... Configure your Internet connection

Please refer to the screenshots on page 339 to complete this How to… activity.

1. Using Windows 7®, Internet configuration and communications set up is a very straightforward process provided you have essential information to hand in advance:
   - the IP address of the default gateway
   - the IP address of the DNS server(s)
   - the IP addressing scheme (or whether the system uses DHCP to issue IP addresses).

For this example, the following addresses are used:
   - the IP address of the default gateway is 192.168.1.1
   - the DNS server IP address is 194.168.8.100
   - the IP address being given to the computer is 192.168.1.99 with a subnet mask of 255.255.255.0

2. Make sure that the network card is correctly installed and the connection is valid to the switch or WAP.
3. Enter control panel > network and Internet > network and sharing center.
4. Click on connections: it may be local area connection or wireless or 3G.
5. Right click and select Properties. On the Networking tab select Internet Protocol Version 4 (TCP/IPv4).
6. You can change the settings, or leave it as is.
7. If it is not working, follow these steps.
   - Check the cable or connection.
   - Check that your settings are correct.
   - Check whether the operating system has recognised the network card correctly.
   - Check whether the switch or WAP is working correctly and is connected to the Internet.
   - Check that you have used the correct addresses when configuring the local IP address, default gateway, subnet mask and DNS server.

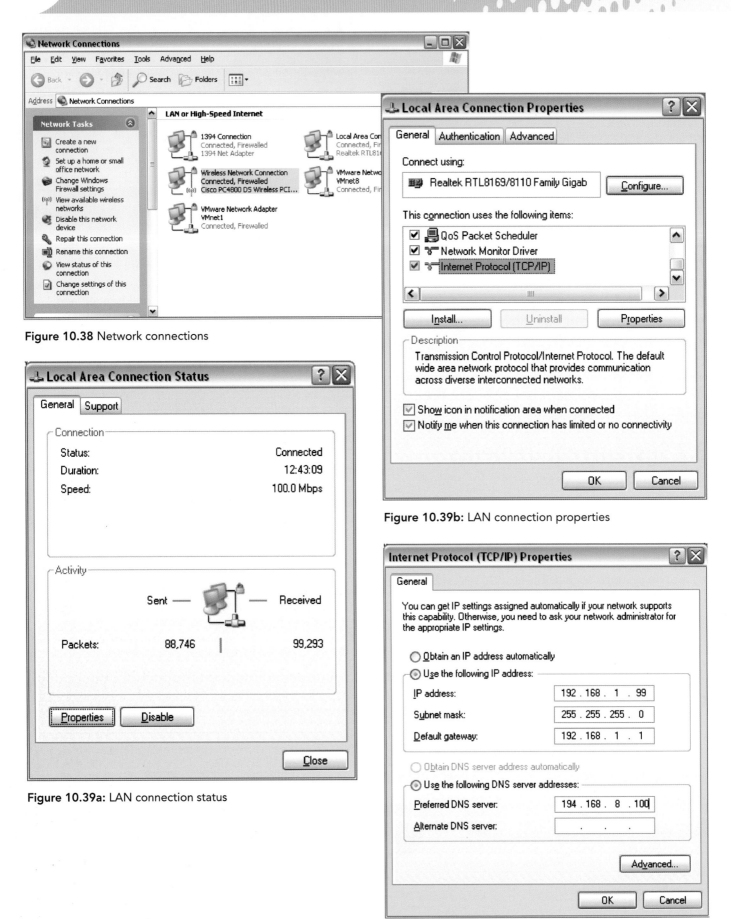

Figure 10.38 Network connections

Figure 10.39a: LAN connection status

Figure 10.39b: LAN connection properties

Figure 10.39c: TCP/IP settings

3.3 Direct communication

Chat

Chat is a simple one-to-one or one-to-many text-based communication system which relies on a central relay server to pass the conversation between all the clients. Systems such as IRC, Skype™, AOL Instant Messenger and Windows Live® Messenger® all support text-based chat. Social networking sites, such as Facebook®, now offer chat as a principal feature, allowing you to communicate with friends when they are online and offline.

Email

Email has been available on networked systems since the early 1970s and the technology has changed little since, with a few minor improvements in security. Email relies on a server acting as a post office, relaying the messages across the Internet to other mail servers in each domain (using DNS as the method for locating these servers).

Your email client could be an application such as Outlook® or Eudora®, or a web page such as Hotmail or Gmail™. Currently email use accounts for over half of all Internet traffic.

Web phone

Voice communication over the Internet differs from communication via mobile phones and land-based phone systems that we use every day. This is an emerging technology and is still improving as you read this section. Web phones are classed as VoIP (voice over Internet protocol) technology. Establishing and managing a voice conversation across the Internet is a complex process as the lines of communication must be reliable and the conversation must not be affected by any interference (delay in delivery of the data).

Protocols such as SIP (session initiation protocol) are used to establish and manage web phone calls, with applications such as SipGate using this protocol to enable free or low-cost calls to your home computer.

Social networking

A large number of readers will already have more than one social networking account via Facebook®, MySpace™ or one of the many other services. The advent of social networking has increased the reach of common communication systems onto many platforms.

Where social networkers will participate using both their home-based systems as well as their mobile devices.

Services such as Twitter, which rely on **microblogging**, demonstrate the power of this when in January 2009 a pilot safely landed a plane in the Hudson river. The first media, was tweeted pictures of the plane in the water from passengers on the ferries diverted to support the rescue.

Video communication and web conferencing

Video communication is bandwidth intensive and was once used only by commercial organisations to reduce the cost of transatlantic trips for essential meetings. With the development of lower-quality (in comparison) webcams and an increase in speed with broadband communications, the average Internet user can easily obtain a webcam at low cost and already has the software installed to support this.

Video communication can take place using the same applications used for chat and can support voice as well as text-based communication.

Skype™ is amongst a range of technologies (such as WebEx, Illuminate, Centra and DimDim) which enable web conferencing to take place. Web conferencing, irrespective of the system used, allows individuals to collaborate via voice and video (as well as chat) communication using the Internet.

Key term

Microblogging – using services such as Twitter™ to share with the world information in a short sentence.

What difference has tweeting brought to the way we receive news stories?

Desktop sharing

Many web conferencing systems allow collaborators to share their desktops either as read only, so others can see their applications, or as a PowerPoint® presentation. This is not to be confused with remote desktop, where you are able to allow others to remotely access your desktop operating system.

Activity: Internet connections

1 Identify how different domain names and URLs are constructed. Compare URLs of different types of organisations, for example educational establishments, charities, commercial websites, etc.

2 Compare different email, chat and video/voice communication systems and identify how their integration is leading to a single common method of communication.

3 Thinking points:

   a) What protocols are in common use on the Internet?

   b) What technologies are used on the Internet and how is this set to evolve?

3.4 Interconnection devices

For an explanation of wireless access points (WAPs) see page 308.

For explanations of bridges, switches and routers, please refer back to section 1.3, pages 311–14.

Mobile base stations

The mobile masts often seen in neighbourhoods are mobile base stations owned by various mobile providers. While the majority of towns and cities are covered by the majority of providers, rural areas can suffer from limited coverage. Some mobile providers are not seeking to cover these areas, and other offer only a limited service. Areas such as the Scottish Highlands and the English Lake District are to date only covered by one provider.

The variability of coverage, once one leaves a large urban area, imposes a limit on the 3G and 4G coverage available. While you may have come to expect a good mobile data service, you are likely to discover that it is more sporadic as you travel through the UK (and worldwide).

Assessment activity 10.3

 **BTEC**

This task could link to the final outcome of Unit 9, as well as many of the other networking and system support units.

1 In a lab context create direct network communication between two users by setting up interconnection devices for direct communication. You will need to demonstrate using more than one interconnection device, at least one direct wired connection and one direct wireless connection. You could use a router and a switch, and a wireless router with a switch for example. **P7 P8**

You must prove that the direct network communication works.

2 Using the wired and wireless interconnection devices you set up, demonstrate the direct network communication between two users by sending messages and files via a number of direct communication methods. For example, you could send a message and image file via instant messaging or email and deliver a short presentation over the network using video conferencing or web conferencing. **P7**

3 Assess the effectiveness of data transfer (e.g. transfer speed) between a direct wired connection and a direct wireless connection. **M3**

Grading tips

- You must clearly document the setting up of the direct communication network using interconnection devices and the direct communication link between two users. The documentation provided for assessment could take the form of a short video, observation evidence or a written summary. **P7 P8**

- For this task, a stopwatch may help. **M3**

PLTS

You can demonstrate your skills as a **creative thinker** by creating direct network communication between two users

Functional skills

You can demonstrate your **Functional ICT** skills by documenting your assessment using a PowerPoint® presentation or creating a short video.

Jacob Smith
Network specialist

I am a network specialist working on a team of network and communications specialists as part of an Internet service provider. Our department supports the daily operation of the telecommunications network and it is our job to resolve any problems with the network.

We make sure the system runs smoothly and that it is protected from threats, both internal and external. As the system grows, we look at traffic and communication load and are expected to ensure a minimal (excellent) service quality.

A typical day

There is no typical day for our team. We have to complete many routine administrative tasks, monitor network traffic, look at load and check logs for any torrent traffic. We support a large customer base that connects to our network for many reasons.

There are sometimes hardware or communication issues that we have to address quickly because if the network or communication technology isn't working then the organisation can't function. We have to quickly set up a way for users to continue working while we get to the root of the problem. We communicate to users that we are fixing the problem and create a solution.

Best things about the job

As a network specialist I get to learn about new network and communication technologies all the time. We also get to evaluate new applications and devices as they become available, to see whether we could put them on our system without causing problems.

Think about it!

1 What have you covered in this chapter, to give you a technical understanding of Jacob's job? Write a list and discuss this with others.

2 What additional skills would you need to develop for this career to become a reality? Work in a small group and create a list.

Just checking

1. How is a PVC used in WAN communication?
2. What is a MUX?
3. What issue may be caused on a network with 'big talkers'?
4. How does CSMA/CD resolve collisions?
5. List the different kinds of servers in use.
6. List the different types of workstations in use.
7. What is the role of a switch?
8. What is the role of a router?
9. What is the role of a 'model' in networking?
10. How does WEP protect wireless communication?
11. What is DTE?
12. What is DCE?
13. What is amplitude and frequency and how are they used in the transmission of data?
14. What mechanisms are use for error correction and detection?
15. What (common) channel types are used?
16. In an Ethernet frame, what are the different 'fields'?
17. What is the role of a datagram?
18. What is the difference between half duplex and full duplex?
19. What are the coloured pairs in a UTP connection?

edexcel

Assignment tips

- Many elements of this unit link to other vendor and non-vendor units in networking, security and systems support. Try to link your experiences from this unit to all the others.
- There are many practical opportunities in this unit. Make sure you take the time to explore them
- Use plenty of diagrams. While a picture is not always worth a thousand words, with supporting text explaining what is required you may find you achieve a merit.
- Evaluation requires supporting evidence. This can be accomplished using tables, presentations or complex (structured) diagrams.

11 Systems analysis and design

Designing a new or revising an existing system is a complex process and it is remarkably easy to produce expensive systems that do not match the needs of the clients or users. Systems analysis provides structured processes that help make sure that the final system is fit for purpose.

In completing this unit, you will gain an understanding of the principles and stages involved in systems analysis and of the documentation involved.

This unit also covers the reasons why organisations undertake systems analyses, as well as the benefits of engaging in such processes.

Different organisations will adopt their own approaches to systems analysis, that meet their needs. Here, you will consider a range of life cycle models and methodologies. In your practical work however you need to focus on only one methodology as agreed with your tutor.

Learning outcomes

After completing this unit you should:

1. understand the principles of systems analysis and design
2. be able to carry out a structured analysis of business systems requirements
3. be able to design business systems solutions.

Assessment and grading criteria

This table shows you what you must do in order to achieve a pass, merit or distinction grade, and where you can find activities in this book to help you.

To achieve a **pass** grade the evidence must show that you are able to:	To achieve a **merit** grade the evidence must show that, in addition to the pass criteria, you are able to:	To achieve a **distinction** grade the evidence must show that, in addition to the pass and merit criteria, you are able to:
P1 outline the principles of systems analysis **See Assessment activity 11.1, page 353**		
P2 illustrate the stages of a development life cycle **See Assessment activity 11.1, page 353**	**M1** discuss the most appropriate uses of different development life-cycle models **See Assessment activity 11.1, page 353**	
P3 explain the benefits of structured analysis **See Assessment activity 11.1, page 353**		
P4 carry out a structured analysis of a specified business process **See Assessment activity 11.2, page 365**		
P5 produce a requirements specification for a business process **See Assessment activity 11.3, page 366**	**M2** suggest alternative solutions **See Assessment activity 11.3, page 366**	**D1** analyse costs and benefits **See Assessment activity 11.3, page 366**
P6 produce a design for a specified system requirement **See Assessment activity 11.3, page 366**	**M3** explain any constraints on the system design **See Assessment activity 11.3, page 366**	**D2** generate comprehensive design documentation independently **See Assessment activity 11.3, page 366**

How you will be assessed

This unit will be assessed by a number of internal assignments that will be designed and marked by the staff at your centre. It may be subject to sampling by your centre's Lead Internal Verifier or an Edexcel Standards Verifier as part of Edexcel's ongoing quality assurance procedures. The assignments will be designed to allow you to show your understanding of the unit outcomes. These relate to what you should be able to do after completing this unit.

Your tutor will tell you precisely what form your assessments will take, but you could be asked to produce:

- written reports
- documented discussions
- PowerPoint® presentations and notes.

Helen Johnson, BTEC National IT learner

After I read the assignment brief the first time I was a little sceptical because I assumed that the 'solution' we might be led to develop would involve an impersonal call centre that actually puts barriers in the way of good customer interaction. I have used some IT-based interfaces myself and get quite irritated by automated phone systems and standard messages. My first instinct was that perhaps we ought to leave the existing manual system alone and not try to automate it – this is because I really do value human interaction.

I was pleased in the end, however, to see that the director also had similar concerns and that going about the investigation in a structured way did allow me to capture all of the requirements and issues. I hope that if the final system was actually built according to my designs, then it would be a system I would be happy to use myself.

The work also helped me to understand wider influences and constraints that impacted on the design and I think that if now I had to do an analysis for real, then I would be in a good position. One thing I do know now is that the first thing to do when given a project is not to start programming!

Over to you

- **In groups discuss your personal experiences of customer service systems and make a list of characteristics of good customer service.**
- **After a list has been agreed, look at each characteristic again and describe what barriers you might encounter when trying to build them into a system.**

1. Understand the principles of systems analysis and design

1.1 Principles

Here are three different definitions of systems analysis.

- The study of a business problem in order to recommend improvements and to specify the requirements for a solution.

- A phase in which the current system is studied and alternative replacement systems are proposed.

- A detailed analysis of the components and requirements of a system, the information needs of an organisation, the characteristics and components of current systems, and the functional requirements of the proposed system.

There are many more possible definitions but there are common themes within all of them. In particular, the study of the current system if there is one, understanding and specifying the requirements, and the design of new or replacement systems.

Fundamentally, systems analysis is a process and, although different companies describe and operate the process in different ways, the key purpose is always the same, as is the need for a structured and organised approach.

This unit will help you to gain an understanding of the principles of systems analysis and design, as well as the documentation involved. Although all stages are important, it is crucial to capture the requirements accurately and fully in order to ensure that the new system is fit for purpose. Remember also that any later testing or review should be based on these requirements.

1.2 Development life cycle models

To structure the systems analysis process, a number of particular models have been developed. One very common model is the waterfall model – so named because the stages 'cascade' in one direction from one activity to the next. Another popular model is Rapid Applications Development (RAD).

Waterfall life cycle model

The waterfall life cycle model has been modified in different ways over time and is often described in slightly different ways, but the essential 'no turning back' feature remains at its core. Just as with real waterfalls, water never goes back up to the top! In the classic version of this developmental model the key stages are as shown in Figure 11.1.

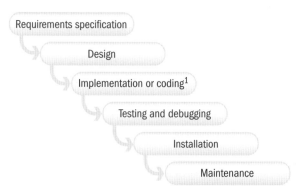

[1]The implementation phase often requires some integration where different parts of the new system that were created separately are brought together into the complete system.

Figure 11.1: Classic waterfall life cycle

The key disadvantage of waterfall development is that, because of the 'no turning back' characteristic, once a phase of development has been completed, it will never be visited again. So, it does not allow for revision or reflection. If one of the stages is not completed well (for example, the requirements are not fully captured or the testing not undertaken rigorously), then the final product may not be fit for purpose. If, of course, each phase is completed with care and the outputs can be relied upon, then the waterfall method can work very well.

Activity: Exploring variations of the waterfall method

Alternatives to the classic waterfall model include modified waterfall models.

- Research some of the modified waterfall models.
- For each of these models, find out how the waterfall method has been modified and why.

Rapid applications development

Rapid applications development (RAD) (see Figure 11.2) is a development model that was devised as a response to the inflexible processes developed in the 1970s, such as the waterfall model. As well as the disadvantages of the waterfall method already described, using it (and other similar models) to build a system could take so long that requirements had often changed before the system was complete. This often resulted in unusable systems.

RAD is a software development methodology that focuses on building applications fast – it involves **iterative development**.

The speed is achieved by using specialist tools such as **CASE** tools that focus on converting requirements to code very quickly. It achieves this using **prototypes** that are iteratively developed into a full system.

The initial prototype serves as a proof of concept for the client, but more importantly it also serves to focus discussions to help define and refine requirements.

A disadvantage of RAD is that the speed can compromise the features available in the final system. Also, it may not be easy to expand or scale up the system later because it was developed specifically to meet a particular need.

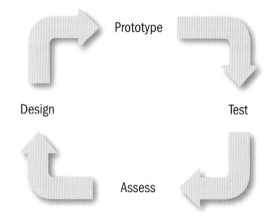

Figure 11.2: Rapid applications development (RAD)

Key terms

Iterative development – repeating the development process until all the required functionality has been developed. It can be used to produce increasingly sophisticated and functional versions of a system in short development cycles.

CASE – stands for computer-aided software engineering and describes the use of software tools to assist in the development and maintenance of software. Tools used to assist in this way are known as CASE tools.

Prototype – a restricted version of the finished product that can be produced in as short an amount of time as possible, preferably days.

Spiral model

The spiral development model combines the features of the waterfall model with prototyping. Typically it is used for expensive, large or very complicated projects. Key advantages are that it is more able to cope with a changing project and that estimates of costs are more reliable.

Benefits

Many of the benefits of structured systems analysis are often invisible. Good analysis ensures that the project implements an appropriate solution that meets needs and because it is the best solution then it is hard to see the cost, time and effort that has been avoided by doing it badly.

There are some specific benefits that can be attributed to the different life cycle models.

Waterfall model benefits

- The model is simple and sequential.
- The processes are compartmentalised in order to give good control.
- The development process moves from one phase to another like a car in a car wash with no repeated steps.
- Deadlines set should be met.

Rapid Application model benefits

- Development is fast.
- There are many opportunities during the whole process to refine and improve the design.

Spiral model benefits

- The model can cope with changes.
- Cost estimates should be fairly accurate.

Stages

Compartmentalising the different activities within a development life cycle and then detailing what happens in each compartment helps to ensure that no important aspect is missed out and that the different activities are undertaken in the most appropriate order.

Although different organisations may divide up the whole in slightly different ways and life cycle models will vary, the list of stages below is fairly commonly accepted as a workable set of stages for a waterfall model.

- Initiation and feasibility
- Investigation
- Requirements analysis and specification
- Design (logical and physical)
- Building systems
- Testing
- Implementation (and then yet more testing)
- Maintenance.

The stages are all important, but the statistics detailed in the case study on page 352 about the causes of project failure do show the crucial importance of capturing the requirements and this relates to both undertaking the investigation with rigour and also then specifying the requirements accurately.

Project initiation and feasibility

At the start, there must be a trigger that initiates, or starts, the whole process of development. Typically this trigger will be one of the key drivers (see section 1.4, page 352). At this early stage, a limited feasibility study is undertaken instead of starting on a full analysis.

The key questions that a feasibility study aims to answer are:

- Should this project be undertaken?
- Can this project be justified?

It is possible that an outcome of the feasibility study will be a decision not to proceed.

A feasibility study will normally be broken into sections, as follows.

- **Purpose of the system:** If the project is to replace or upgrade an existing system, then the purpose might include something about what the existing system does (the **As-Is**), as well as the requirements of the new system (the **To-Be**).

Key terms

As-Is – short-hand phrase meaning the current system as it is now.

To-Be – short-hand phrase meaning the new system that is to be completed.

- **System scope:** This section identifies what parts of the wider system are to be considered. As the project develops, the impact on other parts of the system may be discovered and it is important to revisit the scope from time to time. IT systems cannot be developed in isolation and so the scope will include changes to such things as connected administration procedures and job functions.
- **Problems and requirements:** This section can be difficult to write without a full investigation. This might involve a limited set of interviews with some key people and a review of any documents. If possible, the analyst should interview people who actually use the system as well as the managers of the organisation or department. Capturing things that work well, as well as those that do not, is important. At an early stage, these requirements will often be in the form of prioritised lists. The requirements may then be translated into what it means for the system and documented using similar

techniques to those used when undertaking the more in-depth investigation and analysis. A typical method will use **DFDs** (data flow diagrams). Later on, these diagrams will be reused and refined. (For more on DFDs, go to page 359–360.)

- **Constraints:** Key aspects should be identified although others may emerge later.

- **Recommendations:** One possible recommendation might be not to proceed with the development. There may be a number of recommendations and alternative solutions and each possible solution has to be documented with sufficient information to allow managers to make a decision.

Did you know?

Customers are frequently asked to formally sign-off key documents – this is partly self-protective on the part of the analyst, but also serves to focus the customer, as they recheck and confirm that the project is still on track.

The Investigation and the Requirements analysis and specification stages are covered later in this unit in section 2 starting on page 356. Design is also covered in this unit under section 1.3. These stages will revisit some of the work done in the feasibility stage but in greater depth. Different specific systems or companies will group stages in different ways.

Logical and physical design

The physical design of computers – hardware and software, database files, manual files etc. – is relatively well understood by developers. The logical design, involving the data and process components of the resources, is less well understood despite being as important, if not more so, than the physical design.

The physical components describe 'how' the logical design will be implemented and because the physical implementation is ultimately based on available technology there may be many different ways of doing it. In contrast, the logical side represents the inherent nature of the business process and only changes if the business changes. It is therefore considerably less volatile than the physical.

It is important to understand that logical design always takes place *before* physical design.

Activity: Getting started on projects

1 Why might people be optimistic about the costs of development projects?

2 Identify the problems that could develop if the system scope is not sufficiently clarified at the start of a project.

1.3 Developmental tools and techniques

There are a number of methodologies used within life cycle models that employ a series of developmental tools and techniques. One methodology and an established set of tools is Structured Systems Analysis and Design method (SSADM), which works best within a waterfall-type life cycle (see below).

Other developmental methodologies, such as the **object-oriented** Unified Modelling Language (UML), work best within other life cycle models such as RAD (see page 348).

Key terms

DFD – stands for data flow diagram.

Object-oriented – where the whole system is broken into a number of objects that are designed to interact with each other to produce a working system. Object-oriented methods are becoming more popular and are particularly useful in large and complex systems.

Structured Systems Analysis and Design

Although SSADM is certainly a waterfall-type method, some of the terminology used is different from that used in the classic waterfall. In addition, SSADM focuses mainly on the early stages of this model, the capturing of the requirements and the design of the new system.

The whole system development process can be broken down into six stages:

- project initiation and feasibility
- investigation and analysis

- design
- implementation
- testing
- maintenance.

The last three stages are not covered in this unit. Please see *Unit 14 Event driven programming pages 369–400* for more on these development stages.

Feasibility as an iterative process

Although the SSADM methodology is a type of (one-way) waterfall method, it is likely that a discussion of the recommendations made in the feasibility study might raise more questions. So the analyst could be asked to revisit some of the work undertaken in the the feasibility study in order to clarify some of the detail.

At the end of this part of the activity, there would normally be a 'sign-off' of the final feasibility report and a documented acceptance of the requirements of the new system. It is also possible that, at this stage, the analyst will need to make commitments about such things as timescale for the full analysis process, costs (whether they are internal or external to the organisation), reporting and interim reporting arrangements.

Several modelling and structured analysis tools are available within SSADM. Other methodologies provide alternative tools and methods. These tools can be used at various stages of the process and might include:

- data flow diagrams (DFDs) – see pages 359–60
- entity relationship diagrams (ERDs) see page 361
- process descriptors – see page 361–2.

Data flow diagrams are key to the logical understanding of what the system does.

1.4 Key drivers

Given that the development of new systems can be fraught with problems and delays, what drives organisations to develop systems? These drivers will be very different in different situations.

The most important drivers come directly from the needs of the business and are often not related to technology, but require technological solutions. Examples could include:

- the organisational needs to grow or acquire other companies in order to extend their market share
- a change in legislation that requires organisations to develop new or adapt new systems and processes
- a need to reduce staffing costs.

1.5 Structured analysis

During the process of designing and producing a new system, it can be very tempting to cut corners to save time or maybe to skip aspects that seem obvious. Experienced professionals will always advise against this and quote a number of benefits of keeping rigorously to the process.

Those benefits include:

- a reduced risk of projects running over budget or over time
- the building of good-quality systems that are more likely to meet requirements
- keeping projects manageable
- building maintainable and resilient systems.

It is common in the press to hear of projects that end up costing far more than anticipated and furthermore, it is often tacitly assumed that they will not complete on time. The impact of either of these can be significant and in some cases a late finishing can have drastic consequences – think of the side effects of an Olympic Stadium not being ready for the Olympics or even a new network for a school being installed during the summer that is not ready for the beginning of term.

The whole purpose of systems analysis is about ensuring that the requirements are met. As the CHAOS Report (see case study below) shows however, this cannot always be assumed!

Case study: CHAOS Report

The 1995 Chaos Report was the first survey made by the Standish Group. The report is a landmark study and is often quoted in papers or presentations where reference is made of IT project failure.

Reason for IT project failures	Percentage
Lack of user involvement	12
Unrealistic expectations	11
Lack of management support	9
Requirements changed	10
Lack of planning	9
Incomplete requirements	14
Others (for example resourcing problems, system not needed anymore, technological illiteracy)	35

1. In small groups discuss whether poorly completed systems analysis could have been to blame for each of the reasons quoted above.

2. See if you can find any references to later CHAOS reports and find out how the situation is changing.

Did you know?

- There are a number of different life cycle models that can be used in different situations.

- Many apparently well-designed systems fail to meet the requirements when actually implemented.

- The drivers behind new systems must directly relate to business drivers.

PLTS

Assessment activity 11.1 provides opportunities to develop as a **reflective learner** as it requires you to reflect back on the understanding and skills acquired in order to summarise and communicate the key issues back to others.

Functional skills

It is important to ensure that the evidence produced for Task 1 is written at the appropriate level of detail and takes account of the intended audience. Both the written reports and any records of verbal discussions could very well contribute to the evidence you may be putting together for Functional **English** skills.

Assessment activity 11.1  BTEC

Scenario

Parry's is a retail company that sells electrical goods in the high street. It has a small team of three customer service assistants, managed by a customer service manager, who respond to customer queries. The assistants do not get involved with selling new products – only with after-sales service.

The customer service unit is quite informally structured, but over the years two of the assistants have developed specialist knowledge – one in music systems/TV/radio and the other in kitchen items, such as microwaves and fridges.

The manager of the company feels that there are some issues with the service that they offer and wants to improve it and put it on a more formal and sustainable basis for the long term. He engaged an external consultant who started off the investigation, but has recently had to withdraw.

You have been asked to take over the investigation and complete the analysis and design. An assistant has been provided who has little experience of systems analysis and you have been asked to mentor him so that in the future he can work independently. The assistant is currently undertaking a part-time degree in IT.

You have been given some notes and transcripts of interviews (see Case study on pages 354–55).

1. Prepare three sets of slides that can be used by your assistant to gain a better understanding of the following:
   - Outline principles of systems analysis
   - The stages of a development life cycle
   - The benefits of structured analysis.

   In each case illustrate your slides using references and examples from the scenario so as to more effectively help the assistant understand. **P1 P2 P3**

2. You have been contacted by the tutor of your assistant and asked to participate in a teaching session. Prepare some background notes for a proposed tutorial discussion meeting with your assistant, his tutor and the rest of his class. The title of the seminar is 'Appropriate uses of different developmental life cycle models'. Rehearse the discussion with someone else, possibly your tutor, and record it or document it in some other way. **M1**

Grading tips

In respect of the merit grade, check out the benefits again of two life cycle models and consider situations where these benefits would be valuable. For all of the tasks check before you hand in your work that you have met the criteria in the grading grid. **M1**

Case study: Parry's Electrical Store

Investigation material relating to Customer Care Development Project

This material is a combination of the following:

- Summary of 130 customer satisfaction surveys
- Interview questions and responses from two of the customer service assistants
- Record of meeting with customer service manager
- Record of meeting with managing director
- Blank query form.

Summary of 130 customer satisfaction surveys

	Yes	No
Satisfied with speed of response	72	58
Satisfied with quality of response	110	20
Would you use us again?	88	42

Notes from consultant

At first look, the results are a little worrying. I rang up a number of the people who were dissatisfied and one of the issues raised on a regular basis was that the person they actually needed to talk to was not in the office, or on another line, and no one else could help.

In my observations I calculated that the two of them were busy for about 60% of their time – the third assistant (Z) was busy for about 95% of his time, but many queries are lost because at times no one is available to answer the phone and no records of missed calls are made. If the proposal for a queries database was implemented, and if they all had access to a centralised store of answers and some way was found to extend the hours someone was available, they could perhaps get by with only two assistants.

I was a bit concerned that some of the assistants are not filling in any records and also that the records that are completed do not seem to be referred to. There must be a need to store this information and make good use of it to improve the service.

I have explored the cost of an automated phone system and it will be around £5000. Maybe another £3000 for other costs and perhaps two days of training needed.

Key quotes from interviews with assistants

Assistant Y

Q: Can you explain what you do?

I work from 9.00 a.m. to 5.00 p.m., just like the others, and when the phone rings I check that they are actually a customer who has bought a product and if they are then I take down the details on this form (see below) and if I can then answer the question. If I cannot answer it I pass the form over to someone else and if it is a complaint I tend to give it to my manager. If it is a query about music, TV or similar I always give it to Z.

Q: Can you see anything that needs improving?

We need more people certainly as there are times when all of us are talking to customers. I also noticed once when I ate my lunch in the office that the phone rang all the time, but normally the three of us go out from 1.00 p.m.–2.00 p.m. together.

Assistant Z

Q: Can you explain what you do?

Same as everyone else really, but I am the expert for all music and TV products. I have been told a few times by M that I must fill in those query forms each time I am talking with a customer, but I can never be bothered and I think customers would prefer me to be talking to them and solving their problems instead of wasting time filling in forms.

Q: Can you see anything that needs improving?

Yes - I should be paid more than the others because I know more things. We all get twice minimum pay rates and work 40 hours per week. I have been thinking about moving on from here as it looks as if my manager will be here for the next 20 years. It can take ages to find out if the customer is a valid one and the printouts are always out of date anyway – we need to have access to an online up-to-date database.

(cont.)

Case study (contd.)

Key quotes from meeting with customer service manager (M)

The process is simple – when the phone rings, whoever is available picks it up and at the same time starts filling in one of my forms. They first have to check if the customer is a valid one and has bought something in the last year. They check that from a printout that I update and hand round each week. Once they are sure it is a genuine enquiry they complete the rest of the form and answer as best they can. If it is a difficult complaint then I tend to take it. They should store the forms in my in-tray and I then store them in my filing cabinet.

I sometimes do need to go through the filing cabinet if a customer has a follow up query, but I admit that it can be difficult to find a particular old form.

I am dependant on Y a lot and if he ever left we would be in trouble. I have tried to get more staff, but the director always says no – he sometimes sees all of us sitting around doing nothing – especially on Friday afternoon.

Notes from meeting with managing director

Key drivers: director intends expanding and taking over other stores. He is aware of the importance of good customer care and wants the function to be made more formal and able to be centralised. The director is very keen that the service does not become impersonal, however, with complex phone menu levels and endless meaningless messages. Very much aware of the dependence on customer service operator Z, but knows that when he is here and talking to customers directly, he gives a good service.

Customer query form

Customer _____ Phone _____

Date _____

Product bought _____

Nature of query _____

_____

_____

_____

_____

Response _____

_____

_____

_____

_____

Query passed to _____

2. Be able to carry out a structured analysis of business systems requirements

2.1 Investigation

Techniques

There is a variety of techniques that can be used to gather information about both the current system and the required system. The five basic techniques are:

- observation
- document analysis
- interview
- questionnaire
- data analysis.

Normally, an analyst would not depend on one technique only and would choose the techniques appropriate to the situation.

Interviews can be an excellent way of collecting detailed information and also allow an open dialogue in which the interviewee has the opportunity to bring up issues that the analyst had not considered. Typically, the analyst will start by interviewing or meeting with the managers and decision makers in order to get an overall picture of the issues. They will also gain an understanding of the organisational structures, the people involved and any areas of sensitivity.

Questionnaires can be used to obtain information more quickly and cheaply from a larger selection of people.

Observations need to be undertaken carefully and with some sensitivity, as they could result in employees becoming worried about what is happening and how it might affect them. In addition, the employees observed may not be typical of other employees. A good systems analyst will engage with the individuals within the organisation and explain what is happening and why.

Document analysis might be undertaken early in the investigation. The issues identified in the documentation can be used to construct questions for questionnaires or interviews. A wide range of documentation should be looked at, including possibly: procedure manuals (to compare with observed practice), complaints files, paper records or files, etc.

2.2 Analysis

In one sense the process of analysis is simply following the procedures detailed in the chosen methodology. However, there is no doubt that an experienced systems analyst can add further value from perspectives gained in previous work.

It is recognised that a systems analyst requires three key sets of skills in addition to analysis and they relate to:

- technical knowledge
- managerial understanding
- interpersonal skills.

Technical knowledge helps systems analysts understand what is possible, including the limitations and potential of the hardware platforms. Many analysts have previously worked as programmers and can therefore define new systems in terms that programmers understand.

Managerial understanding helps systems analysts in managing projects and resources as well as risk (risk management). It is likely that one of the key drivers identified earlier (see page 352) will relate to finance or resources. Perhaps the company needs to cut costs or expand without incurring additional costs. This facet can be captured in a cost–benefit analysis (see page 358).

Interpersonal skills help systems analysts work with end users and also with people on the technical side of the system. It is important that some sensitivity is shown to the people that are involved in the system, as a new

Interviews can be an excellent way of collecting detailed information.

Table 11.1: Advantages and disadvantages of investigative techniques

Method	Advantages	Disadvantages
Observation	Workloads, methods of working, delays and bottlenecks can be identified.	Can be time-consuming and therefore costly. Users may put on a performance while under observation. Problems that take place infrequently may not occur during observation. Employees may not cooperate.
Interview	A rapport can be developed between interviewer and interviewee. You can adjust questions as the interview proceeds. Interviewees may identify issues, problems or requirements that have not already been identified. You can add more in-depth questions to find more information.	Can be time-consuming and therefore costly. Poor interviewing skills can lead to misleading or insufficient information. May not be feasible for a large organisation – it is important to identify key people to be interviewed in depth.
Document analysis	Good for obtaining factual information, for example data stored, procedures, volume of sales, inputs and outputs of the system.	Not all aspects will be documented and employees may not always follow the defined procedures. Manuals and paperwork may not be up to date.
Questionnaire	Many people can be asked the same questions – this is a relatively cheap way of accessing large numbers of people. Anonymity may encourage honest answers. Questionnaires can be processed electronically.	Questions need careful design, e.g. tick boxes are simple and easy to answer but do not allow shades of responses. Need to avoid ambiguity. Questions may require interpretation. Cannot guarantee return rate and the people who do respond may not be typical of all involved.
Data Analysis	Data analysis is a process of inspecting, analysing and modelling data. It can help to summarise and highlight useful information as well as suggesting conclusions, and supporting decision making. If the data can be relied upon then outcomes are objective and valid, as well as providing insights that might be difficult to identify by other means.	Very dependent on the quality, completeness and reliability of the data. Ideally any conclusions drawn or recommendations made should be cross referenced by other investigation techniques.

system potentially can mean significant change and that may be viewed as threatening.

Analysis tools

There is a variety of tools and techniques that can be used to undertake the analysis. Data flow diagrams for example are visual tools that can be used in early investigations to capture an emerging understanding of parts of the system but can also be used to illustrate both high-level overviews and detailed breakdowns of large and complex systems. DFDs can represent the As-Is logical models of the current situation and also the To-Be models of the future system.

Cost–benefit analysis

A cost–benefit analysis is often described as an informal or inexact process. The costs of a project are often complex, but can be determined and calculated with some degree of accuracy. The benefits, however, are often less easily quantified. An example of a benefit might be 'improved customer satisfaction', but such a statement is very difficult to translate into any anticipated financial benefits.

2.3 Requirements specification

In most medium to large companies, individuals or teams will specialise in particular stages of the whole life cycle process. Some work can be given to external contractors, but unless the requirements are translated fully into a formal specification then this can result in vital information being lost. In the case of an individual in college or school undertaking all of the stages of a limited project this may not be a problem, but in a commercial environment it is very different.

A typical minimum requirements specification should include:

- scope of the work
- inputs
- outputs
- processes
- cost–benefit analysis
- recommendations
- alternative solutions.

Determining and agreeing the scope of the work early is crucial to ensure that the whole development focuses on the agreed areas and neither misses important aspects nor covers those that are not required. It can be useful to specifically detail aspects that are out of scope as well as list those in scope to give clarity.

Inputs, outputs and processes are covered in more detail later on in this unit, as is the cost–benefit analysis.

Recommendations and alternative solutions appear straightforward, but require a degree of creative and lateral thinking in order to be of value within the specification. It is important that the systems analyst maintains an integrity in these sections based on the results of the investigations and does not simply reflect the opinions of the managers who contracted the work in the first place.

These general headings can appear to concern only the flow and processing of information, but the analyst must ensure that all of the requirements are represented, including less well-defined ones. Furthermore, the actual purpose of the new system must be clearly stated – either perhaps within the scope section or together with useful other background in an introduction. It is unlikely that a single layout and structure for a requirements specification will suit different projects.

As the investigation develops and additional information is collected and analysed, it is likely that the original statement of requirements as identified in the feasibility study will need some modification. The end of the investigation phase is likely to be a key decision point in the whole systems analysis activity. It is also likely to be marked with some further detailed dialogue with the customers resulting in an agreement or signing-off on the requirements.

3. Be able to design business system solutions

3.1 Design

Proper design documentation is vital if all of the hard work in the earlier stages is to be converted into a new system that is fit for purpose.

Formats for design documentation will vary, but a typical minimum will be:

- summary of the requirements
- overview of the whole system, including details of interfaces with other systems or procedures
- input specifications
- output specifications
- process descriptors
- test strategy and plans (not covered in this unit).

Although it is hoped that such a document will never need to be revised, it is likely that some issues will arise in the build phase. In such cases, further versions of the design documentation will need to be produced, each one given a new version number.

The document is likely to be long and, in most situations, readers will not want to read it all from the start, but will want to jump to particular sections as needed. For this reason, the document needs to have a contents page and to be well indexed and referenced.

As at other key stages of the whole development life cycle, at the end of the design stage the customers of the system should formally review the design and sign off before the build phase.

Inputs and outputs

In many situations, the input and outputs are easy to identify and define. For example, for a process that calculates the VAT to be charged on an order, the input is the value of the order and the output is the VAT to be charged.

For most situations, the inputs are best described and represented using proposed screen designs or data capture forms. In this way other aspects can also be represented, such as the order in which different items are entered and the visual layout including logos, titles, prompt text and so forth.

Outputs can often be in the form of screen or hard copy reports and again output designs represented in these formats can be the most effective in not only capturing what outputs are required, but also giving the customer a chance to feed back on the look and feel of them.

Other forms of input will be present in many systems, for example bar codes, voice, joysticks – even the use of pressure and movement sensors, as in WiFi applications. Similarly, outputs are not restricted exclusively to screen and printed reports – for example, the physical feedback mechanism that controls the speed in a cruise control car system.

Data

Data flow diagrams

A data flow diagram (DFD) is a graphical representation that shows the 'flow' of data through a system. Elements of DFDs are external entities, processes and datastores – these are connected by arrows that show the direction of data movement.

> **Did you know?**
>
> Data cannot travel between datastores or from an external entity into a datastore without going through a process.

What examples of data capture methods are there?

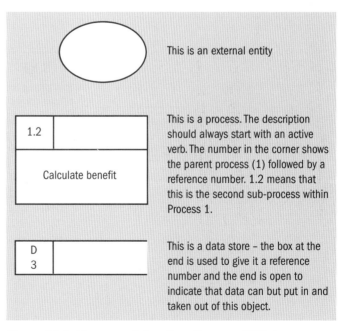

This is an external entity

This is a process. The description should always start with an active verb. The number in the corner shows the parent process (1) followed by a reference number. 1.2 means that this is the second sub-process within Process 1.

This is a data store – the box at the end is used to give it a reference number and the end is open to indicate that data can but put in and taken out of this object.

Figure 11.3: Elements of data flow diagrams (DFDs)

In most cases, a number of DFDs at different levels of detail are needed to describe how systems operate.

At the highest level, the system within scope is shown as a single rectangle and the only data flows shown are those that link outside the system with external entities. Sometimes this highest level diagram is described as Level 0 or the context diagram.

As an example, consider the data flows that are involved when a learner applies for a short part-time course at a college. The external entities might only be the applicant and their referee and the context diagram might be as simple as shown in Figure 11.4. The arrows show flows of information and are normally numbered with details provided separately. For example, arrow 1 will be a request made by the admissions service for a reference and arrow 2 will be the actual reference from the personal referee. The application database (D1) might in this case simply be a store of the application forms in a filing cabinet rather than an electronic database.

The main point of a Level 0 DFD (context diagram) is to clarify the links with external entities. Note that every arrow must have a direction and must be labelled to show what information is transferring.

The next step is to break up the one process into a number of processes and to add further data flows that show internal data transfers. The next level of detail is called a Level 1 data flow diagram (see Figure 11.5).

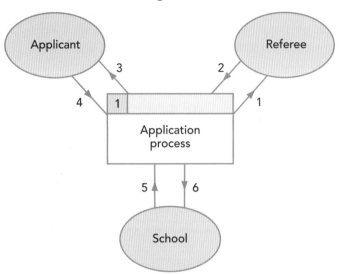

Figure 11.4: Level 0 DFD (context diagram) for a college applications system

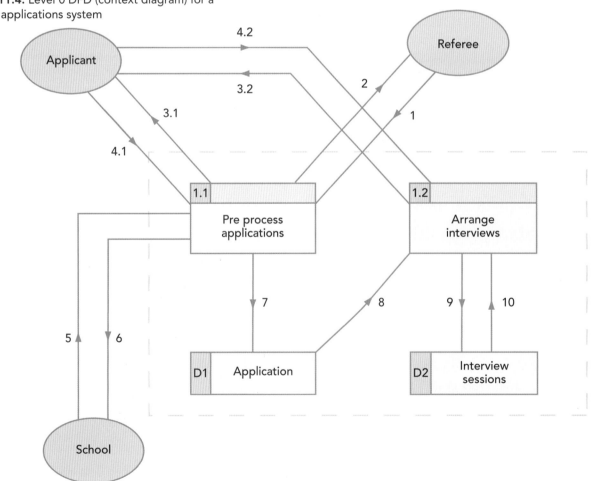

Figure 11.5: Level 1 DFD

Activity: Refining a DFD

Just before the term starts, information about successful applicants who have confirmed their place is used to create an active student database to be used to allocate students into teaching groups. Adapt the Level1 DFD from Figure 11.5 to show this process.

The symbols used in these data flow diagrams are always the same to assist people in understanding a diagram that was created by someone else. Data stores need further detail, including field names, key fields, field types and sizes, etc. All of the details for all of the data stores will be stored in the data dictionary. If one of these sub-processes is particularly complex, it too will need breaking up into further detail. All of the data flows must match up when moving from one level to another.

Data dictionaries

In large or complex systems, it can be very difficult to keep track of all of the different tables and data items. If different tables are constructed over time, or by different people, then different or inconsistent naming conventions can cause errors and confusion. A data dictionary is a centralised store of information about all the data in a database. The expectations of particular employers and methodologies are likely to vary, but there will be a core set of details that will always be necessary.

- Table names and descriptions.
- Relationships between tables (i.e. entities) – often shown using entity relationship diagrams (ERDs).
- Field names (attributes) and the table(s) in which they appear.
- Field definitions, including field types and lengths and meanings, if not self-evident.
- Additional properties for each field, including format and validation controls.
- Aliases or alternative names for the same field as used in different tables.

For more information about data dictionaries see *Unit 6: Software design and development*.

Entity relationship diagrams

Entity relationship diagrams (ERDs) are the real-world things that are part of the system under investigation and need representing in the DFDs. Examples are products, customers and orders. Attributes are the qualities that are of interest and hence worth storing in a database. The attributes for a product might include its product code and the current stock level. For a customer, the attributes would include name, customer reference, contact data, etc. When stored in a database, it makes sense to use the attribute names for the field names. Most entities will be implemented in a practical way as tables.

One (or more) of the attributes of a particular entity has to be defined as the primary key. This uniquely identifies a particular occurrence of an entity. For example, in a cars table entity, the primary key would typically be the car registration number which should be unique to each car.

Most systems have a number of entities within them, and entities are often related to each other. One-to-many relationships are the most common type of relationship between entities, but are not the only type.

Figure 11.6: Entity relationship diagram (ERD)

For more on entity relationships, see *Unit 6: Software design and development*.

Process descriptors

There are different techniques for defining processes, each having different strengths that may be suitable for different situations. Choosing the best way of describing a process is important.

Having identified the processes needed within the investigation phase, it is necessary to define each process so precisely that there is no ambiguity.

A variety of different methods can be used to create process specifications:

- structured English
- flow charts
- decision tables.

Typically, you would choose one of these techniques to describe a particular process, rather than using all three.

Flow charts are diagrams which show processes linked in a systematic way, with branches according to a number of decision choices. It is important, for clarity, to use the right shapes for each part:

- diamonds for decisions
- rectangles for processes
- ovals or circles for start and stop.

All process boxes should have active verbs, for example send, calculate, etc. All decision boxes should contain questions. You should avoid flow

lines crossing each other. Figure 11.7 is an example of a flow chart and relates directly to the Express Tracks Case study on pages 363–364 and the Process descriptor example below.

Decision tables are useful when there are a lot of different options to choose from and you want to identify what happens in each circumstance. They are used when the equivalent flow chart would be too complex to draw.

Structured English describes processes in an informal way using all words. It might be particularly useful in the early stages when you are providing overview descriptions of processes without providing the detail. Also, if it is known that the solution is to be programmed, then perhaps this technique can be used which almost starts the process of coding.

Process descriptor example – structured English

Here is an example of a process descriptor for paying royalties, written in structured English. It directly relates to the Express Tracks Case study on pages 363–364 and Figure 11.7.

Open bands database
Open track sales database and get details of first track
    Get number of tracks sold
    Calculate royalty payment
    Add payment to be made to band in band royalties database
    Move to next tracks and repeat process until end of tracks
Close databases
Arrange for payment to band

Note the use of indents to structure sections of the text – this is used in a very similar way in some programming languages. If necessary, individual sub-processes, such as 'Calculate royalty payment', may need additional detail – perhaps using a different type of process descriptor.

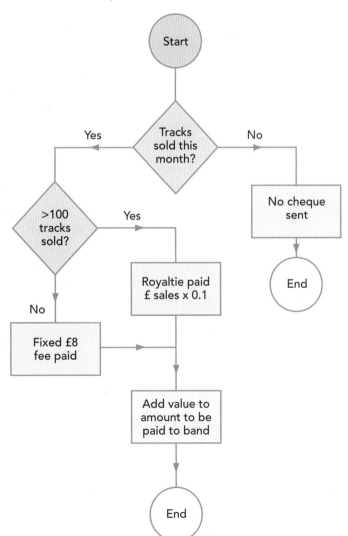

Figure 11.7: Flow chart – calculation of royalty payment

Did you know?

Programmers often design programs using structured English but call it pseudocode. For more on pseudocode, see *Unit 6: Software design and development*, page 187.

Case study Part 1: Express Tracks

Express tracks is a relatively small music distribution company specialising in the sales of individual tracks from new bands over the Internet. The company started when one individual – Pat Kay (now the managing director) started selling his own music using the Internet and then naturally expanded to include other bands. After signing up, bands are paid a royalty fee approximately each month based on the sales.

The volume of tracks and turnover of the company has grown beyond the maximum level for manual management and Pat has asked a systems analyst to produce a feasibility report for the development of their royalty payment system. The analyst learns that Pat's mum, Jane, currently handles the accounts and sends out the royalty cheques. There is a third member of the family involved – Pat's son, Henry – who has increasingly been liaising with and signing up new bands, as well as doing some of the royalty calculations when things are busy. Using the information obtained, the analyst has produced the following report.

Feasibility Study: Express Tracks

System: Royalty payment system

Purpose of the system:

- To record details of bands in a database (contact details, type of music, band members, etc.).
- To record for each track what royalties are due to whom and when.
- To calculate royalties due on a monthly cycle.
- To produce standard reports on demand.

System scope:

- Needs to run on a networked system.
- Analysis only to relate to royalty payments.
- System to provide data to a new, yet-to-be devised accounting system.

Out of scope:

- Networking aspects of linked databases (this will be undertaken in-house).
- Tax calculations related to bands (they will do this themselves).

Current deficiencies:

- Current system requires manual input of data and the process of producing the royalty payments takes too much of Jane's time.
- Mistakes are not easily identified.
- Royalty payments are often not paid monthly and some of the bands need a regular income as they are starting out.

- Details of payments made have to be manually entered into the accounting system.

User requirements:

- Reduced need for manual calculations.
- Faster processing and ability to scale upwards as the business expands.
- Improved accuracy.
- Improved detail on reports.
- Automatic collection of sales data and output of accounting data.

Potential benefits:

- The new system will allow Jane to better cope with the current workload and also cope with expansion.
- Fewer complaints from bands – potentially improving retention on their books.
- Easier and more accurate reporting of payments made.
- Side effect of creating an electronic database for bands means that other tasks will be easier to manage.

Constraints:

- Approximate budget of £5000 for purchase of software and development costs.
- System must be tested and in place by 1 April (for next cycle of payments).

Conclusion and recommendations:

Alternative systems could be:

a) A customised database package using macros and some VBA. This would provide reliability and also relative ease of future maintenance. This could be developed within the estimated budget and would take approximately six weeks.

b) A fully bespoke programmed solution. This system provides the greatest potential for flexibility and additional functions could be easily added into the system. However, the costs would exceed the budget and maintenance would require specialist expertise.

c) A simple spreadsheet that was not linked to the other databases in the network. This solution could be developed in-house and, although it could not link with the existing databases, the data entry could be made efficient and it would achieve some of the requirements identified.

Recommendation:

It is recommended that option a) is taken forward.

Note: the database to be created would need to be linked to the existing networked database.

(cont.)

Case study (contd.)

The costs are not estimated here. However, it is estimated that 'one developer day' would be needed to establish and test these links.

1 An initial comment from Jane queries the need for the system to be networked. Outline briefly the arguments that might be used to justify a networked system.

2 Henry has criticised the feasibility study because no mention of backups is made. Consider the importance of this issue and add appropriate statement(s) to the user requirements list.

3 Identify what the implications on the working practices of the three people involved might be and how you would approach managing their concerns and requirements.

4 Explain the disadvantages of adopting alternative systems b) and c).

5 From the material, identify what you think are the key drivers behind the initiative.

Case study Part 2: Investigating the Express Tracks royalty system

The feasibility study has been presented and a decision to go ahead with a more detailed investigation has been agreed. The systems analyst has now been asked to carry out the investigation stage. Initial thoughts are that at least the following information should be collected.

- **Data types, sources and flows:** Where does the information come from about how many copies of each track have been sold? How does Henry know what percentage to pay each writer? Does all the data come from the same place or does it come from different sources? What other databases, if any, are used and what are their structures, field names, key fields, etc.? Are any backups made of previous amounts paid and to whom?

- **Decisions taken and types of processing:** What equations are used – does everyone get the same percentage? How often are the payments made?

- **Storage methods:** How does Henry store the data used? Where is it kept? Is historic data kept?

- **Documents:** Are there any procedure manuals available? Are past records, letters, reports, etc. available of what has been done before?

- **Types of output:** What are the outputs of the system? How is the money paid to the bands? Does anyone want any new reports? If so, what do the required reports look like? Is any other output needed?

- **Technology:** What is the specification of the existing PC and the network that it is connected to? What storage and backup facilities are available? What are the existing skill levels of the employees?

1 For each area above, identify which investigative method or combinations of methods you think would work best.

2 List the order in which you think the individual investigation activities should take place and who should be involved.

Remember

- Often a blend of different investigative techniques are needed to effectively capture all of the requirements.

- Studies of existing documents and real observation can provide very rich sources of information about current processes.

- Defining what is out of scope can help to ensure that everyone understands what is in scope for the investigation and analysis.

- Maintaining an open mind throughout is important to avoid personal or predetermined opinions dominating the analysis.

Assessment activity 11.2

(P4) BTEC

This Assessment activity is linked to Assessment activity 11.1 on page 353 which you will need to refer back to.

Using the investigation materials provided, carry out and document a structured analysis of the current (As-Is) customer service system used at Parry's.

You are asked to provide DFDs, inputs, outputs and processes. **P4**

Grading tips

Decide on the structure of your report. Read the material provided a number of times and highlight information that is relevant (e.g. a constraint, a process, an output, etc.). For each one decide which section in the report it will be relevant to. Once you feel you have extracted as much information as possible then write the final report using your notes. You cannot 'invent' new material, but you might want to state assumptions. **P4**

PLTS

As an **independent enquirer** there is a wealth of information contained in the materials provided for this assignment. Try breaking it down sentence by sentence to be sure that you have extracted the maximum detail.

Functional skills

There are a number of opportunities to collect evidence that will contribute to **English** Functional skills, particularly Reading and Writing at level 2.

3.2 Constraints

One of the most important constraints on a new system is money and, at this stage, some estimation of the costs of the project will have to be balanced against the potential benefits. The costs are often difficult to estimate accurately and, in many real-life situations, people are overly optimistic.

The costs need to include such things as hardware, software and development costs. In addition to these obvious costs, the analyst must think more widely and consider perhaps the cost of training users in the new system, any changes in employee costs, and so on. The benefits may be even more difficult to identify. Some may be easy to quantify, such as financial savings in linked employee redundancy. But less tangible benefits that might have been stated in the requirements, such as 'improved customer service' or 'increased sales', are particularly difficult to measure.

Other constraints might be organisational policies, timescale, the need to integrate with existing systems, the available hardware systems or staff expertise in the company.

Training users is one of many costs that may arise on a project.

Case study: J P Higgins

A large American DIY chain has taken over three small DIY outlets in the UK as a test run before engaging in further acquisitions. Some preliminary investigation has suggested that that the UK market is more open to self-service checkouts than the US market and a more detailed study has been initiated. Although the chain does have business analysts, it has been decided that a UK-based consultancy, J P Higgins, will be used to ensure good understanding of the UK dimension.

You have been employed by J P Higgins for six months and prior to that you have worked as an analyst-programmer at a large supermarket. While at school and college, you worked as a checkout operator at the supermarket and have completed an HND in Computing. The project has been categorised as a priority and a partner has been allocated to lead it.

1 Construct a memo to the partner asking to be attached to this work. Emphasise what you think you can bring to the project and what you feel are the key aspects of the investigation to focus on.

2 Devise an outline plan for the part of the investigation which deals with understanding the customer side – concerns and benefits.

3 The key driver relates to cost-saving. On the basis of the following assumptions undertake an order of magnitude calculation to decide whether it is possible that the costs will be worth the money saved within a three-year period.

Hardware costs: £100,000

Software costs: £50,000

Estimated annual maintenance of the system and support costs: £10,000

One checkout operator can now look after six tills instead of one till because they are self-service

– annual salary and on-costs per checkout operator = £20,000

– customer throughput remains the same.

State any further assumptions you have made.

Assessment activity 11.3

 **:BTEC**

This Assessment activity follows on from Assessment activities 11.1 and 11.2 (pages 353 and 365).

1 Using the investigation materials, produce a requirements specification in terms of a prioritised list of requirements for Parry's. **P5**

2 In addition, be creative and suggest alternative solutions and also undertake a cost–benefit analysis. **M2**

3 The design specification should include (unless otherwise indicated by your tutor) the following:
   • ERDs
   • data dictionary
   • logical DFDs for the 'To-Be' system
   • process descriptors
   • screen designs
   • report layouts.

4 On the basis of the requirements specification, independently generate and document a design specification. **P6**

5 Explain any constraints. **M3**

Grading tips

For P5 use the suggested structure of a typical requirements specification as a start (see 2.3, page 358) – although you may need to modify it to suit this situation. **P5**

For M2 look for ideas in other small businesses and think about how the Internet might be used, but remember that high-tech solutions are not always the best ones. **M2**

• In your work on cost benefit analysis for D1, it can help to separate 'soft' benefits from 'hard' ones. Soft benefits are ones that are less easily defined in terms of money, but often represent the most important reasons why the system needs to change. **D1**

• To gain D2, you will need to show that you have worked independently. This will be judged by your tutor and if you are targeting this grade then ask for guidance as to how much help they will give before the help they give becomes too much to assign you this grade. **D2**

PLTS

The more significant opportunity is to provide development of **creative thinking**, particularly in questions 1–3.

Functional skills

The production of the written report gives opportunity to provide evidence for **English** Functional skills.

Michael Wagner

Analyst

My name is Michael and I work as an analyst in the IT department of a large retailing company. The IT department helps the business achieve its goals and make the company profitable by redeveloping existing systems and introducing new systems that improve productivity in store and also give the customers better shopping experiences.

I capture requirements, design the screens and reports that will be needed. I am also responsible for the final stages of user acceptance testing before the system is introduced into the stores. This last responsibility is an important one and I am always a little tense when a system is rolled out into the stores in case something goes wrong.

A typical day

There is not a typical day – what I do is very dependent on which life cycle stage of the project we have reached. At the beginning I spend a lot of time with the users (clients), as well as with the business team discussing issues and improvements. I always need to check the costs of the changes and then once we have agreed the detail of the changes, we can move on to the next stage. Later, I check progress of the development, answer queries from the development team and keep the business team and customers updated.

Best things about the job

Every day is different. I enjoy the contact with the business team and the customers and the general sense that I am helping the business move forward. I move from project to project on a regular basis and this brings me into contact with different people in the company, which is interesting. Retail is a fast-moving sector and we also routinely look at leading-edge technologies, which is enjoyable at a technical level.

Think about it!

1 When Michael uses the word 'customers' in the last paragraph, who do you think he means?

2 Michael has a lot of interaction with people. What 'soft' skills do you think you need to develop in order to do this part of the job well?

3 If a global catastrophe caused the end of the technological basis of our society and the world reverted to being an agricultural society, what skills and knowledge related to IT systems analysis would still be of value do you think?

Just checking

1 Why is a structured approach necessary?

2 Name at least five potential reasons why a piece of analysis work might be initiated.

3 What is the main problem with the classic waterfall life cycle model that requires it to be modified?

4 Why are a number of levels of DFDs needed?

5 Why should an analyst spend a lot of time in the investigation phase?

6 An analyst needs to know what is in scope for a project – why might he/she also look at what is out of scope as well?

7 Why use a range of investigation techniques – why not just pick one of them?

8 Name any one potential benefit of a new system that is difficult to quantify.

9 Name a cost that is very easy to quantify.

10 What is a legacy system and why is it seen as a constraint?

Assignment tips

- In your work on cost–benefit analysis for D1, it can help to separate 'soft' benefits from 'hard' ones. Soft benefits are ones that are less easily defined in terms of money, but often represent the most important reasons why the system needs to change. **D1**

- To gain D2, you will need to show that you have worked independently. This will be judged by your tutor and if you are targeting this grade then ask for guidance as to how much help they will give before the help they give becomes too much to assign you this grade. **D2**

14 Event driven programming

Many modern programming languages are event driven, as this is an approach that works well with computers using GUI (graphical user interface) operating systems such as Windows®. This type of programming uses events such as clicking on a button, or moving the mouse pointer over an object as the trigger to run the appropriate code handler, whereas the older style of programming, often called flow driven, only started from one point at the beginning of the code.

As you study this unit you will improve your programming skills, as well as learn how to design and test event driven programs. The designs of these programs should meet identified needs so they fulfil the defined purposes.

You will need to be able to use the tools and techniques of an event driven language by placing controls on to a form and writing code to respond to the events they receive. Code for these event handlers will use constants, variables, loop and selection structures to produce appropriate pathways through the code. You will also recognise the importance of thorough, structured testing of your code using various techniques and be able to review completed code against the original requirements to see how well they have been met.

Learning outcomes

After completing this unit you should be able to:

1. understand the features of event driven programming
2. be able to use the tools and techniques of an event driven language
3. be able to design event driven applications
4. be able to implement event driven applications.

Assessment and grading criteria

This table shows you what you must do in order to achieve a pass, merit or distinction grade, and where you can find activities in this book to help you.

To achieve a **pass** grade the evidence must show that you are able to:	To achieve a **merit** grade the evidence must show that, in addition to the pass criteria, you are able to:	To achieve a **distinction** grade the evidence must show that, in addition to the pass and merit criteria, you are able to:
P1 explain the key features of event driven programs **See Assessment activity 14.1, page 379**	**M1** discuss how an operating system can be viewed as an event driven application **See Assessment activity 14.1, page 379**	**D1** evaluate the suitability of event driven programs for non-graphical applications **See Assessment activity 14.1, page 379**
P2 demonstrate the use of event driven tools and techniques **See Assessment activity 14.2, page 389**	**M2** give reasons for the tools and techniques used in the production of an event driven application **See Assessment activity 14.2, page 389**	
P3 design an event driven application to meet defined requirements **See Assessment activity 14.3, page 398**		
P4 implement a working event driven application to meet defined requirements **See Assessment activity 14.3, page 398**		
P5 test an event driven application **See Assessment activity 14.3, page 398**	**M3** analyse actual test results against expected results to identify discrepancies **See Assessment activity 14.3, page 398**	**D2** evaluate an event driven application **See Assessment activity 14.3, page 398**
P6 create on-screen help to assist the users of a computer program **See Assessment activity 14.3, page 398**	**M4** create technical documentation for the support and maintenance of a computer program **See Assessment activity 14.3, page 398**	

How you will be assessed

This unit will be assessed by internal assignments that will be designed and marked by the staff at your centre. It may be subject to sampling by your centre's Lead Internal Verifier or an Edexcel Standards Verifier as part of Edexcel's ongoing quality assurance procedures. Assignments are designed to allow you to show your understanding of the unit outcomes. These relate to what you should be able to do after completing this unit.

Your tutor will tell you precisely what form your assessments will take, but you could be asked to produce:

- presentations
- case studies
- practical tasks
- written assignments.

Crisold Butler, BTEC National IT learner

It's a little hard, this unit, but after getting a few ideas of what needs to be done and some help from the tutor, I started to understand what programming's about and what to do. We worked in small groups, so we could help and support each other. We got to learn about programming and also how other people understand things.

The assignments were quite long for this unit. The first was easier as it was about the basics of programming, but the others were a bit harder. The final assignment in the unit has made me use all my skills that I have achieved throughout the year. It is not an easy task to get all the grades in the unit, but keeping up with the workload will help you achieve the highest grades.

When I want to make a program at home, it is really easy now. I made one based on our animation exercise at college which takes some jpg pictures and animates them by loading them one after another into a picture box. The program uses a timer control to do this.

If you understand programming you can do anything with computers. I am taking the Networking pathway through my National Diploma, but I know my understanding of programming will be useful to help understand what others do with computers.

Over to you

- **Crisold found programming hard. Can you find three ways your programming language environment helps the programmer to make writing a program easy?**
- **If you were asked to write a program that shows an animation, how would you approach designing it?**
- **In what ways do you think an understanding of programming would be of use to an IT networking practitioner?**

1. Understand the features of event driven programming

1.1 Key features

This section identifies the key features that differentiate **event** driven programming language techniques from the more traditional flow driven programming languages such as Pascal.

Event driven programs are typically used with GUI operating systems, where many types of events are generated, such as when the user clicks the mouse on a button or another **object**. Typical uses of event driven programs include word processors, spreadsheets, databases and drawing packages. This list is just the beginning, as almost all modern software is event driven.

Event driven programming techniques can also be deployed in scenarios other than GUIs and forms – they are typically applied in networking and file-handling operations to handle streams of incoming data within indefinite loops.

These are the key characteristics of event driven programming languages.

- They have **event handlers**, i.e. code that runs when an event occurs.
- Trigger functions are the mechanisms that decide which code runs when an event occurs.
- Events are actions such as a form loading or the user clicking their mouse.

- Event loops are built into the framework to keep checking to find out if an event has occurred.
- Forms are used to contain objects which experience events.

Key terms

GUI – stands for graphical user interface. This means that the operating system can be controlled with a mouse by clicking on buttons, menus or similar objects.

Event – anything that happens to an object when the program is running.

Objects – different from procedures in that they group program instructions and data together. An object may be either visual or non-visual. A visual object is anything on a form, such as a button. An example of a non-visual object is the PrintDocument object of VB.NET which can be used by a program to produce hardcopy on to paper.

Event handler – code that runs when an event occurs.

Service oriented

A lot of networked software applications use service-oriented techniques so that different apps (applications) can reuse code components. Departments within a company could develop and deploy services using different programming languages. Other software apps can then benefit from these services, for example to request data from a database. **XML** is commonly used for interfacing with such service-oriented architectures, though this is not essential.

Service-oriented architectures provide a loosely integrated collection of services that can be used within multiple business domains, good for networks and web-based applications.

Service-oriented architectures are split into components, services, and processes. Components are small program segments that are grouped into services that can be used by programs (processes). A service is a grouping of the components needed to get a program job done. The service offers a single interface for applications and other services to use through a loosely coupled message-based communication model.

Service-oriented applications separate the service implementation from the program interface that uses the service. How a service executes the request by a **service consumer** is irrelevant as all that is needed is for the correct data to be sent back to the service consumer.

Time driven

Time-driven programming is a type of computer programming that is often used in real-time computing, where code execution is controlled by the computer clock. A program is divided into a set of tasks that need to be regularly activated. The activation pattern is stored in a dispatch table, where rules are used to schedule running the tasks.

This programming paradigm is mostly used for safety-critical programs, because the behaviour of the program is highly deterministic. No external events are allowed to affect the program running and rules in the dispatch table will run reliably time after time.

Event handlers

Most modern programs have forms that show when the program runs with **controls** on them. Controls are objects on the form such as a label, button or check box. Many event driven programming environments such as VB.NET (see Figure 14.1) have a toolbox showing objects that can be added to forms.

Most objects have a large variety of possible events, which might include click, double click, mouse down and many more.

A	Label
A	LinkLabel
ab	Button
ab	TextBox
	MainMenu
✓	CheckBox
⊙	RadioButton
[xy]	GroupBox
	PictureBox
[ ]	Panel
	DataGrid
	ListBox
	CheckedListBox
	ComboBox
	ListView
	TreeView
	TabControl
	DateTimePicker
	MonthCalendar
	HScrollBar
	VScrollBar
	Timer
+|+	Splitter
	DomainUpDown

Figure 14.1: VB.NET toolbox objects

Different types of objects have different collections of events. The events appropriate for a text box are not the same as the events for a button, as they are used in very different ways. An event triggers the appropriate event handler.

VB.NET uses **subroutines** for event handling, with the name of the object followed by an underscore then the name of the event, for example btnQuit_Click.

Key terms

XML – The Extensible Markup Language (XML) is an open standard for documents particularly useful for websites as they can include tags for search engines.

Service consumer – an application, service, or other type of software module requiring a service.

Control – a visual object such as a button or a combo box.

Subroutine – a self-contained section of program also known as a procedure. Subroutines in VB.NET must have Sub and the name of the subroutine in their first line with End Sub as the last line with code between these lines.

Trigger functions

Event driven programming languages use trigger functions to select which event handler to run according to which event occurred.

Every object has a range of trigger functions, one for each possible event that can happen to it. A text box in VB.NET has a trigger function for the GotFocus event, another for the TextChanged event and others for all the other events.

VB.NET also allows the programmer to create user-defined controls that can be used in a similar way to other objects in a program. When creating such a control, the programmer must define the trigger functions, otherwise there will be no properties or methods for the control.

A Get structure is written for every property that can be retrieved from the control. Set structures are used for properties that can be changed by the programmer. This part of programming a new control is called exposing the interface.

Events

There are many, many possible events that can trigger the event handlers to run. Here are some examples.

- The mouse events include left click, double left click, right click, and hover.
- The keyboard events include key press, key down and key up.
- HTML object events include clicking on an object which might then connect to a linked web page.
- Form events include the load event when the form appears for the first time and the activate event, used when a form regains focus. See the Forms section on this page for more detail. Form events can also trigger event handlers for objects on the form such as defining accept button code for when the user uses the enter key on a form.
- User interface events include anything that the user does with a GUI operating system or to the form of a running program.

Event loops

Event driven programming languages need to have event loops built into them at a level the programmer would not normally be aware of. The event loops are needed to keep testing the user interface to detect whether anything has happened, such as clicking on a button or typing into a text box.

If an event is detected, the event is passed to the trigger functions, which then call the appropriate event handler to run any code in the program that was designed and written for the event.

Event driven programming languages often include provision for programmers to create bespoke event loops (also known as event listeners) to enhance the functionality of their applications and make them more flexible. This is because it would be impossible for the designers of programming languages to provide events for every imaginable circumstance.

Forms

Forms are a major feature of most event driven programming environments, as they are what the user sees when the program runs.

Forms are used to hold all the controls the programmer used to create the program.

Forms are also a type of control so have a collection of events that may be used by the programmer. These form events are a very powerful way of controlling a program, especially when the program loads and ends. Here are two examples of form events.

- **Load** is the event that occurs when a form is first used. The load event is useful for code which needs to set variables, default values and other matters which need to be done just the once.
- **Activated** is an event that occurs every time the form receives the focus (is brought up). The activated event is very useful for updating a form when the user returns to it from another form. A program might call another form to enter details of a sale. When returning to the main form, the activated event could bring up a summary of the sale on the main form.

Flexibility

Flexibility is a great advantage of event driven programming, as the programmer has enormous control over where to place code and how to start it.

Every object has a good choice of events that a program can respond to. These events give you excellent control over exactly what the program will respond to when the user does something.

A good example of this is the text box. Usually there is a choice of events giving fine programming control over anything typed into it. The programming language C# includes these choices:

- Enter, when the text box becomes the active control (receives the focus)
- KeyDown, when the text box is active and at the start of when a key is pressed
- KeyPress, when a key is pressed
- KeyUp, when a key is released.

KeyDown, KeyPress and KeyUp events all respond in slightly different ways to when a user types into the text box. Many programmers would choose the KeyPress event as this summarises the other two, but there are times when more control is needed, so the program could respond to when the user presses the key (KeyDown event) as well as the exact moment when key is released (KeyUp).

- MouseUp – when the m
  form/control and the m
- MouseLeave – when the
  form/control
- MouseMove – when the
  over the form/control
- MouseWheel – when the
  the form/control has fo
- MouseHover – when the
  the form/control.

2.2 Tools and te

Use of tool boxes an

Controls are objects that
usually by selecting a con
dragging the mouse on to
the control object.

The VB.NET toolbox (see
quite similar to the C# too
have collections of the fol

- Windows® Forms tool:
  form.
- Components for addir
  the form.
- Data for connecting to

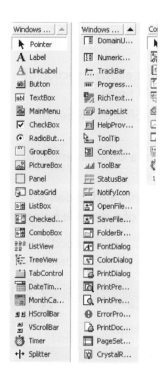

Figure14.10: C# toolbox of

Similarly, there are good choices of events for all the other controls. Figure 14.2 shows some of the events VB.NET offers for a button. Figure 14.3 shows some of the events C# offers for a button.

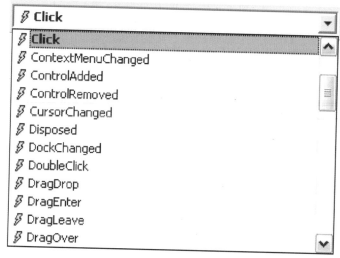

Figure 14.2: Some VB.NET button events

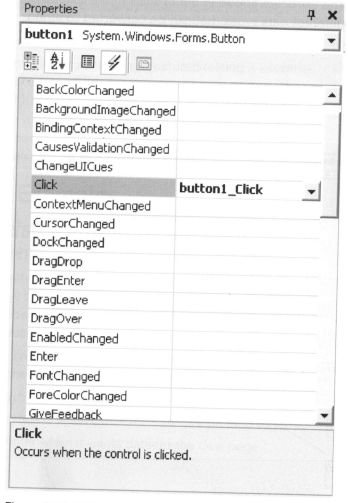

Figure 14.3: C# button

VB.NET events are all available by default, whereas events for C# need to be selected from the Properties box before they are available for coding. The screenshot in Figure 14.3 shows that there is no code for any event of the control shown, apart from the Click event.

Suitability for graphical interfaces

Event driven programs are very suitable for graphical user interfaces (GUIs) as they are an excellent match for each other. A GUI presents the user with a wide variety of graphical choices and menus that can be used with the mouse or keyboard (or other input devices), usually with no set sequence that the user must follow.

An event driven programming language will use this GUI approach to give the user a variety of controls. Each control reacts to events with code that is just right for each event and for how the program is expected to be used.

Most controls are quite independent from each other, so the code will be modularised into event handlers.

Simplicity of programming

Event driven programming languages can make programming very simple compared to traditional flow driven languages, because the programming language is very visual.

A control such as a button can easily be put on to a form from the toolbox. When it is on the form, the programmer can see it. The programmer may choose to see the properties of the control while writing the program (see Figure 14.4). This can simplify programming as there is a lot more information available.

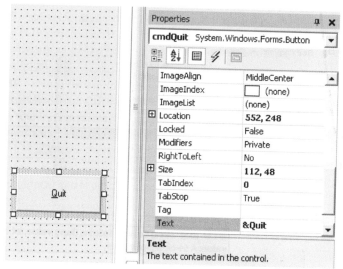

Figure 14.4: C# button properties

2. Be able t
   event dri

2.1 Triggers

Triggers are a wide variety
events. They include:

- key press to trigger eve
  example pressing a key
- alarm triggers, for exam
  paper
- system event triggers, f
  ending or low memory
- touch screen events, fo
  where a stylus has press
- mouse click to trigger e
  user moves or clicks th

Key press

The key press trigger can b
that need to respond to se
validate data entry or to co

Validation should be used
sure that data entering a p
and complete. If bad data
be dire consequences, suc
output from the program d

The key press trigger cou
different keys have differe
direction of travel.

Many business applicatic
respond to the enter key
code to accept and use a

- **Processes** – brings up a window showing processes running on the computer, similar to the Windows® Task Manager, but with a lot more detail and control over which processes are shown; includes the ID numbers of each process which could be useful if the programmer wishes to hook into them.
- **Exceptions dialogue box** (see Figure 14.15) – gives control over how the IDE handles errors and allows the programmer to instruct the IDE to ignore and continue if a specified type of error occurs, for example division by zero, by replacing the system message with one the programmer prefers.
- **Step Into and Step Over** – both run code a line at a time, very useful when the program has been paused by a breakpoint. When code calls a subroutine, Step Into runs the subroutine line by line, whereas Step Over runs all the subroutine as one step.
- **New Breakpoint** – adds a breakpoint to the code; this looks like a brown highlight on the line and will pause the program when it gets there. This is very useful to show the program actually runs the code with the breakpoint or to pause the program so Step Into can be used to run the lines of code one at a time.
- **Clear All Breakpoints** – removes all the breakpoints that have been placed in the program at once.
- **Enable All Breakpoints** – activates them if the Breakpoints window has been used to disable some of the breakpoints.

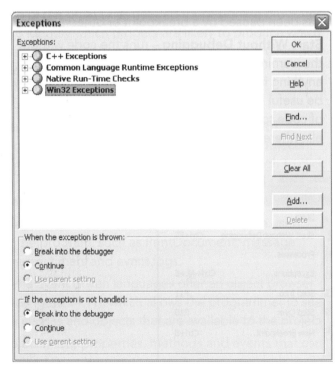

Figure 14.15: C# Exceptions dialog box

2.3 Variables

Most programs need data to work. Data is the name given to numbers, words or other values that are used by a program.

Programs use variables and constants to hold data when the program is running. Data inside a variable can change (vary) as the program runs. **Constants** have their value set once then the value does not change (stays constant).

Variables

A variable is a name used by a program to represent a value that can change.

Some people like to think of variables as similar to pigeonholes (see Figure 14.16), each with a name, for example BookingRef, and holding a value, for example Br2034.

Data types

Every piece of data used by a program has a type which defines the way the data is stored in memory and how it can be used in calculations, comparisons, etc.

Numerics such as 11 or 12 have very different requirements to strings such as eleven or twelve. Not only can the numerics be involved in arithmetic operations such as multiplication or subtraction but they will be stored differently in memory.

Some event driven programs allow variables without having to declare the data types. If there is no data type for a variable, it takes on a default type of variant.

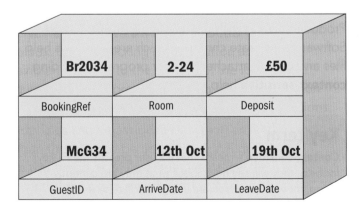

BookingRef	Room	Deposit
Br2034	2-24	£50
GuestID	ArriveDate	LeaveDate
McG34	12th Oct	19th Oct

Figure 14.16: Variables as pigeonholes

Using **variant variables** is considered bad practice as it places unnecessary overheads on the program and reduces reliability.

Key terms

Constant – similar to a variable in that it is a name in code that represents a value, but different in that the value does not change.

Variant variables – variables that respond to the data given to them and adapt as the program runs to whatever is put inside them.

Data types enable programmers to define what sort of data is to be held in each variable. This is useful for two main reasons:

- **speed** – the program will run faster as it will keep data in the most suitable format in memory, allowing faster, easier data manipulation.

- **reliability** – the program will show run-time errors early in testing if unexpected data are assigned to a variable with a declared data type. The program will become more reliable as the programmer will have to reconsider exactly what type of data is correct for the variable and either change the data type declaration or modify the program so the unexpected data arrives in the correct form.

These are some of the many data types available:

- **Boolean** – holds one of two values: true or false.
- **Char** – holds Unicode characters, including those from virtually every language in the world.
- **Date** – holds a calendar date, useful for calculations such as how long between two dates.
- **Floating point** – holds virtually any number.
- **Integer** – holds whole numbers; the integer data type usually has a definite number of bytes in memory:
  - Byte – using 8 bits to store **unsigned** integers in the range 0–255.
  - Smallint, using 16 bits to store **signed** integers, giving a range of -32,768 to 32,767.
  - Int, using 32 bits to store signed integers, giving a range of -2,147,483,648 to 2,147,483,647.
- **String** – holds words and sentences.

The names given to data types may be different in different programming languages (see Table 14.2).

Key terms

Unsigned – when a number is treated as positive. In programming, unsigned usually means that the most significant digit (MSD) of a binary number (the leftmost digit) is simply part of the number.

Signed – when a number is treated as positive or negative. In programming, this usually means that the most significant digit (MSD) of a binary number (the leftmost digit) is used to define whether the number is positive (MSD is 0) or negative (MSD is 1).

Table 14.2: Names given to data types in different programming languages. (Source: Microsoft Corporation®; Visual Studio® help pages)

Storage size	VB	Visual C++	C#
16 bytes	n/a	VARIANT	n/a
Decimal	Decimal (.NET Framework class)	DECIMAL	decimal
Date	Date (.NET Framework class)	DATE	DateTime (.NET Framework class)
(varies)	String (.NET Framework class)	n/a	string
1 byte	Byte	BYTE, bool	byte
2 bytes	Boolean	VARIANT_BOOL	bool
2 bytes	Short, Char (Unicode character)	signed short int, __int16	short, char (Unicode character)
1 byte	n/a	signed char, __int8	
4 bytes	Integer	long, (long int, signed long int)	int
8 bytes	Long	__int64	long
4 bytes	Single	Float	float
8 bytes	Double	Double	double

Declaring variables

To declare a variable the programmer inserts a line of code defining the name of the variable. Usually the declaration includes the data type for the variable. Different programming languages have different **syntax**.

The VB.NET code for declaring a variable named UserScore with data type of integer is:

```
Dim UserScore As Integer
```

The C# code for declaring a variable named UserScore with data type of integer is:

```
Int UserScore;
```

A variable is said to be definitely assigned if it is given a value when it is declared.

The VB.NET code for the definite assignment of a variable named UserScore with data type of integer and value of 12 is:

```
Dim UserScore As Integer = 12
```

The C# code for the definite assignment of a variable named UserScore with data type of integer is:

```
Int UserScore = 12;
```

Arrays

An array is a type of variable that can hold many items of data using a number inside brackets at the end of the variable named called the subscript, to identify which item in the array is to be used.

An array declared as Members(100) could hold 101 items of data, which could be member names (numbering starts at 0, hence 101). This is called a one-dimensional array as there is one subscript.

A two dimensional array has two subscripts, e.g. TestResults(12, 50) which can be thought of as a table-like structure with 13 columns and 51 rows.

Scope of variables

Using a variable outside its **scope** should return an error stating that it has not been recognised.

- **Local variables** have their scope restricted to only the procedure where the variable is declared.

- **Form variables** are declared within the general declarations section at the top of the code for the form. They can be used inside any of the procedures associated with that form.

- **Global variables** can be used anywhere in a project.

Professional programmers are very aware of the scope of variables and ensure that their scoping is tight, with variables only holding values in the parts of the program that need them. Tight scoping limits the available places where values may be changed in variables and thus decreases the likelihood of errors.

Good coding leads on from good design and the closer the program keeps to the design specification the better.

Constants

Constants are very powerful for programs where a value is needed which does not change, but might be different at some point in the future if the program needs modification.

For example, the standard rate of VAT was 17.5 per cent for many years, so a programmer might have been tempted simply to use the number in calculations. The code for a VAT calculation using the number might be:

$$VATcharged = SubTotal * 0.175$$

$$Total = VATcharged + SubTotal$$

However the VAT rate changed to 20 per cent in 2011. In order to carry out **program maintenance**, the programmer would have to find every place in the program where the VAT figure occurs and change it. This could be time-consuming and one or two calculations might be missed, resulting in the program giving inconsistent results.

Key terms

Syntax – the structure and order of the language. In English, 'door to go the' is not understandable as the syntax is wrong, whereas 'go to the door' is very clear as the syntax is correct. Similarly, programming languages need the syntax to be correct or the code cannot be understood.

Scope – how much of the program a variable is usable within.

Program maintenance – the stage in the systems development life cycle (SDLC) when programs are tweaked to remove bugs that are found during use and to make small improvements.

The code for a VAT calculation using a constant might be:

VATcharged = SubTotal * VATrate

Total = VATcharged + SubTotal

In this case, when the VAT rate changes, the programmer only needs to change the one line of code where the constant was defined. This will be quick to do and also result in a program that gives consistent results.

Activity: Program using loops and variables

1 Write a small program to demonstrate the use of these event driven tools and techniques:
- a definite loop
- an indefinite loop.
- menus.

This program will consist of two text boxes on a form with five buttons for next, previous, save and load as well as closing the program.

There will be a 2D array (scoped to the form) dimensioned as People(2,100) to hold some names and ages.

There will be a form variable, LastPerson, to remember how many items in the array have been used.

There will be a form variable, CurrentPerson, to remember which item in the array is currently being shown in the text boxes.

The form load event will be used to assign four names and ages to the array.

The next and previous will each need code to move through the People () array, showing each name and age in the text boxes.

The save and load buttons will each need code to write the People() array to disk (save) as a text file or read this text file from disk into the People() array.

The save button will use a definite loop to go through items in People(), writing each to the text file. This definite loop will use the LastPerson variable for the number of iterations.

The load button will use an indefinite loop to go input items into People(), until reaching the end of the text file. This indefinite loop will set the LastPerson variable to the number of iterations.

Add a menu to allow the user an alternative method of saving and loading the data file.

2 Produce a screenshot of the program as it runs, pasted into a document which has your name, program title and which tools and techniques the program demonstrates.

3 Produce a code print of the program taken directly from the IDE using the File, Print menu option.

This program can be part of your evidence for P2.

Assessment activity 14.2

Your work at Apps R Us is going well (see Assessment activity 14.1). Sabrina needs to prepare for your first appraisal, a meeting you will have with her to formally review your performance as a junior programmer with Apps R Us.

As your job has a strong programming element, she needs to have evidence of your abilities and understanding of event driven programming in preparation for the meeting.

1 You are to produce some small programs to demonstrate the use of the following event driven tools and techniques. Evidence for these will include the following.
- A screenshot of each program as it runs, pasted into a document which has your name, program title and an explanation of how the tools and techniques that the program demonstrates were used.
- A code print of each program taken directly from IDE using File, Print menu of program development environment, with annotations to identify where the tools and techniques were used.
- A small program to demonstrate the use of objects, event handlers and object properties with selection using If.. Then... Else structures.
- A small program to demonstrate the use of menus, loops, both definite and indefinite, with the use of variables. **P2**

To achieve progression in the team you also need to demonstrate skill in report writing.

2 Produce a report justifying the tools and techniques used in the production of your applications. **M2**

Grading tips
- Make sure you produce evidence demonstrating the use of event driven tools and techniques with lots of screenshots, printed code and explanations. **P2**
- You must give reasons why you chose your tools and techniques for your application, so should also include other tools and techniques you could have used, and why your choices were more appropriate. **M2**

3. Be able to design event driven applications

As an IT practitioner you should be aware of how programs are produced, particularly:

- specification – to define what the program needs to do
- design – to plan how the program will look and run
- creation – to produce the program and eliminate the initial bugs.

The stages used to design and create an event driven application are very similar to any other type of program, except that the program is treated as a collection of events with each event identified and its actions defined.

3.1 Specification

User need

The user need is a sensible starting point for most programming projects. A recognised user need is often the initiation of a development life cycle and should be recorded in the specification to ensure the proposed program meets the need.

Purpose

The purpose of the program is stated in the specification. This will be linked to the user need.

Input

All inputs into the program should to be identified, as they must be incorporated into the design. Inputs will be both data and how the controls are to be used.

Data inputs

Data needed by the program should be understood and defined. For instance, if a program is to calculate the amount of paint needed to decorate a wall, the data input will need to include the length and height of the wall so the area can be calculated. The other item of data needed is the paint coverage, that is how many square metres can be covered by a litre of paint. Data inputs should also have their ranges defined.

Control inputs

How controls such as text boxes are used is a vital aspect of planning an event driven program. Processing will need to be planned for each of these anticipated events, such as testing each key press to validate it as a number or to check for the Enter key.

It is important to identify early in the planning what events are expected and what each should do. This will be the basis for which events need coding.

Output

The specification of an event driven application program will include the outputs required, just as for any other type of application. This will usually be the screen and print designs, but may also include any other output device the application will use.

Processes

Processes need to be identified and described in the specification. There will be a process for each anticipated event, as well as processes for shared code, such as a subroutine to update data shown on the form which may be called from any of several controls that take data.

Activity: Job estimator for Pete Taylor

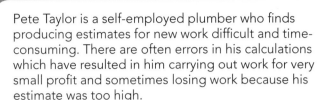

Pete Taylor is a self-employed plumber who finds producing estimates for new work difficult and time-consuming. There are often errors in his calculations which have resulted in him carrying out work for very small profit and sometimes losing work because his estimate was too high.

Pete has approached Apps R Us to get a **bespoke program** written so that his estimates become a lot quicker and more accurate.

The cost of a job includes these elements:

- Labour at £40 per hour
- Travel at £1 a mile
- Plastic pipes at £2 per metre
- Copper pipes at £3 per metre
- Chrome pipes at £4 per metre.

Pete requires the program to run on his laptop, which has a current processor, 2GB of RAM, 120GB of free disk space and a current version of the MS Windows® operating system. The laptop attaches to an inkjet printer that he would like to use to print completed estimates.

1   From these user requirements, produce a design for the form(s) needed by the program. Do this using pencil and paper or a drawing package such as Paint®.

2   From these user requirements, produce a design for the estimate printout needed by the program. This must be actual size, and should be drawn using pencil and paper on to a blank sheet of A4. Careful measurements can then be drawn on to the paper from the top of the page to the top of each object (such as text) on the page and from the left of the page to the left of each object. These X,Y distances will be needed in code to print the estimate.

3   Identify which events are to be used by your program. These will probably be three buttons to produce the estimate, print the estimate and to quit the program.

There are many ways a program like this can use events to meet the requirements – if you design the program to work in a different way, that is fine.

Produce a document entitled 'Data Dictionary: Procedures' with a subheading for each of your identified events. Under each of these subheadings write a description of what the event will do.

4   Identify which variables are to be used by your program, then create a document entitled 'Data Dictionary: Variables'.

5   Produce a test plan for your program.

6   Start a new programming project, produce the form and write code for the events.

7   Test the program to confirm it meets the requirements. Update the test plan with the results of your testing. Document any changes you make to the program when a test is failed.

3.2 Design

After the specification is produced, the needs of the program are understood and the design can be created.

The design is useful as a guide to the programmer(s) and as a communication tool to help management and users understand how the new application will work. This helps avoid wasted effort, as unwanted aspects of the program can be identified before they are actually produced.

Screen layouts

Screen layouts are needed to plan the appearance of forms and how they will be used. Screen layouts may be produced using pencil and paper or using drawing software, as both these methods allow the design to be modified if needed. IT professionals do not use ink for planning, as it is difficult to rub out if changes are needed.

Data storage

Most programs need to store data so that information or documents used by the program are available the next time it runs.

The design will need to identify where data is stored as well as the structure of data. The structure defines what gets saved to disk:

- the sequence – e.g. the data file may have a header section, the main data as records, then a section with **checksums** to ensure no corruption has occurred

- records – what fields are in each record with their data types and sizes.

Key terms

Bespoke program – a program that is written especially for a client. Usually more expensive than 'off-the-shelf' software and more likely to have bugs when first delivered, bespoke is a good option where a client has software needs that are not easily met by commercial, off-the-shelf applications.

Checksum – a calculation on data that is a form of validation, often used during transmissions. The calculation produces a result that is worked out before transmission then sent as a checksum in the last section of data. The receiving computer carries out the same calculation on the data received then compares it with the checksum – if it is different, the data is corrupted and needs to be resent.

Case study:
Cartoon for Anne Merchant

Anne Merchant runs a small music store and wants to purchase a program that will project cartoons on to a large flat screen in the shop.

The cartoons are from a collection of 800 x 600 JPGs and the program should show them in sequence on a form.

Anne requires the program to run on a PC which has a current processor, video at 1024 x 768, 2 GB of RAM, 250 GB of free disk space and a current version of the MS Windows® operating system.

1 From these user requirements, produce a design for the form(s) needed by the program. Do this using pencil and paper or a drawing package such as Paint®.

2 Identify which events are to be used by your program. These will probably be two buttons to start the cartoon and to quit the program.

There are many ways a program like this can use events to meet the requirements – if you design the program to work in a different way, that is fine.

Produce a document entitled 'Data Dictionary: Procedures' with a subheading for each of your identified events. Under each of these subheadings write a description of what the event will do.

3 Identify which variables are to be used by your program, then create a document entitled 'Data Dictionary: Variables'.

4 Produce a test plan for your program.

5 Start a new programming project, produce the form and write code for the events.

6 Test the program to confirm it meets the requirements. Update the test plan with the results of your testing. Document any changes you make to the program when a test is failed.

Event procedures and descriptions

The event procedures relate back to forms and controls and how they are expected to be used. Each event needs a name and description. The description explains what will happen when the event is triggered. This will probably be a paragraph or two of writing for each of the events.

Activity: Booking form for X Ercise

X Ercise is a gym that has approached Apps R Us to have a bespoke booking program written to accept bookings and print out confirmation for the client.

The confirmation print needs this information:

- date of the booking
- time of the booking
- equipment that has been booked
- name of the member of the gym.

The program is to run on a PC which has a current processor, 2 GB of RAM, 150 GB of free disk space and a current version of the MS Windows® operating system. The PC attaches to an inkjet printer to be used for printing confirmations.

1 From these user requirements, produce a design for the form(s) needed by the program. Do this using pencil and paper or a drawing package such as Paint.®

2 From these user requirements, produce a design for the confirmation printout needed by the program. This must be actual size, and should be drawn using pencil and paper on to a blank sheet of A4. Careful measurements can then be drawn on to the paper from the top of the page to the top of each object (such as text) on the page and from the left of the page to the left of each object. These X,Y distances will be needed in code to print the confirmation.

3 Identify which events are to be used by your program. These will probably be two buttons to print the booking confirmation and to quit the program.

There are many ways a program like this can use events to meet the requirements – if you design the program to work in a different way, that is fine.

Produce a document entitled 'Data Dictionary: Procedures' with a subheading for each of your identified events. Under each of these subheadings write a description of what the event will do.

4 Identify which variables are to be used by your program, then create a document entitled 'Data Dictionary: Variables'.

5 Produce a test plan for your program.

6 Start a new programming project, produce the form and write code for the events.

7 Test the program to confirm it meets the requirements. Update the test plan with the results of your testing. Document any changes you make to the program when a test is failed.

Activity: Car for Ray Smith

Ray Smith runs a nursery for children aged 2–4 years old.

The nursery wants a program that can be used by the children to improve their awareness of numbers. The children will choose a number on the keyboard, then drive a car from the form, using the number as the speed of the car.

The nursery requires the program to run on a PC which has a current processor, 2GB of RAM, 250 GB of free disk space and a current version of the MS Windows® operating system.

1   From these user requirements, produce a design for the form(s) needed by the program. Do this using pencil and paper or a drawing package such as Paint®.

2   Identify which events are to be used by your program. These will probably be two buttons to start the car and to quit the program.

There are many ways a program like this can use events to meet the requirements – if you design the program to work in a different way, that is fine.

Produce a document entitled 'Data Dictionary: Procedures' with a subheading for each of your identified events. Under each of these subheadings write a description of what the event will do.

3   Identify which variables are to be used by your program, then create a document entitled 'Data Dictionary: Variables'.

4   Produce a test plan for your program.

5   Start a new programming project, produce the form and write code for the events.

6   Test the program to confirm it meets the requirements. Update the test plan with the results of your testing. Document any changes you make to the program when a test is failed.

Appropriate ways of representing the processing tasks

There are many approaches to representing processing tasks, including: flowchart, structure diagram, pseudocode and action list. The choice of which method(s) to use may depend on the organisation's standards or on the programmer's own view of which method best explains the algorithm.

Flowchart

A flowchart is a diagram that is particularly good at showing program flows. Flowcharts use standard symbols (see Figure 14.17) to represent code, joined by lines to represent the flow of the program from symbol to symbol. These lines are assumed to flow downwards or to the right. Arrow heads may be used on the lines to show if the flow is in a different direction.

Structure diagram

Structure diagrams are good at helping to plan code using a top down approach. Structure diagrams have an implied sequence of top to bottom and left to right (see Figure 14.18).

Pseudocode

Pseudocode is a mix of English and program code and provides a strong feel for how the code will be written, but without the need to actually write and debug it at the design stage of the development.

Action list

An action list consists of bullet points that give the sequence and summarise what the code will do when it is written.

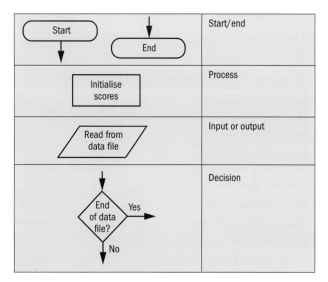

Figure 14.17: Flowchart symbols

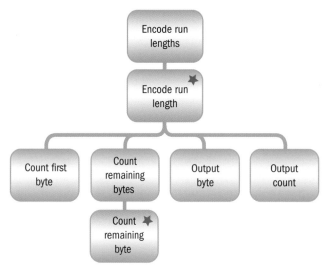

Figure 14.18: Example of a structure diagram

4. Be able to implement event driven applications

4.1 Creation of application

Use of a development environment

Modern event driven languages use an integrated development environment (IDE) (see page 379) to make programming and debugging easier for the programmer – all the tools and facilities are available in the same environment.

Using a modern IDE often has this sequence:

- start the IDE, then either open an existing project for more development or create a new project – for a new project you will need to select the type of application.
- save the new project, giving it a name and creating a new folder for it.
- add controls to the form(s), giving each control a meaningful name.
- add code to the control events that are to be used in the application.
- run the code to correct syntax and simple run-time errors.

Once the program is running reasonably well, the structured testing plan can be implemented.

The VB.NET IDE has these features (see Figure 14.19):

- Solution Explorer – used to keep track of the forms, modules and anything else in the current project, with their names and file locations.
- Main window – shows the forms, code and help screen – the current view is selected using tabs at the top of the window.
- Toolbox – used to select components for the program that can then be dragged on to the form.
- Properties window – gives information and control over the many aspects of components, such as name, position, size, colour, etc.

- Output window – gives debugging information about the current project when it runs, help choices and other information that is selected using tabs at the bottom of this window.

Debugging

Every program needs to be debugged as it is written, otherwise it will not run. There will be a structured test plan later, after the program has been completed, to confirm the program meets the specification.

Event driven languages offer the programmer many tools to help with features such as:

- pausing the program when an error is found, with a message to inform the programmer of the type of error
- Command window used to create a test log or to test code when the program is paused
- Watch window to test values of variables and other objects as the program runs.

Data validation

Good programs do their best to keep bad data out. Bad data entering a program must mean that bad information will be output. (Remember the GIGO acronym from page 380.)

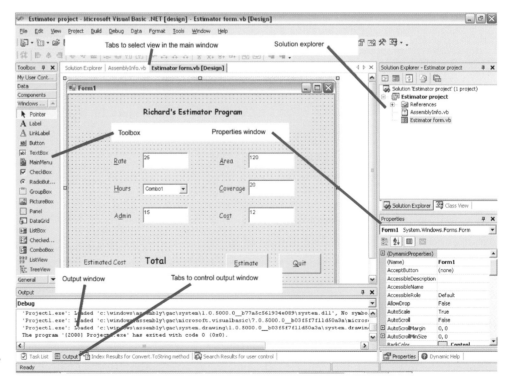

Figure 14.19: Using the VB.NET IDE

Data validation should be programmed into applications to screen out data that is obviously bad. If a date of birth is entered for a new member of staff, then validation should reject any dates where the employee age is too young to be employed or more than the retirement age.

Anything programmed into an application to reject invalid data should give a simple message to the user explaining that an invalid entry has been attempted, where on the form it was entered and also give guidance on what would be valid.

Sensible use of controls can also help keep data valid. A combo box (see page 383) offering all the possible valid choices would make it impossible for invalid data to be entered.

Error handling and reporting

Programs can generate errors when they run, such as expecting to find a disk file which is not there. The error this produces would crash the program. Professional programmers add code to their applications to handle expected errors without crashing and usually send a message to the user to let them know what happened and what to do to resolve the problem. This is also known as handling exceptions.

Sadly, a lot of errors are also caused by poor programming, such as using the contents of a text box in a calculation without the code checking there is something valid in the text box before running the calculation code.

4.2 Programming language syntax

As mentioned earlier (see page 388), programming languages must have the syntax absolutely correct. Any small mistakes and the code will be rejected with the code coloured and underlined to identify where problems are located.

A problem with the code also generates an error message to explain what is wrong with it. Professional programmers are skilled at understanding these error messages to help them debug programs and to make their code work.

4.3 Constructs

A programming construct is when related statements are needed in several lines of code to make a structure work.

Selection constructs include:

- If …then…else, to make a simple selection based on an expression that can be true or false
- Select case, to make a multiple selection, based on a variable or object that can have many values.

Iteration (loop) constructs include:

- For…next, a definite loop
- Repeat…until, an indefinite loop where the condition is tested at the end of the loop
- While…do, an indefinite loop where the condition is tested at the start of the loop.

4.4 Programming standards

Programming standards are there to give guidelines to programmers on how they should approach writing their code. Comments should be used in code to make it self-documenting, with brief explanations of what sections of code do.

The code layout and indentations are usually made by the programming IDE. In older programming languages the programmer needed to indent code to help identify structures in the program.

A common programming standard is the naming of objects with the first three letters lower-case to identify the type of object and the rest of the name as proper noun(s) – so a combo box holding the names of members in a club might be named cboMemberNames.

Programming standards make program code a lot easier to read when everyone in a team writes code in the same style.

4.5 Testing

Testing is always needed when a program is written to ensure it works as expected. Reviewing an event driven application is also needed in order to:

- compare the final product with the original user need
- compare the final product with the program design
- evaluate the ease of use
- identify whether requirements were met and if there are any further development needs.

Test strategy

Testing needs a strategy to make sure that everything that needs testing is checked and to avoid unnecessary duplication of effort.

The test plan strategy may include these sections:

- event testing, to ensure that each of the planned events works without errors and produces the expected results
- **black box testing**, to ensure that pre-prepared test data produces the expected outputs from the program
- **white box testing**, to ensure that all the selections and pathways inside the program code work properly and without errors.

The test plan needs to be kept in a document and should record that corrective actions that are taken each time a test fails. The test should then be re-run to prove the fix worked.

Diagnostic software might be used as part of the testing strategy.

Key terms

Black box testing – when a program is tested without taking into consideration the code inside the program. The program is the 'box' which is 'black', as the tester does not see anything inside it.

White box testing – when a program is tested to make sure each line of the code works. The program is the 'box', which is 'white' as the tester does see inside it.

Diagnostic software – software that attempts to diagnose a problem; it identifies possible faults and offers solutions.

Test plan structure

The test plan is often a table (see Table 14.3). Each row is used for an individual test, with the columns holding information such as:

- the test number – useful so that other parts of the program documentation can easily refer to the test if needed
- a description of what the test is designed to achieve
- the test date – to be filled in when the test is actually carried out
- expected result – so the tester knows what to look for and how the test can be passed

- the actual result must be recorded to show whether the test has passed – if the test fails, this provides useful information for the debugging that must follow
- any corrective action that was taken to fix the bug – this may be a separate section of the test plan documentation.

Error messages

The programmer must be aware of every error message that the IDE shows as the program is written and tested.

Some of these messages can be disregarded, as they will refer to parts of the program that have not yet been written or completed. However, all the other messages will need to be responded to with the issues they identify resolved.

Specialist software tools

Every programming environment provides specialist software tools, such as Debug, which assist in correcting code by giving extra information to the programmer, when needed.

Debug is available to VB.NET, C# and other event driven languages. It can be used to create a log when the program runs and the programmer can examine the log later to see what happened. This can be a very powerful aid to finding errors, as the programmer has a lot of control over when items are added to the log and there is no need to pause the program.

Other specialist software tools for debugging include:

- Locals window – shows the local variables that are in use when the code pauses
- Watch window – creates a collection of variables, the contents of which can be seen 'at a glance' when code pauses.

4.6 Review

A review is needed of every project to confirm that the project is delivering the expected outcomes and is not missing any of the requirements.

Table 14.3: An example of a test plan

Number	Description	Date	Expected result	Actual result	Passed?
1	Main form loads	1/4/10	Form loads without errors	Form loads without errors	Yes

Review against specification requirements

It is essential to review the program against the original specification requirements in order to confirm that the end product is what was originally wanted. Some programmers get side-tracked in their development work (perhaps as a result of solving some programming problems) into producing work which appears to be correct at the time, but which strays away from the original requirements.

This review is also a good check that the end product fulfils the original user needs.

Interim reviews

Interim reviews are useful to check progress both against timescales and in terms of meeting requirements.

Timescales have always been difficult to plan for and meet in programming, as unexpected problems can be discovered during coding which can have considerable impact on the delivery date. The sooner such a problem is discovered the better, as users and management can then be informed of likely delays and, if necessary, extra resources can be put into the project to bring it back to predicted timescales.

Meeting requirements is crucial for the success of the programming. If there is a drift away from the requirements during development, it is important to identify this early on, so that the program can be brought back on course while it is still easy and relatively inexpensive to do so.

4.7 Documentation

Programs need documentation to show the end user what they can do with the program and to explain to other programmers how the program works:

- the user guide is for people using the program
- technical documentation is for the programmers.

User guide

The user guide is there to explain to anyone using the program how to start the program, how to use the program and how to close the program down at the end of a session.

The user guide should have lots of screenshots with simple explanations of how to use the form(s) in the program and their controls, such as combo boxes (see page 383).

There should also be a trouble-shooting section to explain how to deal with any known issues with the program, such as if a default printer needs to be set before the program runs. Such issues would have been identified during the program testing and should have been resolved by the programmer, but any problems that are still there should be identified in the user guide with workarounds.

The user guide will have nothing about programming or code in it, as that will be in the technical documentation.

Technical documentation

The technical documentation is for the programmer, explaining the program design, how it was tested and how the program works. This is useful for any future work that is needed to resolve bugs that are found by users when they work with the program and also for any future modifications that are needed to enhance the application.

The contents of technical documentation will be determined by the organisational standards, including some or all of:

- User requirements
- Program specification
- Program design
  - screen components and their properties
  - data storage
  - event procedures and descriptions
  - data dictionary
  - pseudocode
  - structure diagrams
  - flowcharts
  - form designs
  - print designs
  - test plan and results
- annotated code printouts
- known problems.

The technical documentation will be useful to any programmer needing to modify the code. If the programmer (or programmers) that originally wrote the code makes changes, they will find it useful to be reminded how the program works. If a different programmer needs to make changes they will find the technical documentation makes understanding the code a lot easier.

Assessment activity 14.3

1 The Apps R Us team has been allocated four jobs from clients:
- job estimator for Pete Taylor (see page 391)
- cartoon for Anne Merchant (see page 392)
- booking form for X Ercise (see page 392)
- car for Ray Smith (see page 393).

As the junior programmer you have been given first choice on these jobs so you can choose to produce two programs that are within your capabilities.

2 You will design and implement a working application to meet two of these defined requirements. Evidence for these will be:
- program specification with input, output, processes, user need and purpose
- data storage
- event procedures and descriptions
- planned design for form(s) and printer (if used)
- coding design using pseudocode or flowchart. **P3**

3 Create your program. Evidence for this will be:
- user guide for your program with screenshots of the running program
- code print of each program taken directly from IDE using the File, Print menu option of the program development environment. **P4**

4 Add an on-screen help system. Evidence for this will be:
- screenshots of the help
- written explanation of how the help system was created. **P6**

5 The programs you produced need to be tested:
- written test plan. **P5**

Write a document showing that you have analysed actual test results against expected results to identify

discrepancies. This document should include how you used appropriate debugging tools with explanations of each, including the use of:
- Breakpoints
- Step over
- Step into
- Watch windows. **M3**

6 The programs you produced need technical documentation for the support and maintenance. The documentation for each program will consist of:
- data dictionary
- feedback from other users
- checks against the original specifications. **M4**

7 Produce an evaluation of the program you have written. Include the good and bad aspects your work as well as anything you would do to enhance the program. **D2**

Grading tips

- Make sure your design meets the defined requirements and includes how the program will work. **P3**
- When the program is working, check it again against the requirements. **P4**
- Use a structured test plan and type the results into a table or spreadsheet. **P5**
- The on-screen help for your program should be using .chm files but you could choose. **P6**
- Analyse actual test results against expected results to identify discrepancies. **M3**
- Create technical documentation for the support and maintenance of a computer program. **M4**
- Evaluate your event driven application. **D2**

Functional skills

You will need your **ICT** Functional skills when you enter, develop and refine information using appropriate software to meet the requirements of a complex task as you implement your event driven applications.

The **ICT** Functional skills will also be exercised when you combine and present information in ways that are fit for purpose and audience to create on-screen help and technical documentation to assist users, and to provide support for a computer program.

PLTS

You will demonstrate **creative thinking** when you generate ideas and explore the possibilities to design an event driven application to meet defined requirements.

You are a **self-manager** working towards goals, showing initiative, commitment and perseverance when developing and testing your event driven applications.

You can be a **reflective learner** when communicating your learning by creating on-screen help and technical documentation for support and maintenance of your computer program.

As an **independent enquirer** you will analyse and evaluate an event driven application, judging its relevance and value.

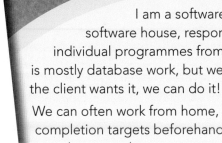

I am a software developer with a software house, responsible for writing and coding individual programmes from client specific requirements. This is mostly database work, but we do get a surprising variety of jobs. If the client wants it, we can do it!

We can often work from home, but my team leader needs to agree with completion targets beforehand. I am expected to be in the office at least two days a week.

I need to interpret written business requirements and technical specification documents then write code to meet these. The specs (specifications) are produced by our systems analysts after consulting with the client.

Testing our software is the most tedious part of the job. To do this we need to investigate, analyse and document any defects we find. This will follow the test plan which is given to us by the analyst with any extra tests we added during coding. The documentation and repetition is the worst part of this. I also maintain other technical documentation for code we write. We maintain programs previously produced for clients and correct any defects or bugs they have identified.

I achieved a 2:1 degree, which was essential for this position. My knowledge of database architecture and design is good and I can easily interpret written requirements and technical specification documents.

The ability to perform under pressure is needed at times, especially when the analyst missed something in the program design and an immovable deadline approaches.

The best thing about this job is that my software products are great and I get a lot of satisfaction from creating an excellent end product software app.

Think about it!

1 Can you identify three types of database applications that different clients might need to be set up and programmed?

2 Search the Internet for three test plan designs. Which would you recommend to John to make testing a little easier?

3 What is a 2:1 degree?

Just checking

1 Can you write a single sentence using the words event handlers, trigger functions, event loops and forms to show how they relate to each other?

2 Provide examples of why an event driven language can make development easy.

3 What is a programming IDE and why is it useful?

4 How many examples of triggers can you identify?

5 What is meant by the scope of a variable?

6 What is an event handler?

7 Can you find an example of a program flowchart?

8 Identify the usage of four tools available in your programming IDE.

9 Can you explain how to debug programs using your IDE?

10 Can you explain the differences between white and black box testing?

11 Identify three benefits that can be obtained from an independent review of a program.

12 How is event driven programming flexible?

13 What are system events?

14 Can you explain what pseudo code is and why it is used?

15 Produce a template for a test plan.

edexcel

Assignment tips

- Make sure the key features you explain relate to event driven programs. **P1**
- Your testing should be accurate and record any tests that fail with the remedial actions you took to correct the problems. **P5**
- This evidence should be a discussion, so outline three or more examples of how an operating system responds to events. **M1**
- You must give reasons why you chose your tools and techniques for your application, so should also include other tools and techniques you could have used with why your choices were more appropriate. **M2**
- You need to thoroughly test your program to analyse or explain why any of your actual test results were expected results to identify discrepancies. **M3**
- If a program you find for this evidence uses a mouse it cannot be suitable because non-graphical interfaces are text and keyboard based only and the use of a mouse is graphical. **D1**
- This evaluation is of the program you wrote, so focus on what you think are the best and worst things about it with any improvements you would make. **D2**

Glossary

10Base-T – the 10 represents the bandwidth in Mbps (megabits per second), the Base is for a baseband signal and the T represents twisted pair cables.

3G – Third Generation of mobile phone technology, includes broadband services.

4G – Fourth Generation of mobile phone technology, includes high speed broadband services.

Abstraction of data – data within the object is hidden from the object's users.

AC – stands for alternating current. It is a type of electricity. The direction of the current alternates (very quickly), providing an efficient way of supplying power over long distances.

Access control method – a system used to control what devices may use and access the network communication system.

Access time – the length of time that RAM takes to write data (or to read it) once the request has been received from the processor. This is measured in nanoseconds (ns) – the fewer ns, the faster the RAM.

ACL – stands for access control list.

Adware – an application (often free) that when installed comes with adverts, either via your browser or in the application itself.

Address book – a book with sections for each letter of the alphabet in which addresses and other contact details are recorded under the name (usually the surname) of each person you might need to contact.

App – shorthand term for a software application.

Architecture – the internal structure of a computer, including hardware, firmware, assembler, kernel and operating system, plus applications.

ARP – stands for address resolution protocol.

Array – a variable which rather than storing one value can store a series of related values (called elements), rather like a table.

ASCII – stands for American standard code for information interchange. It is the format for storing letters, numbers and symbols in documents.

As-Is – short-hand phrase meaning the current system as it is now.

ASP – stands for active server pages. It also allows web pages to connect with databases and online payment systems.

ATM – stands for asynchronous transfer mode.

Attributes – the data that belongs to the class, i.e. the things that describe the class.

Authentication – the use of security measures such as password protection or chip and pin to check that the user is who they claim to be.

Avatar – an image used to represent a user online. This could be an image of themselves, something that interests them or something completely random.

Backup – a copy of the data that is kept in case anything should happen to the original. The term 'backup' is also used as a verb.

Bandwidth – term used to define how quickly data can travel through a communication media. High bandwidth is a general term describing a fast communication, often fast enough to support video.

Base station – a wireless device, used to give wireless network connectivity to other wireless devices.

Bespoke program – a program that is written especially for a client. Usually more expensive than 'off-the-shelf' software and more likely to have bugs when first delivered, bespoke is a good option where a client has software needs that are not easily met by commercial, off-the-shelf applications.

Big talker – the term used for a network device that communicates more than the others, normally a server.

Biometrics – the use of methods of authentication based on unique physical characteristics, such as fingerprints, retinal and iris scans and signatures. It comes from the ancient Greek *bios*, meaning life and *metron*, meaning measure.

BIOS – stands for basic input/output system. It is a chip on every PC motherboard that connects the operating system to hardware, as well as holding the boot program and start-up settings.

Black box testing – when a program is tested without taking into consideration the code inside the program. The program is the 'box' which is 'black', as the tester does not see anything inside it.

Blackberry – the trade name for a mobile phone which combines a keyboard and a large screen and is used liked a PDA.

Blog – stands for weblog.

Bluetooth® – a wireless device enabling connection and an exchange of information.

Boot sector – set aside to hold data about how data is organised on the disk, such as the number of sectors, the number of sectors per track, the number of bytes per sector, the number of FATs, the size of the root directory and the program needed to load the operating system. This last item is the program that searches and loads files needed to boot the disk – if these files are missing, the disk is unbootable.

'Bricks' – any organisation that trades solely using traditional methods. It may have a presence online, perhaps a static website giving the business's contact details, but does not do any business over the Internet.

'Bricks and clicks' – any organisation that trades using both traditional and online methods. It may have been a 'bricks' organisation originally and developed the business to run online as well or it may have set up both businesses simultaneously.

Browser – the software that allows the user to view the web page.

BSD license – a software distribution license from Berkeley Software Distribution (BSD), which is an open source license. The BSD license means the software can be reused and sold without need for payment to BSD, although the software still needs to show a copyright message acknowledging the original source.

Bug – a fault or error in a program which causes it to crash (end unexpectedly) or produce unexpected results.

Cache – a store on a computer hard drive of all the web resources visited by a user. If the user accesses a cached page which has not been updated since the last download, the cached version will be displayed.

Cache memory – a fast memory that is used as a data buffer between the CPU and RAM.

CAD – stands for computer aided design.

Case sensitive – requiring the right mix of upper-case (capital) and lower-case letters. A case-sensitive part of a program will see System and SYSTEM as very different.

Cash flow – refers to ready funds that are available within a business for spending.

CCTV – stands for closed circuit television.

Centralised console – used by a network operator to control the network. A few years ago, network operators would have needed to use several consoles to control separate parts of the network. In current systems these are centralised into one or two consoles.

Certificate-based authentication – a method of cryptography which prevents data being read by unauthorised parties.

Character formatting – affects only those characters selected and can be used to highlight individual words. For example, to make important material stand out, you could change the font colour or present the material in italic, bold or underlined.

Checksum – a calculation on data that is a form of validation, often used during transmissions. The calculation produces a result that is worked out before transmission then sent as a checksum in the last section of data. The receiving computer carries out the same calculation on the data received then compares it with the checksum – if it is different, the data is corrupted and needs to be resent.

CLI – stands for command line interpreter (or command line interface) and is used to describe a non-GUI operating system.

'Clicks' – any organisation that trades solely online. It has no physical presence for trading and all business is carried out over the Internet.

Client – a person or a system which receives a service from another individual or system (for example when you go to McDonald's to order a meal you are a client receiving a service).

Client–server networks – when the server (or servers) control the network and allow clients to log on to the network. The control the server has over the network makes this the network system of choice for most organisations.

Closed question – a question that expects a limited range of answers such as Yes/No.

Closed system – an information system where the outputs are fixed.

Co-efficient – a co-related value, which is any number.

Combo box – A combo box is a control used in many programs, e.g. to select a font in an Excel® spreadsheet or Word® document, where the user can select from the items in the combo box.

Command prompt – this is a window that can be opened in Windows® computers, equivalent to the old DOS prompt where operating system commands can be typed into the C:\>_ prompt.

Computer abuse – a legal, but unethical act, involving a computer.

Computer misuse – an illegal act involving a computer.

Condition – part of a statement which the program understands as representing True or False. For example, *MyVar < 3* would give True if *MyVar* is a variable containing 2 or False if it contains 3.

Constant – similar to a variable in that it is a name in code that represents a value, but different in that the value does not change.

Context-sensitive – means that if a user presses the F1 key for help, they will see help about what they are currently doing, for example if you are using Word® to save a document using F1 will show help about saving files.

Control – an object on a form such as a text box, label or drop-down box. Controls have attributes which decide how they look (such as their colour and font) and behave.

Cookie – A small piece of information stored on the user's computer about them for a specific website, such as the last item they purchased or their choice of display options.

Cracker – a type of hacker who 'breaks in' to a website to display their own version of the site.

CSMA/CA – stands for carrier sense multiple access/collision avoidance. A variation of CSMA/CD, to avoid continuous collisions of network data.

CSMA/CD – stands for carrier sense multiple access/collision detection. It is a method employed by Ethernet to detect continuous collisions of network data.

CSV – stands for comma separated value. It presents data in comma delimited text file format.

Cyber crime – a crime committed over the Internet or a virtual crime.

Datagram – a self-contained chunk of data including the information needed for routing it from the source to destination computers.

Data packet – when data is sent from computer to another it is broken down into smaller units of data (the packet).

DC – stands for direct current. A different type of electricity, where the power runs from negative charge to positive charge, always in the same direction. This works for battery-powered devices where the power has only a short distance to travel.

Decision support software – software that is designed to help users compile useful information from raw data in order to solve problems and make decisions.

Default gateway – a device, which may be a router or switch, which will enable your device to connect to another network, such as the Internet.

Definition – in the context of an anti-virus application, this is a rule explaining which applications are not trusted.

Denial of service – when a service (such as a web server) is sent so much traffic that it slows down to the point of failure, either through the lack of bandwidth or through an increased load for its processor to handle.

DFD – stands for data flow diagram.

DHCP – stands for dynamic host configuration protocol. It is used to issue IP addresses to devices as they log into a network.

Diagnostic software – software that attempts to diagnose a problem; it identifies possible faults and offers solutions.

Diary – a book in which space is set out (months, weeks, days, hours, time slots) to record events (past or future). Also called an appointment diary, this provides a written record of how you have spent your time and what will be on your agenda in the future.

Differential backup – involves storing only changed data since the last full backup.

Dim – the instruction used in the Visual Basic® programming language to create a variable.

DNS – stands for domain name system. It is used to match easy-to-remember domains typed in by the user, such as www.bbc.co.uk, to IP addresses like 82.165.26.58 (which are not so easy to remember).

Domain – a group of networked computers and devices that are treated as a unit and have the same communications address.

Domain controller – a server which is used to manage printers, servers and communications resources across the network.

Dongle – normally a USB device that can be connected to your computer to offer extra services, such as Internet access.

DOS – stands for disk operating system, the name given to a family of operating systems produced for PCs. MS-DOS® was the Microsoft® product, PC-DOS® was from IBM® and DR-DOS® by Digital Research®.

E-commerce – trade carried out online.

EDI – stands for electronic data interchange.

Emulator – a software application which behaves like another system.

Encryption – a method of encoding that is difficult to decipher by unauthorised parties. It uses prime numbers. The higher the prime number, the stronger the encryption.

EPOS – stands for electronic point of sale. It is an automated till system used in many shops and restaurants.

ERMs – stands for entity relationship models.

Event – anything that happens to an object when the program is running.

Event handler – code that runs when an event occurs.

Expert systems – software that is designed to perform tasks that would usually be performed by a human expert. They provide clear answers to questions without any further analysis needed by the user.

Facts – these can be proved: they are either true or false. Data can be collected and hypotheses tested.

False positive – when something is a positive result, but is not the cause you are looking for. 'If someone wins the long distance race, you would think they are the fastest, until you discover all the other contenders had been injured on the way.'

FAQ – stands for frequently asked questions.

FAT – stands for file allocation table.

FDDI – stands for fiber distributed data interface, a standard using optical fiber to connect the network together.

Firewall – a piece of software that protects the system from unauthorised access. This is especially important for web servers.

Firmware – the name given to the instructions encoded onto ROM chips. Unlike software, once written it cannot be changed.

Flash memory cards – a portable medium for data. Commonly used in digital cameras, they can hold your photos until you upload them to your computer or output them to a photo printer.

Flattened – (also called delayering) the reduction in the number of levels of staff and managers.

Fluid pricing – increasing or decreasing prices quickly, depending on circumstances.

Forums – web pages where users can post messages to other users.

Frame relay – a packet-switched network structure. It can be configured to enable multiple systems to communicate on the same structure without any direct communication.

FTP – stands for file transfer protocol. It is used for file exchange and storage.

Gbps – stands for gigabits per second. Approximately a thousand million bits can be transmitted through the media in one second.

Geosourcing – the process of seeking expert skills at the best possible price regardless of location.

GPRS – stands for general packet radio service.

GSM – stands for global system for mobile communications.

GUI – stands for graphical user interface. This means that the operating system can be controlled with a mouse by clicking on buttons, menus or similar objects.

GHz (gigahertz) – hertz are named after Heinrich Rudolf Hertz (1857–1894), a German physicist who studied electromagnetic radiation. Hertz are a measurement of frequency in cycles per second – 1 hertz is one cycle per second.

Giga – one billion. When measuring computer data, giga means 2^{30} (= 1 073,741,824), which is the power of 2 closest to one billion.

Globalisation – having access to products and services from a wider range of sources around the world from which to select the most desirable according to what the organisation seeks.

Goal – the end result towards which your effort will be directed; provides general purpose and direction.

GPS – stands for global positioning system.

Graphical output – information that is presented as charts, diagrams, graphs or pictures.

Hackers – people who are skilled in IT and who like to gain access to networks they have no right to. This might be to obtain confidential information about the organisation and clients or to steal money, although some simply hack for the fun of it.

Hacking – when someone attempts to enter a computer system with the aim of stealing data, damaging the system or just to show that they can.

Handshaking – a process where two communication devices continuously agree a method of data communication.

Haptic technology – touch screen technology which is extremely common in everyday technology in the home and business and can even carried around in your pocket.

Heat sink – a device attached to the processor chip that has lots of fins so that its surface area is maximised and the heat transfer from the chip is maximised. It draws heat from the processor and therefore keeps its temperature down.

Heuristic – in computer science this is a method of arriving at a good solution that works, rather than a perfect solution.

Homograph – one of two or more words that have the same spelling, but differ in meaning.

Hot swapping – connecting (or disconnecting) a peripheral while the PC is turned on.

HTML – stands for hypertext mark-up language. All web pages are controlled and structured using HTML, even if they use other languages as well.

HTTP – stands for hypertext transfer protocol. It is used for the distribution of web pages.

HTTPS – stands for secure hypertext transfer protocol.

ICMP – stands for Internet control messaging protocol. It is used by a variety of management applications, including Ping, to test communication.

Incremental backup – involves storing only changed data since the last backup of any type.

Incremented – when 1 is added to a variable, so it 'counts'.

IDE – stands for integrated development environment.

IDE – stands for integrated drive electronics. It refers to a standard electronic interface between a computer motherboard's data paths (or buses) and the computer's disk storage devices, based on the IBM PC ISA (industry standard architecture) 16-bit bus standard.

Identity theft – occurs when a victim's details are stolen and someone else pretends to be him or her, for example applying for financial products and making purchases.

IEEE – stands for Institute of Electrical and Electronic Engineers.

Independence – someone who has independence is able to act without depending on others, e.g. for financial support, approval or assistance in completing a task.

Infrared – a legacy technology that is still used on some mobile devices to connect them to printers or to exchange data. It uses light at the lower end of the light spectrum, and technology similar to that used by some games consoles and all television remote controls. A mobile device's infrared transmitter can be placed next to a receiver on some printers for a connection. Infrared has been superseded by both Bluetooth and WiFi, with most devices able to print and share files by these means without the need for a 'line of sight connection'.

Input/Output devices – input devices allow a computer user to enter information on to a computer. Output devices enable information to leave a system in many forms, e.g. audio, visual, printed documents etc. Computer input or output devices are known as peripherals.

Integrated system – enables access to separate network management systems by linking them.

Intellectual property – patented products protected by copyright. It is described as 'intellectual' because it has been thought up by someone and the idea belongs to that person.

In-tray – a physical tray for paperwork, or an electronic Inbox such as that provided by email software like Outlook®.

Intranet – like the Internet, but running on an organisation's network rather than the World Wide Web. Many organisations use their intranet to help communications with staff with news, support forms, holiday request forms and many other useful resources.

Intrusion detection system – used to monitor network traffic and analyse if an incursion has taken place.

IP address – in full (Internet Protocol address), this is a unique number that identifies a particular computer on the Internet.

Ipconfig (IP configuration) – a utility program included with Windows® that is used from the command line to show the IP address of the computer running the utility and can show some other network information such as the domain name.

ISDN – is a digital telephone line that shares voice and data communications.

Iteration construct – (also called a loop) a part of a program that is repeated. For example, if you wanted a program that printed out a times table from 1 to 12, the most efficient way to write the program would be with a section of code that repeats 12 times.

JavaScript – in basic terms, provides interactivity between the computer and the user.

Kbps – stands for kilo bits per second. Approximately a thousand bits can be transmitted through the media in one second.

LAN – stands for local area network.

Latency – a time delay that could be better used, for example for processing.

Lead time – the amount of time taken before delivering a service or product.

Legislative – refers to a legal requirement.

Locality of reference – guesswork principle used by the caching system. There are three types of locality: temporal, spatial and sequential. Temporal locality assumes that if a resource (for example a program instruction or a data item) is referenced now, then it will be referenced again soon. Spatial locality recognises that most program instructions are found in routines and that these routines are usually close together and also that the data fields are close together. It assumes that the likelihood of referencing a resource is higher if a resource near it has been referenced. Sequential locality assumes that memory will be accessed sequentially.

Lock and key security – when essential systems are held in rooms and buildings which are secured under lock and key.

Logical operators – AND, OR and NOT are used to combine conditions together using Boolean logic.

Logical topology – how data actually transfers in a network, as opposed to the physical topology. For example, some networks are physically laid out in a star configuration, but they operate logically as bus or ring networks.

Loyalty card – looks like a credit card and identifies the owner and the provider of the card. It can be used to store points or discounts.

MAC – stands for media access control.

MAC address – a unique address burnt into every network card's circuits by the manufacturer. This means that no two network cards are the same and it is useful to help secure network access.

Malware – a hostile, intrusive or annoying piece of software or program code.

MAN – a metropolitan area network (MAN) is a network connecting LANs in an area that might be as small as a campus or as large as a city. A MAN could use wireless, or leased circuits, to allow the system to communicate.

Mass customisation – efficiently mass producing goods and services for customers that have individual needs.

Mbps – stands for megabits per second. Approximately a million bits can be transmitted through the media in one second. (Remember, elsewhere data size is measured in bytes and there are 8 bits in a byte.)

MD5 – an independent code that represents the data inside an application. If the program is altered (by a virus) then the code will change, rendering the application subject to tampering.

Media – the material used in communication. This could be wireless, fiber or copper.

Mega bit – an 'optimal' measurement of data transferred (in the case of wireless). 1 bit is a single binary 0 or 1; a kilo bit is 1000 0s or 1s transmitted per second, therefore a mega bit is 1,000,000 0s or 1s being transmitted per second (abbreviated as Mbps).

Message passing – the technical name for the process by which one class gets another class to do something by calling one of its methods.

Meta-refresh – an HTML tag which redirects the website visitor to another web page.

Meta tags – words that are put into the HTML code of the web page, but are not displayed on the screen.

Methods – functions of a class, i.e. the things that the class can do.

Microblogging – using services such as Twitter™ to share with the world information in a short sentence.

Micron – a thousandth of a millimetre.

Mirroring – a backup server that 'mirrors' the processes and actions of the primary server. If the primary server fails, the backup server can take over without any down-time because it has mirrored the content of the primary server.

MIS – stands for management information system.

Modem – combination and abbreviation of two words: modulator + demodulator. Modulation and demodulation are processes used to convert the computer's digital signal to the method used to transmit the data (such as a phone line) and then back again.

MP4 – a coding format for highly compressed movies to be played on portable media players.

MPLS – stands for multi-protocol labelled switching.

MRI – stands for magnetic resonance imaging, which enables investigations without surgery by generating images of living tissues inside the human body.

MUX – stands for multiplexer. A multiplexer is an electronic device that selects one of many analog or digital signals and sends the input into a single line, therefore allowing many signals to share one device.

MySQL™ – a language for creating online databases. it uses an SQL base, which is the language behind most databases.

Network assets – any components (such as switches) that are used in the network.

Network security – protecting the network from threats to the data contained within it and threats to the software configurations that keep it running effectively.

Newsgroups – a method of posting messages to other Internet users.

NIC – stands for network interface card, part of the workstation hardware that allows connection to a network.

Niche market – a small, specialised section of the buying public that is likely to be interested in a certain type of product or service.

Objectives – these are similar to goals. However, goals are broad and general, whereas objectives are narrower and more precise. Goals are intangible (such as, 'improve your general fitness'), but objectives are tangible (for instance, 'practise until you can do twenty press-ups in one go').

Objects – different from procedures in that they group program instructions and data together. An object may be either visual or non-visual. A visual object is anything on a form, such as a button. An example of a non-visual object is the PrintDocument object of VB.NET which can be used by a program to produce hardcopy on to paper.

Object-oriented – where the whole system is broken into a number of objects that are designed to interact with each other to produce a working system. Object-oriented methods are becoming more popular and are particularly useful in large and complex systems.

OCR – stands for optical character recognition. When a document is scanned into a computer system the software translates the scan into a document with editable text.

OMR – stands for optical mark recognition. When multiple-choice sheets are scanned into a computer system the software translates the respondents' marks into a spreadsheet or database.

Open question – a question that could be answered in a variety of unanticipated ways.

Open source – when the source code of software is available to anyone using the software. Source code is the actual code written by the programmers who created the software, so open source software can be changed to exactly meet the needs of users or to fix bugs.

Open system – information system where the user has a wide choice in how to present the output.

Opinions – these are more complex: they vary from one person to the next and can change within the same person from one day to the next. Opinions can be strong or weak and may be influenced by knowledge – or the lack of it – of relevant facts.

OSI – stands for open system interconnection.

Outsourcing – paying a third party to provide a service that would normally be performed by a member of staff

P2P – peer to peer

P2P file-sharing – programs that are shared between people (P2P = peer to peer) where users don't own a program or a file but pay a small subscription.

Packet – a formatted block of data sent over networks and the Internet. A packet contains the addresses of sender and destination, the data and error checking. The maximum size for an IP packet is 64KB.

Packet sniffing – Looking for data on the network, by listening to network traffic on your connection.

Packet switching – a mechanism which sends network traffic in small manageable data units across the system.

PAN – stands for personal area network.

Paragraph formatting – affects the entire paragraph and is used to control the spacing of lines within, before and after the paragraph. It sets the basic look of the text (font style and size) and may be incorporated into a style sheet or template.

Paraphrase – to say again but using different words.

Parity – equality, for example equal amounts, equal status or equal value.

PAT – stands for portable appliance testing.

Patch – a piece of software designed to fix problems with a computer program e.g. fixing security weaknesses or bugs and improving usability or performance of the program.

Payback – reward in some form or another for using an organisation's product or service.

PAYE – stands for pay as you earn. A system that enables an employer to deduct your tax and National Insurance contributions at source. Depending on any other income, you may be required to complete a tax return to pay any additional tax which has not been collected by your employer.

Pay-per-click advertising – where a website hosts an advert and benefits by earning money every time a user clicks the advert.

PCB – stands for printed circuit board.

PDA – stands for personal digital assistant. PDAs are hand-held computers.

Peer – someone (or something) which is an equal to yourself or others (e.g. your friend is a peer). Peer devices are devices which have equal 'rights' on a networked system.

Peer-to-peer networks – the opposite to a client–server network, with no server controlling the network. Each computer has equal rights and can share folders, printers or other resources. This is the network system of choice for most homes.

Pen drives – small devices that can be used to transfer files between USB-compatible systems and provide a high-capacity alternative to CD-ROMs. They are plugged directly into the USB port and need no batteries for power.

Peripheral – any device, such as a printer, attached to a computer to expand its functionality.

Phishing – involves criminals sending out fraudulent emails that claim to be from a legitimate company, with the aim of obtaining the recipients' personal details and committing identity theft.

PHP – stands for hypertext preprocessor. It allows web pages to connect with databases and online payment systems.

Platform – the foundation around which a system is developed.

Podcast – a media file distributed over the Internet for playback on portable media players and personal computers. The term originates from Apple®'s iPod™ and the word broadcasting.

Polymorphing – a virus that is designed to change its appearance, size and signature each time it infects another PC (just as cells in a diseased human mutate), thus making it harder for anti-virus software to recognise it.

Polynomial – the result of a series of smaller formulae all with the same co-efficient.

POP3 – stands for post office protocol version 3. It is used to collect mail from an ISP.

Port – a technical term for a socket or connection. Provides the link between peripheral and the CPU (central processing unit).

POST – stands for power-on self test. It is a hardware diagnostic routine that is run during the start-up boot sequence and checks configuration settings of the computer.

Primary networked services – when this is the only connection you have to the Internet.

Primary storage – the memory of the computer.

Prime number – a number that can only be divided by itself and 1. This means that by no matter what number you try to divide this number, it will never return a whole value. Prime numbers are mathematically interesting as no one has yet managed to predict the next prime number – they appear to follow no pattern. This property is invaluable in network security.

Prioritising – identifying which tasks are most important and putting these at the top of your 'to do' list.

Probing question – a question that seeks out further information and narrows the responses down to the required answer.

Processor cooling fan – a tiny fan attached to the processor chip or heat sink to prevent it from overheating.

Profiler – a performance analysis tool that measures the behaviour of a program while it is running.

Program – a set of instructions that tells the computer what to do.

Program maintenance – the stage in the systems development life cycle (SDLC) when programs are tweaked to remove bugs that are found during use and to make small improvements.

Proofread – a process of checking, looking for errors within a written piece of text.

Protocol – devices and computer systems use protocols to communicate together so they use the same error checking, data transfer speeds and share other standards, such as data packet structures.

Protocol – a common method of communication and information exchange, following a set of rules, also known as a 'handshake'. If the two computers transmitting data to each other are using the same protocol, the transfer will work.

Protocol stack – term used when data is communicated between computers. There are protocols in place between each of the hardware devices so they can communicate with each other, as in the OSI model. When the data travels through more than one layer and there is more than one protocol used, there is a protocol stack.

Pseudocode – (comes from 'pseudo' meaning 'like' or 'a form of' and 'code') an informal version of programming code that uses the structure of a programming language (e.g. decisions, loops, etc.), but does not worry about the strict syntax (rules) of the language. Flow charts can be thought of as diagrammatical pseudocode.

PSU – stands for power supply unit.

Public key encryption – a method of coding information so that only the people with the right key at both ends of the communication can decode it.

Public/private keys – keys that are mathematically related. The public key can be widely distributed and is used to encrypt data. The private key only can decrypt the data and is kept secret. It is not technically practical to derive the private key from the public key.

PVC – stands for permanent virtual circuit.

Qualitative – personal and subjective.

Quantitative – factual, often number-based, obtained through well-defined processes.

Quarantine – moving a virus or infected file to a safe place on the system to prevent it from doing any damage to the rest of the network.

RAID – stands for redundant array of independent disks. It is used as a live backup mechanism with multiple hard disks maintaining multiple images of the data.

RAM – stands for random access memory.

RARP – stands for reverse address resolution protocol and is used to match IP addresses to MAC addresses on a computer.

Redundancy – a term in computing meaning duplication of information.

Re-engineer the system – a phrase that means starting again with a new system rather than attempting a quick fix.

Registrar – an organisation that manages Internet domain names.

Regulatory – refers to a rule or policy that is not a government law, but is a requirement.

Reserved word – a word used within a programming language as part of a command, for example PRINT.

Resolves – used when referring to IP addresses changing into domain names.

RJ – stands for registered jack. This is an American term for the type of plug used on a connector that has been recognised by a standards organisation.

ROM – stands for read only memory.

Root directory table – has an entry for each file on the disk, the name of the file and the file extension, the file attribute, the date and time that the file was created or last updated, the position where the start of this file is to be found on the disk (cluster number) and the length of the file.

Router – a device which connects networks and makes traffic forwarding decisions based on information learned via its connections or a routing protocol.

RS-232c – stands for Reference Standard 232 revision c.

RSA – stands for the last name initials of the mathematicians who patented the principle for public/private key encryption using prime numbers, i.e. Ron Rivest, Adi Shamir and Len Adleman.

RSI – stands for repetitive strain injury. It is a condition suffered by many PC users.

SATA – stands for serial advanced technology attachment. This is a computer bus interface for connecting host bus adapters to mass storage devices such as hard disk drives and optical drives.

Scope – how much of the program a variable is usable within.

Script – programming code, often short and used as part of another system. The most common web script language is JavaScript®.

Scripts – small pieces of code which are included in web pages to provide additional functionality and interactivity that cannot be provided by HTML.

Secondary storage – a backing store that remains with the computer and provides a greater capacity than the processor can offer.

Serial RS-232 – an older standard used to connect mice, modems and external devices.

Server – a device or an individual offering a service to one or many clients (for example the person behind the counter at McDonald's).

Service consumer – an application, service, or other type of software module requiring a service.

Signed – when a number is treated as positive or negative. In programming, this usually means that the most significant digit (MSD) of a binary number (the leftmost digit) is used to define whether the number is positive (MSD is 0) or negative (MSD is 1).

Smart chip – is an integrated circuit card which can store data, identification, access application and even monetary values.

SMTP – stands for simple mail transfer protocol. It is used for sending emails.

Soft skills – skills that influence how people interact with each other, e.g. analytical thinking, creativity, diplomacy, effective communication, flexibility, leadership, listening skills, problem solving, team building and a readiness for change.

Spam – unsolicited bulk email used for advertising purposes.

Span port – a port on to which all the data on the network is copied.

Spell checker – compares your words with those listed in a dictionary, to ensure that they are spelled correctly.

Spider – a bot (a program that runs on a computer 24/7, automating mundane tasks for the user) which examines websites on behalf of search engines.

Spyware – collects information about a user's various activities without their consent and reports it back to a central server.

SSL – stands for secure sockets layer. It requires a website to issue a security certificate.

STP – stands for spanning tree protocol.

Strategy – a systematic plan of action.

Strong password – uses letters (upper- and lower-case), numbers and symbols, e.g. Jac0b_$m1th instead of jacobsmith.

Structure diagram – a simple diagram that shows how a program will be split into procedures.

Subsistence – living requirements, for example accommodation, food, drink.

Summarise – to sum up the most important points of a communication.

Switch – a switch is a box with a number of RJ45 network ports (sockets) used to connect networked devices together. RJ45 is the usual connection plug on network cabling.

Symbolic language – a programming language where the actual CPU instructions are replaced by English-like key words such as 'If', 'Print' or 'Do'.

Synergy – when two or more elements (in this case computer systems) work together with positive results, the combined effect being greater than the sum of the individual effects.

Syntax – the structure and order of the language. In English, 'door to go the' is not understandable as the syntax is wrong, whereas 'go to the door' is very clear as the syntax is correct. Similarly, programming languages need the syntax to be correct or the code cannot be understood.

Target – an objective or goal; something to aim for.

TCP – stands for transmission control protocol. It is used for the transfer of data which is connection-oriented and must be sent via a reliable system.

TCP/IP – stands for transport control protocol/Internet protocol. It is the very widely used protocol for the Internet, intranets and networks, allowing websites and web surfers to connect and share data.

TCP/UDP – Transmission Control Protocol/User Datagram Protocol (TCP/UDP) is used for streaming audio and video, voice over (VOIP) and videoconferencing.

Technical infrastructure – the development of the management's underlying structure.

Tertiary storage – a store that is destined for transfer to another computer or archiving and needs to be on a portable medium.

Textual output – information that is presented as characters, numbers or text.

Thesaurus – similar to a dictionary but, instead of giving meanings, it lists words with the same meaning.

Third party – in the context of retail and e-commerce, this is an additional organisation that is involved in the commercial transaction. It is called a third party because it is additional to the supplier and the customer.

Time slice – when a portion of device/system time is allocated to a given task.

To-Be – short-hand phrase meaning the new system that is to be completed.

Token ring – a circular network structure, where every device has a fair 'turn' to communicate.

Topology – the structure or layout of the communications network.

Transceiver – both a transmitter and a receiver, a device which may therefore act as a communications.

Trojan – a malicious program that pretends to be a benign application, but purposely does something the user does not expect. Trojans are technically not viruses since they do not replicate, but can be just as destructive. If left in a computer system, provides 'back door' access to the hard drive and data.

Trunking – conduit used in IT rooms to hold the cabling and RJ45 network ports. Trunking is often made from plastic and is usually attached to the walls at desk height.

UDP – stands for user datagram protocol. It is used on connectionless systems; this means that the data may travel different routes and reliability is not a primary concern.

UNIX – a centralised server operating system from the 1970s.

Unsigned – when a number is treated as positive. In programming, unsigned usually means that the most significant digit (MSD) of a binary number (the leftmost digit) is simply part of the number.

URI – stands for uniform resource identifier.

USB (universal serial bus) – a higher-speed serial connection standard that supports low-speed devices (e.g. mice, keyboards, scanners) and higher-speed devices (e.g. digital cameras).

UTP – stands for unshielded twisted pair.

Variant variables – variables that respond to the data given to them and adapt as the program runs to whatever is put inside them.

Viral marketing – marketing that relies on social networks passing on product or service information from person to person.

Virus – a man-made program or piece of code that causes an unexpected, usually negative, event and is self-replicating. It is often disguised as a game or image with a clever marketing title, such as officeparty.jpg, and attached to an email or a download file.

Virus signature – a sequence of characters which the anti-virus software gleans by analysing the virus code.

VLAN – stands for virtual local area network. It is a method used to divide a LAN into smaller logical structures.

Vlog – a blog which uses video as its primary presentation format.

VoIP – stands for voice over Internet Protocol. It is the method used to allow voice telecommunications to take place over a computer data network.

VPN – stands for virtual private network.

Wait state – a time of inactivity for the CPU to allow other devices to catch up with it.

WAN – stands for wide area network. It is a large network, usually covering more than one geographical location and often crossing countries and continents.

Web 2.0 – represents a development in web technology that allows different systems to share data via common methods of data exchange. Many social media resources such as Twitter and Facebook® make extensive use of Web 2.0 technology.

Web presence – Visibility through a website – promoting a product, service, company or individual(s) by featuring their 'presence' on the Internet. Another meaning can be a 'digital footprint' e.g. the number of hits to a website.

Web server – a server that distributes web pages on to the Internet.

WEP – stands for wired equivalent privacy.

White box testing – when a program is tested to make sure each line of the code works. The program is the 'box', which is 'white' as the tester does see inside it.

WiFi – a common method for wireless networking used by laptops, printers and many computers, based upon the IEEE 802.11 standards provided by the WiFi Alliance, initially advertised in 2003 as 'The standard for wireless fidelity'.

WiMAX – stands for worldwide interoperability for microwave access

WIMP – stands for windows, icons, mouse, pointer. It is used to describe a GUI system. The windows are used to show running programs, the icons to start programs, the mouse to control the system and the pointer is an arrow on screen to show the position of the mouse.

WLAN – wireless LAN (local area network) usually following WiFi standards.

Work ethic – a set of values which expects the employee to arrive on time, to work diligently throughout the working day, to show initiative and to be able to work within a team.

Worm – a virus that resides in the active memory of a computer and duplicates itself. It may send copies of itself to other computers, such as through email or Internet Relay Chat (IRC).

www – stands for world wide web.

Wysiwyg – stands for 'what you see is what you get'. In web design programs, it means what you see in design view is the same as if it was published on the internet.

XML – The Extensible Markup Language (XML) is an open standard for documents particularly useful for websites as they can include tags for search engines.

Index